The Star Wars Enigma

ALSO BY NIGEL HEY

Solar System
How We Will Explore the Outer Planets
How Will We Feed the Hungry Billions?
The Mysterious Sun

The Star Wars Enigma

Behind the Scenes
of the
Cold War Race for
Missile Defense

NIGEL HEY

Potomac Books, Inc.
Washington, D.C.

Library of Congress Cataloging-in-Publication Data
Hey, Nigel.
   The Star Wars enigma : behind the scenes of the Cold War race for missile defense / Nigel Hey.—1st ed.
      p.   cm.
   Includes bibliographical references and index.
   ISBN 1-57488-981-8 (hardcover : alk. paper)
      1. Strategic Defense Initiative—History.   2. Ballistic missile defenses—United States.
3. Nuclear weapons—Soviet Union.   4. Cold War.   5. Science and state—United States—
History—20th century.   6. United States—Politics and government—1981–1989.   7.
United States—Foreign relations—Soviet Union.   8. Soviet Union—Foreign relations—
United States.   I. Title.
   UG743.H39   2006
   358.1′74—dc22
                                                                                        2005032894
ISBN-10 1-57488-981-8
ISBN-13 978-1-57488-981-9

Printed in the United States of America on acid-free paper that meets the American National Standards Institute Z39-48 Standard.

Potomac Books, Inc.
22841 Quicksilver Drive
Dulles, Virginia 20166

First Edition
10   9   8   7   6   5   4   3   2   1

For Eddie and Elizabeth

The United States has it in its power to increase enormously the strains under which Soviet policy must operate, to force upon the Kremlin a far greater degree of moderation and circumspection than it has had to observe in recent years, and in this way to promote tendencies which must eventually find their outlet in either the break-up or the gradual mellowing of Soviet power.
—George F. Kennan (1947)

CONTENTS

ACKNOWLEDGMENTS

Many individuals contributed to this book, some through hours of conversation, others through helpful short meetings, telephone calls, and e-mails. Above all I am grateful to my friend and colleague Gerold Yonas for his information, counsel, and criticism; to Lt. Gen. James A. Abrahamson (USAF Ret.) for his insider commentary on the evolution of the Strategic Defense Initiative; and to Peter Zarubin for providing information on the Soviet laser weapon programs, for critiquing my accounts of those programs, and for attempting to explain to me the convoluted organization of Soviet-era military industry. These three, as well as Oleg Krokhin, Robert (Bud) McFarlane, Dmitry Mikheyev, Stanley Orman, Sir Charles Powell, Roald Sagdeev, and Evgeny Velikhov, contributed hours of time, face-to-face, during the six-year gestation of this book. Adm. James D. Watkins (USN Ret.) deserves special thanks for his openness and his enthusiasm for a book project that set out to tell the SDI story in a fashion that would be enjoyed by nontechnical readers.

I am also deeply grateful for the comments, guidance and other assistance provided personally by (in alphabetical order) Donald Baucom, John Bosma, Gregory Canavan, Robert V. Duncan, Eugene Fox, Richard Garwin, Jeff Hecht, Charles Herzfeld, William Hopkinson, Herbert Meyer, Raymond Pollock, Jerry Pournelle, Robert Rankine, John D.G. Rather, Victor Reis, Tom Sanders, Peter Schweizer, George Shultz, Eric Shultzinger, the late Edward Teller, Charles Townes, Al Trivelpiece, Frank von Hippel, and Simon P. (Pete) Worden. My research would not have been complete without valuable aid from numerous libraries and other institutes of learning and scholarship, including the Ronald Reagan Presidential Library, the Liddell Hart Library of King's College London, Chatham House Library, the Committee on International Security and Arms Control (Washington), the Center for International Security and Cooperation (Stanford), and the Kurchatov Institute.

My sources and reviewers contributed the edge of excellence that would not have existed otherwise. However, and particularly since the book continued to develop somewhat after their comments, they are not responsible for errors that may have occurred in the text.

Finally, my thanks to my editor Lisa Camner of Potomac Books, to my agent, Elizabeth Frost-Knappman of New England Publishing Associates, to Ellen D. (Dee) Foster for her comments and criticisms on the general readability of this book, and to other friends and colleagues who read and commented on the manuscript.

For the sake of readability I have made some assumptions in reconstructing several events described in this book. However, I have based these scenarios on careful consideration of each situation and on conversations and bibliographic research, and, where possible, I have checked my prose with the individuals named. I offer my apologies in advance for any inadvertent inaccuracies that may have arisen from this process. I should also point out that, due to secrecy and classification, reliable details about Soviet space systems are scarce. For example, a number of "Orbital Weapons Platforms" were designed, and at least four of them launched, in the 1970s and 1980s. Unfortunately, the information that exists about them tends often to be sensationalist or contradictory, and therefore suspect. While I have noted these reports in the book, I have attempted to name their sources and to gauge their reliability.

SHOOTING DOWN NUKES

1

I do not know with what weapons World War III will be fought. But World War IV will be fought with sticks and stones.
—Albert Einstein

We must beware, lest the Stone Age return upon the gleaming wings of science.
—Winston Churchill

The Strategic Defense Initiative—nicknamed "Star Wars" for the popular film series—was an audaciously attractive feature of the last decade of the Cold War. President Ronald Reagan's administration claimed that SDI would help the world escape nuclear destruction by shooting down hostile missiles with space-age weapons. It was an attractive idea, for in those days U.S. and Soviet missile fleets were enormous, distrust between the two powers was at a high point, and a superpower nuclear exchange was considered a true-to-life threat. Once established, this new program ramped up quickly, exploring elements of an out-of-this-world armory that might have ranged from lasers powered by nuclear explosions to earth-orbiting magnetic guns.

The SDI scenario—a threatening symbol of Western technical genius—troubled Kremlin leaders and threw their plans for military domination disastrously off balance. SDI was technically a questionable notion; it threatened to break high-level international agreements, and in retrospect, it may have been a stupendously elaborate hoax. It remains a premier example of how politics uses the psychologically powerful prestige of science and scientists to further its own ends—a strategy that in this case turned out to be eminently successful.

Few westerners knew that the Soviet Union funded its own colossal, rigidly secret SDI-like programs for almost a quarter of a century, all aimed at using laser technology and/or other high-tech systems

1

against the United States. These programs started with plans to build a nuclear-powered laser in 1963; they crested with the development of the world's most powerful single-shot laser weapon; and they ended with the unsuccessful launch of a giant orbiting battle station in 1987, soon after the conclusion of two major summit meetings between Ronald Reagan and Mikhail Gorbachev.

What, actually, was "Star Wars," and how much did it contribute to the end of the Cold War? The following pages explore the intriguing SDI enigma, largely from the perspectives of American and Soviet space weaponeers who enjoyed—and endured—hands-on involvement in the long battle for space dominance.

※

Evgeny Velikhov, the respected mandarin of Communist Russia's huge nuclear research empire, stirred his bulky frame and stared out bleakly through the scarred Plexiglas window. The airliner was banking gently around to join the traffic out of Washington on the first leg of his long flight home to Moscow. It was March 24, 1983, and the morning newspaper lay on his lap. It was partially unread, for Velikhov, though near-brilliant in his use of spoken English, was not comfortable with an unfamiliar alphabet and a lexicon so different from that of the Slav tongues. But the small, modestly worded headline, at the top right of the *New York Times* front page, wrapped it all up: "Reagan Proposes U.S. Seek New Way to Block Missiles."

The news left Velikhov profoundly upset. There was a needle-sharp mind behind his round, almost-baby face, and a wealth of tactical insight that told him this meant trouble. Toughness and good humor generally managed to reside, improbably, behind the steady pair of brown eyes that were set in that high-foreheaded face—but not now. The Soviets and the Americans had been on Armageddon alert for decades; each had a huge inventory of nuclear-tipped missiles capable of reducing the adversary's cities to piles of radioactive rubble. Now Reagan was threatening the balance that existed between them. If he put real muscle behind his high-tech missile defense idea, and if the Kremlin's more paranoid bureaucrats were sufficiently alarmed, they would soon be demanding more money for their own programs. Some might even propose a preemptive strike on the West. It wouldn't be the first time. The physicist ran a palm impatiently across his thin wash of hair and swore softly.

Velikhov knew that if the Americans put serious money into some new way of shielding their territory from intercontinental missiles— they had been talking about using high-power lasers and other "death ray" weapons—the nervous men of the Soviet missile-defense community would be petrified by the mere possibility that such a plan might work. Old fears, embedded and almost folkloric, would be reinforced. Was it possible that Russia could become vulnerable again, as it had been against the Mongols, against Napoleon's army, and against the Nazis in World War II?

President Ronald Reagan's speech didn't merit a *New York Times* editorial that day. But it did, as *Times* writer Charles Mohr said in his news analysis, promise "a sweeping, long-range change in national strategic doctrine."

Below, towns and farmland drifted by, looking increasingly like a two-dimensional reconnaissance map as the Boeing 707 gained altitude. But Velikhov wasn't interested in the view. Once he returned to Moscow, there would be meetings . . . and meetings. This time, as the Americans with their flair for metaphor would have put it, the shit had really hit the fan. The Russian grunted to himself. It was nonsense perhaps, but dangerous nonsense nevertheless.

Velikhov, forty-nine years old and near the top of his career, wondered whether this new development would affect his aspiration to become president of the Soviet Academy of Sciences. He was already vice president of the Academy and secretary of its Division of Informatics, Computer Science, and Automation, yet he relished his work as deputy director of the I. V. Kurchatov Institute of Atomic Energy. Nothing could match the excitement of fighting for, and ultimately achieving, success with the world's most powerful continuous-wave laser—a carbon-dioxide job supercharged with electron beams—that had been ramped up to several hundred kilowatts just a few years before. And now, as he suspected, the Americans thought they could outdo the Soviets. Reagan probably believed that his country could produce lasers powerful enough—and smart enough—to shoot down Soviet missiles. Right there in front of the television cameras, almost the entire world, he had called on scientists—not just engineers and technicians—to stop the arms race with a new orgy of high-tech wizardry.

Velikhov shifted in his seat as pleasant thoughts intruded on this worrisome scenario. Working with the great laser pioneer Aleksandr Prokhorov and his protégé Boris Bunkin had been a delight to his ego. The continuous-wave laser would never make a weapon, but someday it might ignite a fusion reaction in the laboratory. And energy—nuclear fusion and fission—was Velikhov's game. He had been glad not to be on the military side, but now things might be turning sour.

Velikhov, Roald Sagdeev, head of the Soviet Space Institute (IKI), and a few colleagues had been in Washington for two and a half days of meetings of the Committee on International Security and Arms

Control (CISAC). The committee, a joint enterprise of the U.S. and Soviet academies of science, had met at the headquarters of the National Academy of Sciences, a graceful, neoclassic building on Washington's Mall, with a semiformal garden fronting its copper-trimmed facade. High-energy lasers had been on the program—special attention had been paid to agenda item IV, "Impact of New Technology on the Arms Race and the Role of Qualitative Restraints; Prevention of New Types and Systems of Weapons." But now the American hierarchy was about to spoil everything. Velikhov wondered how much the clever, crafty Hungarian, Edward Teller, had to do with it. Had he won Reagan's support for an x-ray laser? Teller was so much in love with atomic bombs, and with his institution, Lawrence Livermore National Laboratory (LLNL). Maybe he thought he could improve their images by turning nuclear weapons into x-ray-powered missile-killers. What fantasy!

Velikhov dozed off, longing for the moment when he would be skimming away home from Sheremtyevo Airport in the comfortable back seat of one of the institute's black limousines. But it was a troubled sleep, for he knew that soon, in the halls of the Kremlin, the military industry chieftains would be making the most of Reagan's speech, turning it into a threat, and demanding more money for more missiles and, perhaps, a revitalized "Star Wars" program of their own.[1]

George Shultz had, like most of the Reagan Cabinet, been kept in the dark about SDI until the very last minute. The secretary of state, a compact, professorial man with a large face framed by gray bookends of neatly-groomed hair, didn't learn that it was a serious proposal until a February 18 meeting with the national security advisor, William P. (Bill) Clark.* On March 21, Shultz learned that the initiative would be included in the budget speech, but he didn't get his very own, authentic copy of the announcement until the day before it was delivered. A careful and meticulous thinker, he read it over and observed that the wording was so confident that it wrongly implied that a major scientific breakthrough had already occurred; but he did not say this when he gave his required heads-up to the Soviet ambassador, Anatoly Dobrynin. In fact, a lot of top people in Washington were concerned for a number of reasons, but they got nowhere because Reagan had taken hold of a new idea, and it was plain that there was no way he would let go.

*The national security advisor, formally named the assistant to the president for national security affairs, advises the president on national security and serves on the National Security Council (NSC).

Shultz knew something like this had been in the wind for some time. The previous October, Defense Secretary Casper Weinberger hinted to the White House press corps that new anti–ballistic missile technologies might be on the doorstep, sufficient at least to protect the fields of subsurface "silos" from which U.S. missiles could be launched. Only a few months elapsed before Reagan met with a group headed by the industrialist Karl Bendetsen and backed by Teller, which urged the creation of a massive space-based defense program on the scale of the Manhattan Project. Then a National Security Council space policy review noted, with a halfhearted nod to treaty limitations, that "the United States will pursue activities in space in support of its right of self-defense." As the year 1982 wore on, there were reports that Teller had asked Reagan for $200 million a year to spend on a concept that would use x-ray lasers to destroy incoming intercontinental ballistic missiles (ICBMs). By accident or design, forces within the defense community had been quietly putting together the pieces that could lead to only one thing. Even if they didn't actually create SDI, they certainly helped with the recipe.

Just before his March 23 speech, Reagan cleared the way for the Soviet ambassador to visit the State Department for a briefing with Shultz. Dobrynin considered the secretary of state to be taciturn, a reserved sort of individual who tended to keep his own counsel. This time Dobrynin had to listen. He listened very carefully and gravely, showing no anger. After Shultz was through, Dobrynin returned to his embassy, picked up his secure telephone, and punched in the number of Soviet General Secretary Yuri Andropov.

At the Albuquerque International Sunport, two time zones to the west of Washington, Gerold Yonas was waiting for his luggage to chunk down the chute and onto the carrousel when he was approached by a friend whose wife had arrived on the same flight.

"Hey Gerry," he said. "You hear the news?"

Yonas, arguably one of America's best and brightest young physicists, blinked tiredly and without enthusiasm. "What news?" Flights back and forth between Washington and Albuquerque take about a day out of one's life and sometimes seem like two, and he wasn't ready to waste his energy on small talk. "Reagan's budget speech—he used it to start a new program. Wants us scientists to come up with a high-tech way of defending America against nukes. Sounds like lasers to me."

Yonas grimaced and grabbed a bag off the conveyor belt. His

colleague was acting altogether too cheerful. "Yeah, and we'll all be guilty millionaires." He looked his friend in the face. "You're serious about this?"

"Yep."

Yonas shook his head, showed his claim tickets to the luggage inspector, and, his mind swimming with questions, went to the curb to catch a bus to the parking lot. What is Reagan *doing*? What is this all about? What's driving this thing? Yonas was generally able to deal with anything that the world threw at him, but he a hard time coping with this one. It was a non sequitur; it didn't fit.

Driving back to his home in Albuquerque's Four Hills area, Yonas went over the answers. Rather, he tried to find the answers. Not long ago, sitting in on a White House Science Council study, he had decided that there was not much more than a lot of bad ideas sitting out there in the world of advanced military technology. Nobody had a really good idea for lasers powerful enough to shoot down a missile. All he had seen during the study was uncertainty, and little in the way of interest or support for new, exotic weapon programs. Maybe the White House insiders had something else on their minds, something completely different from lasers?

Eleven years earlier, Yonas had started a particle beam fusion program in Albuquerque, at Sandia National Laboratories, followed in 1976 by a relatively small program that was looking into possible weapon applications of particle beams. In both cases the particles were in the form of minute but high-power streams of electrons or neutrons—not lasers, but high-power beams of elementary matter.

The first laser had been demonstrated while Yonas was still an undergrad working for his bachelor's degree in engineering physics at Cornell, and the Department of Defense almost immediately began looking into the use of lasers as weapons. And what of the Soviets? By the time Yonas received his doctorate from Caltech in 1966, they had orbited the first artificial Earth satellite, Sputnik, and sent Yuri Gagarin on the first human orbital flight around the Earth. The Cuban Missile Crisis of 1962, when the Soviets were building a capability to strike the southern part of the U.S. eastern seaboard with nuclear missiles based in Cuba, had shaken the world. This dangerous gambit had been stifled by President John F. Kennedy, but in 1966 the memories were only four years old, and they remained very fresh in young Yonas's mind. The Soviets, backward in so many ways, were obviously a force to contend with when it came to military technology. Finally, Yonas decided not to take the Reagan speech seriously. He'd bet his beard that it wasn't going anywhere. In fact he couldn't believe it was *intended* to be a serious proposal. It had to be some kind of throwaway comment—rhetoric, a political statement—and there wouldn't prove to be anything substantive to it.

Yonas had been rambling on in his mind, and he had to put some thought to the next day's meeting about construction progress at the new particle beam fusion accelerator site. PBFA, the guys at the lab wanted to call it. Yonas believed in pronounceable acronyms, and how the hell would you pronounce PBFA? It sounded like the sad sack in the Li'l Abner cartoons. Joe Btsplk . . . was that his name? No matter; he had work to do, and as for the Reagan initiative, that wasn't in his job description—yet.[2]

⁂

Gen. James A. Abrahamson, chief of U.S. Space Shuttle operations, was at home in Washington, watching television with a glass of wine on the table beside him. His children had left home to make their own lives—one was married and living in California and another was in the Navy—so this was a quiet evening with his wife, watching what by all outward indications promised to be a regular presidential budget speech.

Abrahamson remembers this as being a fairly classic speech, until it came to the end and the president turned to strategic defense, sending waves of excitement running through Abrahamson's brain cells. *He's reversing all these years of strategic thinking!* Abrahamson thought. The Space Shuttle might even be able to play a supporting role. *The Shuttle is the perfect vehicle for all kinds of space tests. We can play.*

Abrahamson was a classical military officer, not a tall man, but alert, clean-cut, physically trim, and the epitome of trustworthiness. While his main preoccupation was the Shuttle, he was also concerned by the nuclear weapons race and wanted to think that there was some better strategy than building more and more nukes. Would Reagan's vision generate a solution to a massive dilemma? "When he finished the speech I thought, 'Well, there's an alternative,'" Abrahamson said. "And, being a technologist, I thought, 'We can do this.'"

Abrahamson was a Vietnam veteran who had also served as an astronaut trainee, an Air Force commander, and—twice—as a NASA executive. As NASA's associate administrator for space flight—in an outfit that ran the Shuttle and had responsibility for Johnson Space Center, Kennedy Space Center, and Marshall Space Flight Center—he was a very busy man, in seventh heaven, working on a job that he truly loved.

"My God!" Abrahamson muttered to himself, "At last we've found a way to get out of this thing!"

Abrahamson—he liked his friends to call him by the nickname Abe—may not have had a deep grounding in space physics, but he was keenly aware of what "this thing" was. It was the Kennedy-era philosophy of mutual assured destruction (MAD), or vulnerability-based deterrence, in which Americans and Soviets alike realized that an attack on either of them by the other would result in terrible retribution—an annihilating storm of multi-megaton hydrogen reentry vehicles. (Technically speaking, *ballistic missiles* are rocket systems that are used to deliver *reentry vehicles*; these reentry vehicles, or RVs, are virtually unpowered missiles that contain explosive nuclear or conventional *warheads*.) No wonder they called it MAD, Abrahamson thought: the world needed to get rid of it.

As a teenager, Abrahamson had been impressed by a movie documentary on nuclear weapons. As he thought of the awesome nuclear devastation that would follow a nuclear exchange, he thought, *"Whoa! We can't let this happen!"*

Abe acquired a leaning toward things technical at an early age; next he determined to pursue a technical education. One year after he received his master's degree in aeronautical engineering, the Cuban Missile Crisis alerted the world to the fact that nuclear war could happen at hair-trigger notice. For the young Abrahamson, it was a sobering initiation into what would become a profound political awareness.

How *might* the Shuttle program help? It could put satellites into orbit, of course. The Heritage Foundation people had been talking up the idea of shooting down missiles with high-energy lasers on the ground, where there was plenty of available electricity and there was no need to put a huge power supply in space. Edward Teller was hot to trot with his x-ray laser. Danny Graham's High Frontier outfit was pushing the idea of arming satellites with small homing missiles. Didn't DARPA (the Defense Advanced Research Projects Agency) already have someone working on an orbiting mirror that could aim laser beams at ICBMs and bring them down? Maybe the Shuttle could be used to put some of those mirrors up there. . . .[3]

Stanley Orman was a Brit in Washington, specifically the deputy ambassador responsible for all defense exchanges between the United States and Britain. A product of London's polyglot, generally undistinguished East End, he had fought his way to the top of his chosen field. Not surprisingly, he relished the Washington experience, where, with his debonair bearing, he tended to look and act as though he had just dropped in from the yacht club. One of Britain's top nuclear weaponeers, he had served on the highly successful Chevaline nuclear warhead program at the Atomic Weapons Establishment in Aldermaston, Berkshire. The year before, while with the Ministry of Defense in Whitehall, an hour's journey from the Atomic Weapons Establishment (AWE) with its police dogs and Uzi-sporting guards, he had the satisfaction of seeing Chevaline come into service, ready to sit securely atop a U.S.-built Polaris submarine launch system.

Orman didn't actually *like* MAD, but he was part of the system. He and his colleagues were confident that the new British deterrent could penetrate the Soviet defenses of the time, more effectively even than anything the Americans had. But it was necessary to keep as up to date as possible on improvements that the Russians might make—so that the British could make the improvements necessary to retain a deterrent posture. When Reagan gave his "Star Wars" speech, Orman paid very close attention indeed.

Was Reagan merely trying to frighten the Soviets into being more cooperative with a clever rhetorical maneuver? Or did he truly believe his technical community could devise a way out of the MAD dilemma?

An acutely insightful man who had adapted the street smarts of his native Hackney to the international scene, Orman had a very strong gut feeling that Reagan was onto something *big*. And if possible, Britain needed to get into the act. Now, just how might that happen?[4]

These five men—Abrahamson, Orman, Shultz, Velikhov, and Yonas—didn't know each other at the time, though Yonas and Velikhov had developed an acquaintanceship as a result of their attendance at international science meetings. Yet each, in his own way, was destined to play a role in the unfolding of Ronald Reagan's Strategic Defense Initiative. Over the next few years, they would be caught up in cascades of confrontation over the presidential initiative—international intrigues, deceptions on both sides, student protests, congressional arguments, Soviet–American shouting matches, even assassinations carried out by the infamous Red Brigades.

What was SDI? The short answer describes a high-tech program to shoot down enemy missiles before they could reach U.S. targets. In fact, it turned out to be an enormously complicated technical, psychological, and political construct. SDI had many layers of meaning, and its significance in ending the Cold War will forever be debated by statesmen and historians. Some have called it a hoax, a trick, or a "sting." Others are true believers who hold that, even if SDI did not end the Soviet empire and the Cold War all by itself, it was one of numerous straws that broke the camel's back. Still others think of it as an expensive mistake of sorts, encouraged by an American military-industrial complex that managed to win the imagination of an aging President Ronald Reagan. Quite possibly it was all of these. Quite definitely it was an enigma, and to a large extent it remains so today.

THE COLD WAR: SURVIVAL AND THE BOLSHEVIK EXPERIMENT

Academics love to argue over unsolvable puzzles, and the origin of the Cold War is one such puzzle. The West had been ready for some ideological confrontation with the Soviets for decades, because Bolshevism had battled the democratic ideal and its backbone of capitalism since it ousted the Romanovs in 1917. The Western powers never trusted Josef Stalin, the much-feared, much-loved hierarch of the 1930s and 1940s, though the Soviet Union was a struggling ally in the war against Nazism. At the Yalta summit of February 3–11, 1945, Stalin agreed with Franklin D. Roosevelt and Winston Churchill that "five Ds"—demilitarization, denazification, democratization, decentralization, and deindustrialization—should dominate the reconstruction of the post-war world. But before year's end, after the Germans capitulated and the three met again in the Berlin suburb of Potsdam, it was a new game. The Soviets transformed the countries of Eastern Europe into colonies, and the initial chill of reaction spread quickly into an unprecedented and dangerous East–West conflict.

By now, two devices, incongruously dubbed Fat Man and Little Boy, had come to symbolize a revolution in warfare, amplifying the confrontation into a quarrel that threatened the very existence of civilization. These were the atomic bombs, developed at Los Alamos as part of the Manhattan Project, that were dropped with horrendous results on the Japanese cities of Hiroshima and Nagasaki. Those bombs were rated at about 1,000 tons of TNT (1 kiloton or 1 kT), but were tiny by comparison with the nuclear weapons that would be developed at the height of the Cold War.

Nuclear warfare is the ultimate in nightmares that might come true. Estimates hold that even a "small" 1-kiloton explosion over Manhattan would kill about 210,000 persons. Nearly half of those killed would die from burns, and about one-third of the remainder would die from blast. A separate estimate projects 830,000 fatalities from a 150-kiloton explosion, plus 875,000 injuries—far beyond the ability of the medical system to cope.[5] It has also been estimated that if a modern multimegaton thermonuclear weapon were detonated outside the White House, it would kill every living thing inside the Beltway, the freeway that rings the city.[6]

The atomic revolution was just six years in the making. Lisa Meitner and Otto Frisch described "nuclear fission" in the journal *Nature* in early 1939. That September, the Hungarian scientists Leó Szilárd, Eugene Wigner, and Edward Teller talked Albert Einstein into writing a letter to President Roosevelt, advising him that "extremely powerful bombs of a new type" might be created through the use of nuclear power.

By March 1940, Otto Frisch and Rudolf Peierls, at Birmingham University in England, had confirmed that it was possible to make nuclear weapons. In July 1941 Britain's Maud Committee determined that "the scheme for a uranium bomb is practicable and likely to lead to decisive results in the war," and the committee produced plans for a uranium separation plant.[7] The report was sent to the United States in October; it had been leaked to Soviet spies a month earlier.

The British set up their development program under the code name Tube Alloys; the Americans named theirs the Manhattan Project. Soon, U.S. and British scientists were pooling their resources. Top scientists from other nations joined the cause, and it was not long before the first nuclear chain reaction was achieved in Chicago on December 2, 1942. Tube Alloys would be merged with the Manhattan Project as a junior partner under the Quebec Agreement of 1943.* Meanwhile, early computers were humming away, providing the calculations that would permit engineers and scientists to detonate the first nuclear explosion in the desert near Alamogordo, New Mexico, on July 16, 1945.

At his research laboratory in Moscow, the great nuclear physicist Igor Kurchatov had been chafing at the bit, hinting strongly to Lavrenti Beria, chief of intelligence and atomic energy operations: "Some 3,000 pages of new intelligence materials show the enormous effort abroad. Might you offer some suggestions for our work corresponding to our great state?"[8] Finally, after Hiroshima, Stalin ordered that the bomb be developed. On August 29, 1949, the Soviet Union tested its first nuclear device, "Joe 1," which, thanks to the fruits of espionage, was a replica of Fat Man. The British decided to make their own bomb, withdrew from their partnership with the United States, and readied

---

*This stage of Anglo–American nuclear weapons cooperation ended with the U.S. Atomic Energy Act of 1946. The act was repealed in 1958, and joint U.S.–British nuclear weapons resumed with the institution of a number of joint operating working groups and U.S. leadership in the provision of nonnuclear matériel for the British program.

their goal on October 3, 1952. France joined the club in 1960, and China in 1964.

Though no natural date exists for the beginning of the Cold War, it most likely began in 1946, a year when Churchill observed that "from Stettin in the Baltic to Trieste in the Adriatic an iron curtain has descended across the (European) Continent." Viktor Mikhailov, longtime head of the Russian Department of Energy, MINATOM, contends that it started in 1941, when the United Kingdom and United States left the Soviet Union out in their early studies of the feasibility of creating an atomic bomb. In his book *The Struggle for the World* (1947), James Burnham suggested it started in April 1944, when communists led a mutiny against the Greek navy in Alexandria Harbor. Edward Teller, on the other hand, argued that the Cold War doesn't deserve to be called a war. In any case, it was institutionalized with the Truman Doctrine of March 12, 1947—in which the U.S. government pledged to counter Soviet expansionism—and with Stalin's response that he would fortify Eastern Europe under his own "doctrine of retaliation."

THE SPEED-OF-LIGHT SOLUTION

Peter Kapitsa was a much-accomplished scientist and a disciple of the great Ernest Rutherford at Cambridge University, but now he had little more to do than putter around his little lab, write, eat, sleep—and figure out a way of escaping the confines of his country house near Moscow. It was 1950, and Lavrenti Beria was still on his case. Perhaps Kapitsa could ensure his safety, even save his own life, by using his knowledge to invent a new way of outgunning the dreaded Americans—an energy-beam weapon, perhaps. The great Russian nuclear physicist knew that Beria's secret police would be watching his house night and day, waiting for him to venture into the streets so that he could be shot as an enemy of the state. Kapitsa might even hope for such a fate, for it would be greatly preferable to what he might face in the dungeons of the Lublianka security complex.

Only Stalin had saved him, and Beria, who had been sycophantic toward the Soviet dictator for so many years, hated him for it. He would have executed Kapitsa long ago for his outspokenness and inso-lence, even for his patriotic insistence that the Soviet Union should build its own atomic bomb rather than reinvent the proven design stolen from Los Alamos. But Stalin had a deep respect for scientists, rooted in the desperate race to build the first Soviet atomic bombs.

Kapitsa thought he might be able to benefit from Stalin's lust for high-tech weapons. Before the Great Patriotic War ended, he had come to some logical conclusions. First, after the ghastly experience of the Nazi invasion, which touched off a conflict that cost tens of millions of Russian lives, the government was terrified that history might repeat itself. Second, German success with missile warfare against Britain proved that they could wage war from a distance without engaging in conventional combat. No modern Hitler or Napoleon would need to use troops to attack the Soviet Union. An effective modern defense—not with rockets, but something fast enough to down the attacking rocket at any part of its flight path—would be just the thing. Kapitsa thought he had the perfect answer: a beam of microwaves capable of penetrating the missile skin and frying everything inside.

Kapitsa summed up the competition; there wasn't any, really. The British had tinkered with the idea of microwave weapons in the 1930s, until their top scientists had been siphoned off into secret work that would lead to the invention of radar; an American Army Air Force group had suggested research on some undefined kind of "beam weapon" in 1946; and that was about it. Most of the interest resulted from fiction, from Wells's *War of the Worlds* to *The Death Box*, a 1926 Russian novel about a scientist who invented a beam weapon.

The time was right. The United States and the Soviet Union had begun ballistic missile programs right after the war, the U.S. effort impeded at first by worries that a rocket could not loft a payload as heavy as a nuclear weapon. America's Stillwell Report, compiled after it was learned that the Nazis had plans to launch a missile attack on New York City, had strongly endorsed the just-announced U.S. anti-ballistic missile program. First there had been ballistic missiles, ultimately capable of covering thousands of miles as they arched into space and back again; now there had to be anti–ballistic missiles (ABMs) to shoot them down.

Kapitsa, a gentle man with a long face and large, far-seeing eyes under what was now a thin, combed-over thatch of graying hair, put pen to paper for the umpteenth time. For years he had corresponded with Stalin (his letters were read but, with one exception, unanswered), but this time he addressed his memorandum to Georgi Malenkov, Party secretary since 1939 and a possible successor to the Great Leader himself.

"Dear Comrade Malenkov . . ."

In a secret Kremlin meeting, six months after Stalin's death on March 5, 1953, a group of generals asked the Central Committee of the Communist Party of the Soviet Union (CPSU) to put the development of an ABM system into high gear. A feasibility study followed, and an exploratory development program began at year's end. Other things happened, too, during this honeymoon of Nikita Khrushchev's regime. Beria was arrested, Kapitsa was freed, and then Beria was executed. Kapitsa invented two new high-power microwave generators in the period 1950–55, but now, reinstated as a well-paid government lab director, he sensibly gave up his interest in microwave weapons and went back to probing the insides of atoms. He was chosen for a Nobel Prize for physics in 1978, six years before his death.

In 1953 there were no jet airliners, no touch-tone telephones, no space satellites, no personal computers, let alone the Internet or video games. Television was in its infancy, and what was available was in black and white. One even had to make a reservation with the telephone company to make an international call. But technology was moving fast in other directions. With the world's arsenals of tactical and ballistic missiles—nuclear tipped medium range missiles like the Soviet SS-6 Sapwood and the U.S. Thor and Jupiter come to mind—beginning to blossom, the stage was set for an epic battle between two superpowers. No one wanted a nuclear war that could lay waste to the entire planet, yet in the name of defense the two great missile fleets were being continuously improved and enlarged.

Gradually, though no one knew it yet, the scene was being set for the era of mutual assured destruction. This theory holds that, if one of two opposing sides were to launch a nuclear attack, both the attacker and the defender would be destroyed in the resulting exchange. It became a plausible idea some time later, after nuclear-armed submarines made it possible to launch a retaliative strike against a first-strike aggressor, greatly enhancing the deterrent previously provided by nuclear bombers. This doctrine would be enunciated by Secretary of Defense Robert McNamara at a United Press International meeting in San Francisco on September 18, 1967. "The cornerstone of our strategic policy continues to be to deter nuclear attack upon the United States or its allies," he said. "We do this by maintaining a highly reliable ability to inflict unacceptable damage upon any single aggressor or combination of aggressors at any time during the course of a strategic nuclear exchange, even after absorbing a surprise first strike. This can be defined as our assured-destruction capability."[9]

While Kapitsa was packing away his notes on microwave weaponry, researchers at Lawrence Livermore National Laboratory were working out another exotic defense against hostile missiles. This program, code-named Seesaw, was run with Advanced Research Programs Agency funding from 1958 until 1972. It and a similar program emerging at a secret lab in Siberia were the first serious proposals for striking missiles with particles rather than beams of relatively weak radio energy. In Seesaw's case, these were high-energy fragments stripped from atomic nuclei and moving close to the speed of light.

Ronald Reagan's "Star Wars" program was still a quarter of a century away, but the race for the ultimate space weapon was already under way. A number of directed-energy weapon schemes would soon be on the books. These had started with high-energy radio waves, moving on to atomic particles and lasers—the latter named "directed-energy" weapons (DEWs) because they consist of energy, rather than matter, deliberately aimed in the direction of a previously identified target at, or near, the speed of light. Someday, it might be possible to place defensive systems such as these in space, along with the offensive weapons they were meant to destroy.

BALLISTIC MISSILE OFFENSE AND DEFENSE

The age of guided missile warfare is a mere six decades old. The German V-2 missiles developed at the end of World War II began a new era in warfare that would eventually enable accurate delivery of weapons of mass destruction to targets thousands of miles from their point of origin. The Soviets first launched their SS-6 Sapwood multistage ballistic missile in August 1957; fifteen months later, the U.S. Atlas ICBM made its first full-range maiden flight, followed by the slightly shorter-range Titan, the ancestor of today's Lockheed-Martin space launcher fleet.*

By the time extremely fast, rocket-borne nuclear weapons became a reality, both the United States and the Soviet Union were developing ways to blast them out of the skies. Development of the U.S. Nike-Zeus (later Nike-X) ABM system began in 1956, during the administration of President Dwight D. Eisenhower. A sleek, super-fast, two-stage system, it was designed to sit beside a field of missiles and flash into the sky at the moment an attack was detected, blasting incoming missiles to smithereens. As this project began in 1956, similar work was moving apace in the Soviet Union.

There were problems with the U.S. and Soviet systems alike. They were nuclear-armed, which meant that a misfire would be disastrous and even a direct hit on a missile would probably rain radioactive debris upon the mother country. Though they were fast, they were

*Ballistic missiles may carry conventional high-explosive warheads or weapons of mass destruction (nuclear, chemical, and biological warheads), and are classed by range. An ICBM has a range greater than 3,400 miles; an intermediate-range ballistic missile (IRBM) 1,500 to 3,400 miles; a medium-range ballistic missile (MRBM) 500 to 1,500 miles; a short-range ballistic missile (SRBM) less than 500 miles.

actually slow compared to a warhead coming from space, and they were not "smart" enough to discriminate between real nuclear warheads and large numbers of decoys.

Various ways of using these new devices were argued, over and over again. Would they be best used to provide a "thin" defense to protect highly populated areas, a defense of the U.S. nuclear deterrent, or a defense of the national command authority? These questions were never answered satisfactorily. Arms control advocates argued that a successful defense would convince the Soviets that the United States was considering a first strike. Then, they argued, the Soviets would be tempted to launch a preemptive strike before the United States could take action.[10] Soviet premier Leonid Brezhnev publicly disavowed the "first strike" alternative on January 18, 1977, claiming, "The Soviet Union has always been and remains a convinced opponent of such concepts."[11] But many in the West remained unconvinced.

Though these systems, U.S. and Soviet, might diminish the effects of an all-out first strike, there was no way they could actually nullify one. Thus, in the years prior to 1983, the best strategy was to convince war planners to not even consider an attack. This was accomplished through nuclear deterrence—in other words, the inevitability of counterattack promised by the MAD scenario. Even if one side leveled the other side's major cities, and/or successfully targeted its missile sites, the other could retaliate with nuclear weapons fired from submarines, hard-to-find mobile launchers, silos that had escaped destruction in the initial onslaught, or aircraft.

Nike-X and its successors were ideas for shooting down missiles from the ground. On the other hand, the idea of policing the world's war machines *from space* had been visualized as early as 1946, in a short-lived RAND Corporation study. While the Soviets force-fed their military might with huge, secret projects that were more expensive than ever will be known, the United States poured money into its Advanced Research Projects Agency. One of ARPA's programs, included under the code name Project Defender, bore the misleadingly Disneyesque acronym BAMBI (Ballistic Missile Boost Intercept). BAMBI came up with one idea that would survive the high-tech gauntlet of the Cold War—small, "smart" weapons launched from orbiting spacecraft.

Apollo, the Space Shuttle, and other space spectaculars like *Pioneer*, *Voyager*, *Galileo*, and *Cassini*, were among the winners in the annals of geopolitical one-upmanship. None of these in itself changed the world. Considered together with the Manhattan Project, however, they were an unbeatable combination. Such feats proved repeatedly that, particularly in terms of science and technology, the United States was by far the globe's most visionary and most capable nation.

In the 1960s and 1970s, a new picture of the United States spread effortlessly into every corner of the planetary hive. This was more than a nation of New York plutocrats, military machines, railroad and rustbelt millionaires, cornfields, and lend-lease. Here was a nation that could take up the most daunting of technical challenges and transform them into tangible reality. Carl Sagan conceded quite readily that *Apollo* was not mainly about science or space, but about world leadership and national prestige. Still, he said, "*Apollo* conveyed a confidence, energy, and breadth of vision that did capture the imagination of the world. That too was part of its purpose. It inspired an optimism about technology, an enthusiasm for the future. If we could fly to the Moon, as so many asked, what else were we capable of?"[12] That was exactly the question the Soviets asked, when SDI came along.

THE SPUTNIK REVOLUTION

Mutual Assured Destruction . . . requires that there be a balance, and the balance is the understanding that if either side initiates the use of nuclear weapons, the other side will respond with sufficient power to inflict unacceptable damage. Mutual Assured Destruction is the foundation of stable deterrence in a nuclear world.
It's not mad; it's logical.
—Robert McNamara[1]

The headlines of October 4, 1957, rocked the world. Suddenly everyone was aware that a small, shiny, sphere made in Russia was circling the Earth, emitting a nonstop series of beep-beep-beep "I am here" radio messages. While the idea of putting a satellite into orbit had been proposed many times, no one had done it before, and Washington's space and defense community cringed. The Americans had invented—and used—the atomic bomb. The Germans, under Wernher von Braun, had demonstrated that rockets provided an awesome means of delivering weapons. Now the Soviet Union's Sputnik was showing, without anyone actually saying so, that a future nuclear war could be waged from space. The Americans knew that they would have to respond to this challenge to Yankee ingenuity. Before long, they would.

The two-faced personality of modern technology had become starkly evident when it was demonstrated that nuclear reactors could be used both to generate civilian nuclear power and to produce uranium and plutonium for weapons. Now the world had to think more seriously about the fact that large rocket systems—and their payloads—could be used either for space research or for providing significant advantage in the delivery of weapons of mass destruction.

The years 1957–66 were arguably the greatest decade in the history of Soviet military science. Following Sputnik, Premier Nikita Khrushchev whipped the nation's science and technology communities into a frenzy of trial-and-error innovation, and he rewarded them with new buildings and new labs—even new cities—in which to do their work. While consumer technology withered, good minds, good materials, and quality manufacturing became the monopoly of the military space establishment. Science theory, overseen by the Academy of Sciences at such centers as the Kurchatov Institute and the Lebedev Institute, was in many respects world-class. But applying scientific ideas to make new products was another matter. In some respects, engineering was as backward as science was refined.

Almost all Soviet military science and technology was hidden in secrecy—only the good news got out, and then with a liberal application of verbal cosmetics. And there was plenty of good news. Just after Sputnik left the world slack-jawed, there was a successful test of the Soviet Styx cruise missile. Then the Soviets tested the first intercontinental ballistic missile, fifteen months before the maiden flight of the U.S. Atlas. The next year, 1958, saw the establishment of a high-level Soviet antimissile defense department.

"After Sputnik I, the authorities' appetite for launches and for the quick political dividend they brought in was growing," said Roald Sagdeev, former director of the civilian Soviet Space Research Institute (IKI).[2] Under cover, the military establishment was sponsoring huge research programs in other hitherto untested fields. Peter Zarubin, former director of high-energy laser programs in the Main Directorate of the Ministry for Defense Industry (Military Industrial Commission, or MIC), noted that "it turned out later that the tendency to embark upon risky and not fully substantiated projects continued to be a weakness of scientists and military for a long time."[3]

The Sputnik III satellite story provides an illustration of the political value placed on space technology. Project engineers suspected the little craft had electrical problems and wanted to run more tests, but the international communist movement needed support in its bid to win votes in an upcoming Italian election. Khrushchev, believing he could improve its chances for victory by demonstrating the might of communist technology, ignored the warnings and pressed the Sputnik III managers to launch their bird in May 1958. The satellite managed to reach its orbit, but, alas, its tape recorders failed to function. It was a lost opportunity. Had the recorder worked as expected, the Soviet Union might have discovered the zones of natural radiation around Earth that came to be known as the Van Allen Belts. The Americans soon discovered them with the Pioneer 1 satellite.

The Soviet drive to exploit new technology was again illustrated during the attempted October 1960 launch of a new ICBM design from Baikonur, the huge cosmodrome located at Tyuratam on the Kazakhstan steppes, downrange from Kapustin Yar. Marshal Mitrofan Nedelin, overly enthused and determined to grasp the opportunity, insisted on having a front-row view, despite warnings from his safety crew. When the rocket blew up on the pad, he and scores of other onlookers were incinerated.

Successes naturally accompanied the failures in this burst of activity. In an October 1961 test, the winged V-1000 antimissile missile downed an R-12 missile, also called the SS-4 Sandal. The Kremlin was jubilant, and it was not long before Khrushchev claimed that the Soviets could hit "a fly in outer space" and Defense Minister Marshal Rodion Malinovsky boasted that "the problem of destroying ballistic missiles in flight has been successfully solved." While these claims were gross exaggerations, the Soviets were determined to capitalize on their well-publicized early success with the V-1000, code-named Griffon by the North Atlantic Treaty Organization (NATO). The missile was first seen in public in 1963, when it was paraded on Red Square. It was to be deployed at Leningrad and Tallinn, but these plans were abandoned after adoption of the A-35 interceptor system, which utilized Galosh nuclear-armed rockets.

The Galosh was revealed on Red Square in late 1964, when Western observers noted with some amazement that it was larger than the U.S. Minuteman ICBM. Sixty-four of these three-stage interceptors, each of which had a 190-mile range, were eventually deployed at four sites near Moscow in the period 1972–90. Concurrently, an improved point-defense system, the A-135, was in the design stage. It included the longer-range (220 miles) Gorgon, which was an upgrade of the Galosh; the short-range (50 miles) Gazelle; and improved radar.

The ability of these antimissile missiles to destroy U.S. ICBMs could not be proven. However, their very existence made a strong statement. The Soviets had erected a symbol to give the world the impression that their technology was ready to deal with a U.S. first strike. Not surprisingly, Soviet Premier Aleksei Kosygin strongly defended ground-based antimissile defense at the 1967 Glassboro summit with President Lyndon Johnson. When McNamara warned that "deployment of a Soviet ABM system will lead to an escalation of the arms race," Kosygin retorted that "defense is moral; offense is immoral!" adding that "the antimissile system is not a weapon of attack. It is a weapon of protection."[4] Twenty years later, the shoe would be on the other foot.

Nukes on the American Doorstep

Sputnik would forever stick in the craws of America's defense chieftains. The United States was also surprised by a feat in which a Soviet spacecraft photographed the otherwise invisible back side of the moon, and then it was inflamed by an intelligence report—later shown to be erroneous—that there was a "missile gap" that favored the adversary. The United States was driven firmly into action in April 1961, after Yuri Gagarin, aboard the *Vostok*, became the first human to orbit the planet. Gagarin had barely finished his welcome-home parties when President John F. Kennedy announced Project *Apollo*, pledging to place American astronauts on the moon by the end of the decade. Then Khrushchev truculently implied that, with the technology used to orbit Gagarin, he could drop nukes from orbit any time he felt like it.

"Sputnik was the starting gun in my technical career," said Gerold Yonas. "It initiated me as a Cold War warrior with an early feeling for the competition in technology, and my interest soared in the science and technology of the time." In 1961, intrigued by the just-invented lasers, he wrote a paper on optical communications at a time when the idea had occurred to few others.[5]

If 1961 was a year of widening eyes and slackening jaws, 1962 was one for clenching teeth. It was a prickly year in which the United States put its first Minuteman ICBMs into service, declared a squadron of Jupiter medium-range nuclear missiles operational at Cigli Air Base in Turkey, and demonstrated, over the Kwajalein test range, that the "B" version of its nuclear-tipped Nike-Zeus ABM system really worked. First used to bring down an unarmed Atlas ICBM nose cone, Nike-Zeus B scored about a dozen more successes—including a satellite kill—before the end of the next year. Its ability to bring down single targets was well proved, but the system was primitive by modern standards and limited in speed and range. Its low-tech radars would have been completely confused by decoys.

Thus the Cold War arms buildup was well under way when, on October 14, U-2 photos showed a missile on a Cuban launch site. Shocked and angered, President Kennedy ordered a blockade of Fidel Castro's island fortress. It was later confirmed that the Soviet commander in Cuba, Gen. Issa Pliyev, had a nuclear force consisting of Luna short-range rockets with twelve 2-kiloton warheads; FKR cruise missiles with eighty 10-kiloton warheads; and six 6-kiloton bombs that could be delivered by Ilyushin-28 bombers. An additional twenty-four half-megaton missile warheads were locked up in a ship's hold, awaiting pickup.[6]

After a series of tense exchanges with the U.S. government, the

Soviets took their nuclear weapons home. It was not a complete loss of face. In return, Kennedy secretly agreed to remove nuclear missiles from Turkey and promised that the United States would never invade Cuba. But Khrushchev's regime remained tinged with humiliation until his removal from power in 1964.

The Cuban Missile Crisis is generally reckoned to be the closest the United States and Soviet Union came to nuclear war, though false alarms would prove the risk of unintentional attack in coming decades. It gave both sides pause to think of the horrendous results that might emerge from nuclear confrontation.

AKADEMGORODOK

Roald Sagdeev was not particularly interested in Novosibirsk, despite the fact that it was his official destination. He had his sights set on a completely new city—Khrushchev's personal dream project—that was rising from the Siberian taiga not far away. In 1958 there had been little there save a hilly birch forest. Then the earth-moving equipment came in: the telescoping gantry cranes, the concrete workers, truck drivers, the electricians, plumbers, fitters of all kinds, and the humble wielders of pickaxes and shovels. Big new lab buildings and lines of apartment houses built of reinforced-concrete block panels flanked the avenues bulldozed from the forest floor.

Academician Mikhail Lavrentiev's sparkling new Akademgorodok, the "Academic City" of the Siberian branch of the Soviet Academy of Sciences, was an unusually large scientific center.[7] It began with a new multidisciplinary university and fourteen institutes; with time, that number would double. Gersh Itzkovich (Andrei Mikhailovich) Budker was one of many top-level scientists who moved there from institutes all over the Soviet Union. Budker, first to arrive from the Kurchatov Institute, was captivated by the dream of building colliding-beam experiments for high-energy physics, similar to those at the Stanford Linear Accelerator Center and CERN. On the side, he dabbled in death-ray weapons.

Sagdeev arrived at the center in 1961. Down the wide boulevards he drove, to the not-quite-finished, five-story Institute of Nuclear Physics, the largest complex in the entire city, where inscriptions on the walls still read, "Implement the historical decisions of the XXII Congress of the CPSU!" and, in praise of the contractor, "The collective of Sibakademstroi is struggling for the honor of being a Collective of Communist Labor."

Moscow was an exciting place for science, but Akademgorodok, three time zones to the east, was charged with enthusiastic, optimistic, idealistic newcomers like young Sagdeev. And of course they were scientists too—already some of them were preparing Budker's awesome VEP-1, the world's first colliding-beam accelerator, for its first shots. A byproduct would be free-electron laser technology, developed after Budker's death and Alexander Skrinsky's appointment as his successor.

Particle beam weapons—also the focus of LLNL's Seesaw project—were part of Budker's bailiwick, though most of his funding was dedicated to development of particle-accelerator technologies. Once he had established an Institute of Nuclear Physics, he persuaded Sagdeev to join his team. Sagdeev before long was involved in discussions of what was called "the beam weapon with charge exchange." Later called the "neutral particle beam" (NPB), it emerged about ten years after the new center opened and became a small but significant part of the institute's overall activity.*

"The beam weapon marked a very interesting period," Sagdeev said. "The original [pre-NPB] concept was that you would accelerate charged particles to high energy. The main problem was that you would be unable to fire it against a target because it would be deflected by the Earth's natural magnetic field."[8] This also was the weak point of particle-beam ideas previously suggested by the Yugoslav scientist Nikola Tesla and others.

On the other hand, a successful space-based *neutral* particle beam could be aimed at a target and fry its electronic brain. Budker had figured out how to solve the magnetic-field problem; but his invention would be too big to put into orbit and its beam would quickly spread over a large area, steadily losing its destructive power with distance. "The problem," said Sagdeev, "was that you would have to have an accelerator on a space platform—and the general impression of high-energy accelerators is that they are huge. The second issue was beam divergence. At the time, the concept was almost science fiction."[9] Budker's NPB—which went no further than accelerator experiments and studies—sparked a debate within the Soviet Academy of Sciences, led by the fusion pioneer Lev Artsimovich and physicist Boris Konstantinov. "Konstantinov said it was nonsense," said Evgeny Velikhov.[10] And that was the end of that.

When Sputnik went into orbit—nearly three years before the first laser was demonstrated—Peter Zarubin was working as a junior elec-

---

*Neutral particle beam weapons could destroy missile electronics with hydrogen ions from a linear accelerator. These would be very penetrating and would also cause the target to give off radiation, providing a signal that would indicate whether this was a reentry vehicle or a decoy. NPBs also have potential use as antisatellite weapons.

tronics engineer, developing computerized systems for Soviet air defense. He had just completed his studies at the Moscow Physical-Technical Institute (MFTI) and had yet to start his way up the professional ladder. "I remember the general atmosphere of admiration and national pride," he said. "There is no doubt that the Sputnik program triumph had a significant influence on the general attitude of the people and the government toward new technologies, and determined many future events in our country."[11]

Possibly because he was both a physicist and an avid mountain climber, Zarubin's first professional posting was an exotic one. He was sent to Antarctica, where in 1959–61 he served as a geophysicist at the Vostok research station. At Vostok he shared the distinction, with his colleague Igor Ivanov, of logging the lowest-ever temperature then recorded on Earth—minus 88.6 Celsius—in August 1960. His first contact with lasers—the first time he heard the word "laser"—was in September 1961, after he returned to the Soviet Union and decided to return to the MFTI for postgraduate study. There he was introduced to professor Leonid Kurbatov, scientific director of the Applied Physics Research Institute in Moscow. Kurbatov invited him to become his assistant both in the MFTI and in the Applied Physics Institute, which participated in the infant Soviet laser program beginning in 1961.[12]

Zarubin joined the Soviet Ministry of Defense Industry (MOP) in 1967, two years before it created the special 8th Directorate for high-energy laser programs. In 1976 he became the 8th Directorate's technical director and a member of the ministry board, with general oversight of Soviet military laser development, a position that acquainted him with influential scientists from Alexander Prokhorov and Nikolai Basov to Yuli Khariton, head of the nation's nuclear science programs. He remained with the ministry until its dissolution in 1990, but he continued teaching, consulting, and (beginning in 1994) advising the director of the Granat design bureau, which develops and produces high-energy laser devices and systems.

PROJECT DEFENDER

U.S. research in space weaponry steadily gathered momentum in the 1950s and 1960s. Inside the Department of Defense's Advanced Research Projects Agency (ARPA)—which was created in response to the Sputnik challenge—the intriguing Project Defender would spend more than $1 billion (in then-current dollars) from 1958 to 1969, for research on military satellites, lasers, and other advanced defense concepts.* Defender was then the crucible of all ballistic missile defense research and a place for out-of-the-box thinkers. "The initial program was rather excessively advanced," wrote Barry Bruce Briggs, "including examination of antigravity, antimatter, and force fields. . . . Defender was a veritable research Disneyland, the greatest toy show since the nova of frantic experimentation of the last days of the Third Reich."[13] By the summer of 1960, Project Defender was well under way, and its leadership had quickly recognized that enemy ICBMs would be most vulnerable immediately after launch, when boost-phase rockets produce a strong and easily detectable flare of infrared radiation.

Among Defender's programs was BAMBI, the breeding ground for a number of ideas for picking off enemy ICBMs in the boost phase. "It was in a sense the intellectual precursor to the actual SDI; I don't think there's any doubt about that," said Charles Herzfeld, who joined ARPA in 1961, directed Project Defender from then until 1963, and served as the agency's director in 1965–67.[14]

The idea of using Earth satellites to launch very small ABM missiles was mentioned in Defender's 1960 annual report. These non-explosive "kinetic kill vehicles" would weigh as little as two pounds each. At the speed traveled by ICBMs, a collision with one pound of material would release the energy equivalent of 6 pounds of TNT.[15]

Convair then proposed Space Patrol Active Defense (SPAD)—a constellation of huge 30-ton "garage satellites," each carrying a number of interceptor missiles—to ARPA. Each 300-pound interceptor would deploy a wire web, studded with small pellets designed to perforate the attacking reentry vehicle at mind-boggling speed, anywhere from 6,000 to 60,000 feet per second.

This was no small project. It might have taken more than five hundred SPAD satellites to provide sufficient coverage of the Soviet Union, plus a "mother satellite" to detect launches, calculate their trajectories, and speed the missiles toward their targets. The first SPAD proposal was reorganized and simplified, and then it disappeared, a victim of complexity, cost, and computing limitations. Herb York, a former director of DARPA, later had this to say about BAMBI: "The concept of this mad-scientist's-dream involved surrounding the earth with a great swarm of small satellites that would detect, attack, and destroy anything that stuck its nose above the atmosphere. Some thought had been given to the question of how to enable friendly missiles and satellites to pass through the swarm, but that was one of

*ARPA over the years has been denoted with both ARPA and DARPA, the "D" standing for Defense.

the least of the problems with this system, and it too never got beyond the study stage."[16] The ARPA Terminal Defense (ARPAT) offered several alternative ABM approaches for terminal defense as missiles approached their targets. "All these were firsts because ARPA was the only game in this town," Herzfeld explained. "One, the air-launched interceptor, worked several times. The tests were complicated. We drove a reentry vehicle into White Sands to get close to ICBM velocities. Anything less would have been unconvincing."[17]

Once ARPA had pulled off a successful test, the project went no further, accepted policy being that, after proof of concept, one of the armed forces would continue with development. "That was the theory," grumbled Herzfeld. "But in ABM few things were picked up by the Services."[18] The ARPA folks were paid to be visionaries, and the uniformed pragmatists were leery about making major new ABM investments. Literally and figuratively, ground-launched interceptors were more down to earth: they called for relatively easy-to-understand technologies, they were relatively cheap, and they thus remained the ABM weapons of choice.

Still, the ARPA people could manage to be philosophical. "A lot of strategic issues are based on what it looks like and what people think it might mean, not what's actually deployed," said Herzfeld. "Many strategic issues are resolved by thinking about what could happen and not what's available right now. And that's both wise and foolish, depending . . ."[19]

BAMBI achieved everlasting fame as a font of early U.S. blueprints for battle stations in space, but it was ahead of its time. With an expensive Project Apollo now on the books, the Kennedy administration cancelled BAMBI in 1962 after coming to the conclusion that it would soak up billions of dollars to pursue concepts that simply would not work—yet. Not only that, but satellites in low orbits over the Soviet Union would make very tempting targets for space mines and other antisatellite weapons. Robert Cooper, who managed BAMBI in the early 1960s, told a congressional panel that this was the main reason for abandoning his program.[20]

John Bosma, a onetime DARPA staffer and one of the most ardent anti-MAD people then on the U.S. political scene, believes that Project Defender could have solved the missile defense problem early in the game. "Had the U.S. gone ahead with the non-nuclear space-based defenses envisioned and prototyped (to hardware but not space-tested) under Project Defender," he said, "we could have had a rudimentary BMD system in low earth orbit by 1964. That system, for all its imperfections, would have terminated the Soviet investment drive, which probably approached $500 billion or maybe more.[21]

As scientists around the world were beginning work on laser weapon concepts, that most tangible reminder of the Iron Curtain, the Berlin Wall, was under construction. East–West tension was mounting, and now, after Cuba, both sides were even more concerned about their ability to defend against weapons that were steadily becoming more numerous and more sophisticated. In the August 1963 issue of *The Atlantic*, Alton Frye reported that "sentiment is building up on Capitol Hill for a more substantial military space effort." Frye went on to remind his readers that "secretary of Defense McNamara has publicly indicated that 'the Soviet Union may now have, or soon achieve, the capability to place in orbit bomb-carrying satellites.'"[22]

McNamara believed that if the United States limited its land-based nuclear missiles to just over one thousand, the Soviets would follow suit, and the 1,000-missile level became official policy in 1965. But as Robert C. "Bud" McFarlane, who would become Ronald Reagan's national security advisor, noted, "the Soviets reached 1,000 missiles in 1968, and kept right on going." This was clear evidence, he said, that the Kremlin would not be satisfied with a balance of power. "They were interested in dominance."[23]

The Soviets and the Americans agreed on one important issue in 1963—the Limited Test Ban Treaty, which banned atmospheric nuclear explosions. It was signed by representatives of the United States, Britain, and the Soviet Union on August 8, a couple of months before the world, including many ordinary Soviets, were shocked and saddened by the assassination of John F. Kennedy.

To some, a breakdown in the MAD model was becoming an awful but credible possibility. The risk of mutual assured destruction was no doubt reducing the likelihood that there would be another world war; on the other hand, it might inadvertently result in the ultimate holocaust. Either way, mutual assured destruction was frightening enough that many thought it might be worth mounting an effort on the scale of the Manhattan Project to free the world of the idea. In time, SDI would provide the vision that many were looking for.

LASERS: LAUNCHING THE LIGHT FANTASTIC

The intriguing history of the laser began in the late 1950s, when Charles Townes of the United States and Alexander Prokhorov and Nikolai Basov of the Soviet Union worked out theories that would result in their being awarded a 1964 Nobel Prize for "fundamental work in quantum electronics which led to production of oscillators and amplifiers according to the maser-laser principle."

Gordon Gould, who broke away from Townes's Columbia University master program to join Technical Research Group (TRG) in 1958, was also extremely active in early laser development. In 1988, after three decades of litigation, he would own four key U.S. patents.[24] Writer Jeff Hecht tells us that Gould gave the Department of Defense a $300,000 proposal to work on the yet-unproven laser concept in 1959, after which, to his surprise, DARPA gave his company $1 million to do the work. With his record of an early (and abandoned) interest in Marxism, Gould couldn't get clearance, couldn't work in classified areas, and never knew what, if anything, the government did with his proposal.[25]

After all of this early research and development by others, Ted Maiman of Hughes Research Laboratory demonstrated the first working laser on May 16, 1960, with TRG, AT&T Bell Telephone Laboratories, and IBM close on his heels. It was a pulsed laser, energized by light from a photographer's flash lamp.*

At first the laser was something of a curiosity, a means of producing a beam of absolutely pure red light from a chunk of ruby held between two carefully positioned mirrors. When they were "pumped" with a flash lamp, chromium atoms in the ruby adjusted to the insult by producing light particles, or photons. The light bounced back and forth between the mirrors, with the photons marching in step. One mirror let some of the light escape each time the light reached it, forming a red beam. To the eye it appeared as light of a single color; in the laboratory it was energy of a single wavelength, many times purer—and more useful—than the white light of the flash lamp. Ruby pulses soon attained enough power to punch tiny holes in razor blades. Gradually the laser became a taken-for-granted part of everyday life. Many types of lasers were developed, using different materials, producing pulses or continuous waves, and available in many wavelengths. They found thousands of uses: for example, in communications, fusion research, cutting and welding, range-finding, surgery, checkout scanners, laser pointers, compact disc readers, image scanning, pointing and surveying, and printing—and yes, weapons.

An Early Soviet Laser Initiative

The laser's "scientific curiosity" stage turned out to be very brief. At the end of 1961, a Soviet rocket designer by the name of Grigory

---

*Bell Labs subsequently made the helium-neon laser, which emitted a continuous beam of a few milliwatts and was electrically, rather than optically, excited.

Kisunko approached his superiors with a peculiar but intriguing idea—why not use lasers to lock onto and track enemy missiles? Radar worked, but bouncing radio waves across the sky in the search for targets was not precise and required a clunky triangulation system. Kisunko's was a timely and fortuitous suggestion, for Basov and Prokhorov were desperate to find ways to make their discovery useful. Basov and his associate Oleg Krokhin already wanted to use lasers to gain new insights into the physics of the hydrogen bomb. Now they were being invited to delve into a new, intriguing, and more immediately practical application. Kisunko's idea was to use lasers to find and track missiles, not to shoot them down. A laser radar system, code-named LE-1, was soon under development and would be officially accepted in 1980. Research into lasers powerful enough to destroy enemy missiles began in about 1963, and a large-scale research and development program was approved in 1966.

The early Soviet thrust in military laser technology—underestimated and unmatched in the West—drew on the resources of a large number of research institutions, led by Vympel, the Lebedev Institute (FIAN), the All-Union Research Institute of Experimental Physics (VNIIEF), and the Vavilov State Optical Institute (GOI). The Kurchatov Institute, which led Soviet nuclear physics programs, also became involved in high-energy laser development through its interest in fusion research. Test facilities for laser weapon and radar projects were planned, among other places, at the Balkhash site of the State Central Research and Development Testing Ground at Sary Shagan.

Soviet research into laser weaponry and other directed-energy systems was carried out in deep secrecy, though it was observed (often with questionable accuracy) by Western analysts during the last three decades of the Cold War. One thing was sure: the research was serious, and it was very big. During the 1960s, in America's Project *Apollo* years, Soviet laser research and development shot ahead, spurred by Prokhorov and Basov. And it continued to expand, notably in a program that began with an early 1960s concept for pumping a laser with nuclear explosives.

"An avalanche-like growth was observed in the number of research institutes and industrial plants, as well as higher education institutes engaged in the research and development of lasers," wrote Zarubin. "Probably a hundred such organizations in the Soviet Union were involved by the mid-1960s."[26] Yonas, who served as chief scientist of the U.S. Strategic Defense Initiative in 1984–86, estimates that one hundred thousand individuals must have been involved in this giant build-up.

Colonel Vitaly Shlykov, a department chief in the Main Intelligence Administration (GRU) of the Soviet military general staff, confirmed that his nation made huge investments in military laser technology. "The laser equipped with an x-ray booster is a Russian invention," he said in an interview conducted after the fall of the Soviet Union. "In this [SDI-related] field we surpassed the Americans in many areas. However, we spent tens of times more resources on all these programs than the Americans."[27] Shlykov could be right; however, his comment on expenditures should be taken with a pinch of salt because it is probably impossible to make a valid estimate of the extent of the SDI-like efforts of the two rival countries, which were organized differently and operated under a markedly different economic system.

The Soviets were also keen to develop sophisticated antisatellite (ASAT) weapons. The first Polyot ASATs, killer satellites armed with shrapnel-firing mechanisms, were test-launched in November 1963 and April 1964. Again, secrecy was airtight. "The Soviets almost certainly have considered systems for use against satellites," the CIA reported, but "there is no intelligence as to the method of intercept."[28]

The Soviet Union's military-space machine now expanded to include serious work on battle-capable space stations. "The Soviets are continuing to voice generalities about manned space stations," the CIA reported in 1967. "They refer to them by a host of terms, such as cities in space, giant flying laboratories, scientific research institutes, refueling stations, etc." But while "references to military applications of space stations have been conspicuously absent," the report continued, "a space station weighing approximately 50,000 pounds and capable of carrying a crew of three or more could probably be placed in earth orbit in the first half of 1968."[29]

In fact, a huge space station—the MKBS—was secretly in the design stage. It would be capable of carrying a number of civilian and military payloads, possibly including a beam weapon.* Where actual technical work was concerned, the Soviets kept their cards close, but public chest thumping continued nevertheless. "Soviet military strategy," wrote Marshal Vassili Sokolovsky in 1968, "takes into account the need for studying the question of the use of outer space and aerospace vehicles.

"This," Sokolovsky continued in florid Stalin-style rhetoric, "must be done to ensure the safety of our country, in the interest of all socialist cooperation, for the preservation of peace in the world."[30]

---

*The MKBS was to use the N-1 launch system, which by now had been freed of its portion of the ill-fated Soviet man-on-the-moon project, but because of the rocket's continued development problems the two were fated to die in 1974.

The U.S. Laser Research Boom

It seems the United States did lag in early development of laser weapon systems—and it would have been absurd for Washington to suggest matching the Soviet Union's commitment of such a large portion of its GDP for blue-sky technical studies. But it did at least as well as the Soviets—and probably a great deal better—in the field of *generalized* laser research. Soon after Maiman demonstrated the ruby laser in 1960, Peter Sorokin and Mirek Stevenson of IBM produced a second type of solid-state laser, one based on a crystal that contained uranium metal. This started a five-year splurge of eye-popping achievements.

Two major advances were made in the following year. Ali Javan, William Bennet Jr., and Donald Herriot invented the helium neon laser—still commonly used as checkout scanners—at Bell Labs; and at General Electric Robert Hall invented the semiconductor laser, which is now used in applications ranging from telecommunications to laser pointers.

A major step in the development of high-energy laser technology occurred in 1964, when C. Kumar Patel of Bell Labs reported a revolutionary "gas dynamic" electric discharge carbon dioxide laser.[31] With further development, this laser exhibited high power levels and by 1968 was being readied for industrial cutting and welding applications. Today it is also used for military range-finding, and for some medical applications.

In 1964, J. E. Geusic, H. M. Markos, and L. G. Van Uiteit of Bell Labs produced the Nd:YAG laser, eventually used in numerous special applications from eye surgery to Lawrence Livermore National Laboratory's giant Nova and National Ignition Facility (NIF) fusion research machines. In the same year, William Bridges of Hughes Laboratories demonstrated the argon ion laser, also used in some types of surgery.

Though no one knew it then, a key candidate for a laser ABM system emerged in the mid-1960s when Jerome Kasper and George Pimentel from the University of California, Berkeley, were developing an unusual device called the photodissociation laser (PDL). Unknown to them, their successes, published in scientific journals, were helping prod Soviet laser experts into launching the biggest laser weapon project of the century.

Laser-guided weapons (which lock on to a target illuminated with laser light) were developed by the U.S. Army and used in the Vietnam War beginning in 1966, but still there were no U.S. laser weapons, which damage targets with their own light. That would soon change, thanks in part to initiatives already launched by the armed forces.

In 1968 the United States held secret laser technology discussions under the code name "Eighth Card." The discussions were sponsored by ARPA and the U.S. Air Force and encouraged by the fact that an Avco-Everett Research Laboratory gas-dynamic laser had achieved the impressively high energy output of 138 kilowatts.[32] "This achievement," wrote Hans Mark in *Defense Horizons*, "made it possible to start thinking about the use of high-energy laser beams as weapons that would have military value."[33]

As a result of the Eighth Card initiative, the U.S. Air Force Scientific Advisory Board launched a study, carried out in 1969–70, of how lasers might be utilized in militarily effective weapons. It appeared that if lethal energy could be directed at targets at the speed of light, the task of aiming such weapons accurately would be much simpler than it was for projectiles that are launched at moving targets at relatively slow speeds. Lightweight mirrors could reflect a laser beam to its target quickly and precisely, and it followed that lasers could be "reloaded" and fired again much more quickly than conventional weapons.

Mark remarked on Edward Teller's interest in an aerial battleship armed with high-power laser weapons, which could be used to defend bombers from enemy attack from aircraft and missiles. "Our subcommittee began to consider Teller's idea seriously, and we looked at some concepts for a prototype," he wrote. "What eventually emerged from these discussions was a proposal to put a large carbon dioxide gas dynamic laser on a four-engine jet aircraft."[34] This became the NC-135 "flying lab," in which the laser was built into a converted Boeing 707 aircraft.

At first the Pentagon thought the gas-dynamic laser "appeared to be scalable to very high energies, and as such it paved the way for serious consideration of a laser damage weapon system."[35] All branches of the armed services tested it, but with limited success because lasers do not travel well through the atmosphere. Useful for fusion research, it proved unsuitable for artillery weapons (unwieldy and ultimately useless systems were prototyped in the Soviet Union, Germany, and France).[36] The original Air Force version, which worked better because it could be used at high altitude, was scrapped in favor of equipping a Boeing 747 with a chemical oxygen iodine laser (COIL).*

---

*One of the challenges with this system is to position it close enough to the target—at the right time—to destroy it during the boost phase. Information on the program is accessible at www.de.afrl.af.mil/Factsheets/ABLHistory.html.

Bullets to Hit Bullets

At the time, laser weapons were not only secret, they were unproven, and most people assumed that only rocket systems could provide a reliable ABM defense. High-velocity missiles already could be positioned to defend an ICBM launch site, a large population center, or a command headquarters.

The U.S. Army pioneered America's ABM rocketry programs in 1957, when it established the Nike-Zeus Guided Missile Defense System Project. However, the program was never popular with President Kennedy and his defense secretary, Robert McNamara, and it was allowed to die on the vine. The concern was that the Soviets might be able to overwhelm it with decoys or high-altitude nuclear blasts, but Bruce Briggs was furious. "Had the orders been given in 1958, Nike-Zeus would have been first deployed by 1963, and would have provided effective ballistic-missile defense against the Soviet Union at least until the early '70s, and against everybody else to this day," he wrote in 1988. "ABM would not have become a football for cynical politicians. . . . America would not have been naked to attack, and would not have been convulsed by frenzy later."[37]

Three years after the Soviet Galosh missile made its first public appearance, in late 1964, McNamara announced that the United States would build and deploy the Sentinel ABM system, deferring a political skirmish with the Soviets by saying that deployment would "deter China from nuclear blackmail." Sentinel was intended to protect U.S. cities and Minuteman ICBM silos alike, but, like the early single-missile Nike-Zeus, this two-missile program (Nike-Zeus missiles plus Sprint missiles) was doomed. Designed to protect U.S. cities from a limited nuclear attack, it attracted widespread criticism from the technical community and from citizens who realized that nuclear-armed missiles would be positioned near their places of residence. When the Presidency passed from Lyndon Johnson to Richard Nixon in 1969, the program was scrapped and replaced with Safeguard, which would protect missile sites instead of cities.*

It took the vice president's tie-breaking vote to win Senate approval for Safeguard, but, while it survived a couple of years longer than Sentinel, it never had much of a chance. The original plan was to build twelve Safeguard sites, but that was cut to two (Grand Forks,

---

*The Sentinel, Safeguard, and the Soviet A-135, employed "layered" terminal defense systems. One type of high-speed missile would intercept incoming ballistic missiles at high altitude and another type at low altitude. In other words, they were positioned to take out the invaders as they approached national airspace, and as they approached their actual targets, respectively.

North Dakota, and Washington, D.C.) with the signing of the Anti-Ballistic Missile (ABM) Treaty. On October 2, 1975, the day after Grand Forks became operational, the House voted to deactivate the system—it could not handle an onslaught from the Soviets' newly developed multiple independently targeted reentry vehicles (MIRVs), and its radars would be blinded by a nuclear explosion, whether from a Soviet reentry vehicle or its own defensive missiles. During Safeguard's ten months of operation, it had been equipped with thirty Spartans (the upgraded Zeus) and seventy Sprints. After its cancellation, U.S. ABM efforts were restricted to investigation of systems that could be used only if the Soviet Union broke out of the ABM Treaty.

U.S. and Soviet ABM systems were able to approach their targets only at the end of a short but extremely important series of ballistic trajectory phases. They could not reach missiles during the first few minutes of flight, when boost-phase rockets give away their presence with a bloom of infrared photons. Nor could the systems reach the ICBM in its high-altitude postboost phase, where the warhead carrier is separated from the engines and releases reentry vehicles (RVs) along with penetration aids ("penaids") such as aluminum fragments and RV-like decoys. Penetration aids confuse the guidance systems of defensive missiles, so that it's likely that at least some invading missiles will get through to their targets. This meant that ABM systems had to operate in the terminal phase—attempting to sort RVs from decoys, and then destroy them—in an extremely short period of time. (The process of reentry lasts between half a minute and a minute and a half. In all, it would have taken an ICBM warhead about twenty-five minutes, no more, to travel the entire distance between the Soviet Union and the United States; a sub-launched warhead would reach its target in about fifteen minutes.)[38]

The nuclear warhead contributed its own set of problems to the early ABM systems, U.S. and Soviet alike. It was included because the extent of its destructive burst would compensate for the relative inaccuracy of the defensive missiles of the day, but the detonation would cause widespread radioactive fallout over its home territory and would blind the very radars that controlled the battle. In the late 1970s and early 1980s, new versions of old concepts emerged for non-nuclear interceptor missiles, sensors and platforms, miniaturized computers, and lasers and particle beam technologies. Superficially the collection of new technologies looked good, but it was far from enough to constitute a useful defense against ballistic missiles. "We did little until 1983," wrote Ronald Reagan's secretary of defense, Caspar Weinberger, "contenting ourselves with some minor research designed to try to improve the effectiveness of the 1970s-vintage ground-based Sprint and Spartan missile systems."[39] He was greatly troubled by the ABM muddle, which he correctly labeled as an exercise in proving what was already known.

In 1969, the United States unilaterally cancelled its biological weapons program, mandated a plan to destroy existing stocks, and restricted its related work to defensive measures such as immunization. If Washington hoped that Moscow would follow suit, it was sadly mistaken. According to Kenneth Alibek, former deputy director of Biopreparat, the civilian arm of the Soviet biological weapons effort, this program was actually expanded after the Soviet Union became a party to the 1972 Biological and Toxin Weapons Convention. "The size and scope of this program were enormous," Alibek told a congressional committee following his defection to the United States. "For example, in the late 1980s and early 1990s, over 60,000 people were involved in the research, development, and production of biological weapons. Hundreds of tons of anthrax weapon formulation were stockpiled, along with dozens of tons of smallpox and plague."[40]

With Alibek's disclosures it became clear that the U.S.–Soviet confrontation had had consequences worse than the even the pessimists dreamed. After an attack from ICBMs carrying separately targeted nuclear and biological warheads, survivors would be wiped out by epidemics of horrific proportion.

A New Wake-Up Call

To westerners the Soviet Union was certainly an evil empire, though it would be unfair to apply the term to the essential Russia, her heritage of science, arts and letters, and her people. The Bolshevik aberration, with its long-standing ideal of converting the world to a mistaken philosophy, had generated a monstrous political system in which basically decent people were cranking the levers for a quasi-religious movement. Stalinism would remain entrenched in the upper echelons of the Kremlin until foreign minister Andrei Gromyko and defense minister Dmitry Ustinov departed from the scene in the early 1980s.

Now the Cold War was working itself into a froth. One might argue that it had been going on for decades, spawned by traditional Russian political meanness, germinating in the brutal excesses of 1930s Stalinism, lapsing into a brooding hibernation during the marriage of convenience with the Western World War II allies, and finally breaking loose during the Truman administration. Would the Soviets have developed nuclear weapons if the United States had not first dropped them on Japan? Certainly. Though smarter, very much more powerful, and the ruler of huge areas of Europe and Asia, Stalin was the Saddam Hussein of his day. To him, nuclear weaponry became the badge of a superpower, and in those days it was still Russia's manifest destiny to spread communism across the world. The gradual easing of this philosophy under Khrushchev and the regimes that followed slowed neither the Cold War nor the nuclear arms race. The world was now a very dangerous place, where the casualties of a single exchange would not be measured in tens or hundreds or even in thousands, but in hundreds of millions.

How could the Soviet Union protect itself from such devastation? The threat of retaliation would certainly help a lot, and no doubt it did. But why not devise a new way of stopping nuclear weapons before they had a chance to do their deadly business? Find them and destroy them with defensive missiles before they could land? The idea was attractive and worth trying, but messy and prone to unreliability. New technology might come to the rescue, as it had in the past. Greatly encouraged by their proven ability to make nuclear weapons, accurate launch systems, manned spacecraft, and interplanetary probes, the Kremlin's defense chiefs opted to try for another leap forward. It proved to be extremely costly, but the Russian people were used to making do with short rations. They were loyal to the motherland, and they would endure.

Relatively speaking, the Eighth Card initiative was a fairly relaxed affair. Hans Mark, Edward Teller, and their colleagues could not know that, at the newly built Raduga laser test center, near the Russian city of Vladimir, a carbon dioxide laser named the 3D-01 was putting out unprecedented amounts of power—and yet was branded unsuitable for beam-weapon use. The techies had something much better in mind. While the Eighth-Carders ruminated, enthusiastic Soviet mega-laser experts were working on a truly massive pulsed laser called the PDL. Their revolutionary photon-belching monster was working splendidly, and it was getting more powerful all the time.

3

LASERS VERSUS MISSILES

The Soviet empire was created and built for the arms race,
confrontation, and even war with the rest of the world.
—Aleksey Arbatov*

Peter Zarubin was not a physically imposing person. He was a guy you could easily miss in a crowd: short, stocky, as unnoticeable as a sparrow and just as quick. Unlike nearly every other Russian, he could speak colloquial English. At times, this little man in nondescript clothing seemed almost American, with a penchant for kidding around, but he also struck anyone who spoke with him for more than half an hour as being very, very smart. During the Cold War, when he bantered about laser technology with his American counterparts, they were bemused when he said such things as, "Well, we did that; it's no big deal," or, "We built one ten times bigger than that; it's no big deal!" They generally thought he was kidding. He probably was not, but the rules of secrecy would not permit him to explain more.

By no means was Zarubin as unremarkable as he looked. "You may wonder why I speak good English," he said to me one November day in Moscow, as I puzzled over this very fact. "It is because I come from a very famous intelligence family." In fact his father was the KGB resident in Washington during World War II, at the time plans for the American atomic bomb were being smuggled back to the Kremlin. Zoya Zarubina, his half-sister and eleven years older, was a fascinating

*Arbatov, a defense expert and Duma deputy, made this observation in a signed article, "The National Idea and National Security," published in *Mirovaya Ekonomika i Mezhdunarodnyye Otnosheniya* (May 1998, p. 8).

37

woman who from the age of twenty was Stalin's protocol officer and translator, serving in these roles at the historic Tehran, Yalta, and Potsdam summits of 1943–45.[1]

Zarubin was not strictly in the intelligence business, though not unnaturally he would continuously troll for information on American laser programs. He was a master secret-keeper, a key insider who spent thirty years working on the Soviet Union's military and nonmilitary lasers, including a remarkable spell in which he controlled the Ministry of Defense Industry (MOP) laser and laser systems directorate. As it had been in the past, from before Zarubin joined the Ministry of Defense Industry in 1967 until after his departure in 1990, nobody *ever* disclosed the inner workings of the Soviet high-energy laser weapons program. Nobody knew that, in just a few years, the laser pioneers Alexander Prokhorov, Nikolai Basov, Oleg Krokhin, and their colleagues from the Lebedev Institute, had rewritten long-held views of what can and what cannot be done in science. To Russian military optimists, it now seemed possible that, in the grand scheme of things, large radars on the periphery of the Soviet Union would detect incoming American ICBMs, super-precise laser radars would locate and lock onto their deadly reentry vehicles, and then perhaps high-energy lasers would take them out.

But lasers were newcomers on the ABM scene, high-tech hopefuls that were upstaged in many respects by the accomplishments of Soviet missile and space technology. By the time Zarubin reported to work at MOP, an independent BMD organization had been operating within the air defense command for nearly ten years, and development of an antimissile missile system was moving ahead quickly.

With fresh memories of the agonies of World War II (as many as twenty million Soviet citizens were killed, seven million of them soldiers), the Soviet Union had good reason for making heavy post-war investments in offensive and defensive military technologies. The war experience, and then the tensions born from the acute ideological mismatch that existed between the Soviet Union and its former allies, provided a fertile breeding ground for a national paranoia that would perpetuate the Cold War phenomenon for decades into the future. Thus, the Soviet offensive rocket program blossomed immediately after the war, and early antimissile research and development began not long afterwards, in the autumn of 1953.

For many years, no one outside the Kremlin elite knew the identity of the greatest contributor to Russia's Cold War space technology. He was Sergei Korolev, and ironically he did not care for Stalin. Korolev was under technical arrest during World War II, and did not get around to joining the Communist Party until after Stalin's death in

1953. After being arrested on trumped-up charges in 1938, Korolev was confined to a gulag, and then eventually moved to a relatively comfortable *sharashka* prison camp that specialized in aviation design. Following World War II, he was responsible for the success of Sputnik 1, and was the guiding light behind the most famous names in the Soviet spacecraft fleet, including the Vostok, Voskhod, and Soyuz manned spacecraft and the Cosmos, Molniya, and Zond unmanned spacecraft. His rival was Vladimir Chelomei, a Khrushchev favorite who played a leading role in the development of cruise missiles, submarine-launched ballistic missiles, ICBMs, and space launch systems.

When given the chance, Korolev championed space exploration over military projects. Yet he was responsible for the early R-7 ICBM and the MKBS battle station, and there are reports that a space bomber from his design bureau, technically known as a "fractional orbit bombardment system (FOBS)," was tested soon after Zarubin reported to MOP. This project, formally approved in September 1962, was known to the CIA, which estimated that such a system could be deployed "by late 1967 or early 1968."[2] Khrushchev's rhetoric, mixed ambiguously with grim humor, made the most of such efforts. "We placed Gagarin and Titov in space," he warned in 1961, "and we can replace them with bombs that can be diverted to any place on earth."[3]

Korolev was also active in antisatellite (ASAT) technology. Design of an "inspector satellite," capable of close encounters with suspect foreign satellites, had begun under his leadership as early as 1956, with Chelomei's bureau beginning work on a maneuverable "space mine," the "Istrebitel Sputnikov" (IS) satellite destroyer, three years later.[4] In November 1963 a Polyot satellite of this type was launched into orbit, designed to carry 900 pounds of explosives into space, approach an enemy satellite, and then detonate the charge. With time, ASAT technology—including the more conventional missile launches from the ground and fighter aircraft—would provide several of many "countermeasure" options available to disrupt and destroy ABM systems in orbit.

The Soviet space program, like its nuclear program, was kept under wraps unless it seemed some political advantage would come out of an announcement—like Sputnik and the early manned flights that might have resulted in a manned lunar expedition. "Russia's predilection for talking in generalities makes it futile to speculate on the future course its program will take," wrote a frustrated Wernher von Braun in his classic 1966 *History of Rocketry and Space Travel*. "Soviet literature contains many references to manned orbital laboratories, space stations, Lunar—and even interplanetary—spaceships, but descriptions of concrete programs have not yet emerged."[5]

But, with success, some of the details began to materialize. The first launch in the pioneering Salyut ("Salute" or "Firework") manned space-station program occurred on April 19, 1971. Technical problems, some of which resulted in fatalities, plagued the program in its first two years as the Central Committee moved Chelomei into a quick-time attempt to get ahead of the U.S. Skylab program. Eventually most of these were ironed out, and from 1977 until 1982 Salyut 6 was visited by sixteen crews, topped by one flight that lasted 185 days. Salyut 7, launched in 1982, was the second large-scale space station of its type. It suffered more technical failures than its predecessor but successfully tested the docking and use of the heavy add-on modules that would make up a large space-station complex.

In 1969, the Salyut bureau completed the design of a prototype for a series of TKS manned transport ships that were intended to resupply secret Almaz military space stations. Three manned Almaz launches would be completed under cover of the Salyut name. Each ship carried reconnaissance equipment and an aircraft cannon, one of which was used successfully on a target satellite. The program was mothballed after this first phase of its long on-again, off-again history, apparently because of criticism within the military establishment. By then, the Soviets' lunar exploration program had flourished briefly and died. Moscow's belief in the military importance of technology, however, remained intense. In a 1969 article published in the classified military journal *Voyennaya mysl'*, Colonel P. Sidirov cautioned that "further intensive development of science and technology . . . is not only a central economic [task] but an important political task as well. At the present stage, problems of scientific and technical progress are acquiring, quite frankly, decisive importance."[6]

The difficulty of "hitting a bullet with a bullet," however, remained acute. Rocket defenses are fast, but how long would it take to verify an attack and locate the incoming weapons? In a desperate game where every second of response time mattered, research into beam weaponry continued vigorously despite the disappointments with the prelaser approaches put forward by Kapitsa, Budker, and others.

Nurturing the Light Fantastic

Soviet laser research began with Aleksandr Prokhorov, a career physicist who suggested the use of ruby as a material for lasers in 1957 and in 1958 proposed that it be used to generate infrared waves.

Basov, the other Russian laser pioneer, was destined to become one of the great genius promoters of high-power laser development.

"Basov and Prokhorov were high-level people," said Zarubin. "They communicated with other people at a very high level of the Soviet leadership, and their opinions were considered to be very important." And then he gave a little grin. "The leaders agreed to listen to what they said, even if they didn't understand what they said."[7]

The brains of Lebedev were a diverse group of personalities. Small black-and-white photo portraits of Prokhorov and Basov still hang above the paneling in the director's office on Leninsky Prospekt. Prokhorov's long, humorous face is seen in profile. Basov looks utterly different, almost bursting out of the photo with energy, the big, broad, thick-lipped face with a receding hairline willing you to say, "Yes! I *do* want to hear about your wonderful new laser experiment!"

Still, Basov could be very stiff and formal. He was an impressive, clear speaker, tending his reputation carefully by publishing reams of technical papers. Some considered him a political animal who made a point of building friendships with Party bosses. In fact, almost all high-level, influential scientists had to cultivate fruitful contacts, if not actual friendships, with the Party leadership. But some scientists quietly disapproved, in the belief that science should be "above politics," and considered Basov to be more acquiescent to political requirements than was *kulturny* among intellectual seekers of nature's truths.

Basov's right-hand man, Oleg Krokhin, was tall and slender, suave and sophisticated, with a finely honed sense of humor. His knowledge of laser physics was unparalleled—he too had been there from the beginning, watching and working at close range.

Prokhorov, a tall, casual, and rumpled figure, was quite different from Basov. Softspoken and friendly, he exuded sincerity, credibility, and intellectuality, and yet he was capable of being quite blunt when the occasion called for it. Born in Australia to an émigré from Tsarist Russia, Prokhorov was considered by his colleagues to be a more independent spirit than Basov. "He was a gregarious man, very nice company," recalled Sagdeev, who reported directly to him at the Academy of Sciences. "You couldn't talk to him without hearing a joke every five minutes. There was an interesting interplay between the two men, and overall they didn't do well with each other."[8]

"Prokhorov was full of jokes, very personable," agreed Charles Townes. "But Basov wanted a lot of power and control, and he was a pretty conservative communist."[9]

"There's a Russian proverb that says that two bears cannot live in the same den," says Zarubin. "Prokhorov was the more outspoken, more humorous. Basov was a little more on the scientific side. But both had one strong part of their nature: they could form teams around them. Each had a team. When Basov became director of Lebedev, Prokhorov immediately said, 'I want my own institute,' and they cut the Lebedev Institute into two parts—the Lebedev Institute and the Institute of General Physics—just because there were these two exceptional men."[10]

In 1963, a letter bearing an impressive seal reached the desk of Mstislav Keldysh, president of the Soviet Academy of Sciences. Keldysh had been expecting it, more or less, and smiled to himself as his eyes scanned the typewritten paragraphs. The message, from Andrei Grechko, the deputy defense minister, suggested that the academy take a very serious look at the potential military applications of lasers. Keldysh naturally liked the sound of this, for he had taken great interest in the work of Basov, Krokhin, and their colleagues for a couple of years, as they attempted to improve the performance of their fledgling lasers. With military support, they would get the funding they needed, and just twenty years later, the U.S. government would take a similar action.

Basov and Krokhin had already started looking into the feasibility of using laser radiation to generate thermonuclear plasmas (as in the current U.S. National Ignition Facility concept) and others were already developing laser radar. But Grechko wanted a deeper, more widespread commitment. Keldysh huddled with Basov, then sent a speedy reply back to the Ministry of Defense: without doubt, the laser had enormous military potential.

That year, the Kremlin agreed to support a laser ABM research program that had been mapped out by the future Vympel Central Research and Production Association (then headed by Grigory Kisunko) with the Lebedev Institute (FIAN) and the All-Union Research Institute of Experimental Physics (VNIIEF). Goals included supporting the LE-1 laser radar and producing a very high-power laser (more than a million joules per pulse) that could blast warheads out of the sky with ease. The program, code-named Terra-3, was engaged in a variety of testing and experimental work. While some of its subdivisions would work on lasers to determine the precise location of invading reentry vehicles, others would figure out ways to use lasers to destroy the missiles.

The national laser research program was split in two parts. Omega, Prokhorov's program, encompassed aircraft defense, with the exception of the LE-1; and Terra, Basov's program, focused on ABM defense. "Omega was concerned mostly with more realistic tactical applications," explained Evgeny Velikhov. "I still believe this may make sense to us sometime, with modern adaptive optics."[11]

Test facilities for Terra antimissile and laser radar projects were later built, among other places, near the Sary Shagan railway station, on the shores of the shallow, brackish Lake Balkash, bordered on the northwest by a region known by the locals as the Famine Steppe. It was reachable from Moscow in four days by rail (not surprisingly, nearly everyone flew) and positioned well for tracking test flights from the ballistic missile range a thousand miles north at Kapustin Yar. It's hard to think of the entire testing ground as a "place," for it is a huge region twice the size of France, spread over the desert and steppes of Kazakhstan, with ballistic missile installations one or two hundred miles apart.

Zarubin first visited Sary Shagan in the late 1960s, when he was a newly appointed member of the laser systems directorate of the Soviet Ministry of Defense Industry (MOP). After his four-hour plane ride, a jeep sped Zarubin to the Vympel LE-1 research center for the first of more than thirty visits he would make over the next six years. When he stepped inside the cavernous concrete building, he was amazed at what he saw—a convoluted network of light beams and mirrors that radiated and folded over a path of one hundred yards or more. "My first impression was," he said, "wow, I have never seen a laser optical system so huge!"[12]

Meanwhile, the people at Lebedev were working hard to please Grechko and Keldysh with a laser that could actually shoot down missiles. Basov and Krokhin first considered using an atomic bomb to energize a very-high-energy laser. It would yield the explosive equivalent of 100 tons of TNT—impressive enough, but very small compared with military-issue bombs that had yields of 25,000 tons.[13]

Investigation of nuclear-pumped lasers apparently continued elsewhere until the mid-1980s, though at a low level of effort. There is speculation that one was built near Dushanbe,[14] but that Velikhov dismissed that program as unpromising.[15] Zarubin agreed: "This project was probably a relatively minor, mostly theoretical and experimental study, and never gained any great importance."[16]

Still, the story persisted that the Russians also developed ground-based, multishot nuclear laser systems in a program that ended in the mid-1980s after the Soviet Union announced a moratorium on space defense systems—and after the puzzling deaths of the two project managers.

But there were other ways of making high-power lasers. Soon Basov and Krokhin started to think about using high explosives to "pump" a laser in a way that was similar to the method they might have applied with a nuclear explosion. Of course, there was no public statement about the Soviet decision to look into laser ABM systems, though in terms of science theory (as opposed to technology, which requires making things) it anticipated the future Strategic Defense Initiative twenty years before SDI was announced. While all this was happening, Ronald Reagan, the future godfather of America's Strategic Defense Initiative, was still on the fringes of American politics, making anticommunist speeches and supporting right-winger Barry Goldwater's growing interest in the 1964 presidential election.

The United States had no way of knowing for sure that a ballistic missile defense organization had long existed within the Soviet air defense command, and that it was pursuing new technology regardless of cost. Between 1964 and 1966, McNamara and other top Department of Defense officials regularly called on the Soviet Embassy, trying to learn more about Moscow's stand on ABM systems. The secretary hoped the two sides could agree that they would be ineffective and too expensive to bother with. They got nowhere.

RUSSIA'S MEGALASER

Basov and Krokhin, working with their Lebedev colleagues, became intrigued with the idea that the molecules of a certain iodine compound could be used in a laser device well suited for ABM defense. It would be an iodine "photodissociation laser," or PDL. Theoretically, nuclear radiation could split the molecules and start the process—but why rule out the radiation generated by chemical explosives? There seemed to be no reason, so long as they could detonate a very large amount of explosive with a very high degree of control.

Basov and Krokhin were greatly encouraged when research at the University of California, Berkeley—announced in one of the world's most respected physics journals—showed that the idea really would work. Iodine atoms released when their parent molecules were zapped with radiation had been supercharged to an "excited" state, meaning that they could be used in a laser.[17] This proof of concept supported the Russians' belief that their own high-energy PDL was suitable for pumping by high-energy ultraviolet radiation sources, including shock-wave radiation in heavy gases (in this case, perfluoroalkyl iodides).

A major step would be to upgrade the system so it would be powerful enough to cripple a reentry vehicle. The problem: it would have to be scaled up sufficiently to produce a pulse ten million times greater than the one joule that had been seen in the American lab. The PDL test program would have to be held at a huge, isolated laboratory that was so secret it was known only by its postal address or, even more cryptically, as "The Installation."

In 1965, Basov won the agreement of Yuli Khariton in a pivotal matter, scientific supervisor in charge of The Installation—actually Arzamas-16, located at Sarov and nicknamed "Los Arzamas" because it was the Soviet equivalent of Los Alamos Scientific Laboratory. In short, Khariton agreed to let Basov conduct high-energy PDL experiments at the site, which had special expertise in precisely machined high explosives, shaped to deliver their energy output in a given direction. Thenceforth, most large-scale PDL experiments took place under Samuil Kormer, a first-class atomic weapons research scientist who had been at Arzamas since 1947. Among many other laser weapon concepts, Kormer's laboratory produced the megajoule-class F-1200, a PDL that was twenty-two meters long and used 2,600 pounds of explosives.[18]

The new partnership was finalized in 1966. The next step, after experiments at Sarov, was to set up a large experimental complex at Balkhash capable of producing PDL pulse energies as great as 10 megajoules. This was an almost unbelievably large amount of laser energy, and at this optimistic time there was little doubt that the beam could overcome the thermal and structural protection of an American reentry vehicle.

Experiments at Sarov soon proved that an iodine PDL was not only feasible, but it could put out high-pulse power and radiation energy at a near-infrared wavelength (1.315 micrometers) that was relatively effective in penetrating the atmosphere. The program soon was enjoying the support of Defense Minister Dmitry Ustinov, his right-hand man Leonid Smirnov, and other top-level military people.

PROVING THE PDL

Zarubin's monitoring of PDL experiments at Arzamas followed procedures reminiscent of the best spy-novel tradition. He would receive a message summoning him to appear at a certain place in the departure hall of the Bukovo airport, an old single-runway facility twenty-two miles southeast of Moscow. There he would meet a man in civilian clothes who, after making sure Zarubin's name was on the passenger list, would escort him to the aircraft—usually a sleek Yak-40 business jet. Once the plane arrived at its destination, uniformed guards checked his documents and those of his fellow passengers before the group was allowed to leave the plane.

Zarubin's other alternative was to go by direct train, using coded tickets that did not bear the destination name. After a 250-mile trip, the train would stop at a border station at the edge of Sarov's huge restricted zone, an area that was heavily guarded and surrounded by numerous rows of barbed wire fences. At this point, Zarubin, other passengers, and the train itself, were checked and searched. The guards would find Zarubin's name on their guest list, then hand him his personal permit. Once the train moved into the unguarded station and creaked to a stop, he was free to meet his escort. When pressed for time, he or other high-level guests could cut short the snail-paced last hundred miles of the journey, debouching from the train at an earlier station and proceeding the rest of the way by car.

So it was that Peter Zarubin arrived by train at a vast city and science complex that, for most intents, did not exist—Sarov was absent from all Soviet maps issued after 1947. The sleeper train had rattled its way eastward from Moscow like any other, the women in their babushka scarves patiently stoking the coal space heaters and arranging flowers on the dining-car tables. Zarubin arrived in a setting graced by a beautiful, birch-wooded countryside, with a seventeenth century monastery standing high above the banks of the Sarova River on the site of an abandoned Tatar fortress.

In this bucolic setting, the Soviet Union had located its version of America's Los Alamos laboratory, the VNIIEF research institute of the Ministry of Energy, Minatom. The lab occupied a hexagonal area measuring almost one hundred square miles, with its headquarters located a short distance from the monastery. It was a pleasant assignment, clean and peaceful, with an ambience that, for many, made it quite possible to forget that barbed wired fences surrounded this oasis of science. Here, since 1946, Yuli Khariton had run experimental facilities for the Soviet nuclear weapon program with a cadre of top-level scientists and engineers who lived safely and well in a kind of gilded gulag. This is not an inappropriate metaphor, for the slim, heavy-lidded physicist had watched cheerfully as his state-of-the-art center was built by laborers brought in from the gulags—places named after the Russian acronym for the "chief administration of corrective labor camps" run by the secret police. The nuclear scientist–administrator Viktor Mikhailov seemed oblivious to such things. In his biography he wrote of the excitement of exploring the wonders of nuclear physics at Sarov: "This, combined with a nice private room in a communal dwelling and a family income that was enough for a completely adequate living, seemed like paradise after the deprivations of student life."[19]

There was one big reason for holding the PDL tests at Sarov apart from secrecy, and this was the special technical expertise available among the resident nuclear scientists. The PDLs consisted of several long, bolted-together metal tubes big enough for a man to crawl through, filled with xenon gas that was spiked with relatively small amounts of the iodine compound. A rod coated with chemical explosive was suspended within each tube. When the explosive was detonated, it produced an immense radial shock wave. The shock wave generated ultraviolet radiation as it heated the xenon; this in turn excited the iodine atoms, causing them to give up the infrared photons that were central to the lasing process.* The trick was that the explosive had to be detonated with extreme precision, just like the explosives used to compress the primary of a nuclear weapon. It had to emerge "flat," squeezing evenly outward toward the outer cylinder, with no bumps in between. If a detonation occurred at one place one millionth of a second earlier or later than another place, the experiment would be a disaster. "This is exactly the same problem you have with the A-bomb," Zarubin explained. "You must explode the charge very, very symmetrically, and those people at Sarov were expert in such things. Except that in this case you didn't need spherical symmetry, you needed linear symmetry."

The wooded southern part of the laboratory site contains a number of experimental facilities and storage areas. When Zarubin arrived, he found a long, straight sausage-string of PDL cylinders containing meticulously applied rods of explosive with their networks of precisely spaced detonators. The experiment was arranged in a rectangular space cut from the forestland that graced the hills around the installation. The site was located away from the main complex because isolated fragments from the PDL explosions could fly some miles before they came to earth. A scant sixty feet from the row of PDLs, a stairway led down to a concrete bunker crammed with people, desks, instrumentation, data processing equipment, and recording paraphernalia, the latter attached to special mounts to isolate them from the explosive shock.

Then it was test time. "Everybody was down in the bunker," said Zarubin, who attended some of these experiments as a MOP 8th Directorate observer. "They turned on the closed circuit TV and a man went out to make the last connection—a single man because after that it becomes a bomb. A lot of measurement equipment had been prepared to measure the beam quality, the energy, the divergence, all these things. They had no computers at this time, or practically no computers, but there were various kinds of meters and a lot of record-

---

*One beauty of this system was that the same xenon used in external flash-lamps was being used in very large amounts *inside* the laser cavity, and its released photonic energy was therefore not reduced by the process of passing through a window into the lasant gases.

ing oscilloscopes and people sitting, waiting for it to start. Then the safety man comes back, and after all the checks were made and everything was ready, the countdown started—30, 29, 28 . . .

"Then the detonators were electrically discharged to start the explosion and all of the building shook because two tons of explosives were going up, twenty-five, thirty meters away. For us, the most important thing was to see the meters that measured the energy. I would look over a technician's shoulder and see a needle moving, or a bright trace on an oscilloscope.

"As soon as we saw the measurements, we had an understanding of whether it was okay or not okay, practically if not officially. We would get the official result the next day, after all those automatic tapes had been deciphered and checked. When I was present, we had measurements of up to 500,000 joules, half a megajoule. Later they made even bigger explosions—yielding up to a million joules of laser energy. The PDL was by far the most powerful laser in history, though naturally its beam would lose power as it spread into the distance.

"Finally, because sometimes a piece of explosive may remain unexploded, a safety man went out to check to make sure everything had exploded. We would go out to collect fragments from the test, including pieces of optical elements.

"I was thirty-five years old and it was very exciting. To celebrate, we did what all ordinary people do in such cases. When we do good work, we deserve a glass of vodka."[20]

Again, as with Sputnik, the first manned orbital flights, and some of the early interplanetary explorations, the Soviets were ahead of the Americans. It seemed that someday the Terra-3 PDL might be able to shoot down RVs with high-energy photon bullets, but they did not advertise the matter. This was a genuine secret weapon.

However, problems were emerging that had been glossed over in the past. Beam divergence, as with all "beam weapon" systems, was a major problem; the internal mirrors were not so damage-resistant as predicted; and the American ICBMs may have been less vulnerable to laser attack than first estimated. The Lebedev team proposed a number of possible solutions, but Vympel was under pressure from the military for faster deliveries of fieldable hardware. At the end of 1968, realizing that the PDL approach would take a long time to materialize, Vympel transferred its laser experts to a new organization, Luch.*

---

*Later, Luch became Astrofizika, an enterprise that, like the American company TRW (now part of Northrop Grumman), had special expertise in defense optics. Here, the efficient and talented Viktor Orlov led the development of high-energy PDLs, solid state, carbon dioxide, and other lasers. Units of the Soviet Academy of Science, including Lebedev, could do research, but were not equipped to create and manage large-scale installations.

In 1969, PDLs were blasting their targets with energies measured in terms of hundreds of thousands of joules (the mechanical energy of a rifle bullet is only about 10 thousand joules).* Plans for the massive new Balkhash complex had been drawn up, and in the early 1970s engineers began to build the reinforced concrete building that would house the giant experiments. Sited a few miles from the LE-1 laser radar pointing system, the complex was designed to stand up to the gigantic shock that emerged as several ganged-together PDLs were exposed to the huge amount of explosive needed to produce a 10-megajoule laser pulse. However, the project was never finished.

"The main opposition to Soviet beam weapons proponents came from Academician Lev Artsimovich, who was the leader of the Soviet magnetic fusion program," explained Evgeny Velikhov. "At the insistence of Academician Khariton, an honest and principled critique was written and handed over to the government, which decided to stop the program around the time the antiballistic-missile treaty was concluded in 1972."[21]

The treaty, however, did not prohibit the continuation of PDL research. Magnetic explosion generators (MEGs), used to reduce costs, produced a pulse of about 90,000 joules in 1974. Construction of test buildings continued at Sary Shagan until 1977, but the entire program was officially dissolved in 1978.

"We succeeded in achieving very high energy with the photodissociation laser, to about one megajoule in a single pulse," Krokhin said. "It could have been developed further, but the program was stopped due to some economical or political reason. I have no idea how it came to this. But it's still possible in principle to increase this figure."[22]

The PDL was an extremely expensive proposition, from the labor-intensive construction job to its large and costly charge of xenon gas. Though it may have been the highest-energy single-output laser ever built (most U.S. weapon lasers were continuous-wave rather than pulsed devices), it was self-destructing, more like a single silver bullet than a machine gun. An impossibly large number of such bullets would be needed to take out a salvo of incoming missiles.

A still stronger pulse was also essential because reentry vehicles, which must be protected against the intense mechanical and thermal shock encountered when returning to the atmosphere, are very tough

---

*Higher energies would have been possible if the beam's pulses could have been concentrated into a shorter time period; as it was, the early PDL experiments had a relatively long pulse—between 10 and 100 millionths of a second. PDL work continued, off and on, and at different sites, until end-century and beyond. Similar technology was proposed for cleaning up space debris.

targets. Even a more powerful PDL would probably have inflicted little damage to a reentry vehicle, though, with the right optics and correction for beam divergence and atmospheric distortion, it could probably destroy a satellite.*

Development of high-energy lasers, especially carbon dioxide lasers, continued at a number of sites, as did work on other types such as the helium-neon laser used in the LE-1. But the carbon dioxide laser is good for fusion research and inherently unsuitable for ABM use—its wavelength is too long—and the Soviet government also let the word trickle out that the notion of orbiting space cannons was no more than another vision that did not work.

Or was it? Later, in a 2001 *Military Parade* article, chief designer Alexander Ignatyev of the Almaz company noted that successful tests in the development of laser-beam weapons had "proceeded since the early 1980s" at his organization, "some of them air-based, for destroying aircraft and, presumably, space objects."[23] Yuri Votintsev, commander in chief for Anti-Rocket and Space Defense, commented that, "in the area of lasers, according to the data I had at the time, in the mid-1980s, the Soviet Union was ten years ahead of the Americans."[24]

THE DEW CHIMERA

Successful directed energy weapons (DEW) technology would rely on cutting-edge innovation in a number of extremely complex fields. There was the weapon system, which consisted of detection, tracking, aiming, and power supply paraphernalia, as well as the actual weapon, or the payload. Almost certainly there had to be a launch system—a multistage rocket required to loft the payload from its launch pad. Similar launch systems can deliver military or civilian payloads alike, for example, an orbiting antimissile systems platform or a spacecraft headed for the moon. Significantly, the moon's changing position can be precisely predicted, but the position of a missile or reentry vehicle cannot. The job of detecting and tracking such a tiny object, launched without warning into the vastness of time and space, is daunting, to say the least.

---

*Basics of PDL weapon technology were used at Sarov to build the Iskra ("Spark") series of fusion-related high-energy lasers, which produced short pulses after being exposed to manmade lightning bolts shot from huge capacitor banks. Iskra-4, operational in 1979, produced a single shot rated at 10 trillion watts. Iskra-5, a 12-beam system, produced 100 trillion watts in an extremely short pulse—between one and two millionths of a second. (Zarubin, personal communication with the author, November 25, 2003.)

Did the Soviet decision to give up the PDL result from an analysis of such problems? Or was it another example of disinformation, aimed at dissuading the West from pursuing similar plans? Perhaps neither, for some suspect that the high-energy laser weapon program continued in even stricter secrecy. At least some Terra funding may have been diverted to another technical enterprise, again with the aim of placing exotic weaponry in space. Indeed, in 1976 the space side of the Soviet defense industry had been secretly tasked with the job of developing a large manned orbital battle station, which if needed (and if the technology were available) could carry small laser weapons, antisatellite cannons, small rockets, even nuclear weapons. Given the code name Skif, it would be a much-scaled-up descendant of the earlier Almaz, which was now hibernating in a large container marked "SECRET." A gigantic new launch system, Energiya, would be needed to put it into orbit.

The Soviet Ministry of Defense and the Soviet research and development community had launched, in 1976, a two-part Fon ("Background") concept which, though it focused on advanced space systems like military satellites, included the investigation of directed energy weapons for possible use with these systems. Fon-1, said to be short-lived, included basic research; the long-lived Fon-2 included systems for neutralizing hostile space weapons. In early 1982, the Department of Defense's Richard DeLauer said, in classified congressional testimony, "We expect a large permanent, manned (Soviet) orbital space complex to be operational by about 1990 . . . capable of effectively attacking . . . ground, sea, and air targets from space" with high-energy lasers.[25] A Department of Defense publication then announced, "The Soviets could launch the first prototype of a space-based antisatellite system in the late 1980s or very early 1990s. An operational system capable of attacking other satellites within a few thousand kilometers' range could be established in the early 1990s."[26] With time, both statements would come remarkably close to reality.

The Soviet laser program was still alive: the main question was, alive and doing what? "It didn't stop," says CIA veteran Herb Meyer, who worked for Director of Central Intelligence William J. Casey during the Reagan years. "Previously there was discussion of it in Soviet scientific and military journals, but then, when they realized what they had, the Soviets stopped further publication about it. They stopped all that. It became very secret."[27]

On May 30, 1972, while the Soviets were still doing well with the PDL and the United States was chugging along with Safeguard construction, something truly remarkable happened in the world of diplomacy. The United States and the Soviet Union signed the Strategic Arms Limitation Treaty (SALT I) *and* the Anti-Ballistic Missile Treaty. The latter stated that "each party undertakes not to develop, test, or deploy ABM systems or components which are sea-based, air-based, space-based or mobile land-based," but it did not specifically rule out ABM *research*. Nor did it single out exotic new developments like laser weapons for inclusion under the ban. "The Russians did not insist on this because, at that time, there was still a kind of obsession that there would be significant developments in laser technology," said Sagdeev."[28]

In the 1960s, the Soviet Union had developed a highly mathematical model for war planning, known as a correlation of forces (COF) analysis. While people must eventually make such decisions, Soviet military thought held that, with COF, "extensive potential has opened up for mathematical description and logical formalization of the laws of warfare. In spite of their complexity, the process of warfare can be described by means of a rigorous mathematical edifice, with a high degree of accuracy in approximating reality."[29]

The SALT and ABM Treaties could be factored nicely into COF planning. Armed with this information, Soviet strategists assumed they could adjust their nuclear forces as needed to ensure superiority over the United States.[30] It was a meticulous, precise plan, but it was also inflexible, and it was an Achilles heel. Two decades later, these strategists were staggered by Reagan's SDI. Though somewhat improbable, the initiative would be credible enough to the Kremlin worriers to unbalance the COF and add momentum to the Soviet death spiral.

U.S. MILITARY SPACE LOBBIES IN ACTION

Boosted by the post-Sputnik adrenalin high, the Americans now had leaped ahead in the nonmilitary side of the U.S.–Soviet confrontation. Soviet hopes to put cosmonauts on the moon had been dashed by a trio of failures with the N-1 launch system, and U.S. *Apollo* astronauts walked the lunar surface for the first time in July 1969. There had been some Russian success with interplanetary probes, along with the early cosmonaut flights, but it seemed fairly obvious that no manned Russian spacecraft would ever land on the moon.

On the military side, the Cold War had settled into fretful fulfillment of the mutual assured destruction paradigm, with both powers quickly building up their nuclear missile fleets—to the disadvantage, some planners on both sides pointed out, of conventional warfighting capability. At the time there were only two ways out of MAD. One was through negotiation and disarmament, which to many seemed an impossible dream; the other was to build more and better antimissile missile systems, which, if they were ever accepted by the U.S. public, might serve as an incentive for the Soviets to build even more offensive missiles.

Then, in 1977, Ronald Reagan, the newly elected governor of California and thus a regent of the University of California, visited the UC-managed Lawrence Livermore National Laboratory at the invitation of its founder, Edward Teller. There, in Teller's words, "I gave him a proposal of a primitive Strategic Defense Initiative. Governor Reagan was very interested. In the end he gave strong support to missile defense, but non-nuclear defense."[31] Why the interest? Plainly Reagan was an ardent anticommunist, a longtime opponent of nuclear weaponry, and a believer in high technology. The idea of driving the Soviet system into oblivion was nothing new to him; Reagan had savored that thought for twenty years or more.

As another, low-key catalyst, some have mentioned Reagan's involvement in the low-budget 1941 film *Murder in the Air*, in which he played the part of a secret service agent who foils a plot to steal an "inertia projector" capable of shooting enemy planes from the sky. Nobody knows whom or what to credit for Reagan's interest in starting a national program in exotic antimissile weaponry. Other individuals may have been more influential in the long run, but Teller claimed to be the first influence.

Then, Reagan's friend Maxwell Hunter II of Lockheed published a paper that looked a little like BAMBI's space defense blueprint, and, on the invitation of Wyoming senator Malcolm Wallop, Hunter presented his ideas to key members of Congress. With expert coaching from Angelo Codevilla, a senior staff member on Wallop's Senate Intelligence Committee, he also briefed executives of TRW, Lockheed, Draper Labs, and Perkin Elmer, thereby giving impetus to a "Gang of Four" who in time would lead the battle for government support of chemical laser ABM weapons. Jeff Hecht, author of *Beam Weapons: The Next Arms Race*, suggests that President Reagan "can legitimately be considered the first major public advocate of the idea," although Wallop supported space defense systems more than three years before he launched SDI.[32]

That year, the magazine *Aviation Week & Space Technology* launched a major discussion of directed-energy ABM weapons, starting with a scathing attack on U.S. military incompetence written by a just-retired Air Force general, George J. Keegan. Keegan said the Soviets were undertaking "extraordinary weapons development projects" that were not being acknowledged by U.S. scientists, whose "egocentricity is functionally incapable of recognizing" that the Soviet work was truly on the cutting-edge of technology. The Soviet ABM program was twenty years ahead of the U.S. program, he said.[33]

Some of Keegan's information was correct, but some of it was no more than guesswork dressed up as fact. John Pike, for decades the lead spokesman for the Federation of American Scientists, would brand one of Keegan's assumptions "one of the major intelligence failures of the Cold War."[34] A site at Semipalatinsk, identified by Keegan as a directed-energy weapons research facility, was actually used to test nuclear rockets.

Accurate or not, Keegan started people thinking. Hecht observed in his book that the general "evidently had been unable to convince higher-ups at the Pentagon of his interpretation of intelligence information and had decided to 'go public' with his analysis. In an interview with *Science* magazine, he said his goal was 'to provoke and make enough people angry' about the situation."[35] That made sense. Gen. Simon P. (Pete) Worden, USAF (Ret.), after years of service in the SDI leadership, noted that "most of the defense intelligence community was criticizing the CIA as being overly sanguine"[36] and suggested that a number of people "probably overstated their case in order to get past the understatements" that represented the general view that Soviet military research was backward. "The truth was that the Soviets were not acting in the way that many people had predicted."[37]

While the decade had begun with the ghost of a hope that Moscow would begin to curtail its rapid production of ICBMs, it was now evident that output had increased. *Aviation Week* believed the same applied to directed-energy weapons. "The Soviet Union," the magazine claimed in its May 2 issue, "has achieved a technical breakthrough in high-energy physics applications that may soon provide it with a directed-energy beam weapon capable of neutralizing the entire United States ballistic missile force and checkmating this country's strategic doctrine."[38]

Ironically, the Soviets were then in the process of wrapping up—or at least cutting back—their existing PDL directed-energy weapon programs, which had been a drain on time and money. This was, of course, a secret as well, with the result that no benefit of hindsight was available to cool down interest in accelerating the infant U.S. beam weapons program.

In fact, U.S. research in exotic weaponry was in considerably better shape than Keegan and *Aviation Week* feared. Significant laser developments had been in progress since the early 1960s—at Bell Labs, Hughes Laboratory, and then, in 1965, the University of California at Berkeley. In 1967 scientists at Avco Everett Laboratory and Los

Alamos started work on a new directed energy approach based on the carbon dioxide gas dynamic laser, and a proposal to use one in a satellite antimissile system surfaced briefly in 1968.* ARPA had been funding an x-ray laser program for some time at the Naval Research Laboratory, and at Lawrence Livermore Teller's team was doing theoretical work on its own x-ray laser concept. Los Alamos was persevering with the NPB. At Stanford, John M. J. Madey and his team demonstrated the first free electron laser, which would be taken up shortly by Los Alamos and Lawrence Livermore.

Work was also getting under way on a concept that, unlike so many others, was destined for life beyond the turn of the twenty-first century. The Navy's deuterium fluoride antiship laser, which successfully shot down short-range missiles in 1978, would with time morph into TRW's continuous-wave MIRACL, and then into a system called Alpha. A similar TRW laser would develop into the U.S.–Israeli tactical high-energy laser (THEL) system for shooting down short-range tactical missiles, used in the successful intercept and destruction of a Katyusha rocket at White Sands on June 6, 2000.

Thin-skinned missiles would make likely targets for DEWs, but only if it were possible to hold a high-intensity spot of radiation in one place long enough to cause damage. Interception of a tough reentry vehicle with a pulsed laser, therefore, seemed an impossible task and, unlike the Soviets, U.S. industry never considered pursuing this technological route. Continuous-wave lasers seemed the only way to go.

By August 1978, *Aviation Week* was in a more mellow mood, reporting that "a major part of the Defense Advanced Research Projects Agency's high-energy laser program is exploring technology suitable for possible space applications."[39] But the Department of Defense's research chief, Ruth Davis, had something more dramatic up her sleeve—a centrally directed U.S.-directed energy weapon program. That September, at her request, a group of fifty-nine specialists met at Los Alamos and put together a multibillion-dollar draft plan. Some wanted particle beams, the Gang of Four wanted lasers, Teller wanted his x-ray laser, and others wanted fast missiles. The technologists contributed ideas for radars, satellites, missiles, and battle management systems, but it seemed the national and global politics were wrong, and there was no money—yet.

At that time, according to the defector Arkady Shevchenko, a former Soviet UN official, it was estimated that Moscow's ABM system could shoot down more than half of the U.S. missiles involved in a

---

*The Soviets would take up the idea themselves, albeit for tactical, theater use, where electrical supplies are easily available and targets appear at short range.

putative attack upon Moscow; with improvement the system would able to shoot down more than 90 percent of incoming missiles. It was an amazing piece of hyperbole, but people were listening. "The Moscow defense was upgraded," Teller growled at a Commonwealth Club meeting. "Our retaliatory missiles were not."[40]

THE PENNY DROPS

Ronald Reagan, now seriously interested in becoming the Republican candidate for the presidency, was strengthening his understanding of national and international affairs. On a visit to Colorado on July 31, 1979, he stopped in at the North American Air Defense (NORAD) Cheyenne Mountain headquarters. He was present when his aide Martin Anderson asked the general in charge, "What would happen if an SS-18 hit somewhere near the mountain?" When the general said, "It would blow us away," [41] the presidential candidate blanched. "Somehow (MAD) didn't seem to me to be something that would send you to bed feeling safe," he wrote.

Nor was the situation getting any safer, for the Russians believed they lacked "parity"—equal destructive power—in nuclear weaponry. Even if the United States slowed down missile production, the Soviets had no intention of following suit. "When we build, they build. When we stop, they build," Carter administration Defense Secretary Harold Brown once told the Senate Armed Services Committee.[42] Output was cranked up to new levels on one side, then on the other, in a cycle that seemed to have no chance of ending.

"It was like having two westerners standing in a saloon aiming their guns at each other's head—permanently," said Reagan. "There had to be a better way. . . . My deepest hope was that someday our children and our grandchildren could live in a world free of the constant threat of nuclear war."[43]

The following February, Lt. Gen. Daniel O. Graham, U.S. Army (Ret.), presented Reagan with what might indeed be a "better way"—a constellation of space-based, homing ABM-killers. Graham had advised Reagan in his first, unsuccessful bid for the presidency in 1976, and he returned again for his successful campaign. The two of them had talked often on the virtues of antimissile defense, with the result that each had steadily become more intrigued with the idea. Now Graham pressed his point home, the effort made all the easier by Teller's earlier tutorial on the benefits of antimissile missiles and Martin Anderson's suggestion that Reagan call for development of a protective missile system as part of his presidential campaign rhetoric. Reagan had chosen not to take Anderson's advice at that time, but in July 1980 he did ensure that the party platform endorsed "vigorous research and development of an effective anti-ballistic missile system, such as is already at hand in the Soviet Union, as well as more modern ABM technologies." Now, with the Cold War showing no sign of abatement, the American electorate chose as its president a man who had been briefed on missile defense by several experts and appalled by his nation's vulnerability during that 1980 visit to NORAD. Ronald Reagan, that longtime, dyed-in-the-wool opponent of both communism and nuclear weaponry, was ready to confront the Soviet Union.

4

REAGAN TAKES
THE REINS

*We have had our last chance. If we do not devise some greater and
more equitable system, Armageddon will be at our door.*
—Gen. Douglas MacArthur (broadcast shortly after the nuclear
bombing of Japan, 1945)

For many it was hard to conceive that an elderly actor could
become president of the United States at the height of the Cold War,
let alone one that was confident he could oversee the demise of a Soviet
superpower that was bristling with nuclear weapons and angry rhetoric. Yet, on November 4, 1980, Ronald Reagan won the U.S. presidency for the Republican Party, trouncing incumbent president Jimmy
Carter with a campaign that promised "A New Morning in America"
and restoration of the nation's military strength. He would more than
make good on both promises.

From the moment he assumed the presidency, Reagan made it
clear that his dislike for communism was at least as ardent as it had
been in his earlier life, when he was the outspoken, anticommunist
head of the Screen Actors Guild. He did not mince his words. In his
very first presidential press conference on January 19, 1981, he made a
noteworthy statement about détente and its aim of pursuing friendlier
U.S.–Soviet relations. A portent of future presidential tactics, it delighted his right-wing supporters and ignited a sense of anger and exas-
peration within the Politburo: "So far détente has been a one-way
street that the Soviet Union has used to pursue its own aims," he said.
"The only morality they recognize is what will further their cause.
Meaning they reserve unto themselves the right to commit any crime;
to lie; to cheat." Reagan and his team had hit the ground running.

A revolutionary new anti-Soviet strategy was already waiting in the wings.

For his secretary of defense, the new president had called in Caspar "Cap" Weinberger, who administered Reagan's budget office during his days as governor of California. A World War II veteran, Weinberger had a Harvard law degree and had been a corporate attorney. Tough but generally mild-mannered, he had earned the nickname "Cap the Knife" while serving in the Nixon cabinet. Like Reagan, he was steadfast in his opposition to the Soviets, only more so. "Caspar Weinberger was utterly convinced that there was no potential benefit in negotiating anything with the Soviet leaders and that most negotiations were traps," commented Jack Matlock, who joined the National Security Council in the spring of 1983, after two years as ambassador to Czechoslovakia.[1] Weinberger also had his own way of doing things, and got away with it. "Cap was not as interested as George [Shultz] in opening negotiations with the Russians," Reagan wrote, "and some of his advisors at the Pentagon strongly opposed some of my ideas on arms control that George supported."[2]

On the other hand, wrote Matlock, "Shultz's qualities complemented some of Ronald Reagan's weak points. Shultz mastered details that bored Reagan, exhibited greater stamina in negotiations, and had a keener sense of the value of consistency in overall policy. In contrast, Reagan was more effective on a public platform."[3]

Very early in the Reagan administration, Weinberger's assistant secretary of defense, Richard Perle, engineered a far-reaching "defense guidance" aimed, among other things, at pushing back a Soviet empire that was fighting for new beachheads in Afghanistan, Angola, Nicaragua, and elsewhere. Main points from this secret document would emerge later in a series of history-changing Reagan-era national security decision directives (NSDDs).

The nation was by now used to the policies of détente and "containment," the latter committed to blocking Soviet opportunities for expansion. But were these measures sufficient? Richard Pipes, a Polish-born Harvard scholar who was looking after the NSC's Soviet and East European desks, and CIA chief William J. Casey came up with a then-novel idea. The present course vis-à-vis the Soviet Union might well lead to war unless the West managed, somehow, *to change the Soviet system*. It was a sobering, challenging opinion from sober analysts, and it found its mark.

Casey was Ronald Reagan's first campaign chairman and, like his boss, had lived through the Great Depression. The two shared a fierce loyalty to the American system and were good friends. But this political drumbeater had been plucked from an unlikely professional career, that of a spymaster in the pay of the U.S. government.

Toward the end of World War II, Casey served as chief of secret intelligence, European Theater, Office of Strategic Services (OSS). He distinguished himself by putting together an intelligence network that penetrated Nazi Germany, something no one had ever done before. After the war, the OSS was reconstituted as the Central Intelligence Agency.

Within days after Reagan took office, Casey was appointed director of central intelligence (DCI) with a specially created cabinet post and a seat in the NSC. A place was reserved for him on the National Security Planning Group (NSPG), a new organization that would sit at the center of the nation's foreign policy machine. He ran the organization in hands-on fashion, riding in a bullet-proof Oldsmobile 98 and flying around the world in his airborne command center, an all-black C-141 Starlifter. He mumbled, he was bald and walked with a stoop, and he was old. But he had style. And he was very close to the president. "He was a self-assured, well-read, devoted Reaganite," wrote Bud McFarlane.

Casey and his special assistant, Herb Meyer, were concerned that the Washington power elite seemed to have more interest in maintaining the superpower status quo than actually winning the game.* Meyer considered that Reagan, Casey, and others like National Security Advisor William P. ("Bill" or "Judge") Clark, Weinberger, and UN Ambassador Jeane Kirkpatrick "were trying to win, to end the Cold War—not to somehow 'make it better.'" It took Reagan to push home the idea of playing to win rather than holding the line. "It wasn't an argument between hawks and doves," Meyer explained. "There was almost a psychological difference between those who were playing to win and those who were playing to 'not lose.' A lot of people just didn't think you could win, that such an idea was beyond the pale. They couldn't even imagine it."[4]

Jack Matlock took a milder view. "President Reagan was in favor of bringing pressure to bear on the Soviet Union, but his objective was

---

*President Dwight D. Eisenhower's Solarium Group had cast doubt on mere containment, which had no mandate to change the U.S.-Soviet confrontation, as early as 1953. This group, which included the much-respected George Kennan and Andrew Goodpaster, proposed two policies that would be adopted independently by the Reagan administration. One recommended that containment be transformed by taking political and psychological action against the Soviets. Another called for covert operations and economic pressure. (Tyler Nottberg, "Once and Future Policy Planning: Solarium for Today." The Eisenhower Institute, 2004. Posted at: www.eisenhower institute.org/programs/livinghistory/solarium.htm).

to induce Soviet leaders to negotiate reasonable agreements, not to break up the country," he wrote in his book *Reagan and Gorbachev: How the Cold War Ended*. Following a November 1985 meeting with senior administration officials, Matlock noted their agreement that U.S. policy objectives should *not* include challenging the legitimacy of the Soviet system, military superiority, or forcing collapse of the Soviet system.[5]

Casey was worried that he might be held back by the inflexibility of an agency that, in Meyer's words, "had become bureaucratic, sclerotic, and woefully inadequate to its mission." So he created an analog of the OSS within the CIA, staffed by a group of outsiders. These included Meyer, whom he recruited from the staff of *Fortune* magazine and installed as special assistant and vice chairman of the National Intelligence Council. Meyer found the agency bland and boring, its analysts cut off from sources that would have made their work more useful. Their reports were in the main presented as bare facts with little reference to what might be happening in terms of the history and culture of the adversary.

Sometimes Casey and Meyer could get the analysts to modify their reports. When this failed, a secret weapon was brought to the fore. Quietly, Casey would authorize members of the closet "OSS" to write an alternative report that mirrored their own judgment. Then, briefcase in hand, he would trot over to the White House and hand them personally to Reagan and other key members of the administration, as Meyer put it, "all the while suggesting—with Bill's version of a wink and a nod—that when they had finished reading the official CIA version, they take a moment to read this, too."

When Reagan took office, the official view of the Soviet economy was relatively rosy. But after he brought in Casey, and Casey brought in Meyer, a new line of memos began to appear. Its commentaries included insights into the Soviet Union's path to collapse, countering other reports—from the CIA and elsewhere—that described a relatively robust Soviet economy.

"Bill would go down to the White House and say, 'Here is the National Intelligence Estimate,' and then reach into his other pocket and say, 'Here, why don't you read this as well,'" said Meyer. "That's the way we did it. We might be accused of screwing around with the intelligence, but we got the right stuff to the president."[6]

Casey knew that a very large part of the Soviet Union's economy was devoted to weaponry and soldiering—it could turn out tanks and bombs, aircraft and missiles, at breakneck speed. The United States, on the other hand, was oriented toward domestic matters and taxpayer interests, its defense budget tightly constrained by members of Congress who wished to please the parochial needs of their constituents. It followed that the Cold War would not likely be won by accelerating the arms race, but by attacking the soft belly of the Soviet bear—its economy, and the technology needed to underpin its superpower status.

Casey told the president that if the Soviet leadership felt warm and cozy at home in Moscow, they'd find ways of staying that way. Any change in this situation would have to come from a new strategy that would generate damage from *within* the Soviet Union and its satellites. If an effective strategy were put in place, internal pressures would mount, making the Kremlin much more amenable to change.

The time was ripe. While Moscow could look fairly prosperous to a chaperoned Western visitor, the Soviet Union as a whole was faltering from a sadly mismanaged agricultural program and could hardly feed its millions; it had put huge amounts of money into industrial projects but neglected to provide the infrastructures they needed. Its nuclear industry—civilian and military—was creating vastnesses of radiation-poisoned land and water. Its successes in military and space technology were marred with a history of wasteful and capricious expenditure, doled out at the expense of ordinary people. Over the protests of many Democrats and some Republican members of Congress, the administration now claimed that Soviet defense spending was 20 percent greater than that of the United States in 1972, 55 percent greater in 1976, and 45 percent greater in 1981—and that the Soviets spent 10 percent more in research, development, test and evaluation in the same period.[7]

The Soviet Union's attempts at neocolonialism only worsened its economic woes. Moscow started to establish a stronghold in Afghanistan in 1978 and took over Kabul in December of the following year. From then on, the Soviets were engaged in a downhill, devastatingly expensive guerrilla war in a country nearly twice the size of Alaska. The Soviets would lose about fifteen thousand soldiers, and perhaps two million Afghans would lose their lives in just under a decade of conflict. Thanks to the clash in Afghanistan, the Soviet Union's infrastructures were weakened even more, making it more likely that new U.S. initiatives would be successful, though Osama bin Ladin would boast that the Taliban eventually brought Moscow to its knees.

On January 30, 1981, with the president seated close by, Casey presented his theory to his NSPG colleagues—Vice President George H. W. Bush, Defense Secretary Weinberger, Secretary of State Alexander Haig, and National Security Advisor Richard Allen. The group favored increasing the defense budget and undermining Moscow's influence in Poland, which already was showing signs of independence.

Reagan then went out of his way to promote the idea of taking the battle right to the Kremlin itself. From that point, things began to move very quickly.

On March 30, outside the Washington Hilton Hotel, where he had just addressed a union convention, Reagan was grievously wounded by a deranged gunman, John Hinkley. Conspiracy theories erupted, but it quickly transpired, bizarrely, that Hinkley was trying to impress actress Jodie Foster, with whom he had become infatuated. At his trial he was found not guilty by reason of insanity and committed to a psychiatric hospital.

Two months later, in St. Peter's Square, a gunman shot and nearly killed Pope John Paul II, who was encouraging the anti-communist Solidarity labor movement in his native Poland. CIA Director William Casey, a regular visitor to the Pope, always suspected the Soviets were behind this assault, with help from KGB operatives in Bulgaria. In 2006 his suspicions were supported by an Italian parliamentary commission, which used new photographic evidence to conclude that KGB or GRU officials orchestrated the attack.[8]

Both men lived to contribute, in quite different ways, to the downfall of the Soviet Union. The Pope relied on popular sentiment to undermine communism—especially in Poland, which, observed Herb Meyer, the Soviet Union considered "the linchpin of its empire."[9] The president followed a more complicated scenario. He unleashed a fistful of tough measures to throw the Soviet system precariously off balance. Though no one could know it in 1981, the success of his strategy would hinge partly on a far-out idea that some at first tried to laugh out of existence—the Strategic Defense Initiative.

Reagan's National Security Council warned him that the Soviets believed they had achieved both nuclear and conventional warfare superiority. In other words, they believed they could fight and win a war with the West. But, that May, a confident Reagan assured a Notre Dame University audience that the Soviet Union represented "a sad bizarre chapter in human history whose last pages are even now being written."[10] This may have been true, but by no means were the Soviets ready to give up. Martial law was declared in Poland on December 13, 1981, to which the United States replied by imposing sanctions on December 23. Then, on January 22, the Polish crisis led to a shutdown of bilateral arms control negotiations.

ASYMMETRIC WARFARE

Two deeply ingrained aversions stuck with Ronald Reagan throughout his two crisis-ridden terms: one was to communism; the other was to nuclear weaponry. He was utterly convinced of the awe-some destructive power of the world's growing atomic arsenals, horri-fied by it, and determined to do his utmost to completely rid the world of nukes. Reagan also held a deep distrust of the policy of nuclear deterrence—mutual assured destruction—as an instrument of contain-ment, and pictured it many times as two people holding guns at each other's head.

It was not a totally unfair picture. "To be most effective," wrote arms control negotiator and national laboratories administrator C. Paul Robinson, "deterrence must create fear in the mind of the adver-sary—fear that he will not achieve his objectives, fear that his losses and pain will far outweigh any potential gains, fear that he will be punished. It should ultimately create the fear of extinction—extinction of either the adversary's leaders themselves or their national independence, or both. Yet, there must always appear to be a 'door to salvation' open to them should they reverse course."[11]

Surprisingly, most Americans mistakenly thought the nation al-ready had a ballistic missile defense system in place, and they continued to do so at least until the late 1990s, when a revised program was taken on by the newly formed Missile Defense Agency. By contrast, the Soviets had a genuine ABM defense in place around Moscow, along with thousands of air-surveillance radars and surface-to-air mis-sile launchers. This array of defensive might was coupled with an offen-sive capability in which a Soviet ICBM needed only thirty minutes' flight time from a silo or launch pad in Siberia to an explosion above a U.S. missile silo in North Dakota—or any other target chosen by the military commissars.

NATO was then planning to bring nuclear-armed U.S. cruise and Pershing II missiles to Europe, to counter Soviet intermediate-range nuclear missiles, most notably the three-warhead SS-20s, which the Soviets began to aim at European allies in 1977. The SS-20 could strike European capitals after a flight of four or five minutes, with greater accuracy and from greater distances than had previously been possible. NATO's Pershings and cruise missiles were nowhere near so capable, and there would be fewer of them.*

The European peace movement rebelled. There were marches, angry speeches, and sit-ins. In one notable case, housewives protested

*The Pershing had a range of 1600 km, considerably less than the 2500 km claimed by the Soviets. The original plan was deploy 108 Pershing IIs by the autumn of 1983, and 464 ground-launched cruise missiles (GLCMs). The slower, jet-powered GLCM has a similar range but takes much longer to reach its target since it is powered by a jet engine, not rockets, and since it follows a computer-generated map in order to evade radar at low altitude.

at Greenham Common in England, which was chosen as a base for ground-launched cruise missiles. Their activities, supported by Czech intelligence operating from a safe house in Reading, started with a march to the base in September 1981. It continued, intermittently and noisily, until December 1983, when an estimated fifty thousand women circled the site and brought down part of the fence.

Sergei Teresenko of the Soviet Foreign Ministry later reflected that he and his colleagues "believed that we would manage to prevent the deployment of Pershings through the peace movement—trying to split Europe and the United States, playing on differences in attitudes among the major European powers."[12] The strategy fit well with Lenin's policy of supporting the communist cause "through propaganda, sympathy, or materially . . . in all countries without exception."[13]

Soon after the October Revolution of 1917, Lenin wrote that socialism is inconceivable "without . . . engineering based on the latest discoveries of modern science." He was not necessarily referring to Russian science. In *The Impending Catastrophe* (1917), he wrote, "We do not invent, we take ready-made from capitalism; the best factories, experimental stations and academies. We need adopt only the best models furnished by the experience of the most advanced countries." Lenin's advice was sorely needed with the outbreak of World War II and its grim segué into the Cold War. The Soviet Union's expertise in science was world-class, but its technology and engineering programs were so outdated that they had to be fortified by vast transfusions of information and matériel from more technologically advanced nations.

The KGB followed this advice assiduously, assisted by intelligence-gathering organizations in other communist states. In the 1940s, U.S. research establishments had been successfully mined by Soviet intelligence for atomic secrets. Espionage continued at a clip after the Soviet Union went nuclear, and in 1970 a widespread campaign to collect Western strategic military R&D information was in progress under Directorate T, the science and technology department of the KGB First Chief Directorate (Foreign Intelligence). National Security Council staffer Norman Bailey noted that the Soviet Union was lagging about fifteen years behind the United States in computer and microelectronic technology at that time, but that "by 1981 the Soviets had closed the 15-year technology gap to three to four years."[14] The program was blown when a KGB engineer-analyst, Colonel Vladimir Vetrov, told his story to French intelligence. At the cost of his life, the informer—code-named Farewell—exposed the activities of a sci-tech collection agency called Line X and spilled the names of more than two hundred operatives working in the West. This information arrived at Casey's office in Langley, Virginia, in the summer of 1981.

Casey was soon devising and implementing a closely held strategy with a handful of allies. National Security Advisor Dick Allen resigned and was replaced in January 1982 by Bill Clark, a tall, bespectacled, and sober-looking intellectual who had served as Allen's deputy. A California lawyer, rancher, and longtime Reagan friend, Clark had little other experience in foreign affairs. This, and his modest air, made him look like a lightweight at first, but he proved to be nothing of the sort. Rather, Clark skillfully manipulated the nation's foreign policy from the shadows: he was a quiet man, but he was also very aggressive.

As his deputy, Clark brought in Robert C. "Bud" McFarlane, the earnest, methodical, even diffident son of a Texas congressman. McFarlane was not very well known, but he had more experience in foreign and defense policy than James A. Baker III, Reagan's chief of staff (preferred by Shultz), or Jeane Kirkpatrick (preferred by Weinberger and Casey), who was just finishing her tenure as ambassador to the UN. The NSC team preferred McFarlane, and they got their way. A Marine lieutenant colonel, McFarlane served on Secretary of State Henry Kissinger's staff from 1973–75. In that capacity, he had carefully studied and come to understand the strategies behind the growth of the U.S. and Soviet Union nuclear stockpiles. This background— which provided him with a keen knowledge of defense issues, along with a wide range of contacts in Congress—made him a rare and valuable bird in the Reagan aviary. McFarlane was deeply concerned that the American star was fading, and he wanted desperately to do something about it.

Meanwhile, Reagan's Department of Defense had been putting together its plan to weaken the Soviet empire. The plan, bolstered by a secret national security decision directive titled NSDD-32, dovetailed nicely with CIA and NSC strategies. Signed by the president on May 20, 1982, the directive called for the development of advanced technologies and declared that the United States would do its best to "neutralize" Soviet domination of East Europe by whatever means necessary short of war.

The CIA had another part of the action. "I believe that it is important today to understand how clandestine intelligence, covert action, and organized resistance saved blood and treasure in defeating Hitler," DCI Casey wrote. "These capabilities may be more important than missiles and satellites in meeting crises yet to come, and point to the potential for dissident action against the control centers and lines of communication of a totalitarian power."[15]

NSDD-32 was the first of three hard-hitting anti-Soviet NSDDs that would be enacted within a year. It affirmed that the United States would weaken the Eastern European states' dependence on Moscow by supporting Solidarity and other anti-Soviet movements, and by increasing anticommunist propaganda. Ironically, it resonated with Soviet doctrine that "Nuclear war is a complex and many-sided process, which in addition to the operation of the armed forces will involve economic, diplomatic and ideological forms of struggle. They will all serve the political aims of the war and be guided by them."[16]

The new directive also legitimized a secret U.S. agreement that was consummated one afternoon in January 1982, when Gus Weiss, an NSC analyst, met with Casey to talk about the Vetrov papers. "I proposed using the Farewell material to feed or play back the products sought by Line X," Weiss recounted, "but these would come from our own sources and would have been 'improved,' that is, designed so that on arrival in the Soviet Union they would appear genuine but would later fail."[17] Casey readily agreed. One Trojan horse was a supervisory control and data acquisition (SCADA) computer program that had been prepared (and doctored) for the Soviet gas pipeline system.* "The result" recalled Tom Reed, a special assistant for national security policy under President Reagan, "was the most monumental non-nuclear explosion and fire ever seen from space."[18]

Technology would be central to the campaign. The United States would accelerate the use of high technology to strengthen its defense posture, and when expedient it would overstate and misstate the high-tech information that was being gathered by and for Soviet intelligence. Washington did everything in its power to strangle the flow of real information—and real high-tech products—to the Soviet Union.

More information on the KGB's tech-espionage operation came through in June 1982, when the KGB defector Vladimir Kuzishkin walked into the British Embassy in Tehran and unraveled more of Line X's workings. "In everything from spy satellites and supersonic fighters to artillery and atomic submarines, the communists were using technology begged, borrowed or stolen from their capitalist opponents," wrote journalist Jay Tuck in his 1986 book *High-Tech Espionage*.[19]

---

*It is worth noting that SCADA attacks by cyber-terrorists became one of the prime concerns of the Department of Homeland Security created by President George W. Bush.

By now, Line X was a problem for the Soviets, not the Americans, and the United States was giving Moscow headaches in yet another department. The Soviets were made greatly uncomfortable by the idea that key strategic decisions were made with the blessings of a man whom so many thought was little more than a slightly loopy old guy who used to play hunk roles in B movies. It's true that Reagan did say some nutty things now and again, yet in some respects he was playing the best role of his career. Indeed, he had been known to refer to the Oval Office as the biggest theater in the world.[20] "It was part of Reagan's strategy to get the Soviets to think he was a little crazy," National Security Advisor Dick Allen told writer-analyst Peter Schweizer. Schweizer was reminded of Herman Kahn's observation that "no one wants to play chicken with a madman."[21]

"The fact that some elements may appear to be potentially 'out of control' can be beneficial to creating and reinforcing fears and doubts within the minds of an adversary's decision makers," Paul Robinson remarked. "This essential sense of fear is the working force of deterrence. That the United States may become irrational and vindictive if its vital interests are attacked should be a part of the national persona we project to all adversaries."[22]

So started a closely held but very resolute "psy-op" or psychological operation, which in turn was part of a very large-scale act of asymmetrical warfare. The Soviets were on edge, and the U.S. administration was determined to make them even more so. The effort would be needed, for, in the words of NSDD-32, "[T]he decade of the eighties will likely pose the greatest challenge to our survival and well-being since World War II and our response could result in a fundamentally different East–West relationship by the end of this decade."[23]

The new Reagan thrust, which favored defense and incorporated his aversion to nuclear weapons, soon established a new U.S. stance in world politics. Here, Reagan's attitude toward to the Soviet Union was fundamental. He had no inborn hatred for Russian individuals, but he loathed their political system and was convinced that it was time to move away from reliance on détente and containment and into a mode where residents of East and West were freed from the threat of nuclear warfare. Students of the time, including Peter Schweizer and Herb Meyer, suggest that DCI Casey played an important role in motivating the president to find unusual and unpredictable ways of disrupting the internal workings of the Soviet Union while, generally, "playing to win."

There are differences between "bringing the Soviet Union down," "playing to win," and "changing the Soviet system," and interpretations of the three phrases make for an interesting evening's discussion. Regardless, America under Reagan did plan to do its utmost to solve the so-called "Russian Problem." In the years following Reagan's accession, the United States played important roles in the dissolution of the Soviet Union, but the Soviets, already weak with mismanagement, would do a fair amount of the work themselves.

SCI-FI WEAPONS AND STRATEGIC DEFENSE

Whatever a technologist does must be useful in general, or useful to someone, or just apparently useful. If a technologist goes through exactly the same process without any intention of producing something useful then he must either be mad or an artist.
—Edward de Bono

In September 1981, at about the time the Greenham Common ladies were starting their long demonstration at the cruise missile site in Berkshire, Gerold Yonas was in Moscow giving a paper at the 10th European Conference of Plasma Physics and Controlled Nuclear Fusion Research. Yonas was enjoying the distinction of speaking at the same podium as Academician Andrei Kapitsa, who like him was interested in electron beam propagation in air, and the directed-energy research pioneer Oleg Krokhin, who of course could say nothing about the PDL laser. Yonas was a man among peers. He had been working on laser concepts as early as 1967–68, and most recently he had been behind the scenes with the RADLAC (radial-pulse-line accelerator) electron-beam machine.*

It's highly doubtful that anyone at the meeting thought of any directed-energy scheme as a candidate for near-term application. For example, while Yonas was interested in electron beams and effects, his Sandia team didn't know how to propagate them effectively. These so-called e-beams could work in all weather, but when it came to making

---

*The RADLAC program encompassed high power electron beam propagation experiments and accelerator development, both for advanced propagation experiments and to develop compact accelerator options for future charged particle beam weapons.

them move in a straight line, the researchers were clueless. Their beams whipped around wildly, like electronic dervishes.

Yonas had come to Moscow at Evgeny Velikhov's invitation. He was given the VIP treatment, complete with tickets to the Bolshoi ballet, and welcomed as Velikhov's guest at the Kurchatov Institute, which was established as the Soviet Academy of Sciences nuclear research center in 1943. Yonas would retain a nagging suspicion that his special treatment was an ameliorative gesture for being briefly detained at the Leningrad airport a couple of years earlier.

It was relatively calm in the conference rooms, but the political scene was tense. Rumors were circulating that Leonid Brezhnev's troops would invade Poland to suppress the Solidarity movement. Reagan had approved production of the relatively small-yield neutron bomb as a warhead for missiles and artillery.* Unknown to the Soviets, the Americans were just beginning to analyze the KGB's sensitive Line X information. And the KGB, then run by a worried future general secretary, Yuri Andropov, had begun another high-priority espionage program. The program's Russian title, *Vnezapnoye Raketnoye Yadernoye Napadeniye*, VRYN, gave rise to the American nickname Operation Ryan.[1] Influenced by memories of Hitler's 1941 Operation Barbarossa surprise attack on the Soviet Union, VRYN's mission was to determine whether it was likely that their current "Main Enemy" would launch a "sudden nuclear missile attack" and to find out whether, among other things, the United States planned to use its brand-new Space Shuttle to drop hydrogen bombs.

Sitting there at the conference with the translators' headset clamped to his ears, Yonas became intrigued by the dual nature of the information he was picking up. Here, developments in plasma physics could only be discussed in the abstract, or as means for investigating fusion and its possible use for producing electrical energy. Yonas suspected—correctly—that a mirror image of the same work existed under wraps in the closely related, classified world of directed-energy beam weapons research. In fact, the dual roles of science had been noted by a 1978 RAND report that said the Soviets were doing pulsed power work for "(1) the achievement of controlled thermonuclear reactions as a national energy source and (2) military applications."[2]

Not unnaturally, while Yonas was speculating that the Soviets might have had a big laser program somewhere that they were not

---

*The neutron bomb is a small thermonuclear weapon that produces a relatively small amount of blast and heat but produces large amounts of radiation over a limited area. Thus, while it could be devastating on the battlefield, it would have a limited effect on structures and on nearby population centers. U.S. production of the bomb was postponed in 1978 and resumed in 1981.

talking about, the Soviets were looking at him, thinking he must know something about a U.S. beam weapon program.[3] The practice of talking publicly about fusion and working in secret on beam weapons took place in both countries. The two-faced personality of plasma physics was an open secret, and it gave fund-raising leverage to scientists on both sides. During the Moscow meeting, Yonas got the idea that the Soviets weren't going anywhere with their high-energy research program, though hints of what they were trying to do managed to leak out. For example, he knew that Velikhov was working on a carbon dioxide laser for fusion, and that others were active in his own specialty area, electron beam generation and propagation.

While the Moscow plasma physics meeting was all courtesy and refined good manners, Yonas said, "There was a lot of talk about the Soviets going into Warsaw, so many thought that Soviet–U.S. relations were collapsing and that there was a real lowering of the threshold for nuclear war." Yonas jotted down comments from other conference attendees in his notebook. The entries illustrate the undercurrents that were flowing through this meeting. For example, he wrote, "The average Russian is being told that the American plan is to bankrupt the Russian economy by creating an arms race."* Another conference attendee said, "We'll starve before we give up our bombs and our planes and our tanks. I'm not in the weapons business, but I have friends who have the clearances and they know." Someone else felt that "things were breaking up between American and Soviet scientists." Others were saying things like, "I like you and I like your people, but your society is corrupt."[4]

Yonas had visited the Soviet Union every year since 1973, and he enjoyed everything from the intellectual milieu to the dark, moist, heavy bread that was served with its coating of fresh butter and a little salt. He knew little of the history of the Soviet Union, and, because he saw only what his hosts wanted him to see, his view of Soviet life was canted toward the positive.

"From what I could see," he wrote, "the average person got to go to the ballet, was rather satisfied with poor food and lousy housing, and at least thought everything was getting better little by little. But the real Soviet Union was a third-rate nation that had sacrificed much

---

*The idea of bankrupting the adversary with a high-tech arms race was not new to the Soviets. In his masterful biography of Khrushchev, William Taubman mentions a 1959 memo in which the Soviet premier, knowing that his country had only four ICBMs in its stockpile, said that if the West joined in an arms race they would be "sucking from their budgets, depleting national economics," and "thereby contributing to the advantages of our [Soviet] system." (William Taubman, *Khruschchev: The Man and His Era* (New York: W. W. Norton, 2003), 448.)

of its limited wealth to have a world-class military and a huge strategic nuclear weapons capability. I did not know at the time that their multi-million-person nuclear enterprise included two closed science cities, where an enormous national investment provided everything from mining raw materials to running the dairies. In this separate world, kids were born and raised, could get an excellent education, got married, and lived out their lives. The populations of these closed cities constituted an isolated, but top-notch, scientific and technical cadre dedicated to a well-focused strategic nuclear weapon capability to deter the U.S."[5]

"Things were tense back then in 1981," he said. "I remember saying goodbye to my Russian friends, thinking we'd never see each other again."[6]

By this time, it had become painfully evident that the dream of détente simply hadn't worked. More aggressive arms control measures, especially bilateral treaties to reduce stockpile inventories, were being pursued vigorously by the "doves," while MAD remained the fallback position that was beginning to cause heartburn for the "hawks." And then there was the question of defensive weaponry.

LOBBYISTS IN ACTION

Some of the rights to claim authorship of SDI belong to Jerry Pournelle, a very bright and assertive World War II combat veteran, science and science-fiction writer, spaceflight enthusiast, and self-confessed "paleo-conservative." Pournelle's Citizen's Advisory Council on National Space Policy, formed in 1980, generally met at the Tarzana, California, home of his colleague and co-author, Larry Niven. These were large and diverse get-togethers catered lavishly by Niven's wife Marilyn, with attendees from the military, science fiction, aerospace, and science communities. There, astronauts Buzz Aldrin and Pete Conrad were mixing with the likes of Lowell Wood, Max Hunter, Dan Graham, Greg Bear, and Robert Heinlein. The group had a common interest in manned space exploration, but soon was involved in SDI-type promotion through Pournelle's preelection association with Richard Allen, the future national security advisor.

Pournelle says his group prepared much of the Reagan administration's transition-team policy papers on space. "I think you will find that most of the intellectual firepower behind SDI was in meetings in Larry Niven's house in Tarzana between 1980 and 1984," he said. The idea went beyond out-gunning the adversary: "The object of defense is to complicate the enemy war plan to the point that he has no confidence in it and thus no incentive to start the war."[7] Pournelle claims that, as a result of his organization's work, "the (National Security) Council wrote parts of Reagan's 1983 SDI speech, and provided much of the background for the policy."[8]

Meanwhile, a remarkable young man by the name of John Bosma—who had been ruminating over Herman Kahn's writings while serving variously as short order cook, logger, commercial fisherman, truck driver, and hitchhiker—came onto the scene. Somehow in the late 1970s he found a job at Boeing's Strategic Defense Analysis Group and became interested in superpower war-gaming, learning to his fright that, in nuclear exchange modeling, "we lost our ass every time." Boeing, unready at that time to countenance defensive systems, sent Bosma to Washington, where he met Dan Graham, became an aggressive congressional staffer, and then eventually moved to DARPA, the old ARPA that in 1972 had its original name changed to *Defense* Advanced Projects Research Agency.

In the summer of 1982, Bosma was hard at work in the Library of Congress Madison reading room, perusing documents for his boss, Rep. Ken Kramer of Colorado. During a lunch break, he found proposals for BMD and air defenses that had been penned for United Nations consumption by Andrei Gromyko in 1962 and 1963. "They came up with the idea of phasing up both types of defenses while reducing bombers and missiles," Bosma said of the Soviet proposals. "Very creative."[9] When he told White House science advisor Jay Keyworth's office about his discovery, the response was immediate, and very positive. A courier was dispatched to Bosma's office to pick up the goodies.

Later, U.S. negotiators used this documentation repeatedly when they attempted to soften the Soviets' antipathy for Ronald Reagan's Strategic Defense Initiative. But Gromyko quickly backed off when the issue was brought up in the summer of 1983, arguing that times had changed; and a similar response met Secretary of State George Shultz at the 1985 Geneva summit.

While Pournelle, Bosma, and other advocates for strategic defense applied their individual talents to the cause of BMD, several powerful groups were thinking very seriously about space-based directed-energy defense. Public interest in strategic defense, preconditioned by science fiction, was building, too. It rather naturally settled upon the use of space- and ground-based lasers, space-based particle beams, and nuclear directed energy weapons. Problems associated with the realization of these dreams were quickly identified by academics, but proved to be so esoteric that they escaped the radar screens of public debate. They extended well beyond the basic problem of up-scaling an energetic beam that happened to work well in the lab. Let's imagine we could put in space a beam weapon that moves in a short straight line with little spread, so that it is able to zap its target with metal-melting power; so far, so good. But lasers in space would need very powerful energy supplies, meaning the overall system would weigh much more, and newer and bigger rockets would therefore be needed to put it into orbit. The satellites would also need some means of defending themselves from attack, a fact that only increases the need for the lifting power that must be provided by the launch system.

But then, the beam need not originate in space. Laser energy could theoretically be generated at a defensible ground station where power was plentiful, then (provided the sky was clear) reflected toward its targets by an orbiting mirror. Such a system would need a laser strong enough, and a beam sufficiently intense, to penetrate even a cloud-free atmosphere efficiently. The challenges of detecting a missile launch, tracking the missiles, discriminating real weapons from decoys, then aiming and holding the spots of laser light on individual targets until they did their damage, were so astronomical that few wanted to think about them.

Finally, whether deployed in space or on the ground, a ground rule was that SDI systems had to be so cheap that the Soviets would no longer gain by adding more offensive weapons to their arsenal. If this were not the case, then deployment of countermeasures and new ballistic missiles would increase and the goals of SDI would remain out of reach. Targets would be home free if they were not zapped within a time frame of a few short minutes. Attack satellites and orbiting mirrors, however, would be forever vulnerable.

Once the lobbyists had decided that such questions were too difficult to bother with, the battle for beam-weapon bucks was under way. Of all the competitors, Edward Teller's x-ray laser sported the most glitz. On the other hand, and although it had a wealth of government funding through the U.S. Department of Energy, it was energized by a nuclear explosion, and Reagan didn't like nukes. Dan Graham, a retired Army general and former chief of the Defense Intelligence Agency, was vigorously promoting ideas originated by DARPA's old but relatively sensible Project Defender. He too had briefed an intrigued Governor Reagan on the need for ABM technology in early 1980, praising Defender's virtues literally to the skies. Graham had a new organization, High Frontier, supported at the time by a quartet of rich, right-wing Reaganite industrialists—Karl Bendetsen, Joseph Coors, William Wilson, and Jacquelin "Jack" Hume.

Though also a member of the Bendetsen group, Teller pooh-poohed Graham's aspirations. "It was not a very hopeful program, and

I hoped to deflect it into different directions," he said. "I thought his optimism was unjustified."[10] For his part, Graham told the *New York Times* that Teller "wanted very much to leave in the nuclear options. The man is carrying a load and has taken a lot of abuse as the 'father' of the H-bomb. Now he wants to see nuclear technology turn out to be the answer in the opposite direction, to save the Western world."[11]

Teller joined High Frontier in the summer of 1981, "hoping that as a member I could help the group put together an optimal technical proposal for strategic defense."[12] Graham preferred to use more readily available technologies; a rift split the two camps and Teller emerged the victor in terms of accessibility to the president, but without being able to break through Reagan's general aversion to nuclear technology. Senator Wallop was another competitor, favoring the orbiting chemical laser proposed by the "Gang of Four."[13]

At an October 2 White House press briefing, Weinberger hinted that a new breed of antiballistic technologies sufficient at least to protect missile silos might be on the doorstep. The same day, Reagan announced his support for basing MXs (the "Missile-X" ICBMs that were intended to replace America's aging Minuteman fleet) in silos, along with his support for production of one hundred B-1 bombers. A background statement noted that "research and development on ballistic missile defense will be rigorously pursued," and that "we will develop technologies for space-based defense."

That December, outflanked by his prolaser colleagues, Graham split away from the Bendetsen group and took High Frontier in a less sexy but ultimately more sensible direction. This favored orbital interceptor rockets which, he reasoned, were technically and economically more attractive and would win greater public approval because they were non-nuclear and used more conventional technology. Bendetsen, Hume, Coors, and Teller then presented their case for advanced space-based ABM weaponry in a secret meeting with Reagan and members of his kitchen cabinet held on January 8, 1982, in the White House's Roosevelt Room. On January 20, Reagan wrote Bendetsen: "You can be sure that we will be moving ahead rapidly with the next phase of this effort." The letter continued: "The antisatellite and ballistic missile defense programs have lagged behind the Soviets. . . . we plan to continue our review of strategic defense to determine what additional steps will be necessary."[14]

Later that year, with Air Force backing, Cap Weinberger made it clear that he had no time for High Frontier and its vision of protecting America with off-the-shelf hardware. "Although we appreciate your optimism that 'technicians will find the way and quickly,'" he wrote Graham, "we are unwilling to commit this nation to a course which calls for growing into a capability that does not currently exist."[15] Beam-weapon ABM capabilities didn't exist, either, but their advocates were better financed and the whole field benefited from its association with the famous name of Edward Teller.

POURING ON THE PRESSURE

In 1982, in front of and behind the scenes, diplomatic maneuvers, public pronouncements, and charged suggestions were thick in the air. In the main they originated from Washington, and they had one primary purpose: to make the Soviet Union so uncomfortable that it would become more willing to implement measures that would genuinely reduce East–West tensions. Ideally, these measures would also provide leverage for neutralizing world communism, consigning the MAD doctrine to the history books, and getting the other superpower to either change its ways radically or implode.

In a May 9, 1982, speech at his alma mater, Eureka College, Reagan called for equal reductions in the number of ICBMs held by the United States and the Soviet Union. The Soviets had most of their eggs in that basket, with relatively small investments in free-fall bombs and shorter-range missiles, and the president either chose to ignore or didn't know that this was the case. Angry Kremlin leaders labeled the proposal further proof of U.S. militarism and general hostility. By their calculations, such a move would leave the United States with three times as many warheads and half again as many strategic weapons. Still, on May 25, the Politburo agreed to talk.

That month, a pastoral letter from the American Catholic Bishops roundly condemned the U.S. nuclear arms buildup. The bishops attacked the deterrence principle, urged "accelerated work for arms control, reduction, and disarmament," and—as it turned out—helped jump-start the U.S. conversion to strategic defense. The Pentagon's five-year plan, "Fiscal Year 1984–1988 Defense Guidance," which was made public on May 29, must have chilled the leaders at the Kremlin to the bone. It countenanced the possibility of a protracted nuclear war and lined out a tough strategy to pressure the Soviet economy, assist China in strengthening its border with the Soviet Union, and bolster U.S. conventional forces. Then came the stroke that caused the Soviets more anxiety than the Americans could ever imagine—a strong recommendation to develop weapons that "are difficult for the Soviets to counter, impose disproportionate costs, open up new areas of major military competition, and obsolesce previous Soviet investment," including "prototype development of space-based weapons systems."[16]

That December, *Science* magazine announced that DARPA was sponsoring development of a nuclear generator "capable of producing millions of watts of electricity for use in outer space."[17]

Reagan flew to Europe in early June, stopping off in Rome for a
secret, yet historic, one-on-one conversation with Pope John Paul II.
In short, the meeting concluded that the United States and the Vatican
had a common enemy, the communist empire, and they would quietly
work together to bring it down.* Before the British parliament in London the next day, June 8, Reagan challenged the Soviet Union to extend basic human rights and hammered home his determination to
contribute to the "march of freedom and democracy which will leave
Marxism-Leninism on the ash-heap of history, as it has left other tyran-
nies which stifle the freedom and muzzle the self-expression of the
people." Afterwards, Margaret Thatcher toasted Reagan "for putting
freedom on the offensive, where it belongs."[18] The atmosphere was
not nearly so ebullient back home in the United States. With his approval rating considerably below 50 percent, the country in recession,
and unemployment at nearly 9 percent, Reagan returned at about the
time that many thousands of demonstrators were crowded into New
York's Central Park, calling for an end to the production and testing
of nuclear weapons.

On June 15, the Soviets made a declaration that they would make
"no first use" of nuclear weapons. Fragmentary reports of spectacular
Soviet space-power demonstrations followed. One stated that a submarine-launched missile, two SS-11 ICBMs, and an SS-20 missile were
test-launched on June 18; that all were intercepted by Soviet ABM-X-
3 rockets; and that for the grand finale a combat satellite was popped
up into orbit.[19] A more modest report in *Nevsky Bastion* said that, during a Soviet strategic nuclear force exercise on that date, a Cosmos
rocket intercepted a mock U.S. Transit navigation satellite.[20]

Reagan then chose a July 4 Space Shuttle landing at Edwards Air
Force Base to review key points of U.S. space policy. "The United
States is committed to the exploration and use of space by all nations
for peaceful purposes and for the benefit of mankind," he said. However, "'Peaceful purposes' allow activities in pursuit of national security
goals." Current policy, he said, encouraged peaceful, and international,

---

*"Only President Ronald Reagan and Pope John Paul II were present in the
Vatican Library on Monday, June 7, 1982. In that meeting, Reagan and the Pope
agreed to undertake a clandestine campaign to hasten the dissolution of the communist
empire. Declares Richard Allen, Reagan's first National Security Advisor: 'This was one
of the great secret alliances of all time.'" (Carl Bernstein, "The Holy Alliance." *Time*,
February 24, 1992. Available at www.mosquitonet.com/~prewett/holyalliance1of
2.html.)

exploitation of space; yet, he allowed, "the United States will pursue activities in space in support of its right of self-defense."[21] These points were included in National Security Decision Directive 42, issued the same day. Following the speech, Reagan met Jim Abrahamson in a side room and pinned on his third star.

ERICE

That summer, Evgeny Velikhov traveled to Erice, Sicily, for the August 19–24 International Seminar on Nuclear War, an annual meeting staged by the World Federation of Scientists (WFS). The federation was founded in 1973 by a group of world-class scientists under the leadership of Isidor Isaac Rabi and Antonino Zichichi. This meeting became famous for "The Erice Statement" on science, society, and peace, signed initially by Paul Dirac, Peter Kapitsa, Antonio Zichichi, and subsequently by more than ten thousand scientists worldwide.[22]

Erice is a picturesque, historical, out-of-the way town that dominates a hill in the northwestern part of the island. It is overlooked by a Norman castle and a fourteenth-century cathedral, and its old streets are lined with stern stone facades that hide scores of houses with graceful, brightly flowered courtyards. It is the home of the Ettore Majorana Center for Scientific Culture, where three restored monasteries provide the setting for what some have called "The University of the Third Millennium." The center and the WFS exist largely to provide international forums for the mitigation of planetary emergencies—a broad swath of real and incipient problems that range from nuclear war to AIDS.

Velikhov and his fellow delegates were treated to a feast of erudite, insightful, and often idealistic lectures, including a presentation on "Openness: A Contribution from Scientists" by Edward Teller, director emeritus of Lawrence Livermore National Laboratory. Velikhov's topic was "How to Avoid a Nuclear War." Soon he made his way through the crowd toward Teller, who was surrounded as usual by fellow scientists, holding his trademark staff with its leather thong hanging about his wrist. Teller was naturally a spirited man, sparkling with intelligence, but Velikhov noted that this time, he was unusually animated.

"Edward gave a speech discussing the importance of defense," Velikhov recalled. "Afterwards we had a number of discussions with Edward, and he said certain things that convinced me that something special was cooking in the United States."[23] In fact, Teller had made a vague reference to a technological "ace in the hole" that would defend the United States against Soviet missiles, and commented that "some of my young colleagues have taken the initiative in defensive weapons and will one day get the full credit for it." Then, in the discussion period, Teller noted that, "in addition to nuclear weapons, we have other new weapons of high technology, for instance the lasers."

Richard Garwin, a physicist and IBM Fellow who opposed placing any kind of weapon in space, started a vigorous exchange with Teller, asking him to explain the "ace in the hole." Teller demurred, "That is a question to which I am not allowed to say yes, I am not allowed to say no, and I am not allowed to say maybe." He did concede that he had asked Congress to support the development of defensive weaponry, adding, "The probability is small that my ingenious colleagues in the Soviet Union have not thought about the possibilities that I have in mind and which I did not invent but others did." Garwin continued to goad him, but Teller refused to yield, congratulating Zichichi for having invited a "lawyer" who was "excellent in cross-examination."[24]

No wonder Velikhov was intrigued. Was Teller making progress in an ABM field that Velikhov's own countrymen had previously been working on? "My feeling was that, while we were discussing the relationship of defense and offense, he was extremely optimistic on defense, especially space defense," Velikhov said, "and for this reason I thought something was going to happen."

But what was it? Surely it had to do with weaponry. "Edward never supported disarmament. He said pacifism was simply not credible, and of course he considered it important that American military power rested upon its nuclear arsenal. Edward was a big believer in technological solutions."[25] Velikhov continued to puzzle over Teller's inexplicable show of enthusiasm for what the Russian reasoned must be some yet-undisclosed new technology. He wouldn't have long to wait for an explanation.

FORGING THE REAGAN DOCTRINE

Soon after Teller returned from Erice, Keyworth invited the physicist to join him for his long-sought-after presidential audience, which was approved after Teller complained of his lack of access to the president on a segment of William F. Buckley's TV show "Firing Line." The meeting was held on September 14, 1982, with the NSC's Bill Clark, Raymond Pollock, and Sydell Gold in attendance. In a tribute published just after Teller's death, Edmund Morris penned this description of the meeting for *The New Yorker*:

> Dr. Teller represented all that the President admired in a scientist, being distinguished, individualistic, sonorously spoken . . . and short of academic circumspection. For half an hour, Teller deployed X-ray lasers all over the Oval Office, reducing hundreds of incoming Soviet missiles to radioactive chaff, while Reagan, gazing up ecstatically, saw a crystal shield, covering the Last Hope of Man.[26]

Teller noted in his memoir that the meeting had been "far less successful than I had hoped,"[27] and Pollock concluded that little of significance resulted from it because neither he nor Gold received any questions or assignments.

Aviation Week & Space Technology reported that Teller had asked Reagan for $200 million a year "over the next several years," to develop the x-ray laser "at the expense of the USAF management plan for space-based, long-wavelength chemical lasers."[28] By now Teller had adopted a universally attractive new slogan—"mutual assured survival," to replace "mutual assured destruction."

On November 29, Reagan signed NSDD-66, pledging that the United States would do its best to squeeze off supplies of critical resources to the Soviet Union. It was followed in January 1983 by the masterful NSDD-75, a directive that declared—ominously for the Kremlin—that the United States would "promote, within the narrow limits available to us, the process of change in the Soviet Union toward a more pluralistic political economic system in which the power of the privileged ruling élite is gradually reduced." It went on to say that "containing and reversing Soviet expansion and promoting evolutionary change within the Soviet Union itself cannot be accomplished quickly." Both NSDDs had been inspired in part by the Farewell disclosures, but mostly by earlier analyses from Casey and Richard Pipes, a Harvard historian then on loan to the NSC. "Playing to our strength and their weakness, that was the idea," Weinberger told Peter Schweizer. "And that means economics and technology."[29]

Matlock called NSDD-75 "the most authoritative policy decisions by the president."[30] His NSC boss, Bill Clark, counted NSDD-75 as a major turning point in U.S. policy:

> My covering memo stated that U.S. policy toward the Soviet Union would consist of three elements: first, external resistance to Soviet imperialism; second, internal pressure on the USSR to weaken the sources of Soviet imperialism; and third, negotiations to eliminate, on the basis of strict reciprocity, outstanding disagreements. We emphasized the second of these

objectives. Internal pressure on the USSR represented a new
objective of U.S. policy.[31]

As Clark put it, "The basic premise behind this new approach was that
it made little sense to seek to stop Soviet imperialism externally while
helping to strengthen the regime internally."[32]

NSDD-75, largely Pipes's creation, has been termed the pivotal
document in changing U.S. policy toward the Soviet Union.
"Reagan's goal was to shift the U.S. strategy from reacting to challenges and limiting damage to a concerted effort to change Soviet
behavior," Matlock wrote. This "altered both the substance of negotiations and the way the dialogue was conducted, but it did not require
the Soviet Union to compromise its own security. Soviet claims to the
contrary, it never threatened military action against the Soviet Union
itself."[33] The directive also ended the era of détente, which assumed
that the Soviet Union was here to stay and that the United States had
to learn to live with it. The economist Norman Bailey, a Reagan NSC
staffer, wrote that NSDD-75 "is a complete strategic document and as
such is unique in the history of U.S. foreign relations."[34] Sometimes
called the Reagan Doctrine, it contributed mightily to the process of
ending the Cold War and placing the United States in the position of
the world's sole superpower.

OLD BMD, NEW BMD

On December 7, 1982, the House of Representatives threw out
Reagan's request for nearly a billion dollars to produce the first five
MX ICBMs. Reagan called the vote a "grave mistake": detractors of
the MX were "sleepwalking into the future." At the same time, there
was an upswing in Reagan's predisposition toward the creation of a
massive strategic defense enterprise. If the democratic process would
not support deterrence to match the increasing Soviet buildup, if it
was not in the mood to support offensive weaponry, then perhaps it
would embrace the idea of a perfect defense.

The biggest problem with MX missiles was that nobody could
decide what to do with them. They could be placed in silos like their
predecessors; alternatively, they could evade attack by being shuttled
around on trains, trucks, or even airships. "They came up with this
stupid idea of running them under the tunnels in Nevada [at the U.S.
Nuclear Test Site] and running them around on TELs [transporter
erector launchers]," Abrahamson commented. "Bring them up so the

Russians could see them, then scuttle around someplace else and launch from there.

"I'd listen to this mess and it was just terrible," he added. "It helped convince me that this whole idea of MAD was just junk. I was not a fan of the idea that we would have to destroy the whole world in order to defend ourselves.

"This is part of how the Joint Chiefs of Staff [JCS] began to say, slowly, that maybe it's time to look at defenses—because they couldn't find a survivable place to put their missiles," Abrahamson added. "The Navy was snug in their comfortable submarines, but the Air Force didn't know what to do."[35]

A broad, nonpartisan consensus for a consistent strategy of offense, defense, and arms control was sorely needed if the United States was to change directions and move away from the prevailing ICBM/ MAD model. But no such consensus ever materialized. It would take an executive decision to get things moving. Bud McFarlane recalled a memorable statement made by Reagan during an Oval Office meeting at about this time. "It's coming, Bud," the president said. "This inexorable building of nuclear weapons on our side, and the Russians' side, can only lead to Armageddon. We've got to get off that track."[36]

Meanwhile, intolerance for the idea of mutual assured destruction, and a conviction that strategic defense was the only way to go, was growing fast in the mind of Adm. James Watkins, the well-made, white-haired nuclear engineer and chief of naval operations who served as commander in chief of the U.S. Pacific Fleet from 1981 through 1982. Watkins had been commander of the USS *Long Beach*, the first U.S. nuclear cruiser, and later would be appointed secretary of energy by President George H. W. Bush.

Watkins, a devout Catholic, had read the American Catholic Bishops' letter, *The Challenge of Peace: God's Promise and Our Response*, and it had impressed him considerably. The letter attacked the morality of U.S. nuclear policy and challenged the authorities to find a way out of the nuclear standoff. Watkins tried to think of alternatives and eventually invited Teller to meet with him for a briefing on the possibility of mounting high-tech ABM defenses. Teller, of course, was pleased to accept the invitation. "He wanted to know one thing— missile defense, how did it work?" Teller recalled on a documentary produced for the Discovery Channel. "I told him we had plans how to work it. We can work it."[37] Teller not unnaturally took this opportunity to extol the virtues of the "pop-up" x-ray laser concept. If brought to fruition, he said, these ABM weapons would be capable of being rocketed from their ground bases immediately on notice of a Soviet ICBM attack, locking onto the invading missiles, and shooting them down.

Though a participant in the creation of the nuclear Navy, Watkins shared Reagan's dislike for nuclear weapons, including the nuclear-pumped x-ray concept that the Teller team now was marketing under the name Excalibur. "I said, forget [developing] Excalibur right now," Watkins remembered. "Do the nuclear-based lasers, fine, but that's research. Don't talk about fielding and putting nuclear weapons in space, floating in space. It's not going to be politically acceptable here in the United States, and you're going to spend all of your time doing it."[38] Teller, on the other hand, said it was a while before he got the message that the admiral was not pleased: "I later learned that the admiral did not like the nuclear nature of the laser but was very impressed that I was optimistic about strategic defense."[39]

Robert McFarlane and his assistant John Poindexter, a career naval officer with a doctorate in nuclear physics, paid a December visit to Watkins at Tingey House, his official residence in the Washington Navy Yard, essentially to encourage him in his zeal for strategic defense and to sell the idea to the Joint Chiefs of Staff. Thus it was that around Christmastime Watkins paid a visit to the JCS chairman, Army general John Vessey. Now captivated with the idea of shifting from MAD to an ABM-based defense, Watkins was prepared to go straight to the White House to present his case. Naturally he wanted the support of the Joint Chiefs, but he knew they had their minds on other things, mainly what to do with the MX. Watkins said,

> I told Jack Vessey, 'I have done my work now for several months. I've listened to briefings from the Joint Chiefs of Staff. I've done a lot of things, and I'm going to present my position that I'm going to give at the White House, absent any other Joint Chiefs position that's acceptable to me. And I want a meeting.' Vessey granted that. But I said, 'Jack, I've got to tell you what I'm going to say over there. If none of you agrees with it, that's one thing, but I'm going to say it anyway. I believe we've got to start shifting in the long range towards a defensive posture.'
>
> I said it's American, the way to do it. Historically we based all the justification for our armed forces on the defense of the United States. And therefore we should get back to that, not offense. Mutual assured destruction is morally repugnant . . . we're stuck with it; we generated it; we know that. We had to go through this phase, but it's over. Maybe in twenty years we can be rid of it. We as a nation should at least be taking a position that over the long haul, with new technology, defense is not illogical.
>
> So I prepared a position paper and delivered it to the Joint Chiefs of Staff. And the Chiefs bought it—as long as it

was an aggressive R&D and we weren't saying, 'Let's do this in lieu of strategic modernization,' which we were not doing.[40]

Watkins met with the Joint Chiefs at the Pentagon on February 5, 1983. The Chiefs were preoccupied with the issue of MX basing and generally disinclined to support strategic defense. "I turned the chiefs around on it," Watkins told me. "I went to them when they were saying no, we're not going to go for missile defense. They even talked about opposing missile defense.

"But I told them you cannot beat the Russians by putting missile systems inside of inverted mountainsides. They'll just blast the hell out of us. So let's get on with new concepts, the things we're best at."[41]

With the Joint Chiefs on board, McFarlane and Poindexter now scheduled a JCS meeting with the president for February 11, to be held at the White House. In McFarlane's mind, "It was clear that getting Ronald Reagan on board was not going to be much of a problem."[42] National Security Advisor Clark was out of town, so McFarlane ran the meeting, though there was no doubt that Watkins would be the star. Weinberger said he felt that the defensive-weapon issue was "finally and completely decided" after Reagan heard from the Navy chief, noting the enormous impact of Watkins' rhetorical question, "Would it not be better if we could develop a system that would protect, rather than avenge, our people?"

"Watkins's phrase," wrote Weinberger, "had summed up most succinctly and simply the great hopes that the development of such a system would bring . . . an enterprise far larger and more effective than simply trying to get the most out of Sprint and Spartan."[43]

"Don't lose those words!" cried a delighted Reagan. In typical style, Reagan had responded personally to events where others might call for a committee meeting. Watkins recalled later that "we knew at that time . . . that we had tapped a bell with the president."[44]

In his short tenure as secretary of defense, Weinberger had missed four opportunities to increase ABM funding in the defense budgets. Only now, after McFarlane had encouraged the president to launch SDI, was anything done. Reagan used the rest of the meeting to strengthen support for Watkins' suggestion among all five of the Joint Chiefs. He worked on bringing those who harbored reservations about a defense initiative around until each of them said yes, he'd support the idea. In the Navy chief's words, "You could see President Reagan almost heave a sigh of relief. And I think he was just waiting for the opportunity to say, 'Can we do it now? Can we go now? Can we do it now?'

"And when we said, 'Yes, Mr. President,' he was extremely pleased."[45]

6

THE PRESIDENTIAL
THUNDERBOLT

*It's politically sensitive, but it's going to happen. Some people don't
want to hear this, and it sure isn't in vogue . . . but—absolutely—we're
going to fight in space. We're going to fight from space
and we're going to fight into space.*
—Gen. Joseph W. Ashy, former commander in chief
U.S. Space Command

The decision to scrap détente, containment, and MAD—
strategies that had taken decades to mature—was made in record time.
In the space of one afternoon, strategic defense became the dominant
keyword of the U.S. position in its relationship with the Soviet Union.
Early 1983 brought the dawn of Reagan's own "shock and awe" campaign—which was prosecuted in a way that was considerably more subtle than President George W. Bush's headlong invasion of Iraq twenty
years later—and it was against a superpower adversary that constituted
a direct threat to the West.

As McFarlane had predicted, the president was more than ready
to move in a radically new direction. "The experience of getting intermediate-range missiles deployed in Europe, and MX at home, all in
support of MAD, had been bruising," said Raymond Pollock, then a
young National Security Council staffer. "So, when offered the chance
to call for defense by people he trusted, he was primed to jump. I think
his view of the Soviet response was that either they would join us—he
really was serious about sharing—or we would bankrupt them."[1]

"The President really wanted a way out of it," said Vic Reis,
then assistant director of the Office of Science and Technology Policy
(OSTP). "We'd gone through the MX dense-pack and the siting is-

sues. Now he was looking at 'Let's think about something different,' and he was inclined toward high technology." Watkins and the Joint Chiefs were very concerned. It was, Reis said, as if the administration was thinking, " 'You've got to do something. Don't just stand there, do something.' And, 'We've got to have a surprise.' "[2]

Following a discussion at Camp David, Reagan and National Security Advisor Bill Clark told McFarlane to secretly draft the rallying cry for strategic defense. It would be written into a previously planned budget speech, scheduled for the evening of March 23. The quick-draw, hush-hush approach was encouraged by Clark and a not-quite-so-enthusiastic McFarlane. When, much later, the president's other advisors got wind of the plot and tried to get a word in, they got nowhere.

Pollock, Gil Rye, and Bob Sims, who worked as a media interface for Clark and McFarlane, became members of team charged with writing the speech insert. Almost immediately after the meeting with Reagan, the NSC's John Poindexter asked Pollock to do "a quiet assessment of the state of advanced defensive technologies,"[3] to be delivered about six weeks hence. Pollock was an expert in nuclear weaponry, with prior experience at Los Alamos and the Department of Energy. Though thoroughly open to new ideas, he was skeptical of the Department of Energy–funded x-ray laser, which he considered more attractive to laypersons than it would be to technical specialists.

Reagan then delivered his celebrated "evil empire" speech of March 8, in which he told an Orlando meeting of the National Association of Evangelicals, "I urge you to beware the temptation to label both sides equally at fault, to ignore the facts of history and the aggressive impulses of an evil empire, to simply call the arms race a giant misunderstanding and thereby remove yourself from the struggle between right and wrong and good and evil."

It was the kind of polemic that the Soviets might use against the United States, and it worked. But U.S. commentators were less than universally approving of Reagan's rhetoric. In the *New Republic*, columnist Richard Strout said Reagan's speech contained "primitive prose and apocalyptic symbolism." On the other hand, as Hendrik Herzberg wrote insightfully in *The New Yorker* (June 28, 2004), "the villains of Reagan's world were like the ones in Frank Capra's movies, capable of change once they saw the light."

On March 17, Pollock had finished his research and was writing his report when he and space specialist Gil Rye were summoned to the office of their boss, Richard Boverie. Boverie headed a group (the NSC defense cluster) that also included Bob Linhard, Bob Helm, Horace Russell, and Oliver North. Boverie told his colleagues that the president would announce a new defensive initiative in his speech the following week. Preparations were to be carried out in strict secrecy by a few select members of the staff; even the secretaries of state and defense would be shut out.

"Dick said the Chiefs had triggered this by telling the president that the future looked bleak and it was time to seriously consider strategic defense, especially BMD," explained Pollock. "Boverie found this quite amazing and thought we just might be present at a truly historic event."[4]

McFarlane, orchestrating from behind the scenes, reckoned the Soviet response would be twofold: "One, it would be very costly for them to compete, especially at a time when they needed to modernize their conventional weapons. And two, they would think, 'You (Americans) really are good at technology, and whatever it is, it's going to be big.' I admit it was a roll of the dice, but I told the president many times that the Russian reaction would be just this. The notion of a Soviet first strike had become implausible." McFarlane told the president he believed the *idea* of building a high-tech strategic defense would be sufficient to win the desired Soviet concessions; it wouldn't have to go to deployment. "Reagan said, 'I hope you're right but we're still going to build it.'"

"I understood the difference between my view and Ronald Reagan's," McFarlane added. "While he didn't think it [fielding SDI] was feasible in his lifetime, bargaining was not on his agenda."[5]

McFarlane pressed for soliciting Allied and bipartisan congressional support for the new initiative, but Clark and Reagan determined that there was time for neither. They reasoned that they had to move quickly, quietly, and determinedly, or the Washington system would brand the SDI as a reckless plan and nibble it to death with bureaucracy, if not scorn. "I told Reagan, 'The idea that you should ignore the Congress would not be a good idea,'" McFarlane recalled. "'And Tip O'Neill [Speaker of the House Thomas Phillip O'Neill, Jr.] is no dummy—you could probably get him on board. You should really engage the Congress.' But he wouldn't go for it. 'No,' he said, 'it would abort the whole thing.'"[6]

Later, McFarlane became a believer. "A vital lesson that the experience of SDI taught was the need for secrecy in launching any fundamental reorientation of policy," he wrote. "The premature disclosure of our planning for SDI would have evoked such a storm of criticism as to assure its abortion. . . . In the Reagan Doctrine, in all its manifestations [including SDI], President Ronald Reagan launched the most comprehensive national security strategy since the end of World War II."[7] Time and time again, without a moment of weakness, Reagan would insist that SDI was not a bargaining chip; he was adamant that it was going to happen. A dubious Soviet Ambassador Anatoly Dobrynin remarked that Reagan "was easily convinced that American ingenuity could overcome great technological obstacles."[8]

At a March 18 Situation Room meeting, Pollock was charged with organizing general support for strategic defense from the scientific community, leaving McFarlane to write Reagan's strategic defense announcement by himself. Pollock thought it odd that Jay Keyworth wasn't present at that meeting, and he wondered whether this resulted from general NSC–OSTP tensions, or from some concern with Keyworth personally. "It would look strange," he said, "if the president were to announce a major technological initiative without involving his science advisor.

"I went to my office, thought for a while, and sent Bud a memo pointing out the absurdity of taking on a major technology initiative while keeping the science advisor ignorant. I also urged that Bob Linhard's wisdom be tapped. In a day or so, Bud agreed. Keyworth and Linhard were brought in, and Jay soon started running."[9]

Keyworth had been a strong supporter of strategic *offense*, and his opinion of third-generation weapons was ambiguous at the time, but he was aware that "tendrils" of SDI had been taking shape. He saw SDI as totally Reagan's concept and for a while was torn between his doubts about the idea's technical feasibility and his desire to be seen as one of the president's team. Keyworth also understood the political reality, however, including the factors that George Shultz would later encapsulate in his statement that "the core issues in dispute are really not technical, but political and moral."[10]

McFarlane was now heavily occupied with the draft of the speech insert. He had called off a family skiing trip at the last minute and now was ensconced in his basement office in the West Wing of the White House, creating the draft on his IBM Selectric typewriter. Here, in the same "cubby" he occupied under Henry Kissinger in the 1970s, he was working 15-hour days on weekdays and 10-hour days on the weekend. Most of the "real work" was done after 6 p.m., when the daily schedule slowed down and he had the luxury of what he called "unhindered time." As a bonus, he had access to an unlimited supply of coffee from the Navy mess next door.[11]

NSDD-75 was McFarlane's guiding light. "The policy included a commitment to stress the Soviet economy, and that is essentially what I thought SDI would do," he said. "It was always in the back of my mind as I drafted the insert."[12] The text itself called for technical and military initiatives; naturally it made no mention of the economic or psychological stresses the administration wished to bring about in the Soviet Union.

On March 19, McFarlane called in Keyworth to take a look at his handiwork. The presidential science advisor paled when he grasped the huge scale of what was being proposed, but those fourteen paragraphs survived without input from the Pentagon, and received only last-minute comment from the secretaries of state and defense. Keyworth and Reis tried rewriting the report in an attempt to moderate its language. "But then, on the Monday," said Reis, "Jay came back and said 'Look, we've lost this one.' Whoever it was who made the decision—I don't know whether it was Bud or whom—said we had to have something more substantive than just a relook at the problem. So we were going to do this ballistic missile defense thing.

"Jay turned to me and said, 'This is a political issue and the president has obviously better political instincts than we do,' and therefore he felt he had to support him. My comeback to Jay was, 'Look, you've got to give the president all the best science advice. Then if he makes a decision you can support him. We can do the best we can, but you can't say the science is there and make it happen.' "[13] Reis had a very thorough knowledge of the laser-defense concepts and was convinced the administration was going too fast, too soon. He and Keyworth had both been antimissile skeptics, but now his old ally was beginning to have second thoughts. Reis's own conviction stuck. He tendered his resignation, effective the following September, and didn't participate in anything to do with SDI from that moment on.

As Gerold Yonas puts it, "Big Science is politics. The space between Big Science and politics is zero."[14] Or, to use Jacob Bronowski's testy words of censure, "No science is immune to the infection of politics and the corruption of power."

After turning over his preparations for the speech to McFarlane, Pollock began writing talking points and messages to embassies; but he was still in the loop. "I recall that the tone kept varying," he told me. "Two or three revised drafts appeared every day for the last few days before March 23. One would be hawkish—'We'll start deploying immediately'—and then the next would be relatively timid—'Maybe we should study the problem for a bit.' The swings in tone were remarkable. Reagan inserted key phrases. I'm sure it was his idea to 'call on the scientists who gave us the bomb to make it impotent and obsolete.' "[15]

As the insiders prepared the seeds of SDI, there came a whisper from the wings. Coincidentally, the OSTP's White House Science Council (WHSC) had just completed the military technology review. "The panel worked for about a year, but we didn't see anything that would really change things very much," Reis acknowledged. "In the ballistic missiles [defense] business, we said, 'Look, there are some interesting concepts that may be worthy of research,' but from a technology standpoint there was nothing that we felt would really make any difference in the short term."[16] Another participant echoed Reis's broad-brush analysis—that the panel felt that certain directed-energy concepts might produce some leverage for small, quiet investment, although in general the field remained immature. The panel's report remained classified in 2006 and was considered virtually nonexistent.

"The panel's report was dead on arrival," summarized the *New York Times*'s William Broad. "By the time science advisor Keyworth sent it to [presidential counselor Edwin] Meese, the White House was on the verge of making public its antimissile vision."[17]

BREAKING THE NEWS

Secretary of State George Shultz first got wind of the proto-SDI idea—the gist of the Joint Chief's meeting—from Reagan on February 12, 1983. "I understood the importance of what he was saying," he said, "but I had absolutely no idea that the views he was expressing had any near-term, operational significance."[18] Shultz learned it was a serious proposal during a March 18 meeting with Clark five days before the speech. Then, on March 21, Shultz received a cryptic message from Bud McFarlane: "The alternative [to MX] is a high-tech strategic defense system that can protect us against ballistic missiles and thereby protect our offensive capabilities."[19]

Defense Secretary Cap Weinberger and his assistant secretary Richard Perle were attending a NATO meeting in Lisbon and had been virtually incommunicado until the night before the speech was given. After a "hurried and surreptitious" call from a White House friend, Weinberger set to work telephoning his counterparts in allied nations, giving them each a necessarily brief heads-up.[20] Perle was a super-smart, middle-class, New York–born Californian who had read strategic studies at the London School of Economics and came to Washington in 1969 as a staffer on Paul Nitze's "Campaign to Save the ABM." By then he had become a fiercely patriotic Cold Warrior, a genuine intellect, and a brilliant yet compassionate man of principle. "Perle camped out on the telephone as soon as he found what was planned," said Pollock. "Shultz too was pretty upset—as indeed were almost all the administration powers except Cap."[21]

Perle worried that the plan was being launched in too much haste and with too little consultation. One of his most important calls was to Keyworth. "Jay," he said, "if there ever was time where a man should fall on his sword, this is it. You must fall on your sword. You must stop this."[22] Keyworth of course could do nothing to stem the tide.

Shultz's immediate reaction was that the plan's proponents didn't have enough scientific knowledge to support it; he was also concerned that possible abrogation of the ABM Treaty could lead to strategic destabilization; and he was mindful of the fact that ICBMs were only one of several methods for delivering nuclear weapons. He protested to the president, but it didn't do any good. Reagan was firmly in the saddle, and nothing was going to buck him off.

Jack Vessey and Admiral Watkins felt Reagan was reaching too far too soon, though of course they had supported an initiative in strategic defense. The word went out that the Joint Chiefs might have some reservations. Even CIA Director Casey may have been taken by surprise. "The CIA didn't even know the Soviet Union was collapsing," said Herb Meyer. "How the hell was it going to know Reagan was going to announce SDI? The only one who would know would be Bill. I assume he did, but I don't know that for a fact. He certainly didn't say to me, 'Oh, you've got to watch the speech tonight, the last 30 seconds are gonna be great!' "[23] Vic Reis said his CIA friends were "dumbfounded."[24] Pollock commented that Casey, a key player in the broader anti-Soviet plan, would have been highly supportive; however, he said, "I saw no sign that Casey or any of his minions were involved in preparations for the speech, and the intelligence folks on the NSC staff were not part of the cabal."[25]

McFarlane gave the White House speechwriters the text of the speech the day it was to be delivered. They knew nothing about it and were flabbergasted too. It was a wonderful scrap of visionary rhetoric, but there was absolutely no detail on what this new strategic defense was, how it would work, how much it would cost, or how a development program might be organized.

Advance notification never got to the Air Force officers who that day had been disparaging space-based laser weaponry before the House of Representatives. Using the system to destroy a target, Gen. Bernard Randolph said, would be akin to pointing a laser from the Washington Monument to a baseball on the top of the Empire State Building, and holding it there while both structures were moving. "I view the whole thing with a fair amount of trepidation," he said.[26] That same morning, Air Force Chief of Staff Charles A. Gabriel had heard a presentation on ballistic missile defense from his deputy chief of staff for research, development, and acquisition, Lt. Gen. Lawrence

(Larry) Skantze. It had been a blue-sky presentation. "We talked about what might be possible someday with investment," recalled Brig. Gen. (select) Robert Rankine, deputy director of Skantze's Space & C3 Directorate and a future SDI executive. "I said the technologies had promise but that a long research program would be necessary before you could have a system to defend against ballistic missiles."[27]

Launching SDI

A throng of eminent scientists were invited for the White House speech—about forty of them, including Edward Teller and his contemporary Hans Bethe, a Nobel Prize recipient and Cornell professor emeritus who would become an archopponent of SDI. They had received mysterious invitations just three days before the speech and now were facing TV screens in the nearby Blue Room, unaware of what was to follow. Just before he took his seat, Edward Teller spied Reis in the audience and poled his way over, famous staff in hand. "Vic, what is this all about?" Reis forced a smile. "I can't tell you," he said, "but I think you might be pleased."[28] Keyworth had a similar reply: "It's what you've always wanted."[29]

McFarlane had contributed a brilliant piece of stagecraft to the presentation by suggesting that the scientists be invited. "You had to know people in the science labs who would give it credence—people like Johnnie Foster, Simon Ramo, Edward Teller—to give it legitimacy," he said, "and then build grass-roots support with the help of the phenomenal communicator in the Oval Office."[30]

Reagan began his speech in grand style as McFarlane watched the show comfortably on his office TV. The president went through the defense budget details, defending increases by emphasizing Soviet buildups in the Caribbean and Latin America and reminding his audience that "we maintain the peace through our strength; weakness only invites aggression." Through a "zero-zero option" offer he proposed to keep intermediate-range missiles out of Europe if the Soviets agreed to remove theirs. Then he went on to strategic defense. "Let me share with you a vision of the future which offers hope," he said.

> It is that we embark on a program to counter the awesome Soviet missile threat with measures that are defensive. Let us turn to the very strengths in technology that spawned our great industrial base and that have given us the quality of life we enjoy today.
>
> What if free people could live secure in the knowledge

that their security did not rest upon the threat of instant U.S.
retaliation to deter a Soviet attack, that we could intercept and
destroy strategic ballistic missiles before they reached our own
soil or that of our allies?

After introducing this emotive vision, Reagan said that "current technology has attained a level of sophistication where it's reasonable for us
to begin this effort," and went on to rally his technical troops, trumping
the nuclear-freeze advocates who merely wanted to stop building and
testing more nukes: "I call upon the scientific community in our country, those who gave us nuclear weapons, to turn their great talents now
to the cause of mankind and world peace, to give us the means of ren-
dering these nuclear weapons impotent and obsolete." Reagan said he
envisioned a program that was treaty-compliant, acceptable to America's
allies, palatable to the arms control community, and a possible precursor
to the elimination of nuclear weapons. It would be "a comprehensive
and intensive effort to define a long-term research and development
program to begin to achieve our ultimate goal of eliminating the threat
posed by strategic nuclear missiles"; further, it would be "an effort
which holds the promise of changing the course of human history."

The speech was stirring enough, but short on specifics. Reagan
did not mention lasers or other directed energy weapons or any other
advanced technologies, leaving his press staff to add these details. He
did say the program would be "long term," devoting itself to "research and development," but these nuances tended to get lost in the
hype that followed. At Keyworth's request, AT&T's Sol Buchsbaum,
chair of the WHSC, had telephoned laser pioneer and Nobelist Charles
Townes with an invitation to attend the speech. Sitting there, Townes
was amazed like everyone else except, possibly, Teller. He thought it
was an audacious proposal, yet, as generalized as it was, there was nothing technically inaccurate in what the president had to say. That said,
Reagan was no doubt interested in space-based directed-energy weapons. Would a "Star Wars" scheme work? Townes recalled that Buchsbaum, who had not been fully in favor of the announcement, was
"cagey" about the idea. The Pentagon people Townes spoke with pro-
fessed to share the president's vision for some "idealistic and specula-
tive" missile defense solution. Bill Clark and Bud McFarlane smoothly
told Townes that "there were some reservations about its practicality,
but nobody wanted to disappoint the president." Weinberger reas-
sured him cheerfully that, "When scientists get going, scientists can
always do these things."[31] Townes wasn't so sure. "For a president
who doesn't know the technology one can see why [SDI] might be
appealing," he said. "It didn't really seem very attractive to me, or

doable. But you can see how from a matter of principle it sounded good to Reagan. It's like an imaginary story of what might be done."[32]

This presidential initiative baffled the rest of the world too, even those who until this moment thought they were White House insiders. As Edmund Morris wrote in *Dutch*, what the president proposed would require some forty to one hundred million lines of programming, and enough money to buy another Navy: "The whole concept was so heaven-filling, so imponderably complex . . . as to pass beyond physics into metaphysics, and thence into metaphor."[33] At one point, Shultz asked Teller, "Are you sure this will be 100 percent effective?" According to a 1990 Teller biography, the physicist wisely replied, "No. No defense is 100 percent effective, but a partial defense is better than no defense if it discourages an aggressor from attacking."[34] In his own 2001 *Memoir*, Teller recalled responding, "Against the largest attack that the Soviets can mount? Probably not."[35]

Hans Bethe's spin was predictably different: "A partial defense is more dangerous than no defense at all," he wrote in 1985.[36] Weinberger saw it from yet another angle—tough but bafflingly simplistic. "The defense systems the president is talking about are not designed to be partial," he said. "What we want to try to get is a system which will develop a defense that is thoroughly reliable and total."[37]

"Poor Weinberger and the White House and Pentagon flacks displayed their ignorance by talking of a perfect shield, and the opposition shouted that any such thing was fantastic," wrote Barry Bruce Briggs. "And the public hype concentrated on space-based directed-energy systems—which were the most far-out and farthest from policy relevance."[38] Some scientific advisors, sickened by the imagery of space Astrodomes and perfect shields, observed that such ideas played well with the public but went down very badly with the technically informed.

Lou Cannon wrote up the speech for the next day's *Washington Post*, winning the leading headline at the top right of page one: "President Seeks Futuristic Defense Against Missiles." It was a straightforward report, such as one would have to write on deadline, and it noted Ted Kennedy's charge of "misleading Red-scare tactics and reckless Star Wars Schemes."[39] That morning, the *New York Post* carried a huge banner headline: "STAR WARS PLAN TO ZAP RED NUKES."

※

After the speech, Reagan lost no time in meeting, finally, with his somewhat shaken cabinet. He knew he needed to gather their support; he had to let them know he was earnest; in short, he had to convince them that this was not merely a new tack in creative saber-rattling. Even if it were, no one had ever rattled such an expensive saber before—at least not in public.

Jay Keyworth recalled how, after Reagan finished his introductory comments, he leaned back and laid down the law. This dramatic moment was captured in "The Reagan Legacy," a 1996 Discovery Channel production. "Gentlemen," the president said, "this is the way it is. You can be either an optimist or a pessimist. If you're a pessimist, then you can believe that if we don't do it the Soviets will do it; and when they do it they will blackmail us to our knees. Or you can be an optimist and think that maybe there's a chance that somehow we can free future generations from the horror of deterrence. Either way, we have to do it. And gentlemen, that's the way it's going to be."[40]

Observers and analysts have speculated that Reagan may have been maneuvered into this position. Yet, as Shultz put it, "you have to sometimes take things at their face value." He then offered a marvelously succinct explanation: "In the president's case, what appeared on the surface was what mattered—namely, that we had this strategic threat; that we had no defense against it; that the idea of wiping each other out was morally untenable; and that he was looking for a better way. And this was, to him, a better way. So he devoted himself to it."[41]

"Reagan had a unique vision for a defense against missiles and a powerful motivation to seek the realization of that vision," wrote international relations analyst Paul Lettow. "He saw in missile defense both a means of precluding Armageddon by protecting people from a potential nuclear holocaust and a catalyst for the abolition of all nuclear weapons."[42]

While talking with reporters on two occasions in March 1983, Reagan as much as said he expected SDI—ideally a shared SDI—to be a stepping-stone to nuclear disarmament, not merely as a bargaining chip but as a real-life, working system. Two days after his SDI speech, on March 25, he expressed hope that when a workable missile defense system was developed, "maybe twenty years down the road," it would be reasonable to ask, "why not now dispose of all these weapons since we've proven that they can be rendered obsolete?"[43] One week later, he said he "could offer to give that same defensive weapon to [the adversary] to prove that there was no longer any need for keeping these missiles." Or he could say, " 'I am willing to do away with all my missiles. You do away with yours.' "[44] It wouldn't take twenty years. Reagan himself would soon have the opportunity to test all of these scenarios.

Good News, Bad News

The American public was ready for good news—or at least an alternative to MAD. In 1981, a *Newsweek* survey concluded that seven out of ten respondents believed the United States was very close to nuclear war.[45] The same year, 60 percent of respondents to a Gallup poll said they believed their chances of surviving a nuclear attack were "poor"; two years later, 69 percent offered that response.[46] But public reaction to SDI was a mixture of hope and incredulity. Many embraced the idea; many believed a ballistic missile defense already existed. For others, while there was a natural desire to believe in the feasibility of building an effective high-tech defense system, it seemed—on second thought—a little too good to be true.

In Moscow it was a different story. Reports coming in to CIA Langley the morning after Reagan's address illustrated that the Soviets had been deeply shocked by the implications of the speech, and reactions in their military establishment ranged between depression and panic. "When we walked into the office the morning of March 24, we could see the intelligence from Moscow start shifting," Herb Meyer said. "There was an instantaneous reaction. They understood that Reagan had fired a bullet right between their eyes. They knew in a second. You could see it; you could see the panic starting. They believed SDI could be made to work. Their nightmare was that we were going to do it.

"One reason for their concern came from the fact that the original idea for strategic defense was Russian. They felt in their bones they could do it. But we had the money. Once we said we were going to do it, they knew we were going to beat them to it. Reagan always described it as a shield over the United States, but it was a lid over the Soviet Union. The Russians knew that. That's why it was so powerful.

"They understood instantly what the real threats were. They had understood that the Pope was a mortal threat to them. That's why they shot him. And SDI was a threat, though obviously in a different way. They understood that 'these are the things that will get us.' "[47]

As Yonas observed, neither the Pope nor SDI represented a technology; rather, both represented ideas. "An idea is always more powerful than any technology," he said, "and SDI was a powerful idea."[48] The possibility that SDI might be deployed threatened a catastrophic effect on Soviet strategic defense calculations—the "correlation of forces" plan, originated in the early 1960s, that guided preparations for war with the West. "It was a sophisticated mathematical technology, and the addition of substantial American defenses raised uncertainty considerably in any outcome," said Pete Worden. "It was now clear that they could no longer dominate a crisis once we had substantial defenses. And the 'substantial' number didn't have to be that great."[49]

"They had extremely tough, tough requirements," agreed Bosma. "With SDI they could not meet their first-strike targeting norms. That started the arms race in reverse. They decided they couldn't meet the norms because of what they thought SDI could do in messing up their first strike. Apparently even a primitive SDI could do it."[50]

"Before this, they thought they would have a winning hand," said Meyer. "Then when Reagan got up and said, in effect, 'No, we'll beat you to it,' it was over. They began to recognize that history was not on their side."[51]

"With the Soviet Union lagging behind the United States in nearly every respect—living standards, production capabilities, quality of life—nuclear parity was the only thing that made it equal, a superpower," said Dmitry Mikheyev, an exiled Russian physicist and dissident who was then working for the Voice of America in Washington. "Once you put SDI in place, it would be difficult to convince anybody in the world that the Soviet Union still had nuclear parity with the United States."[52]

SDI complemented Bill Casey's original recommendations perfectly. First, the United States attacked the Soviet economy and stopped its theft of technology, and Reagan announced new investments in conventional weaponry. That made it increasingly harder for the Kremlin to sustain a military edge. Then Reagan fired his "bullet." Meyer reckons this was the point at which the Soviets finally had to concede that they could not compete in high technology at the Western level of sophistication.

Reaction in Moscow's leadership circles was nervous—if not exactly panicky—despite the fact that many Soviet scientists, including Velikhov, Sagdeev, Krokhin, and even Basov, had expressed strong skepticism, based on their own experience, that SDI could ever work. Defense Minister Dmitry Ustinov's first deputy, the aristocratic-looking Marshal Sergei Akhromeyev definitely got the impression that there had been some kind of breakthrough. "When President Reagan announced his SDI program, it was presented as an impenetrable missile defense system," he told interviewers for the BBC/PBS co-production "Messengers from Moscow." "We were very worried. We had endless meetings, a lot of discussions, and studies of the problem."[53]

"It was a shock. It's like all our hopes for an understanding of the danger of the militarization of space suddenly just evaporated,"

IKI director Roald Sagdeev told a CNN interviewer.[54] Velikhov was more argumentative: "Each new arms race cycle resulted in a less—not a more—secure situation for the United States, in spite of the hopes cherished in the beginning of each new phase by those who initiated and supported it. The same will happen again if the United States starts deploying the anti-missile system, as well as the new generation of anti-satellite weapons."[55]

"We felt defenseless," Aleksandr Yakovlev, a Politburo member who became Gorbachev's closest advisor, told Discovery Channel interviewers. "SDI would reduce our nuclear capability to zero. Our missiles would be destroyed in mid-air if there was an attack by the Americans."[56] Yakovlev knew full well that a Soviet attempt to revive its own "SDIsky" would also accelerate his nation's march to bankruptcy. In 1983 a CIA-led interagency intelligence report estimated that the Soviets could not attempt to match SDI, but warned that they would likely attempt to foil it with countermeasures or—in two darker scenarios—by positioning nuclear or biological weapons in Western cities to be used if the Soviets were attacked, and/or by claiming to have built the ultimate "doomsday" weapon.[57]

The month after Reagan's speech, Lawrence Livermore conducted an x-ray laser test, code-named Cabra, at the Nevada Test Site. It was a failure because the data were distorted, and successes—not failures—were needed in order to ensure continued funding. On April 28 a rattled Teller was in front of the research subcommittee of the House Armed Services Committee. "Charlie Townes publishes beautiful papers about what is happening in the center of our galaxy," he said. "Basov and Prokhorov are working with the Soviet military on lasers. You guess who is currently ahead."[58] The Department of Defense had an answer. That year it estimated the Soviet laser weapon effort to be three to five times the size of the programs then under way in the United States.[59] "We knew that the Soviet Union had an SDI program that was, in people terms rather than financial terms, more than ten times the size of what Reagan was proposing," confirmed Herb Meyer. "They planned to do it. But our economy was surging while theirs was collapsing."[60]

SKEPTICISM, HOPE, AND REALITY

The nation's top scientific minds had been given a job that they knew might be completely beyond their grasp. For a while a kind of havoc reigned in their midst, while the uninformed technical arms of the Pentagon hoped the whole thing would go away. Though a plan of sorts was in place, it amounted to an uncoordinated wish list with no strategic underpinning.

Doubtless many scientists reacted to the SDI announcement much as Carl Sagan reacted to President John F. Kennedy's *Apollo* announcement on May 25, 1961: "It was a kind of *gesture*." Sagan had been advised that "the *Apollo* program is really about politics."[61] And indeed, in 1962, Kennedy admitted to NASA Administrator James E. Webb that "I'm not that interested in space." Then the main point: "Everything we do ought to be tied into getting to the moon ahead of the Russians."[62] Reagan was no more excited about science and technology, per se, than Kennedy, but like him, Reagan was extremely interested in its ability to cause radical change.

The SDI speech pleased U.S. conservatives mightily—and exercised the dedicated hard-liners in Moscow as well. "After Reagan's speech there was an enormous inner joy among the conservative forces and the military," Yakovlev, a small man with watchful eyes and bushy brows, told his interviewers. "You wouldn't have seen it at parades; it was an inner joy, because after that speech they got a huge extra budget for military expenditure."[63] SDI also was wonderful for influence-seeking Washington types, regardless of their political persuasion. It gave them a focus on which to pin restatements of their beliefs—a sexy new bottle for old wine—and a great platform for well-publicized debate. As Bruce Briggs wrote, "the issue became polarized, and those people in the business who actually knew something about strategic defense were buffeted by both sides. . . . Within about eighteen months it became quite uncomfortable for knowledgeable folk to comment honestly on SDI."[64]

Threatening news brings power and new business to people in the military-industrial complex. A threat from the United States would give the Soviet military establishment leverage to get more funding; this would give the United States leverage to get more funding, and so on. As Yonas put it, "The Soviet techies scammed their nontech leaders by telling them we would succeed so they could get more money, and we got more money by telling our politicians we were scaring the Soviets and they might catch up with us."[65] But the United States had a lot of money and the Soviet Union was probably already too broke to sit in on the game.*

"You should never free the enemy of the concern he might have

---

*This kind of euphoria was not limited to the Soviet Union. Llewellyn King, a Washington publisher and broadcaster, reports that when he asked the eminent scientist-administrator Harold Agnew whether he thought SDI would be destabilizing, Agnew replied wryly that it would be "very dangerous. Hundreds of contractors will be killed in the rush to the trough."

for what you might do," Reagan once said. "What I'm saying is that the United States should never be in a position, as it has many times, of guaranteeing to an enemy or a potential enemy what it can't do."[66]

⁂

Immediately after Brezhnev's death in November 1982, a young member of the Central Committee's International Department sat down and wrote what he thought would be needed to bring the Soviet Union out of the dark. This up-and-comer, Anatoly Chernyaev, decided he would get rid of the Kremlin cronies, get out of Afghanistan, tell the Polish Communist Party to take care of its own mess, loosen control on the East European countries, restrict the power of the Military-Industrial Commission, get the foreign ministry under control, and let dissidents and Jews emigrate.[67] Not surprisingly, he would have to wait.

Yuri Andropov, longtime head of the KGB, succeeded Brezhnev as general chairman of the Communist Party of the Soviet Union. Glasnost, the openness introduced later by Gorbachev, was absolutely alien to his worldview—it was not even known that he had a wife until she threw herself onto his coffin as it was being placed in the Kremlin wall. Still, he was a transitional leader. He could see opportunities for Soviet neocolonialism arising all over the world, and he was a reformer at home. He resolved to clean up drunkenness, absenteeism, and corruption, and to revive his nation's economy. This hard-liner was also open—on his own terms—to improving relations with the West. And so was the American president. At a secret February 15, 1983, White House meeting—unusually long at two hours and opposed by his inner circle—Reagan told Ambassador Dobrynin, "I don't want a war between us because I know it would bring countless disasters. We should make a fresh start."[68] Additionally, twice-yearly meetings were being held by the Soviet Scientists' Committee for the Defense of Peace Against Nuclear Threat, sponsored by the Soviet Academy of Sciences and the U.S. National Academies' Committee on National Security and Arms Control. Roald Sagdeev's view is that Andropov was quietly supporting these "back-channel" de-escalation activities and making "attempts to find compromise with America."[69]

In the background, Andropov's protégé, Mikhail Gorbachev, was watching. He was learning fast, especially after Andropov assigned him and Nikolai Ryzhov—young members of the Central Committee secretariat—to look into the prospects for governmental reform.

SDI played perfectly on Andropov's paranoia. As head of the KGB since 1967, he was continuously on the lookout for an unexpected attack, a Pearl Harbor staged by the United States against the Soviet Union. Three days after the SDI speech, Andropov labeled the idea a plot "to militarize space"; then the Soviet propaganda machine began to define SDI as "attack from the skies," and agitprop specialists began to encourage anti-SDI views among Western academic communities. When Reagan said he would share future defensive technology with the Soviet Union, Andropov was completely baffled.

On May 4, 1983, Andropov had glum words for a Warsaw Pact committee meeting in Prague. While the 1970s were "years of further growth of power and influence of the socialist commonwealth," he said, things might be changing. "We cannot allow U.S. military superiority, and we will not allow it,"[70] he insisted. At the same time, Andropov was pushing to outlaw any tests or deployments of space weapons. On August 16 he declared a unilateral moratorium on putting antisatellite weapons in space; according to Western reports, Andropov moved the "Fon" military space program into the engineering and manufacture phase later that year, added a counter-SDI mandate, and upped its budget.[71]

SHARING CREDIT, SHARING BLAME

Who really invented SDI? Who conceived the idea of a comprehensive, coordinated system using space weapons to bring down ballistic missiles, and who had engineered the president's commitment to build it? Teller won the lion's share of credit for drumming up Reagan's interest in actually doing something about space defense. William Broad of the *New York Times* wrote that "Over the protests of colleagues, Teller misled the highest officials of the United States government" into "the deadly folly known as Star Wars."[72] Ray Pollock, however, cautions that Teller's was one of many voices. "I believe his direct role in motivating the speech is exaggerated," he wrote in a 1986 letter to Department of Defense comptroller Bob Helm. "I sat in on the mid-September 1982 meeting Teller had in the Oval Office, at which he outlined his views on so-called 'third-generation' weapons and asked the president for more money for [Lawrence] Livermore [National Laboratory]. Teller got a warm reception but that is all. I had the feeling he confused the president."[73] "I think Teller is one of the smartest—if not the smartest—men I ever met, but he was also a great salesman," Pollock said.[74] In Charles Townes' opinion, "Teller did like the [SDI] idea, later pushed it enthusiastically, and continued to do so long after evidence accumulated that it was unlikely to work, but it was that briefing by the Joint Chiefs that was the spark for Reagan's enthusiasm."[75]

McFarlane agreed. "Teller in the long run was uninvolved," he said. "There was a body of thought centered around High Frontier, and to that extent Teller was involved. But the December 1982 decision to revisit strategic defense didn't have anything to do with Edward.* It was entirely due to our loss of the MX basing scheme and the opinion of Jim Watkins—and to advances in computing speed, guidance technology. A few scientists corroborated this view."[76]

In their book *Edward Teller: Giant of the Golden Age of Physics*, Stanley A. Blumberg and Louis G. Panos make it sound as though Teller's role in "persuading President Reagan to adopt SDI" was an accepted fact.[77] But, during a 1999 conversation, Teller was disinclined to talk about the x-ray laser. He claimed to not even recognize the name "Excalibur," while confirming that he was "in favor of an effective defense that would make nuclear explosives obsolete." While at one time he sought enough money to take the x-ray laser into engineering development, hoping to see it deployed on submarines under the Arctic ice, ready to pop up and engage Soviet missiles, he later downplayed his role in SDI and, at our last meeting, told me he had done very little to convince the president of its worth.[78] Ironically, Teller may have had greater influence on the Kremlin than the White House. Among some Soviet leaders there remained a persistent belief in the high-power laser technology that their own scientists had been exploring.

Some years later, McFarlane told reporter Hedrick Smith that SDI was an "NSC creation."[79] The writer Strobe Talbott, who later joined the State Department, agreed. "More than anyone else in the president's entourage," he wrote, "McFarlane midwifed the birth of SDI."[80]

It would take the historian John Lewis Gaddis to label SDI as "Reagan's most distinctive personal policy innovation."[81] Yet it is nearly impossible to imagine Reagan studying the technical ins and outs and burning the candle low in long and intellectual conversations with a cadre of trusted advisors. Thus, his advisors had few opportunities to stage-manage him. More often the reverse was true; the president acted largely from his gut, and this propensity—personal decision-making after contemplating a wide canvas of information and impressions—served him extremely well.

---

*Teller was termed "a politicized scientist" by Daniel Greenberg in his book *Science, Money, and Politics*; In *Teller's War*, *New York Times* journalist William Broad called him "a good scientist who was a great politician."

Many have observed that films—and the film industry—remained important to Reagan throughout his life, and indeed some storylines from fifty or more years ago bear some resemblance to the SDI vision. Colin Powell even suggested that Reagan's offer to share SDI with the Soviets was borrowed from the plot of *The Day the Earth Stood Still* (1951), in which a humanistic alien tells his Earthling audience that they must work together or perish. The similarity of movie plots with the real-life happenings of the 1980s is remarkable, but nothing tops Reagan's outlandish suggestion that the United States and Soviet Union help each other if attacked from outer space. This is the stuff of presidential folklore, and it did nothing to harm his reputation with the American public, or to soothe the Kremlin.

It was an interesting intellectual exercise, in the spring of 1983, to ponder over the origins of the SDI. Then there was the question of where the idea would go from there. This one had only a single, numbingly easy answer: nobody had the foggiest idea.

Arthur C. Clarke once famously said that, "Any sufficiently advanced technology is indistinguishable from magic," and the Reagan administration clearly believed in such magic. "Reagan and Bill Casey were the same in that the two of them couldn't work a two-button telephone," says Herb Meyer. "But they had a profound grasp of the *importance* of technology. They couldn't do it, they couldn't understand it, but they got it. They had a very profound understanding of the *role* of technology."[82]

"Most politicians think technology is some sort of magic," observed Yonas, "but they like to invent fantasies about it. They believe it is profound, and it is—in a social-political context."[83] The real magic lies in the fact that, paradoxically, technology can make things happen even when it produces nothing.

Those who were in the know about the secret NSDD-75 knew full well that SDI was another serious shot across the bows of an already harassed adversary, aimed at "promoting evolutionary change within the Soviet Union."

"Some Americans, particularly Richard Perle, knew the big picture right from the beginning," said Stanley Orman, who would become head of Britain's relatively minuscule SDI effort. "I told him it would be very dangerous to push the bear to collapse, but he was very firm in his opinion that this would cause them to have an implosion. He was absolutely right, and my concerns proved unjustified."[84]

SHAPING SDI

There is nothing more difficult to take in hand, more perilous to conduct, or more uncertain in its success, than to take the lead in the introduction of a new order of things.
—Niccolo Macchiavelli

By the end of March 1983, McFarlane and his White House colleagues were immersed in the business of selling and defending the new strategic defense concept. On the other side of the table, critics were speaking for U.S. allies, Congress, and various sectors of the American public. Meanwhile, the administrative responsibility for kicking off the new project fell to Richard D. DeLauer, who was the Pentagon's top scientist and a man who had reacted to news of the strategic defense speech—nine hours before its delivery—with a splutter of disbelief.

DeLauer, formerly a top executive at TRW Inc., had been undersecretary of defense for research and engineering since 1981. A Stanford graduate who earned his doctorate at Caltech, he served fifteen years in the U.S. Navy, then joined LANL's nuclear rocket propulsion program before moving on to TRW. DeLauer knew missiles; in fact, he was intimately acquainted with a wide variety of advanced space and defense systems. But the experience didn't help this time; here was a highly experienced, widely respected administrator in an unusual state of perplexity. There was no money in the budget for the president's program—then saddled with the unimaginative title "Defense Against Ballistic Missiles"—and even if there were, how would they get the program into gear? A forward-looking Army BMD program was in existence, as well as a few smaller projects here and there, but now something more comprehensive had to be put together, and quickly. The initial news was surprise enough, but DeLauer didn't yet comprehend how big the deal was.

"I think that at first DeLauer saw the new initiative as a small office of the Pentagon," said Bob Rankine, "maybe only about fifteen people who would provide top-level management of programs executed by the services and DARPA. But Weinberger and others saw it as having a Manhattan Project kind of definition, and wanted to create an Organization."[1]

As Simon P. (Pete) Worden—who was destined to spend the better part of a decade with SDI—put it, "the military services and DARPA wanted to pay lip-service to SDI and go no farther."[2] DeLauer strongly suspected that an effective Soviet antisatellite program would render orbiting SDI assets useless, but he naturally yielded to his boss and assigned a staff member by the name of John Gardner to help put together the very first fragments of a plan.

The presidential announcement had filled DeLauer's boss—Defense Secretary Weinberger—with optimistic energy. He showed no signs of being upset by being left out of McFarlane's secretive prespeech activity. To the contrary, "he was a believer, a staunch believer," said Rankine. "I don't know how connected he'd been to all the maneuverings that had gotten into the president's speech, but from my first contact with him, my task was mainly to try to slow him down."[3]

"Cap understood the game and never allowed such niceties as the laws of physics to bother him," said Yonas. "Colin Powell [then Weinberger's senior military assistant] explained this to me one day and calmed me down after I became fed up with Cap's giving the impression that nuclear-pumped x-ray lasers really weren't nuclear weapons. It turned out this double thinking was needed, since Teller was selling a new kind of nukes at the same time that Reagan was asking to get rid of all of them once and for all."[4] Weinberger told Paul Lettow he "didn't know a lot about" the technical side of SDI but knew it "was a very difficult task."[5] He was not alone. For his part, Shultz relied on Paul Nitze (brilliant, but not a technical man) for advice on such things.

Weinberger questioned DeLauer on x-ray lasers until he got an explanation he was comfortable with. The undersecretary told *New York Times* reporter Hedrick Smith that Weinberger seemed relieved when he finally offered the euphemism "nuclear event" as a descriptor for the laser's energy source.[6] "Cap Weinberger didn't think it was a nuclear weapon," said Reis, "because he and the president were really concerned about nuclear weapons—that there were too many of them and we didn't really need them."[7] In July 1983, Edward Teller tried a new semantic twist, offering his x-ray laser to the president as a way of "converting hydrogen bombs into hitherto unprecedented forms."[8]

In a March 25 decision directive, Reagan authorized two studies—the Defensive Technologies Study, chaired by James C. Fletcher,
a former NASA administrator, and the Future Security Strategy Study,
chaired by Fred S. Hoffman. DeLauer then asked Harold Agnew, who
had come on board to advise him on the allocation of defense research
monies, to co-chair what would become known as the Fletcher Panel.
Agnew, a well-seasoned Manhattan Project veteran and former LANL
director, gave his provisional agreement.

Fletcher was assisted in his new assignment by Pete Worden, then
a young, energetic, smart Air Force captain who was destined to become Rankine's right-hand man. Worden was soon looking around for
people to staff the technologies panel. Agnew thought that Yonas
would be a good man to chair the directed energy subpanel. Worden,
then Fletcher, went along with the idea, and finally Worden put in the
phone call to a "stunned" Gerry Yonas.[9]

Yonas could sometimes be an insubordinate joker, but he was
also an extraordinarily astute man, intimately familiar with the subject
of directed energy weapons. Was Agnew, a humorous and often icono-
clastic personality, deliberately putting a fox among the chickens? Agnew's answer: "At least Yonas was a smart fox."[10] Agnew was helping
the administration, but he soon made no secret of the fact that he
thought the idea, in polite terms, was ill conceived. He was a man who
spoke his mind, and he was famous for his suggestion that world leaders should observe nuclear explosion naked, so they could feel the heat
and begin to comprehend how terrible this weapon really was.

Agnew heard from Gardner about a month after DeLauer had
asked him to help with the Fletcher Panel. The Fletcher Panel was
already assembling in a big building in Rosslyn, a district of Arlington,
Virginia, so Agnew moved in to see what was going on. It was a short
honeymoon. "I thought it was getting crazier and crazier, and they
weren't using any real warheads on their missiles," Agnew said. "When
Fletcher wanted to use what's called an *antiproton warhead*—
somebody told him they should—I thought, 'That's just utter nonsense.' That's when I decided I'd had it, and bailed out."[11]

Fletcher, said Yonas, "knew the realities but was a willing player
even though Agnew ridiculed everything we were doing"[12] Yonas had
reviewed the antiproton idea himself and could tell it wouldn't work,
but it didn't die. "Somebody is trying to bring it up again as a super-
weapon," he remarked in 2004, "proving that nutty things are hard
to kill."[13] Fletcher began his Defensive Technologies Study, staffed by
a group of fifty experts, on June 2, with Yonas serving as chairman of
his directed energy weapon panel. Yonas suspects Agnew supported
him for the post because, at a 1982 dinner, they had an uproarious

time trading stories "about ballistic missile defense, the x-ray laser wars between LLNL and LANL, and other nutty things.

"I was always impressed with Harold because he could see things for what they were and enjoyed the irony of situations that others took so seriously," Yonas said. He recalled being in the audience when Agnew was testifying to a congressional committee, seated in front of a big pile of viewgraphs. When the senator asked him to cut it short, Agnew took a large pair of scissors from his pocket and cut his viewgraphs in half. "The head of the nuclear weapon programs was sitting there and he was furious," Yonas said. "I always wondered why Harold had the scissors."[14]

Reagan had not called for any particular approach to SDI, nor did he direct the study to design a Project *Apollo*–like crash program, as some critics were claiming. Arguably, *Apollo* had a well-defined end goal, whereas SDI did not. But the members of the Fletcher Panel were expected to come up with a plan. "A plan to do what?" Yonas asked, time and time again. It was impossible to get an answer because everybody had a different opinion about what was needed. " 'We're going to do it,' they'd say. And I kept saying, 'What is *it*?' "[15]

"So we said, 'Let's put together a plan to resolve the unknown; it's going to take a lot of money—let's try to do it in five years and at the end of five years we'll tell you whether there's anything feasible here.' "[16]

Yonas soldiered on, working day and night through the months of June, July, and August. "When they weren't calling me Darth Vader, friends would jokingly call me Reagan's ray-gun," he said.[17] "It was an interesting time. My family came to stay with me in Washington for a couple of weeks when the daily temperature highs were 100 degrees. My kids claimed that the cleaning lady, who spoke no other English, would knock on the door every morning and say, 'I want to kill you.' Now, I had chosen Dick Briggs from Lawrence Livermore National Laboratory for the study—he had run their electron beam weapon program for many years—and rejected George Miller. It was an unpopular choice, and I was told by people at LLNL that I would 'live to regret that decision.' Sometimes I wonder if they sent the cleaning lady."[18]

Most of the ideas considered by the panel were retained in the final report. "I thought it was 'premanure' to get rid of any of the concepts," Yonas said, giving in to his predilection for wordplay. "They were not yet manure. It would take a lot of time getting it straightened out; it would take a lot of time and a lot of money. The irony of the thing was we figured we could do a much better job of destroying SDI in space than we could in actually using SDI, and I think the Soviets came to the same conclusion."[19] The shaky genesis of the Fletcher Study was such that it is easy to criticize and even ridicule. But an embryonic structure, and a good deal of good sense, did emerge from the process. "Our understanding," Yonas explained in a *Physics Today* article, "was that we were to evaluate the existing research programs, recommend speeding up or slowing down the present efforts, and propose innovative options that might yield entirely new and effective technologies for ballistic-missile defenses."

As compared with the existing Soviet program, Yonas wrote, "it appeared to many of us in weapons research [that] the U.S. was pursuing an inadequately supported program in ballistic-missile defense. Worse, the program seemed to lack definition, strategy, and goals. It could be characterized, we said among ourselves, by fitful starts and stops, changes in direction . . . between government departments and military services. Despite the rather significant expenditures, the full potential of research on ballistic missile defense was not being realized. . . .

"Critics assert that any ballistic-missile defense system would have to be perfect. They say this knowing that no technological system of such scope and complexity could operate with quartz-clock precision. Simple logic argues that some percentage of warheads, although potentially a small number, would get through.

"The toughest issue [in the Fletcher Panel] was the cost-exchange ratio, weighing the cost of a ballistic-missile defense system against the cost of producing ballistic missiles and delivering them on targets or the cost of countermeasures to penetrate the defense.

"We developed a five-year research program that would thoroughly explore the limits of technology for both offensive and defensive systems to winnow out the least promising defense options. Only in this way could sufficient knowledge be acquired for an informed decision in the early 1990s on whether to proceed with engineered prototypes and full-scaled deployment."[20]

This would be the first phase; there would be a decision about whether it would be a good idea to start engineering development and systems integration of certain promising weapons and components in a second phase. These weapons would be prototyped and tested, a step that would likely breach the ABM Treaty. Ideally, if all of this were successfully accomplished, there would be a third phase in which the United States and the Soviet Union would make significant reductions in their offensive missile forces, while deploying their defensive anti-missile systems. A new stability would then be in place for the "final phase," in which both sides had defensive systems ready to launch against a relatively small number of offensive missiles.

"The criteria for a reliable ballistic-missile defense are survivability, lethality, and cost effectiveness," wrote Yonas. "We have to impose an unacceptably high cost on the Soviets to respond to our missile defense system with greater investments in their own ballistic missiles and countermeasures."[21]

The panel completed its work in four and a half months and delivered the report in October (a final version appeared in February 1984). "I went back to Albuquerque and I thought, 'Wow, we put together a twenty-six-billion-dollar plan which promised to *investigate* technologies over a five-year period!'" said Yonas. "That would allow one to make a decision about whether or not we would spend even more money. And, later, the president said, 'So it shall be.'"[22]

Bob Rankine was still working on the air staff on October 1, 1983, when—as a newly minted brigadier general—he was assigned to the undersecretary for defense, research, and engineering as assistant for directed energy weapons. He shared responsibility with John Gardner for the initial planning of the president's new strategic defense program. Rankine reported to Bob Cooper, assistant secretary of defense for research and technology, who reported to DeLauer. Cooper wore a second hat as director of DARPA, which meant he had an office on Wilson Boulevard in Arlington, as well as at the Pentagon. Rankine and John Gardner were given the job of supporting the Fletcher Study recommendations with a workable budget program. By then, after years in the business, Rankine was well aware that scientists relied heavily on marketing to gain funds, but then, he said, "I've always found that scientists significantly underestimate the time it takes for laboratory science to get into actual weapon system applications."

At the outset, not much marketing was required. "Since it was Weinberger's thing, putting extra money in the budget was not a problem," Rankine said. Transferring relevant projects from DARPA, Army, Navy, and Air Force programs, and adding extra money that had to be prioritized in the budget, raised much of SDI's early funding.

"The services hated us, but mainly because we were removing their prerogatives," he added. "The vice chief of staff of the Air Force came down and kind of chewed me out, but the scientists themselves loved it. For example, the budget of the Air Force Weapons Laboratory at Kirtland Air Force Base jumped by a sizeable amount. They lost Air Force money and got back twice as much SDI money."[23]

That autumn the Fletcher Study was converted into a formal program with the money, program elements, and all the other trappings of Pentagon bureaucracy. At this time, the Soviets weren't expected to attempt a head-on competition with SDI. A U.S. Interagency Intelligence Assessment reported, "We have no reason to expect any major alterations in Soviet doctrine and strategy in the 1980s and beyond."[24] It was wrong. Subtle changes were already under way, and soon these changes would be accelerating, threatening the foundations of the huge Soviet empire. It would be hard to discern any trace of an orchestrated U.S. conspiracy or grand strategy in this period, but a cauldron of complex social, strategic, psychological, economic, and political factors would soon be coming to a boil. With some lucky breaks and good timing, the United States would rid the world of the specter of global nuclear war.

The name "Strategic Defense Initiative" emerged from a Weinberger staff meeting attended by Rankine in late November 1983. "They had been using the term 'Defense Against Ballistic Missiles,' which everybody pronounced 'Dabbum,'" said Rankine. "And the secretary said, you know, that's a trivializing name. Everybody will be saying, 'A Little Dabbum'll Do Ya!' It sounded like the Brylcreem jingle. He said we need a name that is more empowering, something like Strategic Defense Initiative. And everybody said 'YES! Strategic Defense Initiative!'"[25]

LOOKING FOR A LEADER

Months after the Fletcher and Hoffman studies concluded their work, the powers of the Department of Defense were still figuring out exactly what kind of SDI organization they wanted. But there was no doubt as to who the embryonic organization's top boss would be. "I placed that new unit (SDIO) directly under me, with its head reporting to me, so that I would know of everything happening on the project, and would be able to block attempts that I knew would be made to divert resources and support from strategic defense, or to slow or dilute the Department's commitment for the Strategic Defense Initiative," Weinberger wrote in his memoir *Fighting for Peace*.[26]

Nine months after the president's speech, Cooper and Rankine were still talking to Congress, trying to communicate rather abstract technical ideas to a community made up largely of lawyers. Cooper and Rankine were top-flight research people, but the organization also needed somebody to coordinate testimony and work with Congress, and the search went out to look for someone who would fit the description. The Department of Defense's leading candidate to head the SDI program was Air Force Gen. Bernard A. Schriever, who was generally recognized as the father of the United States Air Force's space and missile program. But Schriever was retired and had had enough of the

Pentagon. The much-respected John S. (Johnny) Foster Jr., a former Lawrence Livermore director who previously held DeLauer's job, was known for outstanding technological leadership and was another logical candidate. He was never offered the job formally, because by then he was established as a top man at TRW and was out of the running. Another candidate was Hans Mark, former secretary of the Air Force and deputy administrator of NASA.

The White House dispatched two State Department teams to brief U.S. allies on SDI that February. "The allies had almost come unglued when President Reagan popped this on them," said Rankine, who, along with Gardner, participated in the briefings. "They saw ballistic missiles as providing security, so the idea of changing from ballistic offense to defense was scary to them. It meant eventually leaving the ABM treaty. So the president decided we needed to go out and explain. For the most part it was useful and helpful because we were able to answer a lot of questions, like 'Hey wait, this is only a research program and we're not going to go out and start fielding something tomorrow. There is a logic to it. If you're worried about proliferation of nuclear warheads to overcome defenses, the objective here is to come up with defenses that can be proliferated at lower cost than offenses. It therefore would become a stabilizing element rather than a destabilizing element.' "[27]

Meanwhile, Gen. Larry Skantze was well aware that SDI was still somewhat adrift. One day in March he was at a Joint Chiefs' meeting with President Reagan, chewing over the perennial tar-baby problem of how best to deploy the U.S. ICBM fleet. When the discussion exhausted itself, the conversation went around to SDI—how were they going to get a decent handle on managing *that* one? And, was the president correct in his inclination to have a civilian at SDI's helm? This time Skantze thought he had an answer. There was already a bright, enthusiastic young leader on his staff who knew technology and could also be understood by members of Congress. The candidate was Lt. Gen. James A. Abrahamson, NASA associate administrator for space flight.

Abrahamson's introduction to Cold War weaponry had come, oddly enough, while he was attending Bible camp in his hometown of Williston, North Dakota. There, the high school sophomore saw the now-familiar mushroom cloud in a film about science and religion. Determined to pursue a technical education, he went into aeronautical engineering, receiving his bachelor's degree from MIT and his master's through an Air Force Institute of Technology program at the University of Oklahoma. In that year, 1961, Abrahamson was appointed spacecraft project officer for the Vela nuclear test detection satellite at

Los Angeles Air Force Station, California. One year later, the Cuban Missile Crisis alerted the world to the fact that nuclear war could happen on hair-trigger notice. For the young Abrahamson, it was a sobering initiation into what would become a profound political awareness.

At the time, Abrahamson had no way of knowing that his name had come up during his superiors' behind-the-scenes discussion. As head of an outfit that ran the Shuttle and had responsibility for Johnson Space Center, Kennedy Space Center, and Marshall Space Flight Center, he was a very busy man. "When I heard Reagan's speech I thought, 'My God, at last we've found a way to get out of this thing,'" he said. "I was thrilled to think that maybe the Space Shuttle could have a role in it. But I certainly didn't think I'd be called back to Washington."[28] Abrahamson was aware of the Fletcher and Hoffman studies, and NASA Administrator James M. Biggs had encouraged him to volunteer the use of the Shuttle for SDI. But, a year after the speech, nothing had happened and, as he said, "I wondered, 'Why the hell are we taking so long?' Then, just before the scheduled April 6 STS-41C Shuttle launch—this touched off a demanding mission in which the crew repaired the Solar Max satellite—Abrahamson had a call from Gen. Skantze.

"Larry Skantze said that Weinberger would like to talk to me," Abrahamson recalls. "Beyond that, he told me nothing. So I called [NASA Administrator] Jim Beggs and asked him, 'Do you have any idea what this is all about?' Same response. So the next day I called Colin Powell. 'Your name has come up,' he explained. 'Your name is on the list as being a director of the Strategic Defense Initiative.'"[29]

"It was a hard choice but I decided on the spot," Abrahamson said.[30]

Soon Abrahamson was face-to-face with the secretary of defense. "There were no preliminaries," he said. "He was businesslike. He said he had already talked to the president and I had been very strongly recommended by Gen. Larry Skantze and that the president thought it was a great idea.

"I didn't know Cap at all. Here was this dynamic secretary of defense who all the military people thought was just terrific. When he was at OMB [Office of Management and Budget] he had been known as Cap the Knife. When he was appointed as the secretary of defense, there was all this speculation—would he cut the programs or what? And he became the most articulate advocate for strengthening the military structure. It was a great thrill to see this man."

The two men discussed the driving forces behind SDI and associated policy matters, and commiserated on the MX conundrum. But when the secretary said he wanted Abrahamson to start at once, Abrahamson decided he had to temporize. "But we're about to conduct a launch and a mission," he protested. "It's not that I'm so important that I have to be there, but I am the spokesperson. If anything looks bad for the Space Shuttle, it will look bad for the president because he will have taken one man out of the chain."[31]

"I said, 'I'd like to come right now, but once again, if things go wrong people will pin anything they can on the president. They'll say NASA took a risk because I was not there after I had been in charge of all the preparations.'

"Cap said, 'That's fine, but after you've finished you have three days and then you'll be testifying on SDI before the Senate Foreign Relations Committee, as the new SDI director.' "[32]

Abrahamson had one more point on his list of things to say. "I told him how important open public policy was at NASA," he said, "and that NASA had built up credibility and a reputation because they conducted every mission publicly and the press was invited. NASA didn't wait to go public until there was a successful launch. That was an important issue and they should consider running SDI the same way. He thought that was a great idea."[33] In fact, the openness of SDI—quite the reverse of the Russian way of doing business—and even the hype that accompanied the feeding frenzy for funding, would prove essential to SDI's success in the psychological war against the Soviet empire.

Abrahamson was appointed director on the cool, cloudy, spring afternoon of March 27, 1984, almost a year to the day after Reagan's SDI speech. News of the event was lost in the headlines of major world events—NASA Administrator Beggs had just returned from an around-the-world trip where he asked the Allies to help pay for the Space Station; the Dutch didn't want U.S. cruise missiles on their soil; proxy wars were raging in Angola and Nicaragua; and the UN was saying that Iraq was dropping chemical weapons on Iran.

But Weinberger had risen to the occasion. Would SDI really work? "We have a nation that can indeed produce miracles," he replied, referring to the Shuttle, the pride of Abe's pre-SDI career. When asked whether SDI would violate the ABM Treaty, the secretary of defense replied darkly, "The Soviets have not been troubled by that in the work that they have done in this type of strategic defense."[34]

The SDI organization's first charter gave the Abrahamson considerable leeway in managing the program and specified that he would report directly to the secretary of defense. A national security decision directive, NSDD-119, stipulated that "statements describing the strategic defense initiative should be low key and closely coordinated to ensure that an accurate picture of the nature and scope of this R&D

effort is presented to the public." By the time Abrahamson arrived, Rankine and Gardner had put together the 1985 budget. DeLauer then detailed Rankine to serve temporarily as Abrahamson's deputy. Teller was active on the sidelines, having urged a House Armed Services subcommittee that MAD "must be replaced by mutual assured survival, by real defense. . . . I am not advocating war on people. I am advocating war on inanimate, offensive weapons. Is all this provocative? What is provocative: a sword or a shield? Gentlemen, I speak for the shield."[35] (Reagan invented his own descriptor, "Mutual Assured Security," in 1985.)

Abrahamson was just in time to witness one of the biggest SDI hearings yet. "The back of the Senate was full of reporters, the Democrats in full cry and out for bear," he recalled. Fortunately for Abrahamson, who was fresh from the Cape and knew neither the policy nor the technical detail, Gardner and Rankine had prepared everything. "I was kind of enjoying this," he said, "but the story is so good and yet was so bad in so many ways.

"At one time, one of the Democrats said that surely something like what was being proposed would require the president's release if there had to be a response to an attack. Bob [Cooper], whose life was devoted to technology, didn't challenge any of this. They said, 'How is the President going to be informed? How is he going to be tracked so carefully so that he could release this response right away?' He wouldn't even have the twenty- or thirty-minute flight time of a normal missile flight in which to react.

"Bob invented on the spot. 'We're going to have this really great situational display that the president will always have with him,' he said. Some sort of flat-panel display. 'You mean he'll even take this to the bathroom?' the questioner asked, and Bob said, 'Why sure.'

"I could see the press reporting everywhere that the president's bathroom technology with the super tech machine would help him call the shots on SDI. I got Bob's attention with desperately strong kicks under the table, then probably I took over. I said the release procedures had not been worked out, but that there was a profound difference between SDI and nuclear counterattack scenarios, because this concept was non-nuclear and not targeted against people. I said the idea that it might require presidential release was not at issue, and possibly specious."[36]

Abrahamson was SDI's first regular employee; the second was his personnel officer. "When we started getting too many people to squeeze in, and DARPA's directed energy staff was essentially being moved lock stock and barrel to the SDI organization, we needed more space," Rankine said. "So we went to work with the Pentagon space-mongers."[37] Abe wanted to be in the Pentagon, but everything of any significant size was taken. There were two choices—an old warehouse just south of the Pentagon, and the Matomic building, not far from the Old Executive Office Building downtown and closer to the seat of government. They quickly opted for the latter and took over a couple of vacant upper floors.

THE SDIO IN ACTION

That spring, James Fletcher reported to Congress on the bottom-line result of his panel's deliberations:

> By taking an optimist view of newly emerging technologies, we concluded that a robust BMD system can be made to work eventually. The ultimate effectiveness, complexity, and degree of technical risk in this system will depend not only on technology itself, but also on the extent to which the Soviet Union either agrees to mutual defense arrangements and offense limitations, or embarks on new strategic directions in response to our initiative. The outcome of this initiation of an evolutionary shift in our strategic direction will hinge on as-yet unresolved policy as well as technical issues.[38]

Note the judicious use of the terms "optimist," "eventually," "ultimate," and "initiation" in this statement. As Yonas said in a letter to *IEEE Spectrum*, SDI "is not a program seeking a technological solution to a political problem, but a technology thrust attempting to provide an alternate technology option for what must still be a political process."[39] Further, as Yonas said in an article for *Science Digest*, the Fletcher Panel "agreed from the start that there would not be a 'perfect' defense against a determined adversary." Rather, they wanted to find ways of nullifying the military significance of a first strike. This would "motivate a move toward substantial reductions in armaments."[40]

Then Abrahamson got to work, starting from virtually nothing, in a world far removed from the halls of NASA. He did inherit a set of ideas from the two study groups that made very good sense, even if the presumed outcome was somewhat utopian. The SDI vision could and should be studied in a businesslike way, through a program that would evolve as new information was gathered, as new techniques were discussed and proved, and as special hardware and software were tested and built. It would take time. But Yonas's commonsense approach was from the beginning battered by the political propagandists—Democrat and Republican—and by the machinations of industrialists and scientists who hankered for a share of the SDI pie.

SDI, when packaged as a very serious, integrated presidential initiative, worried the Soviets even more than the Western defense community could have hoped. As Edward Teller remarked, "this was very sensitive because missile defense required scientific advances that were much more readily available in the U.S. than in the USSR. It gave the U.S. a clear advantage."[41]

The Soviets were quick off the mark in denouncing SDI on its home territory, on America's Main Street. A month after the SDI announcement, a letter signed by more than two hundred Soviet scientists denouncing the initiative was published in the *New York Times*. Those who had been active in plasma physics research and directed energy weapons included Basov, Prokhorov, Velikhov, Peter Grushin, Vladimir Semenikhin, Fedor Bunkin, and Vsevolod Avduyevskiy.

Dmitry Mikheyev, a physicist, broadcaster, and economist, is a one-time Soviet prison-camp internee who was forced to immigrate to the United States in 1979, and who then returned to Russia. He argued in 1987 that the Soviet leadership was not so much concerned about SDI-related matters concerning "first strike" capabilities, space militarization, or possible effects on the military balance. "Instead, the Party is mostly concerned about the political ramifications of the technological lag behind the West (which could only be exacerbated by an all-out qualitative arms race); the consequences of SDI for Moscow's ability to project power throughout the world; and ultimately, SDI's effect on the struggle between the two powers for world domination.

"The Soviet perception of SDI as the Grand Plan to Destroy the Socialist System derives not from the actual goals of the president's initiative, but from the nature of Soviet political mentality." At that time, he said, it perceived the world "as divided into two socio-political camps, engaged in a mortal struggle for world domination."[42]

The tremendous breadth of the SDI concept was particularly scary. First, as Mikheyev put it, "it is not a particular weapon, nor can it be based on just one or a few technologies. Instead, it requires the simultaneous development of many technologies." Second, "it essentially represents a qualitative—not quantitative—leap forward in the technological revolution."[43]

"For the Kremlin the problem was that it [SDI] was such a comprehensive program. It was a totally new stage of the arms race that would require taking a totally new direction, particularly in development of miniaturized electronics technology. That's different from developing nuclear weapons or even nuclear submarines or strategic bombers and rockets. It required introduction of computer technology on a wide scale. It required totally new technology, and the Soviets were desperately behind the United States and Japanese. That's why it was such a politically powerful program."[44]

"The 'tank people' couldn't care less about SDI or other complex weapon systems they couldn't comprehend," complained Colonel Vitaly V. Shlykov, who was department chief of the Main Intelligence Administration (GRU) of the General Staff, 1980–1988. He went on to comment that the United States, with its think tanks operating in a relatively open environment, was much better equipped for self-criticism and for flexibility: their overestimates were not so great.[45]

Shlykov, who headed GRU research on foreign military-economic capabilities, said that the SDI was a major driver for advanced weapons programs, so much so that they could become part of a "Revolution in Military Affairs." He agonized that the creaky bureaucracy, the field-artillery bias of General Staff old-timers, and certain special interests of the MIC got in the way of a timely response, and he ridiculed Andrei Kokoshin for calling SDI a bluff.

Gen. Maj. V. V. Larionov, a member of the Academy of Military Sciences and a friend of Kokoshin, took mild exception. SDI was certainly not a "blef," he said, but rather a conspiracy of American disinformation and *maskirovka* (deception). He and Kokoshin had been sympathetic to arguments put forward by Evgeny Velikhov and his Academy colleagues who believed that the grandiose SDI scenario was essentially undoable. Then they went further, moving toward Shlykov's view and seeing the SDI process as a more general plan to develop advanced, high-accuracy war machines. This too was scary, for it could generate a new military revolution that some Kremlinites were now calling "sixth generation warfare."[46] Soviet responses to SDI represented the interests of various bureaucracies and thus were extremely varied. Some factions wanted to compete with SDI; some wanted to increase the Soviet nuclear arsenal even more, to overcome U.S. defense. Others simply said SDI wouldn't work; that they could shoot its space-based components down anyway; and that they should sit back and let the United States bankrupt itself on a useless idea.

This chaotic state of affairs calmed after Gorbachev, having listened to the cacophony of differing views, became convinced that SDI would cause an escalation in the arms race. Reagan's view, of course, was exactly the opposite. But Gorbachev was determined to pressure Reagan into giving up his pet project. At the same time, he would start relatively moderate programs to build defenses against what was considered the American "militarization of space," to fall back upon in the event that Reagan prevailed.

Gorbachev also needed to maintain the Soviet Union's super-power status. Khrushchev is reported to have said, "We are not going to make war on anybody, so it is not that important how many warheads we have. What is important is what they think about our nuclear might."[47] It was a wise if not original observation. But now, to the impassioned optimists in Washington and the impassioned pessimists in Moscow, it seemed the Americans were getting themselves ready to ignore Soviet nuclear might altogether.

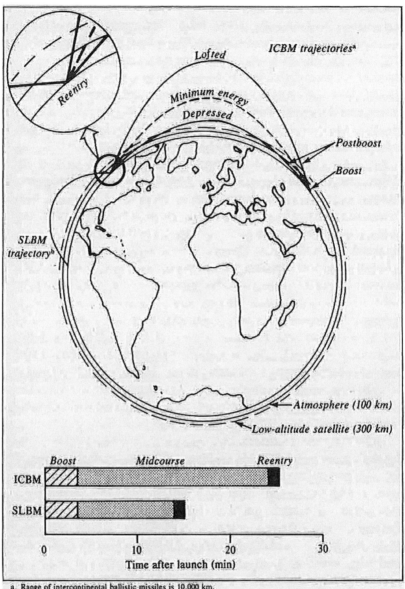

ICBM trajectories[a]

Lofted

Minimum energy

Depressed

Reentry

Postboost

Boost

SLBM trajectory[b]

Atmosphere (100 km)

Low-altitude satellite (300 km)

	Boost	Midcourse	Reentry
ICBM	⧄		
SLBM	⧄		

Time after launch (min)

0   10   20   30

a. Range of intercontinental ballistic missiles is 10,000 km.
b. Range of submarine-launched ballistic missiles is 5000 km.

The trajectories of intercontinental ballistic missiles (ICBMs) and submarine-launched ballistic missiles (SLBMs) follow paths that consist of boost, post-boost, midcourse, and reentry phases. The boost phase lasts a few hundred seconds, during which the missile is visible to satellite sensors. In the post-boost phase, warheads and decoys are deployed on different paths by a "bus" that produces a small, hard-to-detect infrared signature. After the midcourse phase, the warheads reenter the atmosphere and proceed toward their targets. The SLBM and depressed ICBM trajectories pose a problem for missile defense because they provide less time for destruction of the warhead. *Reprinted, by permission of the Brookings Institution Press, from Ashton B. Carter and David N. Schwartz, eds.,* Ballistic Missile Defense *(Washington, DC: Brookings Institution, 1984)*

The Soviet LE-1 laser radar, intended to determine the precise location of invading missiles, emerged from research and development that began in Sary Shagan in 1969. The system was not suitable for actual detection because its search abilities were made poor by a narrow field of view. *Courtesy of Peter Zarubin*

This Soviet-designed AGT-5 Zemskov laser achieved a first in energy output (90 kilojoules) in 1975 when pumped by several iodine photodissociation lasers (PDLs). Combining the energy this way created a single beam that did not spread so radically as a PDL and would therefore have been able to deliver more destructive power to a distant target. *Courtesy of Peter Zarubin*

A Soviet-era explosively pumped iodine laser (PDL) in the assembly shop prior to the installation of optical elements at the ends of the laser body. Extremely powerful PDLs were developed for ground-based ABM applications but never put to use, probably because of their great expense (each time one fired, it blew up) and the fact that these lasers would have to be much more powerful, and therefore even more expensive, if they were to shoot down missiles from the ground. *Courtesy of Peter Zarubin*

President Reagan announces the Strategic Defense Initiative on television from the Oval Office on March 23, 1983, surprising the American public and Soviets alike. A reconnaissance photo illustrating Soviet military presence in Cuba is displayed behind the president. *Ronald Reagan Library*

This intercept vehicle was part of the U.S. Army's successful Homing Overlay Experiment (HOE) in 1984. The dummy warhead and intercept vehicle were launched more than 4,200 nautical miles apart; the HOE vehicle, with its metal net deployed (pictured at left), closed with the warhead at more than 15,000 feet per second, and telemetry data revealed that they hit body-to-body. The test is credited with raising optimism for SDI and reversing a funding crisis. *Lockheed Martin Corporation*

A Titan rocket casing filled with water explodes after being struck by a mid-infrared advanced chemical laser (MIRACL) at White Sands Missile Range on September 6, 1985. This on-the-ground test showed the laser worked when aimed at a fixed target at short distance. The relative ease of the experiment attracted criticism, yet the chemical laser went on to become the most popular speed-of-light ABM weapon concept. *Department of Defense*

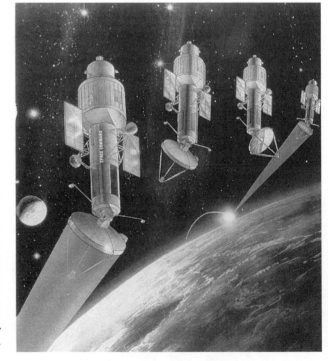

An artist's rendition of a chemical laser concept, the most enduring approach of all orbital directed-energy weapons, typified by the MIRACL and Alpha designs. Chemical lasers operate at high power and hold special promise as orbital speed-of-light ABM weapons because they carry their own fuel into space and do not need a separate supply of electrical energy. *Lockheed Martin Corporation, developed by Lee Lunsford, courtesy of Gerold Yonas*

In a rare 1981 visit to U.S. nuclear weapon facilities, Soviet laser pioneer Nikolai Basov is briefed on electron-beam experiments at Sandia National Laboratories in Albuquerque, New Mexico. Left to right: Gerold Yonas (then director of Sandia's particle beam fusion program), Basov, Sandia physicist Bob Turman, and Soviet physicist G. V. Sklizkov. *Bill Lasker, photographer, Sandia National Laboratories*

President Reagan's first meeting with General Secretary Gorbachev on November 19, 1985, at the chateau Fleur d'Eau during the first arms summit in Geneva. Though little concrete progress resulted here, the summit initiated top-level superpower dialogue in which SDI would figure prominently. Despite Gorbachev's urgings and offers, President Reagan consistently refused to negotiate away his program. *Ronald Reagan Library*

Secretary of Defense Caspar Weinberger talks with members of his SDI technical advisory committee in 1985. Left to right: Weinberger, former Lawrence Livermore director John S. Foster Jr., retired NASA executive James Cornelius Elms, physicist Edward Teller, former president of the National Academy of Sciences Frederick Seitz, SDIO science advisor Gerold Yonas (SDIO science advisor), and Gen. Bernard Adolph Schriever, widely regarded as the father and architect of Air Force space and ballistic missile programs. *Department of Defense*

A White House briefing on Brilliant Pebbles on July 26, 1988. One of the "pebbles" is hidden under the shroud at the far end of the table. Seated, clockwise, around the table: Ronald Reagan; Gen. Robert Linhard; Edward Teller; Lowell Wood; Lawrence Livermore National Laboratory director John Nuckolls; William R. Graham, science advisor to the president and director of the Office of Science and Technology Policy; Lt. Gen. James Abrahamson (in uniform); Vice President George H. W. Bush; and an unidentified attendee. Brilliant Pebbles never went into orbit, but the idea of placing small, smart homing rockets on space satellites has been around for decades and remains on the books for possible future deployment. *Ronald Reagan Library*

In a modern ballistic missile defense test, a target missile takes off from Sandia National Laboratories' Kauai Test Range in 2003 prior to the launch of a "hit to kill" interceptor from an Aegis cruiser. Approximately two minutes later, the two collided and the target missile was destroyed from the force of the collision. *Diana Helgesen, Sandia National Laboratories*

SDI Director Lt. Gen. James Abrahamson trades stories with his former science advisor, Gerold Yonas, at Abrahamson's retirement dinner on January 29, 1989. The two men and their colleagues shepherded SDI from its troubled infancy to a multibillion-dollar research and development program. *Department of Defense*

8

A Year to Test Nations

Nihilism is a dangerous but necessary and a possibly salutary stage in human history. In it man faces his true situation. It can break him, reduce him to despair and spiritual or bodily suicide. But it can hearten him to a reconstruction of a world of meaning.
—Allen Bloom[1]

SDI was plainly of serious concern to the Soviets. But was it worrying them too much? Would it goad them into making a first strike—launching a preemptive attack against the Americans while they still had chance? The Kremlin had some reason to be alarmed. "It was known by then that both Truman and Eisenhower had considered a nuclear strike against the Soviet Union, even though they had finally decided against it," wrote Dennis Healey, who served as a British Labour Party defense secretary and Chancellor of the Exchequer. "Thus there was a real danger that if Washington ever looked like [it was] deploying an effective strategic defense system, Moscow would feel it had no alternative but to get its blow in first, by attacking America's missile bases while they could still do so."[2]

At about the same time, an Office of Technology Assessment report on SDI, commissioned by Congress, warned that development of the proposed "umbrella" would make a preemptive strike more attractive to the Soviets.[3] The conditions under which Moscow might have launched a nuclear "first strike" of their own in the early Cold War years are unknown, or at least undisclosed. Documents available on NATO and its counterpart, the Warsaw Pact, suggest that each side was as aggressive as the other in those days. Some U.S.-originated documentation tends to support Soviet fears of a U.S. nuclear first strike.[4] Llewellyn Thompson, the State Department's top Kremlinologist in the 1960s, thought the possibility of such an attack was "remote," but he recommended that if it ever seemed likely, Washington should launch its own first strike. (Later, it was Thompson who advised JFK to steer a cool course during the Cuban Missile Crisis.)[5]

The first-strike question came up in connection with SDI because enough people believed it could eventually be put into action—and then, like so many technical developments, could be used for "good" or for "bad." It could be a passive network, sitting there just in case there was an attack but otherwise doing nothing, or it could be a tool used in ICBM warfare initiated by the United States—allowing American warheads to strike the Soviet Union while preventing a counterstrike.

Viktor Mikhailov, head of the MINATOM atomic energy agency, reacted by calling for an updated Comprehensive Test Ban Treaty "aimed at preventing the development of the third generation of nuclear weapons . . . the so-called directed energy weapons . . . and at preventing the release of an evil jinn from the research stage to a full-scale development stage at a new spiral in the arms race."[6] Aleksandr Bessmertnykh, head of the American Department of the Soviet Ministry for Foreign Affairs from 1983–86, had his own ideas about what was going on. He counseled that Soviet intelligence "was always alarmist"—a quality he also ascribed to U.S. intelligence. At first, his particular circle thought that the best way of countering SDI would be to build more ICBMs. As they thought more about it, the Soviet leadership came to the conclusion that "there might be something very, very dangerous" in SDI.[7]

There was also the worry that the Americans might put nukes in space, as voiced by Academician Stanislav Menshikov, an economist and the son of a former Soviet ambassador to the United States. "By planning to place nuclear systems into extra-atmospheric orbit for an extended time period," he said, referring to Teller's x-ray laser, "Reagan was spreading the armaments race to outer space, which in Andropov's view was extremely dangerous."[8]

On the U.S. side, Hans Bethe argued, "In a situation of great tension, there would be immense pressure on each side to shoot first, because of the fear that the other would. In a world without defense, and with an invulnerable deterrent, such as we have now, no such pressure exists; each side can afford to wait the crisis out." This argument, Bethe maintained, would remain valid "until some far-off Utopia in which both sides possess a near-perfect defense."[9]

Should Moscow attack the United States before it got its SDI assets into position? Fortunately, everyone knew that it would not be necessary to answer that question for a long, long time. But it was understandably under discussion because, as first Georgi Kornienko, then First Deputy Foreign Minister, put it, the Soviet leadership "began to frighten each other more and more about this program." A few scattered reports that the option was being considered reached the United States, but they were little more than rumors—until after the Cold War, when Hungary's last communist foreign minister, Guyla Horn, assured *Der Spiegel* that yes, some Soviet marshals had indeed advocated an attack "before the imperialists gained superiority in every sphere."[10]

If Washington was an untidy web of speculation and internecine bickering, Moscow was worse. The Soviet scientific establishment was divided between austere Academy pronouncements about a nonsensical SDI fantasy and opposing arguments that "the Americans seem to think there's something in it, so we might as well try it too." The military establishment was torn between the idea—held tenaciously by some of the old heroes of World War II—that tanks and soldiers would win, and the military industrial complex's fascination with the idea that its early, pioneering work in directed-energy weapons could be restored into a viable counterbalance against American weapons of the same variety. Russian moderates, like America's anti-SDI factions, believed that U.S. defensive weapons in space could simply be blown up.

THE POWER OF IDEAS

The consternation of potential first-strikers like Kornienko and Warsaw Pact commander in chief Viktor Kulikov was balanced not only by the academicians but also by the more insightful thinkers of the diplomatic and intelligence communities. Among the latter was Gen. Nikolai Leonov, chief of KGB Analysis from 1973 to 1983. "This idea more than anything was a powerful psychological one," he said. "But of course it emphasized more than anything our technological backwardness and that we should immediately review our place in world technological progress."[11]

"Bingo!" said Gerold Yonas. "Most people think SDI was about ballistic missile defense, but in reality this was only a side issue. Ironically, at a time that so many Soviets were convinced we could solve the SDI battle management problems with our giant computers, we were convinced we did not have a clue how to make that part of the program work. We couldn't even test the software to make sure that we could trust it."[12]

But with time, who knows? The top echelons at the Kremlin, outside the Ministry of Defense, seemed to fit Leonov's profile. "It wasn't SDI *per se* that frightened the Soviet leaders," wrote Robert Gates, then deputy director of intelligence and later head of the CIA under President George H. W. Bush, "I think it was the *idea* of SDI and all it represented that frightened them. As they looked at the United States, they saw an America that apparently had the resources to increase defense spending dramatically and then add this program on top, and all of it while seeming hardly to break a sweat.[13]

"For the Soviets," Gates added, "SDI symbolized the resurgent and diverse strength of the United States—economic, technical, and military—and highlighted their disadvantage in this technology-based competition. Accordingly, constraining SDI became the single most important object of Soviet diplomacy and covert action after 1983."[14]

"I have the impression that the Soviets at first assumed that we were farther along in it than we actually were," George Shultz told me. "I think they also felt that if the American scientific community got moving on defense-type issues, as it had in World War II, there was no telling what would emerge from that."[15]

Charles Townes once observed, "There was a faith, in the wake of the Manhattan Project and the *Apollo* Program, that with enough money and effort, [U.S.] scientists could overcome any obstacle."[16] Townes was describing American sentiments, yet no one experienced that belief—an outgrowth of the "magic" myth of science—more strongly than the Soviets. Competing with the United States in SDI-type technology could not occur without the economic strength that would result from a truly massive, epochal (and, in practical terms, impossible) overhaul of the Soviet system—necessitating, for example, the decentralization of its economy and the introduction of market forces. This feat plainly could not be accomplished, for the Soviet Union was in a sad economic state and poorly equipped to put reforms into motion. Even before Mikhail Gorbachev became general secretary, Richard Pipes said the Soviet Union was in a "revolutionary situation" and that its leaders would have to choose between going to war and bringing about sweeping internal reforms. The new leader would have to take over a tottering system sadly lacking in domestic necessities and in great need of a sound foreign policy.[17]

DEVIOUS DEALINGS

Behind the scenes at the Washington residency, KGB operatives turned with relief from their Project Ryan duties to counter this new threat to Moscow's sense of stability. It promised a welcome change. "In order to please our superiors, we sent in falsified and biased information, acting on the principle, 'Blame everything on the Americans, and everything will be OK,'" one political intelligence officer told *Izv-*

estia in 1999, adding ruefully, "That's not intelligence, it's self-deception."[18]

Vladimir Aleksandrovich Kryuchkov, KGB head of Foreign Intelligence, had vowed to wage his own war against SDI, and the Washington resident, Stanislav Androsov, was eager to join the fray. Yuri Shvets commented that SDI "could not have come at a more opportune time. There was no longer any need to peek into windows, count cars, and cut facts out of whole cloth."[19] Shvets reported, via Tass, that SDI was a bluff intended to intimidate, with the goal of destroying the Soviet economy. Then, at an open Georgetown University debate, he heard Congressman Bob Dornan defend SDI with the observation that "the Russians are frantic; they are afraid of SDI."[20] Whereas Shvets's first report had stimulated little more than a yawn from behind the dirty-yellow ramparts of Dzerzhinskiy Square, this one probably worked because the young spy lied and said Dornan's remarks were made at a closed congressional hearing.

Though no one in Moscow could admit it, their economic and industrial problems already had been compounded by the Farewell revelations of 1981—in other words, by the breakdown of Line X and its subversion by the CIA. The rupture of the KGB-run techno-info pipeline was signaled when about two hundred Line X spies were sent home by European governments.

The Kremlin's conveyor-belt of Western science and engineering know-how had been shattered. In spite of this, or because of it, the Soviet military research machine now began to stir. The severe economic pinch, and the scattered skepticism about SDI, failed to stem the upsurge in advanced weapons research reported by Soviet media following Reagan's "Star Wars" speech. This reportedly included work on particle beam weapons (at Sarov), proton beams and near-infrared lasers (at Krasnoyarsk, Tyuratam, Semipalatinsk, and Krasnaya Rechka), and related fusion research (at the Sefremov Institute, Leningrad).[21]

On August 31, 1983, a Soviet fighter pilot shot down the Korean airliner KAL 007, en route with 269 passengers to Seoul from New York. Shultz denounced the incident in emotional terms; the Soviets stonewalled, then called his comments a "slanderous attack" and did not acknowledge the facts of the case until October 6. By then, anti-Soviet sentiment had flowered anew in the United States, and on television Reagan stated that the Russian pilot knew he was firing on a passenger aircraft—which apparently was not the case. The aircraft had deviated from course, miraculously flown through a gap in the Soviet radar defense system, and been mistaken by controllers for a spy plane. In the brouhaha that followed, U.S.–Soviet relations slipped back yet again.

This was one of a number of serious international incidents that marked the year. On June 14, TWA Flight 847 was hijacked by members of the Islamic Jihad on a flight from Athens and flown to Beirut. Extremely skillful diplomacy ensured the release of 152 hostages (one had been killed by the terrorists), and, on its own terms, Israel subsequently released the prisoners for whom the hijackers were acting. Then, in mid-October, terrorists hijacked the cruise ship *Achille Lauro* in the Mediterranean, and again a passenger was sacrificed.

"I believe the current outbreak of violence is more than coincidence," Meyer said in a memo to Casey. "What we are seeing now is a Soviet-led effort to fight back, in the same sense that the Mafia fights back when law enforcement agencies launch an effective crime-busting program."[22]

Paranoia in the Kremlin

On October 25, two days after the infamous truck bombing of the U.S. barracks in Beirut that killed 241 Marines, the United States, fearing a Marxist takeover, invaded and subdued the tiny Caribbean island nation of Grenada. While this may have been bad news for the Soviet Union, much worse was ahead; November was full of headaches for the men of the Kremlin. The first batch of a planned ninety-six nuclear-capable ground-launched cruise missiles were just about to be installed in England at Greenham Common Air Base—a grave enough development—when the United States staged Able Archer, an exercise intended to test NATO's effectiveness in meeting a nuclear threat from the Warsaw Pact. That was the sum of it, no more, but it sounded very realistic and it scared the Soviets—so much so that some were alarmed enough to label it the prelude to a genuine Western nuclear attack. Western intelligence reported that the NATO exercise had "produced a wave of panic" in Moscow—a situation confirmed, after his defection, by Oleg Gordievski, who had run the KGB residency in London.[23] Washington, realizing that this may have been the most dangerous time since the Cuban Missile Crisis; it pulled in its horns a little, and Reagan's rhetoric become noticeably milder.

At about the same time, U.S. experts were poring over reconnaissance satellite images of a giant new facility that was being built at Abalakovo, near Krasnoyarsk in central Siberia. To the analysts it was clearly a phased-array radar installation capable of detecting large numbers of incoming missiles, and it was a violation of the ABM Treaty. (It was indeed an early warning radar. A U.S. delegation that visited the site in July 1989 reported that, since it lacked either an independent power supply or hardening against nuclear attack, it would be useless in time of war. But then, it would have already completed its job.) The Kremlin made a mess of the Krasnoyarsk radar story. "First," Velikhov recalled, "they tried to convince the world that it was possible to use this radar for scientific purposes, which was nonsense. One of the big problems with the Soviet Union was not only secrecy, but this kind of lying. It was very unpleasant—and stupid, because now it seemed everybody was lying. Its only purpose was for self-protection, inside of our own system."[24]

Jack Matlock learned that during Dmitry Ustinov's tenure as minister of defense, the Soviet foreign ministry had not been consulted until after SS-20s were designed, built, and deployed. And Anatoly Chernyaev, though a senior foreign policy official, knew nothing of the key speeches that Reagan delivered in 1984 and 1985.[25] It was small wonder that, in his *Memoirs*, Gorbachev made the observation that his country's "closed nature and secrecy" were part of what was "wrong with the system."[26]

So, the Soviet ICBM machine continued to churn out its weapons of mass destruction. By 1983 it was estimated at there were 351 SS-20s in service, of which 243 were located west of the Urals; the former number would increase to 441 in early 1986, of which about 270 were west of the Urals.[27] Each SS-20 "Mod 2" had three 150-kiloton MIRVs and a range of about 3,000 miles.

More European NATO governments allowed the American military to install missiles on their soil, and, predictably, Moscow was dismayed, especially when the first Pershing II mobile missiles entered service in West Germany in January 1984. Technically called a battle-field support missile, the Pershing II had a range of about 1,000 miles and carried a W85 nuclear warhead. While the Americans contended that the Pershing IIs did not constitute a first-strike threat to Moscow, a covert campaign appears to have been staged within the Kremlin to present their deployment as an American reenactment of the Cuban Missile Crisis. The idea that these missiles could reach Moscow in ten minutes or less persisted until after the collapse of the Soviet Union. "Those Pershing missiles were a huge worry to us," Gorbachev remarked in a 1996 television interview. "Only three minutes flying time to Moscow, five minutes to the Volga, two minutes to other places. There was nothing we could do to stop them."[28] Votintsev also remained under the impression that "this was a very serious threat and a real possibility of surprise destruction of hardened command and control facilities of the state and the Armed Forces."[29]

"It was absurd for Gorbachev to claim that the Pershing II was a potential first-strike weapon," wrote Jack Matlock. "It did not have the range to come anywhere near most Soviet ICBM silos. . . . it could not even reach Moscow from its bases in Germany."[30]

With this kind of misinformation flying around Moscow, it's hardly surprising that a sort of paranoia reigned until Andropov's death, on February 9, 1984, and Gorbachev's accession to power. It continued even then, in the back rooms of the Ministry of Defense. In retrospect, if Andropov had been in better shape and lived longer, internal changes might have been delayed and the Cold War might have lasted until the century's end, and maybe even longer.[31]

Through all of this, Reagan from time to time managed to say a few things that might have sounded conciliatory to the Soviets. Not surprisingly, they still regarded him as a loose cannon who just might be making such statements to help his popularity ratings. They were not the only ones to be confused by the showman in the White House. Even as he continued to enjoy wide public approval, Reagan remained an enigma to those who studied him most closely. According to Dobrynin, Tip O'Neill, the speaker of the House who was famous for his attacks on the president, at one time called Reagan a demagogue and a "dangerous man" who acted on primitive instincts, while Lawrence Eagleburger, Reagan's undersecretary of state for political affairs, said admiringly that the president was guided by an "inborn instinct."[32] Dobrynin suspected that Reagan's reluctance to hear or read detailed information resulted in a situation where his close advisors, such as Weinberger, had a particularly strong influence in government policy.

"Once the president sensed that his confrontation with Moscow had gone too far," huffed Dobrynin, "he resorted to improvisations prompted by the narrow circle of his closest aides, who were experts in television image-making but knew little or nothing at all about the workings of the Kremlin and how to conduct a dialogue with it."[33]

The folks at the SDIO and its contractors observed all these machinations with a kind of otherworldly detachment. They worked hard and made money, and few dreamed that they might be part of a psychological operation. Abrahamson himself discounts the psy-op idea out of hand. "I don't believe anybody ever had the foggiest idea that the Soviets would just collapse in on themselves," he said. "And if there had been a real plan to do it, I think we would have seen some evidence of it. I don't agree with Gerry [Yonas] on this. I never saw any evidence that we were really a front to break them."[34] Abrahamson's vision of SDI (passed on to its successors) was for a defense against ballistic missiles that, while imperfect, was effective enough to deter an attack, and which for that reason would be an arms control device, or system, much more powerful and much more morally acceptable than MAD.[35] Yonas claims some prescience in this matter. "I knew the thing was not a technological issue, but depended on the Soviet response. Abe never had the time, nor the background, to get into the detailed engineering/physics issues, and never really understood Casey's strategy. I never knew we would pull this 'scam' off, but I understood that it would depend mostly on the Soviet response and whether we could scare them enough."[36]

U.S. information channels fed the fame of SDI with gusto. Some of the worst-kept (and best-leaked) secrets of SDI had to do with weapon concepts that were communicated rather publicly to the Department of Defense and Congress by the research labs, and thence to selected media. One claim glorified the supposed effectiveness of a single x-ray laser against the entire fleet of Soviet heavy boosters. Though certain influential Russians took such hyperbolic claims very seriously indeed, Yonas believes that few if any insiders ever believed in the feasibility of the mega-scale SDI, with its huge, integrated complex of layered-defense systems. "The magic umbrella was never considered by anybody with half a brain," he said.[37] Part of the irony of SDI story was that some out-of-the-box thinkers in the Soviet establishment were convinced that the Americans would never, ever, put up a working Star Wars system.

Velikhov Weighs In

Like nearly everyone else, the U.S. National Academy of Sciences was kept on the outside of SDI policymaking, despite its huge intellectual resources. Officially appointed science advisors also tended to keep their opinions to themselves. As science policy analyst Daniel Greenberg reported, "the regulars who had been appointed to provide scientific advice for the president of the United States were outside, unheeded, and impotent" and "political fealty took precedence over scientific integrity."[38] Russian scientists, on the other hand, did speak out, probably as a result of the status enjoyed by Academician Evgeny Velikhov. Soon after the SDI announcement, an analysis of the U.S. program was produced under the auspices of the Soviet Scientists' Committee for the Defense of Peace Against Nuclear Threat. Velikhov was the first-named editor; his co-authors were Roald Sagdeev of the Space Institute and Prof. Andrei Kokoshin, a historian with an engineering background who had been seconded from Georgi Arbatov's Moscow Institute of the United States and Canada.* Other contribu-

---

*Arbatov, who covertly worked for the KGB, was loud in his denunciations of U.S. commentaries on the Soviet talent for dirty tricks, including KAL-007, possible implication in the papal assassination attempt, and alleged use of chemical agents in Afghanistan.

tors included Arbatov's son Alexei (later a prominent figure in the Russian Federation Duma) and others representing the physical and social sciences. A separate, classified report on the potential of SDI, requested by Defense Minister Ustinov, came out later in 1983. "Our intention," Velikhov said, "was to give him a very real picture of the unreality of particle beams or lasers in space, and that while at some time it might be possible to use the 'Brilliant Pebbles' concept [to attack ICBMs with small, space-based kinetic-kill interceptors], there are simple countermeasures against it."[39]

Velikhov was well prepared to take on the vagaries of SDI. "In 1977 our designer for rockets, V. N. Chelomei, who made big rockets like the SS-18, proposed that we develop antiballistic space stations similar to those proposed earlier by Korolev," he explained. "Chelomei proposed using small, smart rockets—like 'Brilliant Pebbles'—on a small version of the [U.S.] Shuttle. It was a very old idea—it was BAMBI. Brezhnev asked us to make an assessment of the Chelomei proposals. After a very detailed assessment [under the chairmanship of deputy defense minister Vitali Shabanov], the commission concluded that Chelomei's proposal would not work against U.S. nuclear attack. In parallel, the idea of using particle beams was discussed by Academician Budker, and we could see that this idea would not work either.

"Since this was a very complicated debate, it prepared us to deal later with the much more complicated SDI problems. It had been a long debate, including the question of high-powered lasers that were mostly being pushed by Basov."[40]

Velikhov and his team gave their study the English title *Weaponry in Space*.[41] To say the least, this was an unusual book to consider bringing out under the tightly-held publishing rules of Andropov's Soviet Union. "We had trouble," said Velikhov. "And again, the problem was the result of excessive secrecy. When the military people gave us permission to publish, they asked us to put a disclaimer on each page, saying, 'This is not my view, it is the view of American scientists.' I said this was my book, and it was pure physics. It was very controversial, but we didn't include the disclaimer. Our purpose was just to give scientific reasons why SDI wouldn't work, and how simple the countermeasures could be.[42]

"We tried very hard not to base anything on classified reports because the book was completely open. Mostly we wrote it for our political and military leaders, to convince them because, as usual, the other side [the military industrial complex, MIC] would say to the government, 'We need money; we need financing . . .' We tried to stop this. We said, first of all, that space defense does not work. Secondly, we said that to have some sort of assurance against SDI, you need to start to look at countermeasures. It's so much cheaper."[43]

Predictably, the first draft of the SDI analysis, finished in the summer of 1983, met with a mixed reception. The authors had raised a number of what Sagdeev calls "critical arguments—that 'this is bad,' 'this is bad,' 'this wouldn't work,'" and some in the establishment were concerned: "'Do you think it is good to call the attention of the Americans to the weak points in their program? Maybe it will help them to improve it.'

"After publication, there were letters saying that 'Sagdeev and Krokhin are traitors; they are helping Reagan to improve the SDI,'" Sagdeev said, twenty years later. "It is a funny story. People were always asking us, 'If you believe as you argued in your report that SDI would never work because the physics is flawed, or whatever, why are you so worried about it? Why do you spend so much time saying that it is a bad idea?'"

Prokhorov, too, was openly skeptical of Reagan's SDI aspirations, and Basov somewhat reluctantly concurred, despite the fact that their operations would benefit financially from a Soviet response to "Star Wars." "I knew Prokhorov very well, and I knew Basov as well," said Sagdeev. "The general feeling was that nothing promising would come of laser weaponry. From my point of view, our main motivation was to launch a preemptive verbal attack on SDI, to make sure that we could kill any appetite for similar programs within the Soviet military-industrial complex." It was a sound strategy. "If SDI were not demystified in the press, and in the debates, there was a serious chance that these guys [from the MIC] would go to the government and tell them, 'Give us money and we will build it here, in Russia,'" Sagdeev explained.

"There was a direct attempt to bring this about, but we were fortunate. Soviet efforts along the lines envisaged in Washington were already on the dying curve after the supernova explosion of previous decades."[44]

For Sagdeev, SDI was a dream with little or no basis in fact. Velikhov, who was acutely aware of the overblown but secret Soviet DEW programs, all but spilled the beans at a press conference when he commented that "research already carried out shows that to create a highly efficient space system would be practically impossible."[45]

The Velikhov-Sagdeev gambit was not completely successful. "The Soviet military were particularly apprehensive of a possible revolutionary U.S. breakthrough in related military technology," said Menshikov. "Top physicists in Moscow were more skeptical, but the leadership tended to side with the military in assessing Reagan's move."[46] The military and military industrial complex trumpeted that

Velikhov and his colleagues didn't know what they were talking about––that U.S. technology was more powerful than they realized, that SDI was a means for the United States to get away unscathed after executing a first strike, and that it was likely a cover for all sorts of space weaponry that no one had yet talked about. In other words, at least some Soviets were ready to start competing. "Many leading scientific and technical people in the USSR were anxious to get government money for their respective labs under the umbrella of SDI-type [or anti-SDI-type] programs," says Peter Zarubin. "That's why many of them would not be willing to disclose and did not reveal their real attitudes to the problem, even if their attitudes were reserved or skeptical."[47] Neither side succeeded in totally convincing Gorbachev, who simply believed the arms race would continue if the United States insisted on exploring nuclear missile defense. But when they heard that the United States wanted SDI to be operational in 10–15 years, Defense Minister Ustinov and Leonid Smirnov, chairman of the Military-Industrial Commission, channeled new SDI-like funding into the 11th Five Year Plan (1981–1985), and the Baikonur and Plesetsk launch centers were reorganized. It appeared to some that there might be renewed interest in laser weaponry, and it appeared that the star of a controversial figure in that community might be rising.

Nikolai Ustinov, the son of Dmitry Ustinov, acquired the academic credentials of a scientist, but after years of working his way up through the system, his value lay almost wholly in management skills and politics. He was characterized by Zarubin as "not a great scientist himself" but nevertheless "rather an influential person" whose participation "objectively facilitated the development of laser activity."[48]

Ustinov started his laser career in the early 1960s as a junior engineer in a then-small laser laboratory at the Moscow home of the Vympel Design Bureau, where Grigory Kisunko had been developing masers (the microwave version of lasers) as low-noise radar amplifiers. Step by step, over a period of perhaps ten years, Ustinov became head of the project, an administrator rather than a working scientist. He was now a chief designer, responsible for providing the conditions necessary for technical development.

Sagdeev acknowledges Nikolai Ustinov's administrative skills but calls his election to the Academy of Sciences "one of the most shameful moments in the history of the academy."[49] Nikolai liked jokes and popular music, smoked up to five packs of cigarettes a day, and (by contrast with his workaholic father) was not known for his industriousness. While he was an educated man and an avid reader, he would not have won many popularity polls. He was also a hard drinker and his parentage attracted petty jealousies. But Basov, Velikhov, and many others were dependent on him. Sagdeev could not resist making a grim joke during a meeting of colleagues: "There is a tradition of kidnapping kids of prominent parents and holding them for ransom. What would we ask for Nikolai?" Velikhov caught up with him later: "Roald," he said, "are you counting on me to deliver your bread at the gulag?"[50]

Zarubin said that the elder Ustinov was disinclined to exert his influence to promote his son's career, because privately he was not optimistic for the future of laser weaponry. But Yonas saw Nikolai moving vigorously ahead, and with Basov, "pushing big programs that were totally oversold and poorly thought through. It took maybe fifteen years before they realized they were beating a dead horse. They were going down a blind alley; they were wasting vast amounts of money." He paused. "Well, what did *we* do? We really didn't get going until the president said go."[51]

Velikhov says Dmitry Ustinov was skeptical about space defense not only because of the new reports prepared by his team, but because he had been involved in the evaluation of various space-defense ideas, including the Chelomei proposals. "From one side he was quite skeptical, but on the other side as Minister of Defense he needed to be careful," Velikhov said. "Some people in the Ministry of Defense, and some people in the Ministry of Foreign Affairs—and I think in Intelligence—were captivated by their impression of the Americans' drive to get the job done. Some were absolutely convinced that America had the capacity to install the space-based antiballistic missile defense by 1990.

"They remained convinced from 1983 to 1990, during the time of Gorbachev. I tried to convince them otherwise, but they did not believe us. Unfortunately the problem was not just the military, who had no experience of this type of exotic weapons, and for whom it looked like something real. *Perception* was very strong. In Russia as in America, it was the time of Star Wars. It was on television. And the people looked at it as reality, as if it existed, while all the time it was pure fantasy."[52]

Since 1980, Velikhov and Sagdeev had been meeting twice yearly with the U.S. National Academy of Sciences' Committee on International Security and Arms Control (CISAC), one of numerous "back channels" that were smiled upon by both Moscow and Washington as means of facilitating semiofficial communication. They remained in close touch with science and government leaders on both sides of the Cold War divide, and soon Velikhov had built a small but influential constituency for himself in the United States. He encouraged anti-SDI sentiments in Congress among such Democratic Senate leaders as Les

Aspin of Wisconsin, Joe Biden of Delaware, J. Bennett Johnston of Louisiana, and William Cohen of Maine, along with Alan Simpson of Wyoming on the Republican side. He had a natural affinity for declared U.S. opponents of SDI—people like Jeremy Stone of the Federation of American Scientists, Tom Cochran and Christopher Paine of the Natural Resources Defense Council, Richard Garwin of IBM, and Sid Drell of Stanford. Nor did he steer clear of the opposition. He knew and admired, with reservations, the redoubtable Edward Teller. It was his job to sit across from the "gray cardinal," Richard Perle, in U.S.–Soviet negotiations, and he had no fear of stepping into the lions' dens; for example, he paid personal visits to Paul Nitze at the State Department.

For all his diplomacy, Velikhov stuck to his guns and refused to compromise his principles—to either side. He was a survivor; and he kept his dry, sometimes grim, but always witty Russian humor. In a speech at the seventieth anniversary of the eminent American physicist Victor Weisskopf in Boston in 1988, he called on the ghost of Trofim Lysenko, a man who endeared himself to Stalin's regime after cooking up a Marxist-Leninist "genetics" theory—that individuals are wholly products of their environments—that was completely at odds with classic Mendelian theory. Velikhov suspected that SDI too was a foil for political opportunism, and chose to make his point by targeting another guest, Edward Teller.

"Edward was very unhappy," Velikhov recalls with a sly grin. "I said I thought that SDI came from the same roots as Lysenko's philosophy in the field of biology. He was very upset. Afterwards he spoke to me. 'It is very unfair,' he said, 'to make such a comparison.' "[53]

For their part, Velikhov's political and military counterparts were in no mood for humor. The specter of a nuclear first strike was, once again, a possibility. SDI reminded the Kremlin of Russia's technical backwardness; worse, if it worked it would make their formidable missile arsenal obsolete. How else, except with a first strike, could Soviet Russia protect its superpower status, which depended on its nuclear weapons and the MAD balance? But what would be the consequences of such a strike? No one wanted to think about them. The political situation was also grim. Grenada had been an embarrassment, a failed proxy war in miniature. There was the peculiar personality of Ronald Reagan to deal with, not to mention the conflict in Afghanistan, which with American help had become a zone of deadly guerrilla warfare. The world had suddenly become harshly unpredictable, a situation that this creaky regime was ill-equipped to handle.

Velikhov's clear voice tried to cut through the bureaucratic angst—and he was right to assert both his scientific opinion and his distrust of secrecy. But hardly anyone was listening.

9

RESCUING THE INFANT SDI

It's not possible to have a perfect defense, but there can be a defense so good that the Soviet leadership, or anyone else contemplating a direct attack on the U.S. with long-range ballistic missiles, would have to ask, "Dare I launch a 5 percent effective attack?"
—Daniel O. Graham[1]

Jim Abrahamson officially took office on March 27, 1984; the SDI Office (SDIO) was chartered on March 29 and made indelible by presidential decree on April 27. The internal tugs-of-war among various sectors of Soviet officialdom seemed, and were, very far away. Abrahamson was scratching his head in his tiny office—"a kind of a closet in the Pentagon where Bob Cooper and Bob Rankine sat"—trying to figure out who would fit best as his second in command.

One possible candidate was Gen. Daniel O. Graham, who had spent thirty years in the military, much of it in intelligence with a specialty in Soviet affairs and expertise in missile defense systems and satellite surveillance. In the 1970s he was appointed deputy director of the CIA, then director of the Defense Intelligence Agency. A military hawk, he advised Reagan on defense matters in two campaigns. He had been intrigued by Project Defender's BAMBI missile-defense concept, and in 1981 he created High Frontier Inc., a policy organization intended to study and promote defensive systems in space. Graham was fond of the nightlife and a connoisseur of fine food, and he had an extraordinarily creative, unusual personality. "Danny Graham was a colorful guy," Abrahamson said. "He once wandered around in the Pentagon in a Russian general's uniform, just to see if anyone would notice, and he never got stopped. He proved his point.

"There were some people who were extremely committed to the concept, and anxious to go immediately into some deployment program. But I knew we would never get through the political gauntlet with that kind of people. I needed balanced technical judgment, someone who was credible and could not be stereotyped as being over on the wild side."[2]

And then there was Gerry Yonas. After running the directed-energy part of the Fletcher study in the summer of 1983, he had returned to Sandia unconvinced of the merits of SDI and with the full intention of returning to his work in inertial confinement fusion research. But not long afterward, in November, he received a phone call from Bob Rankine summoning him back to Washington. When Rankine explained he needed help to "put some flesh on the Fletcher proposal," Yonas was incredulous. "The twenty-six-billion-dollar thing? You really want to get on with it?" When Rankine affirmed that yes, he did, Yonas heard himself saying, "Okay, I'll do it."[3]

"We thought it was important to have a scientific element in the panel, since a lot of our opposition was in the scientific community," explained Pete Worden. "I'd gotten to know Gerry a little bit on the Fletcher study. He had a wicked sense of humor, and I thought he could bring a different perspective to the group. When Abrahamson met him, he liked him instantly."[4]

"I didn't know about Gerry before that," admitted Abrahamson. "But when I learned of his reputation, his name rose to the top very quickly. Several people said he was the right man. So I started calling him."[5] Abrahamson said everyone he talked to "admired Gerry and thought he had the right personality at this critical time when there had to be a lot of interfaces with the public."[6] There would be times, however, when he would question his early opinion that Yonas was not canted to the "wild side."

Abrahamson then called a group of candidate staffers to the Cape for his first SDI meeting. "Naturally Abe needed help, so he looked at all the likely suspects," recalled Yonas. "He phoned me and said, 'I'm down here at the Cape and I'm launching these Shuttles. Would you please come down and tell me some background on SDI and give me a jump start.'" Yonas flew down to Orlando and drove to Cape Canaveral in a rental car. "It was the first time I had met Abe," he said. He appreciated the general's forthrightness and his businesslike mien. "I was very much impressed by his outgoing personality," Yonas said, "and his willingness to get input and listen."[7] About a month later, they met again at the Pentagon. After an initial discussion, Yonas said, "You know, we'd like to help you out at Sandia Labs." And then Abrahamson popped the question: "If you want to help, come and be my deputy director."

"No problem," said Yonas, surprised and not giving himself time to think. "When do you want me?'

"Tomorrow," replied Abrahamson.

He meant what he said. "He was serious," said Yonas. "Abe was always totally convinced of his dreams. . . . he was totally genuine, with total enthusiasm."[8] The plan was that Yonas would be loaned to the Department of Defense for a couple of years as Abrahamson's deputy director. But back home in Albuquerque, George Dacey, a Bell Labs veteran and Sandia director, determined that Yonas could not accept that position while working at the same time for Sandia. Abrahamson solved the problem by making Yonas his chief scientist and *acting* deputy director.

It took Yonas about two months to find a school for his younger daughter, Jodi, find a house in Washington, rent out his house in Albuquerque, pack, and move. Once in Washington, the family camped at a hotel for a couple of weeks with their two kids and two dogs, waiting for their effects to arrive.[9] Eventually the Department of Defense moved the Yonases into a house that the previous tenants had left with dirty walls and ceilings. Yonas's wife Jane, undoubtedly his match for irreverence, enjoys recounting the time when, just before Abrahamson was about to visit their house, she wrote "SDI Sucks" on the ceiling with blasts of 409 cleaner. She explains that she did it because, "I wanted Gerry to wash the ceiling." He did.[10]

Why did Yonas join SDI when he had decided, by the end of the Fletcher study, that the idea had little chance of succeeding? He is unable to provide a well-defined logic for the decision, other than he liked Abrahamson. Jane Yonas said it appealed to his sense of adventure. "It was a challenge; it was fun, exciting," she said. "And there's always that glimmer of hope."[11] Yonas didn't dispute the point.

"After delays of about two months," said Yonas, "I showed up for work in the Matomic building at 1717 H Street, Northwest, and found two dozen demoralized people housed in a dilapidated office building without air conditioning, without security, and without a clue of how to go about managing a $1.5 billion, rapidly growing program. The first person who saw me said, 'Thank God you're here!'

"When I asked to see the classified proposals that industry was sending in, I was taken to a room that was open to the public corridor and filled with unlocked safes brimming with secret documents. There were no guards, no access control. I was told the safes were unlocked because they were borrowed and nobody had combinations for them." Yonas immediately told the colonel in charge to rent an eighteen-wheeler, load it with the safes, and drive around and around on the Beltway because he thought that would be more secure. When the baffled colonel said it couldn't be done, Yonas told him to lock the safes and get a locksmith. Thus, the SDIO began to learn Yonas's way of doing business—first the nonsense, then the reality. "Eventually the program grew to hundreds of people housed in plush office space created out of the old bus tunnels under the Pentagon," he recalled, "but that first year of the program was wild and woolly."[12]

SDI consolidated the missile defense research and development programs of the U.S. Army, Navy, and Air Force, along with those of the Department of Energy and the Department of Defense's DARPA and Defense Nuclear Agency. From the Air Force, SDI inherited what would be the Boost Surveillance and Tracking System, Space Surveillance and Tracking System (originally conceived for more conventional defense), and the Strategic Laser Technology Program.

Yonas stayed with Abrahamson from 1984 to 1986, providing technical management, oversight, and strategic planning during the SDIO's formative years; playing a key role in emerging programs; creating the new organization's international programs; and studying early deployment strategies. Above all, he marketed the program. Yonas saw absolutely no technical way to do what Reagan said he wanted. On the other hand, what did the president actually say? The fact was that Reagan had no plan at all. Yonas figured that maybe there was a reason for that. It might be that only perception mattered. Even if you don't have the technical means to do what you say you want to do, "it is not that important, and does not matter, as long as you win the mind game." SDI was nothing new. Even deterrence—mutually assured destruction—did not consist simply of having a counterstrike force sufficient to beat the other side to a pulp. "Deterrence is a mind game. There was never anything real about MAD—the whole thing was a game of bluff, a game of chicken."[13]

Within one week of his arrival in Washington, Yonas was on the road explaining the program to thousands of anxious contractors, who were ready to dip into what they hoped would be a treasure trove of funding. "What really was happening, however, was practically nothing." The contractors loved Yonas—cupboard love—but it was a different matter when he began meeting with academic audiences. "You'd think this was the most evil thing that ever happened, he said. "I would go to anywhere in the Northeast—to MIT or the University of Chicago—and they would burn me in effigy and they would have epithets written on their T-shirts. SDI was such an *evil* thing!"[14]

The outlook was far from bullish. Yonas was experiencing plenty of challenge but this was worse—he was winning absolutely no sup-

port. Congress really wasn't that interested; more than that, most senators and representatives plainly didn't like SDI. The man from New
Mexico began to get very worried. "I thought, 'My God, what have I
done?'" he said. "I'd rented my own house to somebody, I rented
another house in Washington, I put my kid into a private school in
Washington, my [elder] daughter was going to start at Stanford—now
I was on the East Coast, and I was stuck. At SDIO, we didn't have
any money other than what we had inherited—about half a billion
dollars—and we were talking about spending twenty-seven billion dollars. So it was obvious from the start that we had to get an appropria-
tion. We had to get some real money. But then Congress really wasn't
all that turned on by all this stuff.

"A lot of the people in the Pentagon didn't like it either. It was
clear the money was going to come out of their hides because Weinberger had clearly said, 'The money's going to come out of your hide.
So you will all ante up in this poker game, and all the chips are going
to go to . . .' We didn't actually know who was going to get the chips,
but Weinberger said, indicating me, 'Here's this guy who's going to
hold all the chips, and maybe you'll get some back, depending how
good your proposal is.' "[15]

Then, that June, a wonderful thing happened. It was the most
significant thing ever done for SDI, and yet the SDIO had nothing
whatsoever to do with it. The Army was working on a project called
the Homing Overlay Experiment (HOE), using a modified Minuteman ICBM to launch a missile that, when it went to work, looked like
a rocket with an umbrella on the end of it.* The Army launched from
Kwajalein (later renamed the Ronald Reagan Test Site) in the South
Pacific, seeking a Sandia-designed target launched from Vandenberg
Air Force Base. It missed three times. There was only one HOE missile
left, and a lot of skepticism; the project looked quite hopeless. But the
fourth missile found its target.

Until this happened, Yonas was seriously concerned that his move
to Washington had been a terrible mistake. "All of Washington sniped
at SDI," he said. "Things were going badly and I was feeling misera-
ble. We had maybe half a dozen professionals, trying to put together a
program to manage two and a half billion dollars. We said we'd get the
money, but there seemed no hope of getting it.

"But this thing, the rocket-borne umbrella, hit. It hit dead on.

---

*Once the sensor locked on its target successfully, the HOE system would unfurl
a 15-ft. umbrella-like net, and collide with the dummy target, a technique reminiscent
of SPAD, one of ARPA's BAMBI systems. But SPAD rockets would be launched from
satellites too big to be orbited by then-available technology.

There was joy in Mudville. It was a home run. And from then on it was, 'Hey, this thing works. We can do this thing. We have proof of principle, and proof of manhood, and we were credible.' "[16]

Abrahamson, Worden, and Fred Hoffman of the Fletcher Commission described the HOE experiment with these words:

> [A] mock warhead was fired from Vandenberg Air Force Base in California to the Kwajalein missile range thousands of kilometers away in the Pacific Ocean. When radar sensors at Kwajalein detected the incoming warhead, a missile containing the non-nuclear KEW interceptor was fired. After leaving the atmosphere, this device opened up an infrared heat-seeking sensor that detected the incoming warhead. A computer controlled a rocket engine on the interceptor to maneuver it into the path of the warhead and execute a direct collision over one hundred miles up in space.[17]

The HOE legend is entangled with a conspiracy theory that was given to the *New York Times* by spokespersons from the American Physical Society (APS). The Army, the APS claimed, had made sure that a radio-controlled explosive was concealed within the target rocket, so that it would appear to be destroyed by the collision with the interceptor even if the experiment was a failure. But Yonas was convinced of its success. The flash of plasma-produced light from the event was bigger and more extensive than could have been caused by a small explosive. Even the Soviets, watching from their trawlers, must have noticed this.

"HOE gave us the leverage to play the mind game on the Soviets even though there was no thought-through approach to make it happen," Yonas said. "There was no conspiracy—no plot, no plan, no smoke and no mirrors. HOE was one of those lucky strikes."[18]

"I believe HOE was the single most important event in the entire SDI story."[19]

Sen. David Pryor of Arkansas would attack the HOE results again in 1993, generating a front-page article, an editorial in the *New York Times*, and a congressional request that the General Accounting Office (GAO) take a look. The GAO report confirmed that the first two of the HOE series featured "a deception program," but that the second two did not. "GAO found no evidence that DOD deceived Congress about HOE-4 intercepting the target," it concluded. "Analyses of HOE-4 test data are consistent with the Army's conclusion that the interceptor and target collided."

As Maj. Gen. Eugene Fox, who was in charge of the Army's

BMD program at the time of HOE-4, put it, "President Reagan, as part of his Strategic Defense Initiative, wanted non-nuclear defensive weapons, and HOE proved it was possible with conventional kinetic energy weapons." [20]

While Velikhov still thinks HOE was a staged show, others—like Soviet Col. Gen. Yuri Votintsev, who had general oversight of Sary Shagan and witnessed the success of the Soviet antimissile missile epic—were inclined to be believers.[21] If the APS scenario had been true, and the explosion over Kwajalein had produced the wrong kind of plasma signature, the Soviet leadership would likely have taken an entirely different view not only of HOE, but of SDI as well.

Congress appropriated $1.4 billion for SDI in Fiscal Year 1985, $2.67 billion in FY 1986, $3.27 billion in FY 1987, $3.6 billion in FY 1988, $3.74 billion in FY 1989, and $3.6 billion in FY 1990. But Weinberger noted, in his book *Fighting for Peace*, that he had to battle against "deeply entrenched support for the theory of Mutual Assured Destruction, and the congressional feeling that anything that violated MAD had to be bad."[22] Each year's appropriations had to be "wrung from the Congress after protracted and highly confrontational hearings."[23]

From the beginning, Abrahamson and Yonas realized that managing SDI could become a gargantuan effort: if ever the project went into high gear it would almost certainly rival the Manhattan Project. Directed-energy weapons projects (missiles, space-based lasers, ground-based lasers, x-ray lasers, and particle beams) were just one part of SDI, accounting for only about 25 percent of its budget.[24] Surveillance, acquisition, tracking, and kill assessment required a large investment. Then there were issues of survivability, lethality, and "key technologies" that included power supplies, launch vehicle needs, and methods for protecting the overall system. But the most critical element was system architecture and battle management—creating the intricate spider's web of technological magic that would join this organism of man and machine together and make it work in battle, real-time and fail-safe.

In addition to HOE, four or five other kinetic energy weapons—KEWs or kinetic kill vehicles—were under development at various sites at this time, identified with such acronyms as ERIS, FLAGE, and HEDI. Defensive weapons of this kind theoretically could be deployed in space or on the ground and, unlike systems of the Nike-Zeus type, did not do their damage with nuclear explosions. Their time would come. But for now, laser and particle beam weapons held the center stage because they were flashy devices operating at or near the speed of light. Like the rail gun, many would be hard to put in orbit because of their power consumption—the public would frown on having a nuclear generator in space and building a completely new heavy-lift launch system to put it there. On the other hand, lasers energized by chemical reaction would carry their own short-lived energy supply into orbit. Orbiting mirrors, computer-controlled and unbelievably precise, might be used when necessary to flip the lethal beams onto their thin-skinned targets.

Neutral particle beam research had been under way for decades at Los Alamos, where scientists were working on a project code-named White Horse. On July 29, 1989, the first NPB device in space was launched aboard the BEAR (Beam Experiments Aboard a Rocket), lofted with an Ares rocket at White Sands Missile Range. By then it had been established that an NPB weapon could discriminate between real RV warheads and decoys.[25] However, the weight problem was not solved, and again the public was leery of the idea of putting nuclear reactors in space. NPBs became all but forgotten, except as esoteric start-up sources for use in the ITER international fusion program.

Whatever the mechanism, high-tech weapons in space were a dream fit to send sci-fi enthusiasts and techno-nerds into a state of nirvana. But it wouldn't just happen. The administration had imposed caveats upon itself, almost as if to dampen the ardor of SDI's supporters. Frank Miller of Weinberger's staff testified before a subcommittee of the House Committee on Foreign Affairs on July 26, 1984:

> If at some point in the future, the end of this decade, the beginning of the next, the administration decided to come to the Congress to ask you to fund full-scale development and beginning deployment, that administration would have to convince you, as well as itself, that such a system would be effective; that it would be cost-effective; and that it would be survivable. Whether a defense system can be developed with these three characteristics is what this entire [SDI] research program is designed to find out.[26]

Richard Garwin used these prerequisites to underscore his contention that, in SDI, "myths are not benign." If the three proofs were not met, he wrote, "then SDI can compel an offensive arms race rather than quench it; it can provoke nuclear war rather than prevent it. Therefore, even the attractive myth (if such it were) of effectiveness, survivability, and low cost for SDI would be downright dangerous."[27] In the autumn of 1984, Fletcher published a detailed and somewhat more positive article in *Issues in Science and Technology*, a National Academy of Sciences publication.[28] The article projected confidence that SDI was "doable," and that deployment of just two of the four phases could protect "perhaps 90 or even 99 percent" of the U.S. population and infrastructure.

"These critical technologies may well require research programs of ten to twenty years before they are ready for deployment in a ballistic missile system," Fletcher said, though "it may be possible to begin deploying portions of the system in the 1990s." Admiral Watkins doubted this. "Reagan got it all screwed up, and so did Weinberger, saying you could deploy such a thing within twenty years," he said. "We never said that. Never did the Joint Chiefs say that. All we said was, 'Let's have an accelerated R&D program and not get involved in ABM Treaty violations.'"[29] Shultz, too, harbored some doubts. He commented later that he had "a certain amount of exposure to salesmanship" from scientists and engineers during his time at MIT and Bechtel, and he thought the SDI labs had come up with some "extravagant claims." He was concerned that Abrahamson might be passing these claims on to the president.

It may be an understatement to say that the Soviets were deeply divided over what to do about SDI. The Military Industrial Commission and parts of the Ministry of Defense thought they should mount their own "SDIsky." Others, like Velikhov, suspected it would be just as well to wait and see, and to rely on antisatellite weapons if the Americans managed to build space ABM assets. Meanwhile, KGB Directorate T's priorities for 1984 were worded to include intelligence on missiles and "the development of qualitatively new types of weapons (space devices for multiple use for military purposes, laser and pencil beam weapons, non-acoustic anti-submarine defense weapons, electronic warfare weapons, etc.)."[30]

The CIA's Herb Meyer sensed a "growing sense of pessimism and looming decline" in mid-1985 Moscow. "In a vague but very profound way," he wrote to Casey, "Soviet leaders are starting to recognize that something has gone hideously wrong. We are not talking here about merely a bad stretch in relations with the U.S. or a temporary run of bad luck; we are talking here of a perceived fundamental shift in the balance of future power. History is no longer on Moscow's side—if ever it was—and Soviet leaders sense the lack of the wit, the energy, the resources, and above all the time, to win it back." He was also concerned that the Soviets might yet attempt a first strike, cautioning that, "at all costs we must be so strong defensively that even in their worst moments, Soviet leaders won't be tempted to let their missiles fly in some sort of desperate, last-ditch gamble to destroy everybody in hopes that they will emerge in control of the wreckage."[31]

Jay Keyworth and others were stumping for SDI while vocal critics, and numerous luminaries including Bethe and Garwin, were engaged in a vigorous counteroffensive. The two sides published opposing articles in the Fall 1984 issue of *Issues in Science and Technology*, with Keyworth describing a world where nine billion tons of nuclear explosive power—his estimate of the combined U.S. and Soviet arsenals—was poised to wreak holocaust upon the Earth. "It is clear," he said, "that a large portion of the earth's population—perhaps a quarter billion people or considerably more—could die as the result of a global thermonuclear war involving even a fraction of present-day arsenals." High-tech defense was presented an attractive option: "We must start to play our trump—technological leverage."[32]

Yonas was bemused that, while the science and technology aspect of SDI was well documented in this period, the story was never put into a deeper sociological and psychological context. How was it that even after reputable scientists said SDI would never work as advertised, Soviet decision-makers were still afraid of it? Surely it was clear that something was at work beyond the points brought out by U.S. science-establishment critics. As patriots, why did they fight SDI if they thought the Soviets were worried by it? Were they concerned that the SDIO was trying to steal money from real science, were they trying to straighten out the misguided Soviets, or were they just fighting for what was right—the idea of physics as the search for some kind of universal truth—and the integrity of science? Yonas suspected that the main reason they opposed it was basically simple: it threatened their long-standing respect for deterrence and the ABM treaty.[33]

Another Secret Space Spectacular

While the Americans were arguing fine points on whether HOE was a success or a deception, the Soviets took it very seriously indeed and made a sudden decision. They would build a titanic space battle station, with a new ultra-heavy-lift launch system, Energiya, to put it into orbit. If certain Americans had known what was planned, and the various armaments that had been proposed to put aboard this space-age behemoth, they would have gone into orbit as well.

For years the Soviet Union had been designing orbital battle stations, even before 1976, when Energiya's chief designer, Valentin Glushko, took over the top-secret Skif project. Early in its history, there were two Skif versions, one equipped to attack low-Earth-orbit targets with lasers, another to attack higher-orbit targets with missiles. The concept evolved considerably, and in 1981 developmental work was transferred to the Salyut design bureau (for the station itself) and Astrofizika (for a giant 60-ton laser). A third element, the heavy-lift booster, was being developed by Energiya.

Immediately after the success of HOE-4 in June 1984, a great flurry of activity began at Khrunichev, the former Moscow auto and aircraft plant that Chelomei had transformed into a spacecraft production center. At last the grand concept of the mid-1970s—Skif, redesigned and publicly named Polyus—was to emerge from its experimental stage and become a real, honest-to-God orbiting battle station, complete with radar-fooling stealth features. Polyus went into production on July 1, as a breakneck, crash program watched closely by the Soviet missiles and space minister, "Big" Oleg Baklanov, and his second in command, "Little" Oleg Shishkin.

"As a rule, no excuses were entertained," recalls a writer familiar with the Soviet's Buran Space Shuttle program, "nor was the fact that almost the same team of developers was simultaneously carrying out the great work on building 'Buran.' Everything was dedicated to adhering to the deadlines which had been set—a clear example of 'administrative team' leadership methods: an ambitious idea, ambitious execution of the idea, ambitious deadlines, and—'money is no object.'"[34] Some time later, Chief Designer Yuri Kornilov of the Salyut Design Bureau called this a capricious project and added that the conditions of the breakneck construction effort had been "unacceptable."

The Polyus model was enormous—more than 120 feet long and thirteen and a half feet in diameter—and it reportedly had four sustainer engines, twenty orientation engines, and sixteen stabilization engines.[35] The spacecraft would weigh 80 tons and the launch system would need 2,000 tons of rocket fuel. It was once estimated that this type of "Orbital Weapons Platform" could deliver nuclear warheads to any point in the United States in six minutes. With the passage of time, all sorts of information—leaks, rumors, speculations, with perhaps some truth mixed in—surfaced about Polyus's likely payload, which might include laser weapons, nuclear space mines, satellite launchers, and/or laser and radar targeting systems. Naturally not all would fly, and perhaps none, but the list went on—and it was awesome.

All this, and nobody in the West knew a thing about it. Baklanov did plan to put a laser in the Polyus, albeit mostly for show. "We set great hopes on laser weapons for a number of years," lamented Igor Bobyrev, a ministry of defense industry deputy department chief.[36] But it wasn't going to happen. While several types of lasers were being developed for possible future space use—chemical, carbon-dioxide, solid-state, etc.—none was ready for full-scale application. Baklanov had pressed on regardless, for he believed his spaceship would represent a dazzling political success. Launching any kind of "space-based laser" (in itself a magical term) could be interpreted as a great victory over the American rivals. And who knew? A successful launch might provide some limited technical information for his design team.

Debating on the Home Front

On August 2, 1984, as Soviet engineers were settling into their heroic 24/7 routine at Khrunichev, Nevada's dry lakes shook with yet another x-ray laser test, Correo, this time staged by the Los Alamos lab. The Lawrence Livermore lab had reported the first evidence of x-ray lasing with the Romano test of December 16, 1983; but after Correo, Livermore's feisty lab sister gave up the idea and concluded that Teller's people based their results on readings from faulty instrumentation. In his book *Teller's War*, William J. Broad published a report that LLNL's assistant director for nuclear design, George H. Miller, received a "caustic" letter from Paul Robinson, then at Los Alamos. It said, in effect, that "Los Alamos doubted that the existence of the x-ray laser had been demonstrated and that Livermore managers were losing their credibility because of their failure to stand up to Teller and [Lowell] Wood."[37]

But Teller and his protégé Wood weren't yet ready to give up on the x-ray laser. If anything, Teller was encouraged by a new DIA report that a Soviet space-based beam weapon might be ready for testing in the 1990s.[38] It would help him raise money. Others wondered how the Russians could build such a system when (1) America was concerned about having enough computer muscle to underpin its own program, and (2) the Soviet information technology effort was lagging behind the West by fifteen years.[39]

By the end of 1984, U.S. support for SDI was still fairly strong but beginning to flag. A Gallup Poll indicated in October of that year that 47 percent of Americans were opposed to SDI, and another conducted by CBS and the *New York Times* found that 48 percent believed it would escalate the arms race.[40]

Not surprisingly, the media were having a field day with strategic defense. The *New York Times* published hundreds of thousands of words on the SDI debate in 1985—including two lengthy series—in an editorial adrenalin rush that earned the newspaper a Pulitzer Prize. Media historians may well muse upon whether this phenomenon provided the vital spark that scared the Kremlin enough to take SDI even more seriously, whether that fear turned the political tide of Soviet history, and whether this was the tiny straw that broke the Bolshevik camel's back. *Aviation Week*'s coverage, though the magazine was also very much respected in the Kremlin, could be said to be the writings of a journal committed to the U.S. military-industrial complex and its lifeline of advertising dollars; but not the words of the revered *New York Times.*

That same spring, Abrahamson took on Harold Brown, a nuclear physicist and formerly President Jimmy Carter's defense secretary, who had called the potential for SDI's success "negligibly low." In March, Abrahamson told the *Times:*

> There is very little question that we can build a very highly effective defense against ballistic missiles someday. The question is how soon and how affordable and what degrees of effectiveness can initial steps allow us. . . . What is really happening is that there are a large number of dedicated, talented people working on this in Government and industry. And when they all have a goal to march to, and that's what the President gave us, you just cannot stop the progress they are making and that progress is what's happening.[41]

John D. G. Rather, a high-energy laser consultant, told the *Times* that an *offensive* laser attack against ground targets could "take an industrialized country back to an 18th-century level in 30 minutes." After all, he said, "anything that involves large amounts of energy can be used for good or evil purposes. A system of space battle stations designed to stop a nuclear attack also may have the potential to attack selected targets in space, in the atmosphere, or down on the surface of the earth." Rather predicted that the first country to have space-based laser weapons would have "the capability for unilateral control of outer space and consequent dominion of the earth."[42]

As the media and others dissected the technical and arms-control aspects of SDI, the initiative evolved into an enormous geopolitical football. Yonas was perplexed when, in debates with opposition spokesmen like Dick Garwin and Greg Canavan, they seemed to want a simple answer to the question, "Will it work?" To him, the issue was more complex. "I kept asking, 'What is *it*?'" Yonas said.

Gerold Yonas had Russian friends but had no illusions about their nation's insistence on continuing the nuclear arms race. "The expectation that the ABM Treaty would lead to strategic arms limitations has been shattered by the consistent buildup in Soviet strategic forces, predominantly directed toward ICBMs that are capable of destroying hardened targets as well as toward submarine-launched ballistic missiles, or SLBMs," he wrote in 1985. "In numerical terms, the Soviet

Union now has close to 3,000 long-range ballistic missiles, compared with about 1,700 in 1970, and in the same 15 years its nuclear warheads have quadrupled to more than 10,000."[43]

Yonas had little more to say publicly about what the Soviets might or might not be doing in space weaponry, but he was very knowledgeable about their defensive systems. When he characterized them as "awesome," people tended to believe him. "It includes 7,000 air-surveillance radars," he wrote, "some 10,000 surface-to-air missile launchers, 12,000 interceptor aircraft and about 100 ground-level launchers located around Moscow in the world's only operational ABM system."[44]

For their part, the Soviets had been trying to figure out why the Americans, despite their high degree of technical advancement, were backing a new missile defense idea that had pretty much failed in the Soviet Union. "Once we realized that it would never work, we began to suspect that those who were trying to promote it were cheating; that they wanted to hide something behind the façade of SDI," said Sagdeev. "I think that the moment Gorbachev understood that SDI wouldn't work, he decided that those who were trying to push a futile system must have some kind of hidden agenda. Even some military spokesmen thought it was obvious that SDI would not work for the purpose it was advertised. So they reasoned that those who were trying to push it forward probably were planning to use the cover of SDI to deliver nuclear weapons from orbit."[45]

The KGB wasn't much help; in fact it seems they tended to think that SDI might be a winning proposition, for whatever reason. Evgeny Velikhov was not privy to the reports on SDI compiled by the KGB First Directorate (external intelligence). "But," he said, "I suspect that they overestimated the potential of SDI. This is understandable because they had no real knowledge, while we knew exactly what the laser weapon represented: how difficult it is to make, the quality of propagation, the quality of light, how it works—we knew all the details and they did not. They knew more than ordinary people, but still it was not what one would term real knowledge."[46]

In 1985 Velikhov put together a study group from the Academy of Sciences and military institutes to evaluate a number of advanced concepts including lasers, electromagnetic guns, and electrodynamic weapons. Again he expressed deep skepticism for the efficacy of directed-energy weapons for ABM defense. The view was quite different in the United States, where a Defense Intelligence Agency report hazarded that a Soviet ground-based laser ballistic missile defense system might be ready by the early- to mid-1990s, with a prototype space-based NPB ready for testing in the late 1990s. It went on to suggest that several high-power lasers, for air defense, antisatellite, and ABM use, were under development at Sary Shagan.[47]

MARKETING, MANAGEMENT, AND MOVEMENT

While rhetoric raged in print and lecture halls (some 2,300 scientists signed a declaration that they would not take SDI money), SDI research was recording some interesting dual-purpose results. For example, on September 5, 1986, the SDIO completed the Delta 180 program, which approximated parts of a boost-phase intercept and collected information on the infrared "signature" emitted from such targets. The experiment, held at the Air Force Eastern Test Range at Cape Canaveral, strongly suggested that the United States could "hit a bullet with a bullet." It was also a successful political hit, scoring a special impact in the Soviet Union. "It demonstrated to the Soviets that we intended to move forward very aggressively," Worden said. "It was a good thing to do to show that we were ready to move very quickly.[48]

Boost-phase intercept would be ideal. But, musing over the program at his house in the leafy environs of Washington, Yonas knew that the most feasible near-term approach to SDI, if there were any, would be a ground-based system for midcourse interception. That, again, was the HOE idea. But then something else might come up. He liked to say that his team operated on the Yogi Berra principle—when you come to a fork in the road, take it! They didn't know exactly what they were doing, but they kept moving.[49]

Abrahamson toured the contractors, checking their progress and giving them what he called "the ultimatum," which was the delivery date. The ultimatum was particularly hard on Ford Aerospace, who was behind schedule in the production of a 26-pound gizmo—a multi-spectral infrared sensor—that would track a target up to the point of impact.

"They were a little bit behind schedule," said Abrahamson. "I told them, 'You're going to be on this launch one way or another, either with your sensor or with twenty-six pounds of lead weight, but we're not waiting for you.' So they actually created this 26-pound lead weight in the shape of the sensor package. Whoever was the most behind in the sequence ended up with this lead weight on his desk. He couldn't get rid of it—it just sat there until he got out of the hole in his schedule and the weight was passed on to the next guy.

"It was a very clever approach. It was so good I wanted to show it to the president. I called the Secret Service and said, 'I've got this

26-pound lead weight that I want to bring in on Monday morning before the Cabinet meeting.' 'We can't x-ray a lead weight,' they said. 'Do you know what's in it?' I said it contained nothing, 'It's just a lead weight.'" After a few minutes of wrangling, the security people finally let Abrahamson put the strange-looking object on the president's desk. The experiment was a success. "It was a kind of management motivational approach that Reagan could really latch onto," Abrahamson said. "He thought it was great: he understood motivating people."[50]

While Abe attended to the myriad administrative details of SDI, Yonas alternated between various personas—the marketer, the scientist, the social philosopher. But, as he said on several occasions, "My business is show business.

"In a year we placed about 850 contracts and committed a billion dollars," he said. "We figured out how to look for answers. Our motto was, 'You have to kiss a lot of frogs to find the prince.' And we were in the frog-kissing business.

"After the president's speech, I had asked for seven billion, eight billion, for my beam weapon program. I said, 'Let me have seven or eight billion dollars, and at the end of five years I'll tell you whether or not there's anything here.' And they said, 'You want seven or eight billion dollars? What are you offering us? An enigma inside a paper bag, surrounded by a "Secret" cover?' And I said, in a low key way, with a kind of a simple look, 'Well, the president wants it.'

"We had laid out plans for huge, *huge* ambitious programs. It was mind-boggling. We were fearless; we were going to do it; we were going to build these things. If we ran into trouble, we had plenty of options. We were going to kiss all the frogs. One of them was going to work!"[51]

Abrahamson and Yonas were selling SDI and the Soviets were working out what to do to counter it—even suggesting to Reagan that, among other things, the two sides work toward cutting nuclear stockpiles and preventing the militarization of space. These efforts would, with time, be completely transformed by the arrival on the SDI scene of two world-changing political personalities: Margaret Thatcher and Mikhail Gorbachev.

RONNIE, MAGGIE, AND MIKE

Science is unstoppable: it will not be stopped for being ignored. The deployment of SDI, just like the deployment of nuclear weapons, must be carefully controlled and negotiated. But research, which necessarily involves testing, must go ahead.
—Margaret Thatcher[1]

Margaret Thatcher was indeed the Iron Lady. On October 12, 1984, she and her husband Denis escaped a massive bomb attack at the Conservative Party conference in Brighton, which killed five and injured thirty-four. Thatcher, though she was shocked and powdered with concrete dust by the blast, was defiant. "All attempts to destroy democracy by terrorism will fail," she declared.[2] An Irish Republican Army note retorted, "Today we were unlucky, but remember, we only have to be lucky once; you will have to be lucky always."[3] She was undeterred.

Bomb or no bomb, there was a wide world beyond the watery confines of little England, and Thatcher believed her destiny lay there too. She was concerned about how SDI might affect world stability and who would replace the rapidly failing Soviet general secretary, Konstantin Chernenko. She went over the possibilities repeatedly in her London flat perched in the rafters high over the black Georgian door of No. 10, and in the graceful comfort of Chequers, the Elizabethan country retreat of successive prime ministers and the closest British equivalent for Camp David.

By this time Thatcher was a good friend of Reagan and an SDI expert. She and Jim Abrahamson also had developed a mutual respect, the general observing that "the sparks just flew around her intellect and her questions."[4] She had been briefed by General Keegan. And she understood technology. "Of all the people that understood what we were doing and the implications of it, Mrs. Thatcher was best," he said. "Most of the world leaders I had an opportunity to brief just didn't understand the technical stuff."[5] But now Thatcher needed to develop her relationship with other side of the equation—the Soviets. Accordingly, at her invitation, Mikhail Gorbachev and his wife Raisa arrived at Chequers at lunchtime on December 16, 1984, accompanied by Aleksandr Yakovlev, the behind-the-scenes anti-Stalinist whom history would proclaim architect of perestroika and the father of glasnost.

Thatcher had scored a Western first in arranging this meeting with the future Soviet leader. She "felt she had discovered him, in a way," said Sir Charles Powell, then her private secretary and later a life peer with the title Lord Charles David Powell of Bayswater. At Chequers, after arguing briskly throughout lunch, what was billed as a forty-five-minute conversation blossomed into a three-hour meeting. "I think he valued her ability to interpret what the Americans were thinking," Powell said. "Both were very talkative. At one time it seemed she talked without drawing her breath for about twenty minutes. I remember sending her a handwritten note, 'PM, I think you're talking too much.' She read it without stopping. Then, again without stopping talking, she wrote a note and pushed it back. 'I know,' it read."[6]

Reagan's second term was about to begin, and Gorbachev was eager to pump Thatcher for all she knew about the president. Was Reagan someone he could do business with? What were his views on nuclear weaponry? And what were her opinions of SDI? Thatcher portrayed Reagan as a trustworthy and peace-loving man, said she thought he would be interested in arms control, and assured Gorbachev that this might be a good time for negotiation. But her support was not without reservation. "I made it clear that, while I was strongly in favor of the Americans going ahead with SDI, I did not share President Reagan's view that it was a means of ridding the world entirely of nuclear weapons," she wrote in *The Downing Street Years*. "This seemed to me an unattainable dream—you could not disinvent the knowledge of how to make such weapons." On the other hand, she made it clear—twice—that "there was no question of dividing us: we would remain staunch allies of the United States."[7] Gorbachev, she felt, had spent an inordinate amount of time on SDI, urging her to convince the president not to go ahead with "space weapons"

They discussed, they argued, and they developed mutual respect. "It was clear," she wrote, "that we could negotiate in a different way with a different kind of person who was beginning to allow people in the Soviet Union to have freedom of worship and freedom of speech."[8]

Gorbachev was a refreshing surprise for westerners who were used to hosting elderly, party-lining Soviet bureaucrats in ill-fitting suits. He and his wife Raisa were well dressed, affable, and relatively young. Gorbachev radiated power, tempered by a sense of humor and knowledge of English culture. Thatcher felt that she established a good personal relationship at this meeting, and indeed a certain mutual understanding and respect—notwithstanding the tough negotiating style of each of them—would pervade their future association.

Immediately after the Gorbachev meeting, Thatcher and her close advisors flew to Hong Kong, where she would sign an agreement sealing the return of the crown colony to mainland China. Then they continued to Camp David for Thatcher's first visit to the presidential retreat in green and rural Maryland. At the back of Thatcher's mind was the suspicion that the president was being battered about by competing arms control proponents in his administration. In consideration of this apparent uncertainty, she felt she might need to lobby for a position that would be acceptable to Western leaders. The British position on SDI was mapped out in the PM's executive airliner, hours before the group arrived at Camp David. "We had a lot of time on our hands, so we were extremely well prepared by the time we arrived in America," recalled Powell.

The American and British contingents met on Saturday, December 22. "Shultz was there, but not Weinberger, much to his [Weinberger's] vexation," Powell said. "We went into a small room with John Kerr of the British embassy and sketched out the Camp David points. Then we took it off the typewriter and gave it to the Prime Minister. She agreed with the wording and handed it to Reagan, who handed it back and said it looked fine. Later she presented it more formally and this time Reagan handed it around. There was only one small change."[9]

Thatcher lectured Reagan for more than an hour, defending nuclear deterrence, warning that U.S. withdrawal from the ABM treaty could break up the alliance with Europe, and counseling against advanced SDI testing and deployment. Reagan had the right response. He would continue to observe the ABM treaty. He soothed her with the assurance that SDI was no more than a research program, and that many years would pass before anyone knew whether it was a practical proposition.

On November 17 Reagan had heard from General Secretary Chernenko, who stated that the Soviet Union was ready to go back to the negotiating tables with the purpose of cutting nuclear stockpiles and preventing the militarization of space. Now he talked to Thatcher with passion and idealism, describing SDI as a concept that was wholly defensive, that was not intended to give the United States a one-sided advantage, and that, if it was successful, would be shared with other countries. Not only that, but "he reaffirmed his long-term goal of getting rid of nuclear weapons altogether." The latter made Thatcher very nervous. As for sharing SDI, Thatcher said, "I was horrified to think that the United States would be prepared to throw away a hard-won lead in technology by making it internationally available."[10]

Reagan then reminded Thatcher that he was aware the Soviets could only squeeze so much money out of their pockets: their efforts to compete in the SDI arena would further overburden their shrunken budgets. But she had already seen a grand design behind the technological scenario. The important thing was "the likely reality rather than the grand vision"—Reagan's determination to complete a broad, crippling assault on the Soviet system. As was the case with so many people who dealt with the president, she was impressed by his ability to get above and beyond the details. "As so often, he had instinctively grasped the key to the whole question."[11]

The joint SDI policy put together by the Thatcher contingent contained four main points. While George Shultz believed they placed unnecessary limitations on the United States, Thatcher said they were "clear and defensible" and would ease the concerns of other European leaders. After undergoing a minor massage at Camp David, those points were

- The U.S., and Western, aim was not to achieve superiority, but to maintain balance, taking account of Soviet developments
- SDI-related deployment would, in view of treaty obligations, be a matter for negotiation
- The overall aim was to enhance, not undercut, deterrence
- East–West negotiation should aim to achieve security with reduced levels of offensive systems on both sides[12]

The statement slid into U.S. policy with lightning speed. "I wouldn't say the Brits came. I would say Margaret Thatcher came," Shultz said. "Reagan and Thatcher had a one-on-one on it, and they wound up agreeing on a statement."[13] At Camp David, Reagan gave it to National Security Advisor Robert McFarlane, who passed it to Shultz—and the deed was done. Weinberger might have raised a word or two against the accord, but he wasn't present and was furious when he heard what had happened in his absence. With time, some would refer to it by the grandiose title, "The Treaty of Camp David."

McFarlane went through a number of private agonies during the Thatcher visit, which started with what he considered to be "a withering attack" on the SDI concept. The idea had already caused havoc in the Soviet Union. "In a Strangelove-like way SDI had worked," he protested, and "Thatcher could have brought it down." She might have been a tad less resolute in her opinions that SDI was overly expensive (deterrence was better), that it would separate the United States from Europe (by removing the U.S. nuclear umbrella), and that it would support a first-strike capability.[14]

Since Reagan had not been able to rebut these points on the spot, McFarlane (who said the president had been "hand-bagged") and Colin Powell prepared a presidential statement making it clear that SDI was a research program and U.S. allies would be consulted if there were ever any intention to deploy it, and released it to the media.

"We papered over the differences as best we could," McFarlane said, "but it was clear there were issues. Ronald Reagan said, 'This is not good; it could affect the acceptability of SDI to the Congress. You'd better go over there and see if you can change her mind or at least mute the critique.'

"So in January I was at No. 10 Downing Street. I had only been talking for a few minutes when she interrupted, and I could see I wasn't going to change her mood. So I played the only card I thought I had. I had talked to Weinberger about subcontracting to British firms. 'But,' I said to her, 'the president wants us to work together. We have about $300 million in projects that we would like the British to help us with.'"[15] After that, he felt that she moderated her criticisms a little.

Sir Charles Powell may have thought that the Americans overreacted. "We didn't want to challenge SDI," he said. "We wanted to champion the idea that valuable research could be done in that area."[16]

From the beginning, Thatcher was a thoughtful believer in nuclear deterrence and favored deployment of U.S. intermediate-range nuclear missiles in Britain and elsewhere in Europe. "But," she wrote, "I soon began to see that SDI would strengthen not weaken the nuclear deterrent. Unlike President Reagan and some other members of his Administration I never believed that SDI could offer one hundred percent protection, but it would allow sufficient United States missiles to survive a first strike by the Soviets." Since there would then be a counterstrike, she concluded, "It follows that the Soviets would be far less likely to yield to the temptation to use nuclear weapons in the first place."[17]

Soviet Defense Minister Dmitry Ustinov died in December, and his son Nikolai, then general director of Astrofizika, subsequently disappeared from the high-energy laser scene. With the two Ustinovs gone, laser-weapon proponents in the military-industrial complex lost some of the political backbone from their remaining research and development apparatus. Chelomei died the same month, from an arterial blockage following a freak car accident at his dacha. But the complex's interest in putting large military systems in space continued unabated. A horde of engineers, technicians, and laborers remained on their 24/7 schedule, riveting and welding the giant Polyus orbiter together at Khrunichev, Chelomei's former production center.

Even as Velikhov and his colleagues were dabbling with their "asymmetric" response to SDI (Sagdeev suspects Gorbachev used the idea primarily "for propagandistic, rhetorical purposes"[18]), a 1985 Defense Intelligence Agency report hazarded that a Soviet ground-based laser ballistic missile defense might be ready by the early- to mid-1990s, with a prototype space-based NPB system ready for testing in the late 1990s. It went on to suggest that several high-power lasers—for air-defense, antisatellite, and ABM use—were under development at Sary Shagan, and it added that "a laser weapons program of the magnitude of the Soviet Union's effort would cost roughly $1 billion per year in the United States."[19]

Thatcher not only had a special relationship with Reagan—she had special access, too. While this put some cabinet noses out of joint, the Central Intelligence Agency had reasons for applauding the Reagan–Thatcher relationship. "Most of what CIA knew in 1985 about Gorbachev's personality and style was from his visit to Canada in 1983 and his visit to Britain in December 1984, where he had been such a hit with Prime Minister Thatcher," wrote Bill Casey's deputy and successor, Robert Gates. "We were embarrassingly hungry for details from our Canadian and British colleagues."[20] The Reagan–Thatcher relationship was unusual, and unnerving to some, but it worked. Reagan happened to be an Anglophile who idolized Winston Churchill but he was, after all, the commander in chief of the United States, and arguably of the NATO alliance as well. He was, as Sir Charles Powell put it, "the ultimate chairman of the board."[21] Margaret Thatcher, on the other hand, was a trusted advisor, a political Tory descendant of the great Sir Winston, and someone with whom Reagan could not only do business, but whom he could also admire.

And she valued SDI. Thatcher would visit Washington once or twice a year and meet Abrahamson for SDI updates during her trips to the Pentagon. When Abrahamson visited the United Kingdom, similar briefings were arranged through Stanley Orman.

"When we went to the U.K.," said Abrahamson, "we'd brief her intelligence people on what the Russians were doing, and then I would give her an update on the program. We shared our intelligence with her staff several times.

"We would meet at No. 10, but most often out at Chequers, which was a wonderful place, just beautiful. We'd show up at maybe ten in the morning and then we'd have a couple of hours of discussion and we'd break for lunch. Denis [Thatcher] would come and join us for lunch and then he'd leave. And then in the afternoon we'd discuss SDI."

Abrahamson was bemused at first that Thatcher never invited anyone from the Ministry of Defense to these meetings, though that she always let it be known that they were conferring. So it was, said Abrahamson, that "on Monday I would be the most in-demand speaker over at the MOD. They had two standard questions—'What did you tell her?' and 'What did she say?' She set up my entrée for these guys even though they weren't very pleased with the way she did it. Except for Stanley Orman's involvement and his ability to get things done, we never had what I would call an enthusiastic or cooperative activity with the MOD. They wanted to know exactly what we were doing in the Thatcher bureaucracy, but weren't going to divert a lot of effort from their own priorities."[22]

And, he chuckled, "Mrs. Thatcher gave very clear guidance. It didn't bother her that I was an American working an on American program for President Reagan. She'd say, 'I like this, and this, and I'd like to see this.'

"She also probably got me where I live more than any other person," he added. At one time she asked him to draft a program in which British scientists would contribute to the SDI. When he complied and showed her the draft, she was not impressed. "She answered, 'I expected a vigorous program, and you gave me a miniprogram,'" Abrahamson said. "Something like that. I had always prided myself on being an independent and hopefully grand thinker, yet somehow I delivered something to this lady who I admired so much that was just trivial. We broadened the program as fast as we could.

"I think she had a lot of influence on the Reagan government, and personally on the president. I think he valued her advice and therefore would defer to her ideas, which were usually at the policy level."[23]

At one time, Reagan sent Thatcher a group photograph from an event that had been held in his honor at No. 10. In it, Thatcher, flanked by the president and George Shultz, is eulogizing him at a dinner speech. Reagan, perhaps tongue in cheek, had added a message below the image: "Dear Margaret—As you can see, I agree with every word you are saying. I always do. Warmest friendship. Sincerely, Ron."[24]

Excalibur Moves On

To most it was obvious that President Reagan would never countenance the idea of exploding a nuclear device in the atmosphere in
order to energize a laser weapon. His interest in "non-nuclear defense" had been repeated time and time again. Yet Edward Teller's
protégés at Lawrence Livermore National Laboratory in California
were still flogging their dying horse. The x-ray laser was pictured now
not as a vulnerable, continuously orbiting system, but one that could
be "popped" up into space when a Soviet launch was detected, to zap
the missiles early in their flight path. The revision neither hindered nor
helped the popularity of the idea. Yonas simply didn't believe it would
work. "Fast-burn boosters would outwit it," he told William J. Broad
of the *New York Times*. "The x-ray lasers could never get there in
time—period."[25]

More expensive x-ray laser tests were scheduled for Nevada and
would be performed as planned, at huge taxpayer expense. But the
story was all but over. One of the most damning statements—almost
an epitaph and all the more powerful for its succinctness—was issued
in December 1987 by Rep. George Brown of California, who pronounced that the Teller/Wood line consisted of "politically motivated
exaggerations aimed at distorting national policy and funding decisions."[26]

By mid-1985, the x-ray laser episode meant little to the Kremlin,
whose analysts of course were familiar with the president's aversion to
all things nuclear. Just that spring, in his foreword to a detailed pam-
phlet titled "The President's Strategic Defense Initiative," Reagan had
again specified that he was interested in achieving "a truly effective
non-nuclear defense."[27] But Soviet peace of mind was again shattered
when the MIRACL laser was used to destroy a Titan missile casing on
September 6, 1985.* After a few seconds' irradiation from about a
half-mile distance, the casing exploded. The next month, Abrahamson
told Congress that MIRACL "demonstrated graphically the lethality
of this technology." While Abrahamson hailed the experiment as a
great success, predictably the Federation of American Scientists expressed grave doubt, as did Roger L. Hagengruber of Sandia National
Laboratories. Paid to be constructively critical as Sandia's director of
system studies, he told Broad, "These demonstrations have the potential to be what we call 'strap-down chicken tests,' where you strap the

---

*At the time, MIRACL (mid-infrared advanced chemical laser), a powerful
megawatt-class deuterium fluoride laser originally built for shipboard use, was being
studied for its antisatellite capabilities.

chicken down, blow it apart with a shotgun and say shotguns kill chickens. But that's quite different from trying to kill a chicken in a dense forest while it's running away from you."[28]

Yonas encountered the formidable *Los Angeles Times* reporter Bob Scheer at the MIRACL test at White Sands Missile Range. At one point, Scheer had turned to him and asked, "Could that laser go through cloud?" Yonas gave him a quick "No" and forgot the matter—briefly. The next morning the *LA Times* headlined its report with the banner, "Cloudy Day Ruins SDI."

"Weinberger was very upset," said Yonas. "A few days later the U.S. Air Force shot a laser (and illuminated a satellite) from the top of Mount Haleakala, in Maui. The idea was, 'This proves it works.' But there were no clouds on Haleakala. I went to Colin Powell, and I said to him, 'I think the secretary needs to call the press together and tell them he misspoke.' "[29] It didn't happen.

Sandia, a sister lab of LANL and LLNL, was more conservatively managed, by people who were technology-oriented and perhaps the world's top experts in "systems integration." It had a relatively small program in particle beam weapons (the use of high-energy ion beams to shoot down targets), but analysis of directed energy weapons from a broad systems viewpoint generated so many questions, and uncovered so many needs for technologies that did not yet exist, that Sandia chose not to participate in a major way. Sandia did contribute to SDI with system architecture studies, directed-energy weapons research, and radiation-effects testing. Most significantly, it played a major "black hat" role in countermeasure analysis, with the none-too-popular job of showing that practical methods existed for making midcourse intercept very difficult indeed.[30]

SDI AND THE ABM TREATY

Two months after Chernenko suggested a new round of superpower talks, Shultz had flown to Geneva to meet with Andrei Gromyko, accompanied by a small retinue that included McFarlane, presidential arms control advisor Paul Nitze, and Richard Perle. At that January 7–8 meeting, Shultz and Nitze finally managed to convince Gromyko of the U.S. determination to press ahead with SDI research. Had the Soviet Union not championed strategic defense twenty years before? But Gromyko, a dour hard-liner of the old Stalinist school, was not amused—that had been a different time, with different circumstances. And the ABM Treaty was in place. Nevertheless, Shultz and Gromyko agreed that the two sides would have formal talks on reducing nuclear and space arms, setting the stage for the November Geneva summit.

There would be a lot of things to discuss. For example, it sounded as though the Soviets were doing naughty things at Krasnoyarsk. But how guilt-free was the United States? Was SDI legal under terms of the ABM Treaty? This treaty says, "Each party undertakes not to develop, test or deploy ABM systems or components which are sea-based, air-based, space-based or mobile land-based." Research was okay, so long as there was no testing of "components," such as new radar and interceptor prototypes. ABM launches from static sites were still kosher, as was the use of "kinetic energy weapons," typified by nonexplosive antimissile missiles. The United States declared that SDI was legal because it was limiting its research to subcomponents of ABM systems; Mikhail Gorbachev would denounce this stand when he met with Reagan in Geneva. SDI, he said, was plainly illegal.

That summer, Perle asked Philip Kunsberg, a bright young Pentagon lawyer who worked for Fred Iklé, Weinberger's undersecretary for policy, to analyze the ABM Treaty and its implications for SDI. Kunsberg, reported Jay Winik in his book *On the Brink*, "concluded that the Soviet Union had never accepted restrictions on space-based ABM systems if they employed 'new physical principles' such as laser beams, directed energy systems, and other exotic technologies."[31] As Thatcher said, "The Soviets had started out with a 'broad interpretation' of the treaty which they narrowed when it later suited them."[32]

Perle was surprised and delighted—he had never liked the ABM Treaty—and the State Department, dismayed, had their own lawyer, Judge Abraham Sofaer, retrace Kunsberg's research. Sofaer conceded that the treaty did not proscribe space defense research and testing, opening the way for its "broad interpretation," though deployment was another matter. In other words, he found that the treaty did not prohibit the testing of space-based missile defense systems, including directed energy weapons.

That September, during a Colorado Springs conference, McFarlane turned to a friend, sighed, and said, "I guess I've created a Frankenstein monster, haven't I?"[33]

Early in October, the Senior Interagency Arms Control group met at the White House with McFarlane in the chair. Perle and Iklé argued for broad interpretation of the ABM Treaty, and no one publicly objected. The next step was to socialize the idea with Congress and U.S. allies, to get their support. But McFarlane jumped the gun and spilled the beans in an October 6 broadcast of the NBC program *Meet the Press*. Predictably, congresspersons, allies—and the Soviets—were furious. And so, of course, was Richard Perle. "If he [Perle] had to guess," Winik wrote, "he felt McFarlane was trying to sabotage SDI—because this was certainly no way to promote it. After having deftly maneuvered the situation to just where he wanted it, now he would have to engage in damage control. Again."[34] Shultz then tried to ease the situation by explaining that, while the broad interpretation was justifiable, the U.S. would stick to the narrow interpretation—at least for the time being.

Paradoxically, the ruling brought about the most difficult time in Abrahamson's SDI career because it seemed so transparently tailored to favor his program. "It was devastating to the program, even though it was intended to help," he said. "It caused such a reaction in the Democratic majority in Congress that the program got infinitely harder."[35] To this day, Abrahamson believes this event cost him his fourth general's star.

GENERAL SECRETARY GORBACHEV

Konstantin Chernenko died on March 11, 1985, a week after he voted in front of television cameras, using a set that had been built around his hospital bed for the purpose. Gorbachev became general secretary of the Communist Party of the Soviet Union. Without wasting any time, but after a Saturday afternoon briefing with Abrahamson at Chequers, Thatcher went to see Gorbachev in Moscow.[36] There, among other points, she again reminded Gorbachev that she favored continuation of nuclear deterrence. Nuclear weaponry was Britain's strongest guarantee of survival, were there ever to be a war in Europe. At least partly for this reason, the Iron Lady's stance may have been even more rigid than the pro-nuke factions of Washington and Moscow.

The international community naturally knew that Gorbachev would try to improve his country's lot—and much more vigorously than his predecessors—but they were not ready to bet in favor of the likelihood of his success. Economically and politically, the Soviet Union remained in a mess.

"My own guess is that the Communist Party is too far gone to transform itself, let alone the country," Herb Meyer wrote in a memo to DCI Casey. "On the other hand, should Gorbachev try and fail—or decline to try at all—the Soviet Union will enter the most dangerous, decisive period of its history . . . in a 'use it or lose it' situation." It would have to decide whether to use its awesome military power—or not use it and drift down into the second rank of nations.

"Should Gorbachev fail," he continued with remarkable prescience, "we and our allies soon will be safely and irrevocably beyond reach of the Soviet Union—or as the Soviets would see it, hopelessly beyond their grasp. Global power would shift from a bi-polar, U.S.– Soviet focus to a multi-polar focus, with the U.S. preeminent and with power shared among ourselves, Japan, Western Europe, China, and whatever becomes of the Soviet Union and its satellites. That would be a very different world; more complex in some ways but on the whole less dangerous."

Meyer also predicted, accurately, that the U.S. "anti-defense crowd" would regain their vocal momentum: "One specific objective of their next campaign will be to stop SDI at all costs by doing to the concept of strategic defense what they have already done to the concept of nuclear energy: discrediting it politically despite its technological merit."[37]

SDI's critics were indeed winning considerable ink in the national dailies, particularly in the *New York Times*. "In the Administration, officials have made ambiguous and contradictory signals as to the actual goal of the Strategic Defense Initiative," wrote the *Times*'s Charles Mohr in March 1985. "They have alternated between describing it as a thoroughly reliable system to protect the United States civil population and the easier-to-achieve protection of missile silos and command posts . . . some analysts say they doubt the program will have the desired strategic and political effect on Soviet leaders, and cite Soviet statements to underline this doubt." Mohr quoted Ray M. Garthoff of the Brookings Institution as predicting that SDI would "certainly inhibit" hope of a reduction in nuclear stockpiles.[38]

SERIOUS ANALYSIS, SERIOUS JOKES

To Gerry Yonas, it mattered little that the *Times* detected ambiguous and contradictory signals within the administration. He was on a roll, spreading the science-technology story, building esprit de corps. But it was a complicated subject, this SDI business, and difficult to explain. In an August 1985 letter explaining SDI to Edward A. Torrero, technical editor of *IEEE Spectrum*, Yonas wrote, "The question is difficult to pose and is much more complex than the standard, 'Will it work?' The real question is, will what work against what threat to what targets, how well by what date, and at what cost. The technology challenge is probably less than half the story, with the crucial strategy and policy issues clearly dominating all other issues."[39]

Yonas also was frustrated by the public perception of strategic defense. "We find even now," he wrote, "that many people still think he [Reagan] called for development or deployment, or even an up-grading, of *a defensive system that they mistakenly think already exists*," (emphasis added). Most people, he said, would be surprised to learn "that we have intentionally placed ourselves in a situation where our only responses to an attack are either to retaliate or surrender, but not protect ourselves."[40]

The public was interested in death rays, but Yonas pointed out that any version of SDI would require development of a huge and expensive array of support systems—"generic means for hardening boosters and the lethal effects of various weapons against those means; development of multimegawatt, space-based electrical power supplies, nuclear and non-nuclear, for weapons, sensors, and computers; and development of low-cost, heavy-lift space launchers capable of carrying perhaps one hundred tons or more to orbit, rather than the space shut-tle's current capability of twenty to thirty tons, at one-tenth the cost."[41]

Maybe the public should have curbed its enthusiasm, even if just a little.

On the job, Yonas maintained his jocular habits. At one time he was asked to go with Vice President George H. W. Bush to invite the Allies to sign up for SDI. Things were looking ominous in Europe at the time, and Yonas simply didn't want to go. When Abrahamson heard this, he summoned Yonas to his office and said something like, "I hear you're going to go to Europe with the vice president. I'll stay here. Don't worry about my feelings." "Abe," Yonas replied, "I'd give anything for you to go." [42] The trip was called off following a terrorist incident, but Yonas had proved his talent for impertinence yet again. "I didn't know how irreverent he was going to be," Abrahamson ad-mitted many years later.[43]

Stanley Orman, later Britain's SDI chief, said that although Yonas was exceptionally bright and easy to work with, "Gerry was very hard to get to the bottom of because he's such a joker."[44] Yonas admits he was all of these, but claims a good reason. "Perhaps my own humor softened the craziness by creating another level of craziness," he said. "Frankly, nothing was as crazy as the fact that we had tens of thou-sands of nukes, and they had tens of thousands of nukes, and in addi-tion had bio weapons so they could kill all of the survivors."[45]

"Maybe my sarcastic jokes and occasional practical jokes were not that funny," Yonas acknowledges. "But I never took much too seri-ously, because if I had, I would have gone crazy, since there were so many contradictions. My ability to deal with contradictions, confusion, and unsolvable problems requires an ability to see the humor in what is otherwise not logical."[46]

Sometimes the wackiness came looking for Yonas, self-contained and with no need for enhancement. At one time, a reporter repeatedly accused him of unfairly withholding information about the propulsion system of an alien spaceship that the reporter believed the SDIO was hiding on an island in the Pacific. The reporter accused him of being the designer of that system and believed that was why he got the job in the Pentagon. Incredibly, a formal review followed at the congressional level, in Abrahamson's office. Not surprisingly, Yonas denied the charges. "I kept a straight face when the Senator [Dennis DeConcini (D-Arizona)] and the reporter confronted me," he said. "However, at one point I could no longer avoid the inclination to giggle, so I just ran from the room when they 'proved' that I had been in cahoots with the aliens all along."

As in many such cases, there was a thread of truth in the story. Yonas actually knew about the MHD propulsion system that supposedly had been expropriated by aliens, had presented a paper on it in 1962, and the reporter had found it. "Exposed as an alien sympathizer," he said, "what else could I do but run!"

Abe had plenty of occasions to roll his eyes in response to Yonas's antics. But it was okay—these were part and parcel of a whole bundle of unusual qualities that he had recognized in his chief scientist. Yonas's mind was a multilevel, continuously multitasking organism in which plasma physics was the province of just one gray-matter pigeonhole. If he was a great speaker—and he was—he was also a peerless and sometimes merciless conversationalist. At the podium or over cocktails he was simultaneously witty, wily, and wise. His manner tended to be slightly offbeat, and confrontational in a friendly sort of way, and this would put others off balance. He was exquisitely aware of this talent and its drawbacks: "People did not always know when I was serious and when I was kidding."[47] This meant he could try out iffy ideas, analyze the responses, and then back off and say, "Only kidding!" if he got tired of the situation. It was not a technique so much as a habit. His verbal acrobatics could raise hackles, but then he had a bottomless store of stories and jokes to ease the tension, and before long another aspect of his personality would reluctantly show itself—an intrinsic good nature that was perfectly capable of humility.

Selling SDI Abroad

Reagan thought that sharing SDI work with overseas partners would ease their opposition to the program and its apparent linkage with the abolition of nuclear weapons. It seemed like a reasonable,

NATO thing to do, but there was more to it than that. The Soviets could see that international technical participation could strengthen the U.S. initiative, as it had done in the Manhattan Project, and they worked hard to find ways of turning U.S. allies against it.

"If the United States could get Japan, Germany, Great Britain, and France to provide their technology, then the United States could develop SDI within ten years," said V. N. Lobov, an army general and former chief of the Soviet General Staff. "If all the technologies were assembled under one roof, they could have achieved a technological breakthrough, perhaps in an area other than SDI."[48]

"Whatever the assessment of its actual feasibility," wrote the sociologist Vladimir Shlapentokh, "the Kremlin perceived SDI as a direct threat to the geopolitical status of the USSR. While military experts in Moscow may have doubted the viability of creating an impervious shield against all incoming nuclear missiles, the Kremlin believed that Reagan's SDI, regardless of its success or failure, would mobilize and integrate the technological resources of all major Western countries. In effect, SDI would act as a springboard for Western technological advancements in all military areas."[49]

Weinberger was acutely aware of the Russians' position, and determined to pull America's allies in, no matter what. Yonas, Weinberger's point man for this task, went on a number of international trips to negotiate, in particular with Britain, Germany, Israel, Italy, and Japan. But, he said, "they had a very different point of view. We were in this head-to-head competition with the Soviet Union and we were playing to win, and all they wanted to do was get money from us."[50]

Yonas had no need to visit Paris. Reagan had already courted French president François Mitterrand on the subject of SDI, and it had not gone well. "Reagan went to see Mitterrand and talked about the French being *le souscontracteur*," Yonas said. "You know how long that lasted? Almost immediately the French announced their own European program, Eureka."[51]

But then, the French thought they had reason to be skeptical. Their representatives had been particularly keen to have a briefing on the 1983 Velikhov–Sagdeev–Kokoshin report. "The first third-country visitor I had was from the French government," recalled Roald Sagdeev. "I gave him the draft manuscript before the book was published, and my recollection is that my French guest was very pleased with the conclusion that what the Americans were planning to do would never work."[52]

SDI perplexed the West German government thoroughly. "The issue has pushed the Germans into what is for them the most uncomfortable of positions," wrote John Newhouse in the *New Yorker*, "having to choose between America, their protector, and France, an old enemy but now the other half of a partnership that anchors Europe's political and economic stability. The contesting pressures from Paris, which is openly hostile to Star Wars, and Washington, are heavy, and may become intolerable; a choice between the two places isn't one the Germans can make. They need both."[53]

Despite opposition in Europe and within her own cabinet, Thatcher instructed her defense minister, Michael Heseltine, to sign a memorandum of understanding to work on SDI with the United States. He did so, and asked the Americans for £2 billion to fund the British effort. His ministry of defense colleagues were aghast. "I believe he got this sum out of thin air," said Orman. "No one I spoke to had considered this realistic."[54] In the event, SDI collaboration agreements were made with Britain in December 1985 (British organizations would receive $55.8 million in SDI funding between October 1985 and December 1988). "The whole issue of missile defense was poorly received in Europe and as a result most of the [British] Cabinet was against Reagan—with one exception," said Orman. "Margaret Thatcher really understood the issues that were behind it. She was the only European leader who understood the big picture."[55] Thatcher's support also helped win more SDI participants. Peter Schweizer went so far as to say that "the vocal and public support of Margaret Thatcher proved central to moving SDI from a president's dream to a research program pursued by leading scientists across the Western world."[56]

Germany would sign up in March 1986, Israel in May 1986, Italy in September 1986, and Japan in July 1987. "The Europeans signed up to work with us because they didn't want to be left behind," Yonas said. "They saw the technology, particularly the sensor and information technology, as a gold mine. They knew that some time there'd be a new technological revolution that would run away with economics. It didn't happen until ten years later, this science and technology revolution. But the boom that we saw in the late nineties in the United States began in the 1980s, when SDI was getting started."[57]

At a Commonwealth Club presentation, when someone from the audience asked why he continued to back the program, Edward Teller was his old stubborn self: "I am supporting SDI on the basis that we need it, the French need it, the Israelis need it—and the Soviets already have it."[58]

Meanwhile, the medium-range nuclear defense buildup was going well for the West, and badly for the Soviet Union. The first Pershing II mobile missiles had entered service in West Germany in January 1984. More than a thousand jet-engined, air-launched cruise missiles were available for deployment by B-52 bombers by early 1985.

Hundreds of sea-launched cruise missiles were ready for service in submarines and surface ships. Deployment of ground-launched missiles had started in England in late 1984; in all, 464 were to be based in Europe.

In April 1985, Gorbachev placed a moratorium on further deployment of the medium-range SS-20 missile. Later, on October 2, he would reduce the number targeted on Western Europe to the level of June 1984. These were small palliatives, for it was generally known that there were already enough to destroy every important target in Western Europe. Perhaps he hoped the United States would follow suit in some way. It didn't.

Mr. Chevaline

Stanley Orman served as coordinating authority for Britain's submarine-based nuclear deterrent while he was based at the British Atomic Weapons Establishment in Aldermaston, Berkshire. The deterrent, put into service in 1982, was the Chevaline, a warhead built to ride atop U.S. Polaris missiles launched from British submarines. When Reagan gave his "Star Wars" speech, Orman was deputy ambassador in Washington and was responsible for all defense exchanges between the United States and Britain.

"When I heard Reagan, watching his speech on my living room TV, I thought, 'I wonder if he believes it,'" Orman said. "What I didn't understand was whether he was very clever in thinking, 'I've got something here that will really put them over a barrel,' or whether he thought, 'We've got something that works.'" [59]

Orman immediately wanted to get into the act. Chevaline was widely respected for its clever use of penetration aids, or penaids, which are devices intended to fool defensive missiles into attacking the wrong targets. "I had been working seven years on how to defeat an ABM defense network," said Orman, "and here was the president talking about directing an ABM defense. So it seemed obvious that Britain had much to offer. Like a poacher turning gamekeeper, we knew the game from the other side." [60]

Orman was called back to Britain in 1984, to serve as deputy director at the Atomic Weapons Establishment. He was then tasked by Sir Richard Norman, chief scientific advisor to the Ministry of Defense, to undertake a joint study between Aldermaston (nuclear weapons) and Farnborough (space technology), to analyze what realistically could be done in missile defense.

Orman left Aldermaston for a second time when he was made

director general of the Ministry of Defense's new SDI Participation Office at Northumberland House in central London, not far from Whitehall and No. 10 Downing Street. He then had his first meetings with Abrahamson at Washington's Matomic Building. "He was stretched to the nth degree," Orman recalled, "because he was Mister Outside, selling the program to everyone—to Congress, the president, the secretary of defense—and talking to international leaders. And he was also Mister Inside."[61] From then on, Orman was regularly asked to give the European view on proposals, both privately and publicly, at conferences. "I'd appear and do the European thing," he said.[62] Not so in London. A chasm existed between the Ministry of Defense and Orman's small SDI office. While he provided the prime minister with regular written briefings, Orman was never to meet with Margaret Thatcher. "She requested a one-on-one meeting, which MOD officials did not want," he said. "They procrastinated until the demands ceased."[63]

Orman was reasonably skeptical about SDI. "I did not believe that the Americans could erect a defense that would nullify a Russian attack," he said. "The physics was sound, but the engineering was way more difficult than anyone had yet envisaged, and the systems engineering was going to be very complex. Genuine belief in a fieldable SDI, while it could be espoused by great scientists, was inversely proportional to one's breadth of knowledge in engineering. My conclusion was that while it might be possible eventually to produce a missile defense, the time scale was decades longer than the Americans were talking about. I told them it would take decades, not years, to deploy a space-based SDI system."[64]

CATCALLS AND DEATH THREATS

For all his bravado, and despite his droll ways, Yonas had to put up with some tough sledding in his home country. Some of the academics, and the political left, were plainly incensed. Yonas bore the brunt of U.S. anti-SDI sentiment in 1985 when he went around giving speeches that were intended to boost interest in the program. "I was called all kinds of names," he said. "I was burned in effigy, people used to yell at me and scream at me, and anywhere near the northern part of the United States I was considered a knave and a fool and a scoundrel."[65]

Nor did Abrahamson entirely escape satire. "When I showed up for a speaking engagement at Wright State University," he recalled, "someone dressed as Darth Vader met me at the back of the auditorium and, as the 'Star Wars' theme struck up, escorted me down the aisle to the front. And I said, 'Yes, there is a similarity . . . the good guys are winning.' "[66]

At about the same time, in Britain, Orman opted to attend a meeting of Oxford academics who ran an organization called "Just Defence." "Their whole concept was, concentrate on defensive efforts and get rid of nukes," Orman said. "Several of them peered at my badge and said, 'You're Deputy Director at Aldermaston, why are you here?' I said, 'Do you think I'm deputy director because I'm in favor of nuclear war? I work at Aldermaston to prevent nuclear war.' They couldn't grasp the idea."[67]

Yonas was quietly incredulous: "Many of us joined the fray with naïve notions of how the game was played and were faced with abuse and even ridicule from the battle-hardened anti-defense forces; but it was the vocal Soviet opposition that kept the public convinced that our struggle was worth pursuing."[68]

The Soviets meantime were attacking SDI behind the scenes, through propaganda and much worse. "There was no way to stop us with these propaganda attacks," said Yonas, "but the Soviets had other dirty tricks up their sleeves. After I spent several weeks in 1985 touring Europe and meeting with leaders in government and industry, there were widely publicized death threats from Soviet-backed terrorist groups in Europe." [69] These, as it turned out, were more than rumors.

In late 1985 the Office of Technology Assessment (OTA), responding to a mandate from the House Armed Services Committee and Senate Foreign Relations Committee, provided two controversial reports on SDI.* In short, the White House didn't like their conclusions. "More than any other subject examined by OTA during its twenty-two years of operation," wrote Greenberg, SDI "strained politicians' tolerance of independent scientific scrutiny of politically sensitive issues."[70] In brief, the OTA found that development of the proposed "umbrella" would make a preemptive strike more attractive to the Soviets; that strategic defenses might eventually be able to defend U.S. missile silos, but not the general population; that it was impossible to tell whether the system would be affordable; and that opportunities would have to be balanced against risks "in the face of considerable uncertainty." It also aired difficult questions about upsetting the strategic balance of power, the unpredictability of the Soviet

---

*The combined reports, named "Ballistic Missile Defense Technologies," (052-003-001008-9) were published by the U.S. Government Printing Office, along with an excellent summary, "Ballistic Missile Defense Technologies," Document OTA-ISC-255, published in September 1985.

response to U.S. advances in ballistic missile defense, and the riddle of whether or not BMD would be the best way to provide U.S. missile survivability. However, "The technology is reasonably well in hand to build a BMD system that could raise significantly the price in nuclear warheads of a Soviet attack on hardened targets in the United States; such a system, if combined with a rebasing of U.S. ICBMs, could protect a substantial fraction of those U.S. land-based missiles against a Soviet first strike."

The OTA would issue another cautionary report on SDI in May 1988; in 1995 it was gone, the victim of a cost-cutting splurge. On the political side of the Cold War debate, Herb Meyer continued to write dispatches on the state of the Soviet Union, relentlessly broadcasting his keynote message that "Throughout the world now, it's becoming obvious that history, after all, is not on the Soviets' side but on our own."[71] The United States was very effectively attacking its adversary by nonmilitary means, with measures that ranged from trade restrictions to counterintelligence and counterinsurgency. Meyer's confident prose, which must have struck its Kremlin readers with immeasurably more impact than the messages received from their own Washington sources, left no doubt, in the spring of 1985, that Reagan was determined to win by means of non-nuclear space defenses:

> As the U.S. continues on course toward SDI . . . the Soviet Union's opportunities will evaporate to use the military power which has become that country's sole claim to superpower status. More precisely, within the next ten years at most, new Western conventional weapons will make it virtually impossible for the Warsaw Pact countries to overrun Western Europe; the Pact's four-to-one advantage will be as useless in the face of NATO high-tech defense weapons as was the Polish cavalry in the face of Nazi tanks. And by roughly the end of this century we will have the means to intercept rockets in their boost phase, which means the Soviets will no longer be able to threaten the West with nuclear annihilation.[72]

Now it was time for serious business. Ronald Reagan and Mikhail Gorbachev were tooling up for the summit, with Margaret Thatcher fretting in the background. It would be the first meeting among the world's superpowers in six years, and supposedly a time for hope. Yet behind the scenes the Cold War went on. The Americans were undermining their Soviet adversaries' economy and political power wherever possible, the Soviets were building their orbital space cruiser and, at Dzerzhinsky Square, KGB planners were preparing their European surrogates for the wet work of assassination.

11

SHOWDOWN AT
THE CHATEAU

*By saying that I espouse the tragic view of technology I mean to ally
myself with those who, aware of the dangers, and without foolish
illusions about what can be accomplished, still want to move on,
actively seeking to realize through technology our constantly changing
vision of a more satisfactory society.*
—Samuel Florman[1]

It was difficult for West to communicate with East in the early
1980s, and, as if to worsen the situation, three of the Soviet Union's
leaders died in the years 1982–85. "As much as we tried to initiate
dialogue, nobody was home, nobody was on the other end of the
phone," Assistant Secretary of State Richard Burt recalled. "One of the
big devices of diplomacy in that period was actually going to funerals."

"There were three (general secretaries) in the first few years of
my Presidency, and I couldn't get along with any of them," Reagan
grumped.[2]

But the new man, Gorbachev, was different. Reagan sensed this
from the start. Vice President George H. W. Bush and Shultz, representing Reagan at Andropov's funeral, came home with a favorable
impression of the new general secretary. Though it had been a short
visit, it seemed he could very well be the man described by Thatcher.
Perhaps so, though as Gorbachev remarked later, in his first year "I
spoke of our country's unchanging foreign policy course, stating that
there was no need to change it."[3] Shultz soon sought out Dobrynin at
the Soviet Embassy and told him that Reagan wanted to get a bilateral
dialogue going, now that the Soviets had a new man at the helm. From
this was born the Geneva summit of November 19–20, 1985.

Shultz, Robert Gates noted in his memoir, "discerned in Gorbachev's rhetoric and proposals much more potential for fundamental change in Soviet direction than we did."[4] For this summit, the keyword was "preparation." On the home front, the White House was defending the administration's record budget—which for the first time had reached a deficit of beyond $1 trillion—and preparing Reagan to veto a congressional tax increase. Behind the scenes, White House staff worked overtime for months, preparing for a key meeting at which the head of the Soviet Union would be taking the measure of Reagan's power. Gorbachev would be thinking, "Not only is the United States an important country, but look at this guy across the table from me— what is the measure of his own power?" In a quasi-scientific way, the goal was to learn the facts of each nation's strategic intent. But in truth this exchange would center on each individual leader's impressions of the other leader's resolve to carry out what he thought was best for his country.

That spring, McFarlane began sending Reagan a series of twenty-five short, in-depth papers about the Soviet Union—a kind of mail-order education that the president devoured. It was, after all, part of the leading man's script for a great role. The Geneva preparations brigade also had the president give four major speeches, designed to boost his ratings on foreign affairs before the summit. They successfully engineered a joint congressional resolution offering support for U.S. Geneva positions. And, at a summit of G-7 leaders, Thatcher (Britain), Mitterrand (France), Bettino Croxi (Italy), Helmut Kohl (Germany), Yasuhiro Nakasone (Japan), and Brian Mulroney (Canada) added their own blessings.

"Wow!" whooped McFarlane, "Suddenly Gorby realizes that everyone from Europe to Asia is saying, 'Right on, Ron!' "[5]

On September 27, the new Soviet Foreign Minister, Eduard Shevardnadze, gave the White House a path-finding Kremlin proposal that might not have been possible under his predecessor, Andrei Gromyko. "The contrast between him and Gromyko was breathtaking," Shultz wrote. "He could smile, engage, converse. He had an ability to persuade and be persuaded."[6]

The new proposal recommended that the two sides discuss reducing their ICBM strength by half while concurrently banning space weapons—SDI. Separately, there would be talks on reduction of medium-range missiles in Europe.* Weinberger repeated the mantra that

---

*Joint Chiefs of Staff Chairman Adm. William Crowe advised the president *not* to propose a "zero ballistics" proposal in Geneva, and Margaret Thatcher gave him the same advice, "discreetly and confidentially."

SDI was not negotiable. When, in early November, Shultz and McFarlane traveled to Moscow for a lengthy talk with Gorbachev, it was a repeat performance. Cautious and realistic, Dobrynin feared that Gorbachev overdid the anti-SDI polemic, because it "would merely reinforce Reagan's belief in its importance."[7]

Nitze and McFarlane may have wanted to use the ABM treaty as the basis for a grand compromise at Geneva, trading SDI for major reductions in the Soviet ICBM force. But someone leaked to the press a letter in which Weinberger reminded Reagan that he had agreed to the broad interpretation of the treaty. The *Washington Post* and the *New York Times* put it on their front pages. McFarlane, incensed, indicated that he believed Perle had leaked the letter, but Perle merely replied that someone else must have done it to make the Pentagon look bad.[8] In any case, no trade was in the offing. The president himself would not agree to that. "I have never entertained a thought that SDI could be a bargaining chip," Reagan wrote to his friend Laurence Bellenson, a former Screen Actors Guild attorney.[9]

The utopian dream of a nuclear-free world had submerged for a while below the surface of Reagan's more pragmatic strategies, though, as Bud McFarlane put it, "he surely believed deeply that he had a moral obligation (and mandate) to seek such a world."[10]

GENEVA

Reagan drew heavily on his film-industry experience as he prepared for the summit, and it served him very well. An adept, committed practitioner of the theatrical, he set the physical details of the stage and crafted his script—the negotiation plan—as carefully as he had worked out his talks as president of the Screen Actors Guild in their strike negotiations many years before. "You know," he wrote Bellenson, "those people who thought being an actor was no proper training for this job were way off base. Every day I find myself thankful for those long days at the negotiating table."[11]

"Reagan was in high spirits, crackling with energy," wrote Bud McFarlane. "He had all his reading on the Soviet Union behind him, well-digested, and now he was itching to get started. He couldn't wait for the call: lights, camera, action. He was an actor, after all, and he was about to walk onto the most important sound stage of his life."[12]

The first day of the meetings was cold and overcast. Gorbachev's shiny ZIL limousine came to a stop beside the stone stairway of the nineteenth century Fleur d'Eau chateau, and he stepped out into the cold wind, a short but dapper figure in a winter coat and hat, a blue patterned scarf at his neck. And suddenly there was Reagan, who had hurried down the stone steps, coatless in a blue suit, to meet him. Gorbachev took off his hat to take the president's hand, and then Reagan put his hand under the chairman's arm and walked him up the dozen stairs to a point above a planter of red flowers. All of Reagan's body language indicated that he expected to remain courteously in control. Gorbachev commented on Reagan's lack of a coat, and then they turned to the crowd, the fresh-looking seventy-four-year-old Californian president and the bundled-up fifty-four-year-old Soviet general secretary. The next time they met, Gorbachev was careful not to wear a coat and hat. As Dobrynin commented, "Gorbachev himself was a very good actor."[13]

For the Americans, the Geneva choreography couldn't have been better. "I felt that we lost the game during this first movement," said Sergei Tarasenko, who served as principal policy assistant to Shevardnazde in 1985–91. "We had come prepared with a chess game that started with the wrong move. It produced a contrast which was not favorable to our side, unfortunately."[14]

In Geneva, Gorbachev led off strongly. The Soviet Union was not economically stressed, it was doing fine in high tech, and it was not striving for military superiority. He seemed to believe it or, more likely, hoped that Reagan might believe it. Seated at the chateau's negotiation table, the two heads of state went through their verbal foreplay, Reagan citing a list of individuals he would like to have Soviet exit visas, then arguing over civil rights. Then they moved on to the nuances of SDI. Early in the discussions, Gorbachev tried to convince Reagan that his country was not concerned about the military ramifications of SDI. "If your laboratory research motivates you to create such a system, considering that obviously America has a great deal of money," he said, "our response will be different, asymmetrical." The general secretary, however, thought that the United States wanted him to start a military space race and showed every sign of being concerned. "We will not deploy SDI," he repeated later. "We have another concept."

If Reagan rose to the bait of Gorbachev's question-begging, there is no public record of it. No one explained exactly what was meant by the Soviets' "asymmetrical" response. Was Gorbachev thinking about his antisatellite weapons or something altogether different? Was there some new idea with which the Soviets could shoot SDI out of the sky?

"Everything was designed, in all these diplomatic offensives, to slow down the American SDI program," the dissident physicist Dmitry Mikheyev observed." It shows how serious they were."[15]

That afternoon, during a fireside meeting in the chateau's comfortable boathouse on the edge of Lake Geneva, Reagan handed Gorbachev an envelope containing proposed discussion guidelines. These called for a 50 percent cut in strategic offensive forces, and agreement from both sides that "their strategic defense programs shall be conducted as permitted by, and in full compliance with, the ABM treaty." There was no specific mention of SDI—meaning it would continue— and, for Gorbachev, that made the proposal a loser. At the end of the day, Reagan again proposed sharing SDI. Colin Powell, who was in a position to know, took this as a thoroughly genuine offer, but Gorbachev didn't believe a word of it. "Excuse me, Mr. President," he retorted, "but I do not take your idea of sharing SDI seriously. You don't want to share even petroleum equipment, automatic machine tools, or equipment for dairies, while sharing SDI would be a second American Revolution."

Reagan later said that this response meant Gorbachev was "judging others by his own country."[16] Gorbachev recalled saying, "Why should we believe you'll share SDI with us? We're not so naïve."[17] Gorbachev was decidedly uncomfortable. He felt that Reagan was lecturing him. And such may have been the case, as Reagan took the philosophical high ground with his younger companion, explaining that the United States would not allow itself to be out-weaponed by the Soviet Union; that a renewed arms race would result if there were not an agreement to cut it back. Gorbachev wasn't ready to agree to what would appear to be a U.S. initiative, and he was taken aback by the president's tone. "I stopped him right away," he told a television interviewer. "I said, 'Mr. President, you are not the prosecutor and I am not your pupil. We are leaders of superpowers. Don't forget that.'"[18]

Some of the "lectures" were downright sneaky. At one time the president challenged Gorbachev with a story. "What is the difference between a scientist and a communist?" he asked. When the Soviet leader shrugged, Reagan smiled and said, "A scientist would have tried it out on rats first." Herb Meyer suspects this was the moment that Gorbachev realized that Reagan was not the idiot he'd been told he was. "That's right up there with what Lincoln said to Gen. George McClellan, who was the commander of the Union forces, when he wouldn't fight," Meyer said.[19] (After McClellan failed to move against Confederate forces in 1863, the president wrote him: "If you don't want to use the army, I should like to borrow it for a while. Yours respectfully, A. Lincoln." McClellan's respect for his president improved considerably from that point.)

When the summit reconvened at the Soviet mission the next

morning, Gorbachev sounded almost playful: "Your people say that if Gorbachev attacks SDI and space weapons so much, it means the idea deserves more respect. They even say that if it were not for me, no one would listen to the idea at all." He may have been right, but Reagan didn't want to play. He went back to his nukes-free-world pitch: "What the hell use will ABMs or anything else be if we eliminate nuclear weapons?" It was a shock reply, one that the Russians would store away for future reference. But not at this summit.

As expected, Gorbachev launched a salvo against SDI. The idea sprang from emotion, not fact, he said. "Was it science fiction, a trick to make the Soviet Union more forthcoming," he wondered privately, "or merely a crude attempt to lull us in order to carry out the mad enterprise—the creation of a shield which would allow a first strike without fear of retaliation?"[20] Openly, he argued that it would overturn years of arms control negotiation; it would start a new arms race in space; it would cost huge amounts of money; it would impair the security of both sides. Reagan was of course ready for Gorbachev's attack, responding with a powerfully delivered defense, characterizing SDI as a program that would not merely protect the United States: it would increase the security of the entire world. In the afternoon, Reagan told Gorbachev that SDI would not be used to launch a first strike, but Gorbachev replied, "It's not convincing. . . . It opens up an arms race in space."

"We're prepared to compromise," Gorbachev told Reagan, "We've said we'll agree to a separate agreement on intermediate missiles. We'll talk about deep cuts in START [the Strategic Arms Reduction Treaty]. But SDI has got to come to an end."[21] Though he very much wanted to reduce strategic nuclear stockpiles and ban shorter-range nuclear missiles from Europe, Reagan met this statement with stony silence. Gorbachev realized that he had come up against an impenetrable barrier. Dobrynin felt that "Gorbachev had gotten himself unreasonably fixated on American military research on space weapons"; so much so that the general chairman considered resolution of the matter "a precondition for summit success."[22]

"Gorbachev was animated, gesturing, leaning forward, really engaged," recalled McFarlane. "He led off with the usual warning about taking war to the heavens. Reagan talked about the danger of reliance on offensive weapons and massive stockpiles and argued the merits of each side deploying defensive systems. Gorbachev came back again: 'No, no, no.' Then Reagan came back again, 'Yes, yes, and here's why . . .'

"After two hours of repetitive sparring, Gorbachev just lapsed back in his chair. The animation was completely gone. The sense of drama in the room was palpable. After a long pause, Gorbachev took a deep breath and almost whispered, 'I disagree with just about everything you have said.' There was a long pause, then he looked up at Reagan. 'But I will reconsider.' "[23]

"I thought to myself: '*Clang*, like a coin dropping,'" said George Shultz. "Ronald Reagan has . . . nailed into place an element of the U.S. position as something that, as far as he is concerned, in its essential nature, he is not going to compromise.' "[24]

Gorbachev then knew his military-industrial complex would lobby even harder to reintroduce a Soviet "Star Wars" effort, even though the negative Velikhov–Sagdeev report had been right on track. "The lasers I was selling were designed to blow up Soviet missiles shortly after they took off and probably would have worked some day, because the physics was not wrong," Yonas said.[25] "But we didn't have a clue how to do the real engineering, and while there were some [Soviets] who said, 'Calm down; let the Americans waste their money,' I don't think they were listened to."[26]

Even if he agreed with his SDI detractors, Gorbachev preferred to bring a complete stop to the U.S. program so that his military-industrial complex could move ahead relatively slowly and in secret. But since Reagan did not go along, perhaps his best option was indeed to launch Skif/Polyus, hoping that this *tour de force* would oblige the Americans to agree to a mutual ban on space defense. From that point, summit discussions centered on human rights and regional conflict, and particularly on Afghanistan.

During the course of the summit, Gorbachev said, time after time, that the only reason for SDI was to allow the United States to launch a nuclear first strike, then protect itself from retaliation. Reagan, just as often, replied that this was not so—that a nuclear disarmament schedule could be put into process while SDI research proceeded, and that it would help keep the peace if and when disarmament became a reality. The meeting ended with disagreement on SDI, but with an implicit agreement to prohibit intermediate-range nuclear missiles in Europe, a pledge to seek a 50 percent reduction in strategic nuclear arms, a promise not to seek military superiority, a statement that "a nuclear war cannot be won and must not be fought," and an exchange of invitations to Washington and Moscow. The two sides agreed on a scientific, educational, and cultural exchange program and, remarkably, Gorbachev agreed to a human-rights statement committing the Soviet Union to the resolution of "humanitarian causes in the spirit of cooperation."

Geneva was a tough summit, especially for the Soviets, but Reagan and Gorbachev had developed the beginnings of a liking for each other. The two leaders had come to know each other's styles, and having done so, were able to communicate despite their deep disagreements. Dobrynin wrote, "It turned out that the two were able to talk, and not as irreconcilable antagonists, but as leaders looking for practical solutions. This meeting opened a new epoch, which eventually led to a drastic change in relations between the two countries and elsewhere.[27]

"On the plane home," he added, "Gorbachev said that Reagan had impressed him as a complex and contradictory person, sometimes frankly speaking his mind, as when he defended SDI, and sometimes, as usual, harping on propaganda dogmas in which he also believed."[28] As Edmund Morris, appointed Reagan's official biographer in 1985, noted in the *New Yorker*, this "key moment in forty years of Cold War brinkmanship" left Gorbachev "confounded as much by the President's power of belief as by his lack of hostility."[29] But the big question of SDI remained. "There were two people who were absolutely sure that SDI would work—Reagan and Gorbachev," Herb Meyer said. "They knew this in their bones, because we'd made everything work. Also, the Russians knew that this was the kind of project that Americans were very good at. There's a sequence to it. There's the Panama Canal, the Manhattan Project, the *Apollo* Project, and then SDI. Gigantic engineering projects that all the experts say won't work. And we're good at that kind of thing. Reagan knew it and Gorbachev knew it."[30] Though Gorbachev's misgivings would mellow, he still would have to placate his fearful (and greedy) military and military-industrial leadership.

The White House was pleased with the Geneva summit, especially when Reagan's popularity index soared, and even the Politburo acknowledged that the meeting was, overall, a positive step. The State Department's Max Kampelman did not attend, but he heard the president's comments soon afterward, at a National Security Council meeting in Washington. His theme, Kampelman said, was, "Maggie Thatcher was correct. We can do business with Gorbachev."[31]

Most of America's allies were unimpressed. Reagan had refused to budge on SDI. "The Europeans, Thatcher excepted, never approved of SDI," said Stanley Orman." They wanted it to go away. They believed it would die when Reagan completed his second term. So the offer to the Soviets was almost disregarded. The real concern was that the summit ended because Reagan would not give up SDI. That really concerned Europe."[32]

McFarlane tendered his resignation to the president on December 4, 1985, and handed the job over to his deputy, John Poindexter. He was buoyed by the success of the summit but exhausted by it, and not a little disillusioned by the slings and arrows of life in the executive branch. He was resigning as National Security Advisor, he said, "with a deep sense of gratitude, sadness, and fulfillment."[33]

BETWEEN SUMMITS

The first half of 1986 was a period punctuated by the *Challenger* Space Shuttle disaster of January 28 and the catastrophic Chernobyl nuclear reactor explosion in April. The magnitude of the Chernobyl affair (between thirty and fifty were killed and as many as 9,000 may die as the result of longer-term radiation) had a profound effect on Gorbachev, who recognized it as a result of the sloppy, corrupt way in which his nation was being run. Soon he began to promote perestroika (restructuring) and glasnost (openness) as means of remedying these failures in the system.

Chernobyl also prompted Soviet war-planners, to wonder what would happen if the United States targeted their reactors, spreading radioactivity throughout the country. It helped underscore the point that no one could win a nuclear war and, in Jack Matlock's words, "provided an impetus both for internal reform in the Soviet Union and for more urgent efforts to reduce the danger nuclear weapons posed to mankind as a whole."[34] But this also proved to be a year of asymmetrical mischief. Several Soviet arms control plans encouraged anti-SDI factions; at mid-year, terrorism would burst into the picture.

In January 1986, Gorbachev sent Reagan a letter and then published it in Moscow. The president commented,

> He said the Soviet Union wanted to eliminate all INF (inter-
> mediate-range nuclear forces) weapons from Europe, in effect
> accepting my 1982 zero-zero proposal for intermediate-range
> missiles in Europe while trying to make it appear that it was a
> Soviet idea; he proposed a moratorium on nuclear weapons
> testing; and he called for the elimination of all nuclear weapons
> by both sides by the end of 1999—but only if the United
> States renounced "the development, testing and deployment
> of space-strike weapons," a reference to SDI. It was propa-
> ganda, yes, but we couldn't ignore it.[35]

As Dobrynin remarked, Gorbachev was trying to wean himself off his preoccupation with SDI. "Maybe it is time to stop being afraid of SDI," Gorbachev said that February. "The United States is counting on our readiness to build the same kind of costly system, hoping meanwhile that they will win this race using their technological superiority. But our scientists tell me that if we want to destroy or neutralize the American SDI system, we only would have to spend 10 percent of what the Americans plan to spend."[36]

Still, Gorbachev was profoundly worried. "The West clearly wants to pull us into a second scenario of the arms race," he told a session of the Communist Party of the Soviet Union. "They are counting on our military exhaustion. And then they will portray us as militarists. And they are trying to pull us in on the SDI." Meanwhile: "We are stealing everything from the people, and turning the country into a military camp"[37] Then he shared his thoughts publicly on television. "The U.S. wants to exhaust the Soviet Union economically through a race in the most up-to-date and expensive space weapons," he told a television audience on October 14. "It wants to create various kinds of difficulties for the Soviet leadership, to wreck its plans, including the social sphere, in the sphere of improving the standard of living of our people, thus arousing dissatisfaction among the people with their leadership."[38]

And yet the Soviet Union seemed to be exhausting itself. Soviet defense expenditures were projected to rise by an amazing 45 percent in the next five years, as Moscow prepared to (with uncertain accuracy) drive itself farther and farther into debt. By 1986 it was estimated to have around 1,200 ICBMs and 6,300 reentry vehicles in service; the United States had about 1,000 ICBMs and 2,100 reentry vehicles.

The formidable Soviet SS-18, housed in hardened silos, was a large and sophisticated MIRVed ICBM, capable of carrying ten to fourteen individual reentry vehicles, each with a 500-kiloton warhead. The START II Treaty was written to ban land-based MIRV systems largely because of the SS-18's capabilities, and because it was seen as a potential first-strike weapon. In 1983, SS-18 "Mod 4" missiles were believed to be capable of destroying between 65 and 80 percent of U.S. ICBMs by targeting each with two nuclear warheads. After such an attack, more additional SS-18 warheads could be available for a second strike.

Congress finally agreed to the deployment of fifty MX Peacekeepers to boost the United States counterstrike deterrent (Reagan had asked for one hundred), and operations began in early 1986 at a base near Cheyenne, Wyoming.* How effective could they be? The Soviet defector Arkady N. Shevchenko told an LLNL audience later that year that the Kremlin believed Moscow's ABM defenses could stop more

---

*Reagan started calling the MX (Missile-Experimental) the Peacekeeper in a speech of November 22, 1982.

than half of incoming weapons and that, with upgrades, it would be able to stop more than 90 percent of them.

At the twenty-seventh annual congress of the Communist Party of the Soviet Union in 1986, Gorbachev expressed a "sincere desire to throw off the burden of 'Star Wars' and of the arms industry in general." The U.S. military-industrial complex, he said, was "the locomotive of militarism," and America and its allies were "subverting the cause of peace in Poland and Afghanistan."

DEATH AND DESTRUCTION

That summer, things had turned decidedly nasty. Several senior advisors to European governments were killed in 1986 and 1987 because they or their organizations supported SDI. It is almost certain that the Kremlin and its allies—the Red Army Faction is reckoned to be among the latter—orchestrated these assassinations as part of a savage campaign that was waged on a number of fronts against SDI. "Since last July," wrote James Denton and Peter Schweizer in a July 1987 issue of *National Review*, "there have been seven terrorist bombings, three assassinations, five highly suspicious 'suicides,' and one disappearance among European scientists, researchers, defense contractors, and military and government contractors."[39]

In a memo to DCI Casey, predicting that "from now on the Cold War will become more and more of a bare-knuckles street fight," Herb Meyer warned that Moscow might opt to "raise the level of violence" and "attribute the increased violence and danger to the inevitable result of reckless U.S. policies." To implement this strategy, he continued, "the Soviets would not need to commit each and every act of violence themselves. They would commit some, arrange for others to be committed by surrogates or allies, and generally create an atmosphere in which violence flourishes. This last element would be especially fruitful, for there are always those who stand ready to murder for one cause or another when the timing seems right."[40]

Anti-SDI violence centered in West Germany and spilled over into France and Italy. Less than a week after Reagan's speech at the Brandenberg Gate, the terrorists struck. Karl-Heinz Buckerts, director of research at Siemens, an SDI contractor with whom Yonas had recently spoken, and his driver were killed by a remote-control Red Army Faction bomb on July 6, 1986—ironically, in the meeting he had criticized "Star Wars," saying it would drive a wedge between the United States and Europe. The Fraunhofer Research Institute in Aachen, which was working on an SDI-related laser, was bombed on July 24.

On July 25, the Dornier offices in Inimenstaad were bombed—the company was working with Sperry on a space targeting system. Thomson CSF's Paris headquarters was bombed in August 1986, shortly after it took on an SDI contract. Gerald von Braunmuhl, a West German foreign ministry advisor on SDI, was shot dead by the Red Army Faction on October 10, 1986. IBM's Heidelberg research center, which had four SDI contractors, was bombed on November 16, 1986. MBB (Messerschmitt-Bölkow-Blohm) personnel moved out of their homes to escape possible Red Army Faction attack. Gen. Licio Giorgieri of the Italian Defense Ministry, who like Von Braunmuhl had been involved in SDI negotiations with the United States, was assassinated on March 20, 1987. Giorgieri's death was claimed by the Union of Fighting Communists, which produced a fourteen-page letter explaining that he had been killed because of his support of SDI. The missive ended, "No to Star Wars."

No direct involvement with the KGB could be proved. Yet, wrote Denton and Schweizer in their article, "Murdering SDI," "in view of the Kremlin's preoccupation with killing SDI, its cozy relationship with various terrorist groups, and the pattern of its past behavior, it would be naïve and irresponsible to ignore its possible complicity."[41] Indeed, Red Army Faction members had been schooled in terror technique at a camp set up south of Berlin by Erich Mielke, a four-star general in East Germany's police force and head of its Ministry of State Security. Members of various terrorist groups gathered there for training by Stasi specialists in the use of weapons ranging from small arms to grenade launchers and car bombs.[42]

The European SDI killings were suspected to be KGB-connected, but was this truly the case? "I always assumed there was a connection but I don't know that for a fact," Meyer said. But, "There are no coincidences. Guys don't suddenly start picking off guys at Siemens for nothing."[43] It's quite possible that Gorbachev and his advisors didn't know the real answer, either, for after Andropov's death the KGB had become virtually independent. "Its chairman was in a position to report what he pleased to the general secretary," Matlock wrote. "There was no mechanism to make sure that the reports were honest or complete."[44]

One U.S. National Intelligence Estimate did address the question of whether the Soviet Union was involved in state-sponsored terrorism: the CIA analysts insisted it was not. "But look," Meyer protested, "we know there are terrorist training camps in Soviet-bloc countries—we have pictures of them. It just isn't possible those governments are unaware of these camps. The Soviet Union must know about these camps, and if they know about them and allow them to operate, that means the Soviet Union is involved." The analysts responded with what Meyer called a classic CIA reply: "We have no evidence of that." Meyer said his frustration with the analysts' consistent failure to connect the dots was "sometimes excruciating."[45]

In the United States, some scientists were simply refusing to work on SDI projects. Donald A Hicks, Department of Defense Research Director, retaliated with the suggestion that federal research grants be denied them. "Freedom works both ways," he said. "They're free to keep their mouths shut. . . . I'm also free not to give the money."[46]

COUNTERMEASURES

After President Reagan refused to abandon SDI at Geneva, Soviet military design bureaus energetically continued their work despite criticism from the Soviet Academy of Sciences and Gorbachev's own desire to call a stop to the expensive development of space weaponry. It centered on countermeasures—earlier described as the centerpiece of the Fon-2 program.

In the middle of April 1986, Gorbachev convened a meeting on space science and technology planning at his small Kremlin office—Roald Sagdeev gave an illustrated talk; Evgeny Velikhov was there to head up the government's science interests; and officials from the rocket industry represented the actual builders. Among the last-named was Oleg Baklanov, minister of general machine building (his organization's name—MinObcheMash, or MOM in Russian—was a cover for the Soviet missile and space ministry), and his deputy, Aleksandr Dunayev. Baklanov headed the Soviet space industry throughout the Gorbachev years, during which time he was appointed secretary of the Central Committee of the CPSU, responsible for the defense industry as a whole. Six or seven people were seated around the table. After Sagdeev's presentation, the conversation was punctuated by the eager voice of Aleksandr Dunaev. "Mikhail Sergeyevich," he said, "why are we wasting our time with space mission when we can do missile defense better and cheaper than Americans?"[47]

There was a momentary silence. "Can you imagine!" Sagdeev reflected later. "Better and cheaper!"[48]

Dunaev and his boss, of course, lost the day. As Foreign Minister Aleksandr Bessmertnykh remarked, Gorbachev was well aware that "any attempt to match Reagan's Strategic Defense Initiative . . . would do irreparable harm to the Soviet economy."[49] "Of course, many of the military industrial complex wished to receive funds and money for these purposes," said Velikhov. "But this never happened. They failed.

They continued financing the old systems under the general umbrella of countermeasures, but these were more or less rational programs, like intelligence satellites, communications satellites, and so on."[50]

Still, the idea of fielding a Soviet "Star Wars" program was not dismissed outright. "Our group, the scientists, produced the evaluation that SDI was futile and dangerous," Sagdeev explained. "Then two other groups of players, one from the military industry, the other the military themselves, joined the debate. After the military industry de facto decided to lobby in favor of a Soviet version of SDI, everything depended on the military [leadership] to break the deadlock." Finally, Akhromeyev applied the coup de grace to "SDIsky." "After he said it was stupid—that we should not do it—Gorbachev put together all the analyses and made the right decision," said Sagdeev. "Perhaps Akhromeyev reasoned that SDI would cause a strategic destabilization between offense and defense, or maybe it was technologically unrealistic, or perhaps it would cost too much money—I don't know, but it was a smart decision."[51]

"We could have competed in terms of basic science and ideas. However, bringing these ideas to life was beyond us," admitted I. S. Belousov, who served as Minister of Shipbuilding 1984–89.[52] "Some of our scientists argued that SDI was feasible," agreed M. A. Gareev, an army general and onetime deputy chief of the general staff. "Others, however, myself included, argued on both economic and technological grounds that it was not necessary to launch an analogous program. We developed our own program, 'The destruction of the enemy's cosmic systems.' In this way we undermined SDI."[53]

Countermeasures were now in vogue—and perhaps a serious dose of bluff as well. "There could be many types of countermeasure," said Velikhov. "It depends on what kind of system you face. The threats are complicated, including decoys, updated systems, shorter [rocket] burn period. There were many possibilities, all cheaper than building the SDI. We tried to convince the world of this, but we did not try to convince the government to build all of them—it was not necessary because the Americans would never be able to build their system. You would never need to implement countermeasures, just to be prepared for them. This was the philosophy we tried to sell to Gorbachev, and which he brought out at the Geneva summit."[54]

"Each particular group in the area of exotic missile defense technology came with its own asymmetric scenario," Sagdeev recalled. There were many different ideas—EMP was there, smokescreens in space, plasmas, decoys that would radiate in the infrared to distract heat-seeking interceptors . . .

"Prokhorov pointed out that the lasers that had been proposed to incinerate incoming rockets would never do the job—but that we could use less powerful lasers, for a cheaper price, to render warhead or interceptor electronics useless. This statement sent a signal to supporters of various decaying exotic technologies: 'Oh, maybe we still can have a role! Maybe we cannot incinerate the targets but maybe now we can find an easier way of doing it!' "[55]

Plans were also continuing for the first flight of the giant Energiya system, which was to carry Polyus into orbit. This too might have been considered part of the countermeasures program—Prokhorov's laser concept might have made an ideal addition to the Polyus manifest. But despite all the research and development that had gone into battle-station hardware, little or nothing was ready to make the trip. At one time Salyut's general designer approached Sagdeev to talk about the payload for the first Energiya launch: "Would you like to say this is your payload? I'll give you a contract." Sagdeev refused: "I said absolutely not." Eventually the launch would carry what he called "old trash."[56] But the possibilities were so varied that it could have been an intriguing mixture of old trash nevertheless.*

The Gorbachev government decided that there had to be a simple means of beating a potentially sophisticated SDI and by the end of 1986 had created an integrated countermeasures program by bringing all related efforts together under a single umbrella. "If they had succeeded they would not only have messed up any SDI, but also have taken the high ground in military capability," said Yonas, "and we would have had to fight back in space with the real 'Star Wars,' but shooting, and not with viewgraphs."[57]

In truth, the once great Soviet research establishment was melting away, as one of the many casualties of the harsh economic realities that were being addressed by the Gorbachev regime. "I feel that Gorbachev has to take the blame for the attempt to demolish the military-industrial complex," wrote Viktor Mikhailov. "He almost ordered that the directors of our enterprises be squashed, treating the talented scientists and organizers like bedbugs."[58]

THE YONAS LEGACY

Yonas left the SDIO in August 1986. Before he left, so much "secret" material had been published about the closely held goings-on of strategic defense that he created his own mischievous leaks, at the

---

*Mark Wade's startling inventory of a possible Polyus payload, posted at www .friends-partners.ru/partners/mwade/craft/polyus.htm, differs radically from the "trash" described by Roald Sagdeev, head of the Soviet space institute IKI.

time of the Fletcher Panel and sporadically afterwards. He wrote bogus memos, scrawled information on boards that he did not erase, left made-up notes in his wastebasket, and created viewgraphs about a fictional Pluton bomb. But while Yonas was convinced that hints of the existence of the bomb would appear in print, nobody took the bait. His colleagues, however, enjoyed the spoof, and when he returned to Sandia they gave him a t-shirt emblazoned, "Father of the Pluton Bomb."

Yonas then joined Titan Corporation as president of Titan Technologies, taking over the company's activities in electro-optics, computational fluid dynamics, and pulsed power. He was also responsible for corporate development of strategic planning, as well as mergers and acquisitions of emerging high technology companies. He would rejoin Sandia as a vice president in 1989.

But he was still haunted by SDI, and kept on writing about it. While President Reagan suggested sharing SDI with the Soviets, Yonas had the idea of sharing an early-warning system with them. But when he gave speeches promoting the concept, he was ridiculed. It was a good idea, but its time had not yet come. Fifteen years later, the United States and the Soviet Union agreed to share just such a system.

Between his stints with the Fletcher Study and SDI, he wrote a paper for the Spring 1985 issue of *Daedalus*, the journal of the American Academy of Arts and Sciences. He made the point that opponents of SDI had, in an attempt to defeat the entire project, seized on the fact that the conclusions of the two Fletcher panels—on policy and technology, respectively—were never fully integrated. Yonas was acutely aware that the program should ideally have integrated the two panels' findings, but methods for accomplishing this act were, if they existed at all, an occult art. This aspect of multidisciplinary thinking would plague analysts into the new century, by which time the problems of complex, multilateral threat had become far more widespread.

In Yonas's mind, the most important thing he learned from "Star Wars" was that, as he wrote in *Daedalus*, "the problem of integrating human behavior and political institutions with rapidly evolving technology may prove to be the most difficult and crucial challenge to humanity's long-term survival."[59]

As for SDI's real purpose, "It was a program about human behavior, as indeed deterrence was always a program about human behavior. It was never something to write equations about. It was about psychology."[60]

Now another barrage of applied psychology was on the way—at the decisive Reykjavik summit of October 1986.

12

THE BEGINNING
OF THE END

I think science, as a diplomatic tool, is great.
—Condoleezza Rice, U.S. Secretary of State

The Cold War was waged at a brisk pace throughout the first half of 1986, despite the increase in East-West negotiations. President Reagan had increased U.S. warfighting capability and was still promising "a shield that could protect us from nuclear missiles just as a roof protects a family from rain."[1] The Soviets, meanwhile, were winning worldwide admiration for orbiting the 20-ton Mir core module satellite, a combination control deck and living quarters. With the addition of other modules, Mir became a 250-ton sensation that would survive the breakup of the Soviet Union, playing an important international role in space sciences until its retirement in 1999. The core module included basic technologies that would be used in Oleg Baklanov's new monster, the Polyus space station, which was nearing completion at the Khrunichev factory.*

In the less glamorous inner world of the SDIO, significant changes were afoot. In December 1985, following the MIRACL experiment, two studies recommended changes in the organization. One called for an administrative sort-out after finding that the SDIO was "critically short" of the people and skills needed to carry out its responsibilities. The other concluded that, whereas the required computing resources and software "could be developed within the next several years," this challenge amounted to "the paramount strategic

---

*Mir had a long pedigree, dating back to the early Salyut, TKS, and Almaz programs. Almaz had morphed into the Skif/Polyus concept n 1976.

defense problem." Abrahamson responded to both studies by reorganizing the SDIO and setting up a "National Test Bed" at Falcon Air Force Base, near Colorado Springs, Colorado, to help solve the problems of battle management.

The organization was also sharpening its focus. In a March 7 speech, Yonas told a Commonwealth Club audience that "the most straightforward and best-proven approach to interception of a high velocity object in space is with a very smart homing projectile—essentially a space version of an advanced conventional munition.

"That's the kind of technology we're pursuing," he said.[2]

Directed-energy weapons were consistently winning publicity, but Yonas had a hunch that in the long run they would be more useful as a means of discriminating decoys from real reentry vehicles than actually destroying the space invaders.

SDI research carried out in the first three quarters of 1986 brought little new hope for fieldable SDI technology, though billions of dollars had been committed for the program. Reagan, despite the dearth of actionable results, remained confident, even ebullient. Most SDI proponents were now backing a partial SDI defense, but he was still perpetuating the umbrella idea. "Even now," he said in a June 1986 speech to graduates of Glassboro High School, nineteen years after the city hosted the Johnson-Kosygin summit, "we are performing research as part of our Strategic Defense Initiative that might one day enable us to put in space a shield that missiles could not penetrate." Then he reproached the Russians for doing too little to achieve "real and verifiable" arms reductions. "I have come here today to say that the Glassboro summit was not enough, that indeed the Geneva summit was not enough, that talk alone, in short, is not enough," he said. "I've come here to invite Mr. Gorbachev to join me in taking action."[3]

Reagan repeated that he had a two-pronged solution in mind—arms reductions linked with strategic defense. In an August 1986 letter, he told Laurence Bellenson, "My own view is that we may be able to develop a defensive shield so effective that we can cause it to rid the world once and for all of nuclear missiles." The system would be kept in place "in the event a madman comes along some day and secretly puts some [nuclear weapons] together."[4]

Reagan's use of words like "might," "may," and "could"—instead of "will"—kept him honest. Amazingly, outside the inner circle of scientists and White House spin-doctors, there was a general feeling that Reagan's dream could indeed come true. SDI opponents like Richard Garwin, Hans Bethe, and Carl Sagan had a hard time matching the rhetoric of the Great Communicator and his aides, however implausible. Many Americans had grown up with the successes of project *Apollo* and had been thrilled to see men walk upon the surface of the moon. Many had been captivated by the *Star Wars* movie trilogy and the great novels of science fiction. They didn't like the grim visions of nuclear war, either, and they *wanted* to believe in SDI.

The detractors also had an image problem. They were detached "academics seeking to expose the truth"; they had a "liberal," "left-wing," even "commie" agenda. And so the majority of the American public was unsure about taking them seriously. In Moscow, nobody wanted to believe in SDI, but they felt they had to—even if they had a gut feeling that they should be more skeptical. There was an abiding belief, even awe, in the success of Western technology: any Soviet who had visited the West could rhapsodize about the technical reliability of its infrastructures. So in a large part the Soviet leaders heard Reagan's words as assertions and promises rather than dreams. Could they crank up their directed-energy-weapons program and compete successfully with the United States in this new department? Some in the military-industrial commission may have protested otherwise, but the answer was a bleak "no," not even if they wanted to.

Roald Sagdeev, like Richard Garwin, knew the physics of SDI and had a broader perception of the nature of the competition between the United States and the Soviet Union than most. "I think it was one of the most important and impressive achievements of Gorbachev that he did not accept the challenge posed by Reagan's SDI program," Sagdeev said in his 1992 Tanner Lecture on Human Values. "The 'asymmetric response,' even as vaguely as it was formulated, prevented huge Soviet expenditures in the area of antiballistic missile defense."[5]

A Lesson in Math

There were now about two thousand U.S. sites—missile silos and the like—that could be considered as targets by Soviet war-planners. Jim Abrahamson and Pete Worden estimated that the Soviets had enough ICBMs to place two or three warheads on each U.S. missile silo. It followed that an ICBM attack would be totally devastating if the United States still lacked an ABM strategic defense system. But the new Abrahamson-Worden math nullified the Kremlin's treasured Correlation of Forces model. The two experts expressed confidence that the SDI program they envisaged, when completely deployed, would totally eliminate the problem. To overcome it—that is, to destroy 90 percent of these targets—the Soviets would have to accomplish a feat that was both impossible and absurd. They would have to aim five hundred warheads at each target.*

In fact, at this point the Soviets had no intention of launching a first strike against U.S. silos or U.S. population centers, though in theory it could take out ten closely spaced cities on the U.S. East Coast with just one salvo from an SS-18. A more logical course would be to deploy countermeasures for use if the United States were ever successful in deploying SDI.

Abrahamson and Worden said their analysis clearly showed that SDI was "a means whereby both the Soviet bloc and the Western nations can forge a better and far safer strategic relationship."[6] Gorbachev had already come to believe that there was no real threat of war with the United States, and he told the Politburo as much. "Until now, during the period of stagnation, we had assumed in our planning that a war is possible, but now, while I am general secretary, don't even put such programs on my desk," he said.[7]

In the summer of 1986, Gorbachev was vacationing at a Black Sea resort, mulling over the Cold War dilemma. "What are we going to do about Reagan?" he asked Anatoly Chernyaev. The foreign policy advisor had a letter from the president with a routine reply penned by Shevardnadze. But Gorbachev had no time for that. "We've got bogged down," he told Chernyaev. "We're getting nowhere. We're stuck—we must get things moving. This can only be done by two leaders, president and general secretary."

There at his Black Sea dacha, in shorts and t-shirt, Gorbachev said he wanted to schedule an urgent meeting with Reagan. Displeased and impatient with the foreign ministry's missive, he told Chernyaev he wanted to get things moving by having a face-to-face meeting—in Reykjavik. Shevardnadze dutifully delivered the suggestion to Reagan at a September 19 meeting. Gorbachev then told Dobrynin he intended to accept significant cuts in strategic missiles in exchange for America's giving up SDI. "We should propose sweeping reductions," he said. "If they are accepted, we can bring real détente. Real disarmament." Dobrynin was cautious. "In general it's a very good idea," he said, "but I doubt very much that President Reagan will accept demolishing SDI. It's a very dear child of his and he will not change it."[8]

---

*The rationale in brief: If the U.S. had a three-layered defense with 80 percent effectiveness per layer, the Soviets would need "200 warheads per target to destroy 50 percent of those targets and 500 warheads per target to destroy 90 percent with their current confidence level." James A. Abrahamson and Simon P. Worden, "Technologies for Effective Multilayer Defenses," in Fred Hoffman, Albert Wohlstetter, and David S. Yost, eds., *Swords and Shields: NATO, the USSR, and New Choices for Long-Range Offense and Defense* (Washington, DC: Lexington Books, 1987), 180.

It didn't take another summit to remind the world of the president's strong stand on SDI at Geneva. Despite this, the compromise faction within his own administration worked hard to soften his position. Robert E. (Bob) Linhard, an Air Force two-star general, advised him that space defenses, while not a bad thing, were not near-term prospects, and that therefore Reagan could afford to accept limits on near-term deployment. This sort of talk alarmed the people who wanted to bring a conclusive end to the Cold War, rather than merely continuing it under less dangerous conditions.

"We all knew that if you had a moratorium on a deployment, for some number of years, the money would go away," said Worden. "This would be the death-knell. So we needed to make sure that we could counter that by letting the president know that there *are* options for near-term deployment."[9]

Apparently Reagan was also convinced by Weinberger and others that an SDI limited to laboratory research could not win funding from Congress. Shultz did not oppose this argument. To Matlock, it was unfounded. "Ten years in laboratories would not have killed SDI," he wrote. "It could have preserved the concept since there was at least that much research needed to determine what technologies were most promising."[10]

To press home his point against a moratorium on deployment, Worden wrote a *National Review* article that said that the United States could have several thousand space-based rockets and a few thousand ground-based missiles by 1995, which would be able to "disrupt" a Soviet first strike for less than $100 billion.[11] Prepublication copies of Worden's article had been carefully circulated prior to the summit, and for a special reason. "Various people were quite concerned that Reagan was being persuaded by the National Security Council staff to give away the farm for deep offensive reductions," Worden said. "When the NSC people read the article in the *National Review*, they were pretty upset, but apparently Reagan read it and demanded that they bring Abrahamson over to tell him what we could and could not deploy. Which he did, and that changed Reagan's attitude. From that point he was not inclined to give away anything."[12]

In June 1986, a group of thirty "former Soviet scientists" used the Washington media to publish a warning that Moscow still supported SDI-type defenses, that a similar plan remained "part of the Soviet Union's global strategy against the non-communist world," and that its leadership "can be expected to continue working on their 'Star Wars' system, either overtly or covertly and with high priority." For the most part, the message was treated for what it was—the unreliable rhetoric of angry dissidents.

The official Soviet machine was setting the stage for a victory of its own at Reykjavik, and working hard to reach into the heart of public opinion. The KGB even made use of the Iran-Contra affair, which became entrenched in December 1985 after Reagan approved a plan whereby an American intermediary would sell arms to Iran in exchange for the release of a hostage being held in Lebanon. Funds from the sales were sent to anticommunist Contra rebels fighting in Nicaragua. The KGB orchestrated the "discovery," in a crashed plane in Nicaragua, of forged papers detailing U.S. aid to the Contra movement.

KGB foreign intelligence chief Vladimir Kryuchkov apparently thought that Gorbachev would want to use this ploy to snooker Reagan into believing that the Soviets had huge amounts of information on the Iran-Contra affair. His naive assumption was that Gorbachev would offer to keep the information quiet if the president gave up SDI. But Kryuchov's archrival, Anatoly Dobrynin, was proposing the now-familiar strategy favored by Gorbachev in their Black Sea discussion—to trade SDI for large-scale reductions in nuclear arsenals.[13]

A New Bid for Early SDI Deployment

While Excalibur struggled in its death throes, other directed-energy concepts, including the space-based chemical laser, the ground-based free electron laser, and the neutral particle beam, were still being investigated. At the same time, adaptive optics* was becoming a way of compensating for atmospheric disturbances (a major problem when trying to take aim at a small, faraway target from the ground); and there was new hope for methods of sending laser beams efficiently through the atmosphere.

Then, impressive results emerged from a September experiment at the new National Test Bed. The experiment, wrote Worden, proved that there are "no show-stopping technical obstacles" that would prevent the creation of an initial global defense weapons system.[14] Not only did it show that the system would work flawlessly from more than one million lines of computer code, it also provided encouragement for development of space-based kinetic-kill missile interceptors of the kind described by Yonas—smarter and more capable, semi-autonomous descendants of Convair's old "garage"-based orbital defenders.

---

*Adaptive optics is used in optical systems to compensate for turbulence in the atmosphere. This is achieved by making adjustments in the light path, generally by rapidly changing the shape of a thin mirror. It is used in modern telescopes to produce sharper images of distant objects.

This idea would survive the century, though at this time most serious thinking was concentrated on ground-based missiles and lasers.

Perhaps just as importantly, though these did not catch the public eye, significant advances were being made in reconnaissance technique, target acquisition, and general battle management technology that would make use of space assets. "Star Wars" was still alive, and the Soviets knew it.

Pro-SDI forces became impatient following a successful test at Cape Canaveral, which was acclaimed "a tremendous success both from a launch and orbital support standpoint."[15] Delta 180 was the first-time equivalent of a boost-phase intercept, and it involved a number of sophisticated sensor experiments, including the collection of data—from space—from a simulated enemy booster launched from White Sands Missile Test Range in New Mexico. "You've got a booster coming up into space and you see the wake behind, a mixture of hot gases confined by the atmosphere," said Abrahamson. "Then, as it goes out into space, you can watch the wake blossom." In this test, Abrahamson and his team wanted to see if computer models accurately showed what the wake would look like to real-life optical sensors—they did—and to make sure that the computerized guidance and navigation commands were correct.[16]

A group of very influential Republicans—including Senators Malcolm Wallop (Wyoming), Dan Quayle (Indiana), and Pete Wilson (California), and Representatives Jack Kemp (New York) and Jim Courter (New Jersey)—began to press hard for SDI work to be accelerated so that parts of it could be deployed for regional theater defense by the early 1990s.

"The early fruits of SDI work can be used in the next half-dozen years to deter war in the Middle East, and to defend our European and Asian Allies from attack with shorter-range Soviet ballistic missiles," promised a letter written by the group to President Reagan. It went on to say that advanced SDI systems could defend the Western alliance against Soviet sea-launched missiles "even in the 1980s," and warned that the Soviet Union might deploy such defenses even if the United States did not.[17]

Meantime, from his aerie in the Department of Defense, Perle could see that McFarlane and Nitze were attempting to use SDI to further their arms control ambitions, and he decided to go the other way. His ideas were more closely aligned with Reagan's, except that he could never bring himself to believe in the dream of building an impregnable shield over the entire United States. Point defense for missile fields, yes; an antimissile umbrella, no. Even the more limited vision might render Soviet missiles useless; and as a side effect it might bring an end to the ABM Treaty, which Perle had come to despise.

REYKJAVIK

Reagan and Gorbachev's summit meeting was scheduled for Reykjavik on October 11–12, 1986. Not surprisingly, DCI Bill Casey had reminded an October 7 NSC meeting, "We think Gorbachev will press hardest on limiting SDI . . . He will have to use the appeal of nuclear reductions to get you to agree to constraints that would effectively block SDI and eventually kill the program."[18]

This was certainly true, but more was in the offing—a dramatic interchange between the two heads of state, dynamic and at the same time confusing, that flipped the decisive card in the house of cards that was the flimsy, secretive, and debt-ridden structure of Soviet bureaucracy. This summit would mark a historic change in the evolution of the Cold War.

Just before Reykjavik, Chernyaev recommended that Gorbachev make strategic weapons his first priority, regardless of SDI, and do away with medium range missiles in Europe without reference to the existing British and French nuclear weapons. Gorbachev was doubtful. While he never admitted that the Soviet leadership was afraid of SDI, it remained his main interest. Reagan had not yet indicated that he might agree to total elimination of nuclear weapons. His main intent was to build on what already had been discussed in Geneva. SDI was nowhere near reality at that time, but it was treated as if it were so. This was now a war of nerves and ideas, not of hardware, and the Kremlin was hoping to spring a trap at Reykjavik.

The U.S. and Soviet teams met at Höfdi House, a two-story, white-painted residence overlooking the Atlantic that had been formerly occupied by British diplomats. One of its peculiarities was that it seemed to be haunted—pictures tended to fall from the walls without explanation. Iceland is an active volcanic region, but the Brits apparently didn't take that into consideration. They moved out.

Very gradually, and invisibly to most, Reagan's faculties had been failing since the attack by a would-be assassin. With a bullet wound close to his heart bleeding profusely, he had managed to summon his strength and make it to the hospital door before collapsing. The ability to summon his energy and play his part immaculately, no matter what, was the special talent of an actor, or of an actor playing the part of a hero. True, every once in a while he would be caught off guard in public, stumbling through a speech, forgetting a question. But for the grand occasions he was always totally there. Preparing for Reykjavik, Reagan was old and internally frail, but the character that kept him on his feet outside that Washington hospital was intact.

Gorbachev started the meetings by opening up his shiny brown leather briefcase and unveiling a set of proposals so detailed—and substantive—that they looked nothing like the typical noncommittal Soviet gambit. (In private, perhaps as a palliative, the general secretary told Reagan that the KGB would not worsen the Iran-Contra affair, and made an order to this effect on his return to Moscow.[19])

By lunchtime, Reagan had suggested eliminating all "strategic offensive weapons" and proposed that if a new strategic defense system turned out to work, the country developing it would share it with the other. He repeated that SDI could not be considered part of an offensive or first-strike strategy—especially since his idea was now to do away with nukes before the system was deployed.

That afternoon, Gorbachev countered by suggesting that each leg of the nuclear triads be cut by 50 percent, and that (as in the original Weinberger-Reagan "zero option") all intermediate range missiles in Europe be dismantled. Gorbachev then asked for commitment to a ten-year extension of the ABM Treaty, and, accordingly, restriction of SDI to laboratory research and testing. Reagan flatly refused on the latter, but the Intermediate-Range Nuclear Forces (INF) missile agreement was home free.

As the heads of state argued, their advisors met informally on the second floor. Here, Peter Schweizer writes in his book *Victory*, Sergei Akhromeyev gave John Poindexter a blunt analysis of the conspiracy he saw behind SDI. This program, the Soviet first deputy defense minister declared, "is an attempt to shift the correlation of forces in your favor."[20]

Early on the second day, Shultz presented Reagan with a Perle-Linhard proposal that would also ensure a ten-year period of compliance with the ABM Treaty. But in its first five years, strategic nuclear arsenals would be cut in half, and again in a second five years if all ballistic missiles were eliminated during that time. Then, after ten years, each side could deploy a strategic defense system. Reagan commented, "He gets his precious ABM treaty, and we get all his ballistic missiles. And after that we deploy SDI in space. Then it's a whole new ball game."[21]

Negotiations continued well past their scheduled midday adjournment. Shortly after 3 p.m., Gorbachev endorsed a modified scheme whereby U.S. and Soviet strategic arms would be eliminated entirely by the end of 1996, but only if research on space components of SDI were confined to the laboratory. Reagan responded by proposing a similar schedule, but allowing defensive weapon research, development, and testing as permitted by the ABM Treaty. After more discussion, the president, frustrated, called for a break. There was more word-wrangling, and then they took another break.

The Americans retired to a specially-built "secret bubble," an electronic-eavesdropping-proof room that had transparent walls and was mounted on blocks. The vision of a world without nuclear weapons was so compelling that Reagan for a moment considered taking the Soviet offer and restricting SDI to the laboratory. Some of the contingent strongly favored taking this course, but pro-SDI aides encouraged Reagan in his resolve: no antimissile system could be proved within the confines of a building. As Pete Worden put it, "Reagan understood that he had to change the game and never give up his trump card, regardless of what was offered."

Worden had absolutely no faith in the total disarmament concept—in his mind the Soviets would go for "deep reductions," and that was the sum of it. "Arms negotiators frequently made ridiculous offers that everyone knew they weren't serious about," he said. "In this case the negotiators were offering the impossible to get SDI on the table."[22]

Late that afternoon, the two leaders seemed to be making piecemeal progress. As the sun dipped low over the Icelandic sea, Reagan said it would be fine with him if all nuclear weapons were eliminated, and Gorbachev concurred. Shultz said, "Let's do it," and Reagan proposed that an agreement be drawn up and signed in Washington.

But they still had not dealt with SDI, and Gorbachev would not leave it alone. He made a last-moment attempt to get the president to agree to the words, "The testing in space of all space components of missile defense is prohibited, except research and testing conducted in the laboratories." Needless to say, the gambit failed.

It was an unbreakable deadlock. "President Reagan wrote a note and pushed it over to me," recalled Shultz. "'Am I wrong?' I looked at him and whispered back, 'No, you are right.'"[23]

"It was the right decision because providing a defense against nuclear missiles was an important long-term goal," Shultz told me. "When Gorbachev said, 'If we get rid of our ballistic missiles, why do you need a defense against them?' President Reagan said that, because there will be rogue states and other states that will make them, we need an insurance policy, 'and you need it too.'"[24]

Gorbachev, who had overestimated Reagan's commitment to disarmament, was stunned; Reagan was stiff-lipped; and again the world was baffled. "Some invisible force suddenly stayed the hand of the President of the United States," Gorbachev wrote in his *Memoirs*.

"Reykjavik became the site of a truly Shakespearean drama. . . . SDI proved an insurmountable stumbling-block."[25]

When the doors of Höfdi House finally opened, it was dark and the waiting crowd could see there had been no agreement on SDI and strategic disarmament. Reagan waved with his head down and there was an even shorter wave from Gorbachev as they continued somberly down the front stairs, looking neither right nor left, an angry Reagan bareheaded in his light raincoat, the disgruntled Gorbachev in his hat and dark winter coat. Photographs of their parting show two men who were not only angry, but also sad. Both had been captivated by the prospect of doing away with nuclear weapons. But that opportunity had been lost.

Nancy Reagan, stranded in the States and watching the summit on her home television set, saw the two as they parted company. "I knew from Ronnie's expression that something had gone wrong," she recalled in her memoir. "He looked *angry*, very angry. His face was pale and his teeth were clenched. I had seen that look before, but not often—and certainly not on television. You really have to push Ronnie very far to get that impression."[26]

Reagan's decision illustrated that, for him, there were no trade-offs in priorities between arms control and SDI. As Paul Lettow remarked, "While Reagan allowed SDI to be used to bring the Soviets to the negotiating table, he refused to allow it to be traded away as a bargaining chip."[27]

Why did Reagan turn down the opportunity to fulfill his dream of doing away with nuclear weapons? As Shultz indicated, other states might pose a future threat even if the Soviets did not. The President also no doubt harbored a lingering mistrust of Soviet intentions and good faith, suspecting that they might keep some of their nuclear missiles even if a treaty were agreed. He would want to have some protection to help America guard against that eventuality. His philosophy in making the decision may well have been, as McFarlane put it, "Trust, but hedge your bets."[28] In addition, Reagan was aware that giving up nuclear deterrence was a giant step that would be unpopular with America's NATO partners—Margaret Thatcher above all had made this clear. Thus, helped by the impetus of anxious whisperings from George Shultz's staff, he would have been reluctant to trash this linchpin of allied deterrence without informing them or, better still, consulting with them.

Others had a different rationale for hanging on to SDI, but not merely to bankrupt the Soviet Union: for all intents and purposes this had already happened. It was to use SDI in the larger plan to aggravate the Soviet Union's pre-existing problems in finance, military planning, human rights, consumer technology, etc.—in a way that would force substantive, widespread, and permanent change in the Kremlin's way of doing business.

Perception was, and is, everything. The "Star Wars" program did not offer protection then, and possibly never would. It could not provide protection from a lunatic with a ballistic missile, a cruise missile, or a model airplane loaded with anthrax. If a promising system were fielded, the bad guys could always a find a way to attack without the use of long-range ballistic missiles. Whether he realized it or not, Reagan's real ABM weapon proved to be psychology—including getting angry and upset, and making decisions based on how he felt at the time. The Soviets perceived strongly that the United States had something up its sleeve—it could have been SDI, or SDI could have been a cover for something even bigger.

Half an hour after the VIPs left Höfdi House, Raisa Gorbachev wept at a press conference as her husband presented a positive (and ultimately accurate) veneer on the summit proceedings: "In spite of all its drama, Reykjavik is not a failure—it is a breakthrough which allowed us for the first time to look over the horizon."[29] A few years later, Margaret Thatcher would write, with a tinge of triumphalism,

> The President rejected the deal and the summit broke up. Its failure was widely portrayed as the result of the foolish intransigence of an elderly American President, obsessed with an unrealizable dream. In fact, President Reagan's refusal to trade away SDI for the apparent near fulfillment of his dream of a nuclear-free world was crucial to the victory over communism. He called the Soviets' bluff. The Russians may have scored an immediate propaganda victory when the talks broke down. But they had lost the game and I have no doubt that they knew it. For they must have realized by now that they could not hope to match the United States in the competition for military technological supremacy and many of the concessions they made at Reykjavik proved impossible for them to retrieve.[30]

Reagan recounted his impressions of this meeting vividly in his autobiography *An American Life*, from which the following paragraphs are extracted:

> While a truly secure and verifiable U.S.–Soviet agreement eliminating nuclear weapons by the year 2000 was something I wanted, too, what about the Qaddafis of the world, or a lunatic who got his hands on an A-bomb? The Strategic Defense Initiative, if it proved practical, would give us the insurance we

needed even after we had banned nuclear weapons—and on this, I decided, Gorbachev was up against an immovable object.

At Reykjavik, my hopes for a nuclear-free world soared briefly, then fell during one of the longest, most disappointing—and ultimately angriest—days of my presidency . . . But that is not to say important changes were not occurring in relations between our countries.

Despite a perception by some that the Reykjavik summit was a failure, I think history will show it was a major turning point in the quest for a safe and secure world.[31]

As Reagan remarked, it's possible that a Reykjavik "success" would have failed. If the two sides had agreed on nuclear disarmament, this would have been significant, but in reality no more than the first step in a long, difficult, and perhaps impossible process. First it would have to be embodied in a treaty. Then it would have to be ratified by the two nations, each of which had special-interest groups that would likely torpedo the effort, though some aspects, like the 50 percent reduction of all strategic nuclear weapons in five years, might have been acceptable.

Something completely new and wondrous started to gestate at Reykjavik, although nothing really new was brought up except for Reagan's proposal to ban nuclear weapons outright, and both heads of state left in an unhappy state of mind. Gorbachev apparently began to question his own opinions and predispositions, and to consider whether they were wise or otherwise. The reform-minded Anatoly Chernyaev believed that, in 1986, Gorbachev's ideas "were still contaminated by ideological and class mythology, and influenced by an outdated view of the situation."[32] But a radical period of transformation began in 1987, a year of many changes that included Gorbachev's long-delayed awareness that yes, the West had reason to fear a Soviet threat.

It was at Reykjavik, Dobrynin said, "that Gorbachev put away passion and decided that he could and would work with Reagan. He saw in him a person capable of making great decisions."[33] As Gen. William E. Odom, Army assistant chief of staff for intelligence from 1981 to 1985 and director of the National Security Agency from 1985 to 1988, observed, "Gorbachev never again referred to him as a 'fool and a clown' or lamented having such an incompetent man as the leader of a superpower, as he had frequently done in the past."[34]

"If you had to pick one moment at which the Cold War ended, it was when Reagan got up from the table and walked away," claims

Herb Meyer. "And if you had to pick any one thing that ended the Cold War, it was SDI. At Reykjavik Gorbachev offered almost anything Reagan wanted if he would give up SDI. Reagan said no, and that was it. That was the night Moscow lost the Cold War, because the Soviets now understood they couldn't stop SDI.

"SDI was the bullet between the eyes."[35]

THATCHER'S END RUN

At that time, however, Margaret Thatcher's mood was anything but euphoric. When she heard of Reagan's public proposal to eliminate all nuclear weapons after ten years, her reaction was "as if there had been an earthquake beneath my feet."[36]

"I think a world without nuclear weapons is a dream," she told writer Chris Ogden. "It's like a world without crime. You cannot disinvent knowledge, and there is always the danger that someone will have them. Therefore, there is always a need to deter that danger."[37] French President François Mitterrand shared her attachment to nuclear deterrence, and West German Chancellor Helmut Kohl protested, in person, that Reagan should not eliminate all intermediate range nuclear missiles in Europe because the Warsaw Pact had a huge advantage in conventional warfighting capability.

"Reagan was a very righteous man who believed evil weapons needed to be neutralized," Sir Charles Powell observed. "On the other hand, Margaret Thatcher thought the nuclear weapon was an excellent thing, which in the right hands enabled you to protect yourself against an alien threat." The more closely she examined the implications of nuclear disarmament, Thatcher recalled, the worse they seemed to be. So she got together with Percy Cradock (special advisor on security matters) and Powell, and they compiled a set of talking points that she would use to hash out the deterrence problem with Reagan.

Reagan, in his desire to abolish nuclear weapons, had been, in Powell's words, "perilously close to success" at Reykjavik. So Thatcher and company again "hastened to Washington to put matters right."[38] As Thatcher put it, "I had to get over there," for the president "was a genuine believer in a nuclear-weapons-free world," and this was "one of the few things we disagreed about."[39]

Thatcher was nervous about this meeting, for she felt that the defense of Europe now hung on her relationship with the president of the United States. At times Reagan's dream sounded like Fortress America, a scenario in which the United States would withdraw its defenses to its own perimeters and leave its allies—whom the Soviets had left out of the equation—to their own devices. If they were left in the cold, Britain and France would need to rebuild and expand their own relatively modest nuclear defenses, perhaps with the help of other European nations, involving a huge expense in building a completely independent nuclear deterrent for Europe.

Thatcher arrived in Washington on the afternoon of November 14 and went over her talking points with Shultz and Weinberger. By the time she left for Camp David the next morning, Shultz had helped her team polish a draft statement. It was evident that she planned a repeat of her 1984 Camp David performance. And it worked. To her delight, Reagan agreed with the statement, which she then announced at a press conference. In her words,

> We agreed that priority should be given to: an INF (Intermediate-Range Nuclear Forces) agreement, with restraints on shorter range systems; a 50 percent cut over five years in the U.S. and Soviet strategic offense weapons; and a ban on chemical weapons.* In all three cases, effective verification would be an essential element.
>
> We also agreed on the need to press ahead with the SDI research program which is permitted by the ABM Treaty.
>
> We confirmed that NATO's strategy of forward defense and flexible response would continue to require effective nuclear deterrence, based on a mix of systems. At the same time, reductions in nuclear weapons would increase the importance of eliminating conventional disparities. Nuclear weapons cannot be dealt with in isolation, given the need for stable overall balance at all times.
>
> We were also in agreement that these matters should continue to be the subject of close consultation within the alliance.[40]

Thatcher also announced that Reagan had reaffirmed U.S. intent to go ahead with strategic modernization, including the Trident sub-launched nuclear missile, and that he also supported modernization of Britain's independent deterrent, of which—except for the nuclear device and the boat itself—all parts were now U.S.-supplied.

Thatcher believed the new Camp David statement had a profound effect on the politicians in Moscow. "It meant," she wrote, "the end of the Soviets' hope of using SDI and President Reagan's dream of a nuclear weapons-free world to advance their strategy of denuclear-

---

*The West did not then know about the secret Soviet biological weapons program and the fact that they had bio-weapons on their missiles.

izing Europe, leaving us vulnerable to military blackmail and weakening the link between the American and European pillars of NATO."[41]

In November 1986, the Iran-Contra scandal, which had been building all year, emerged publicly. The scandal—the government violated the mandates of both Congress and the UN while managing the details of this proxy war spinoff—broke on November 25, 1986, when circumstances forced Edwin Meese, now the U.S. Attorney General, to admit the program's existence.

Iran-Contra caused irreparable damage to the reputation of the White House, the president, and his staff. But even an issue of such magnitude was dwarfed by the fact that Ronald Reagan's administration had already performed the greatest service possible for its people and for the world. It had started the Cold War on its path to oblivion.

But the Soviets hadn't given up yet.

13

The Velvet Revolution

It is impossible to predict the time and progress of revolution. It is
governed by its own more or less mysterious laws.
But when it comes it moves irresistibly.
—Vladimir Ilich Lenin, 1918

Baikonur Cosmodrome is the Cape Canaveral of Eurasia. It was
founded in 1955 on the right bank of the Syr Darya River, in then-
Soviet Kazakhstan. Where alligators prowl the marshy environs of
Florida's launch complexes, camels and wild horses tramp the parched
drylands around Baikonur.

Baikonur's claim to fame is manifold. It was the launch site for
Sputnik, the takeoff point for Yuri Gagarin's *Vostok* spacecraft, and the
springboard for hundreds of missiles and spacecraft, from the first Soviet ICBM to the tragic R-16 explosion of 1960, from the ill-fated N-1
moon rocket tests to the triumph of Mir. Now, in the bright sunshine
of May 15, 1987, seven months after the Reykjavik summit, Baikonur
was poised for what could be its greatest feat ever. Unknown to the
rest of the world, and despite the ongoing diplomacy and the Soviet
peace offensive, Gorbachev had allowed construction to continue on
his huge "Orbital Weapons Platform," variously known as Skif or Polyus, with a giant Energiya launch system to put it into orbit.

The two—the cylindrical black Polyus attached to its booster like
a U.S. shuttle attached to its launch system—lifted off as expected, not
long after Gorbachev had repeated that the arms race should not be
extended to space. In January, the general secretary had forbidden the
testing of all Polyus's capabilities in orbit—this was intended to be a
"demilitarized" launch. "He didn't know what it was, and all the
things it had on it, until he went to the launch," the SDIO's Pete
Worden heard. "When they told him, he told them that would ruin
the political effort."[1] This turned out not to be a problem. Soon after

launch, the huge craft crashed, its control system hopelessly confused and unable to do anything other than aim directly at the waters of the Pacific Ocean.

Unconfirmed rumors claimed that the launch was purposely aborted. This would have been a wise decision because Western analysts would have no way of verifying what the spacecraft contained and would be justifiably alarmed. A successful launch would almost surely have blocked the Intermediate-Range Nuclear Forces (INF) treaty, which, while agreed upon by Reagan and Gorbachev, had not yet been signed. Space exploration advocate and writer Krzys Kotwicki remarked on his website, "It appears that the nuclear warhead launch control system for the Orbital Weapons Platforms was being developed in a very rushed manner and the instability of the Orbital Weapons Platforms scared the Soviet leadership."[*] The rush was genuine; the rest, however, seems to be information borrowed from a proposal for a 1981-vintage Skif, an early version of Polyus that reportedly was to carry "nuclear rocket heads with laser defeat systems,"[2] and based on erroneous interpretations of a Polyus diagram originally published by Vadim Lukashevich of the Molniya organization.

Years later, Oleg Baklanov said in a Russian television documentary that Polyus was connected with development of "a laser system which had to shoot down air balloons launched by the Americans from Europe towards our territory—they would carry out propaganda exercises and so on and so forth." This sounds strange in a time of instantaneous global communication, but it seems to be a garbled cover story for what were actually experiments on balloons resembling those used to fool antimissile weapons. Igor Bobyrev, a Baklanov deputy department chief, disclosed that there was not enough power available aboard Energiya to produce the expected yield from even a scaled-down model of the intended laser.[†]

Baklanov confirmed, as did others, that there had been no working laser on board Polyus, merely a model of the device.[3] It was probably intended to point and track decoy balloons released from the spacecraft.

---

[*]This quotation, posted at http://k26.com/buran/Info/Polyus/polyus-energia.html, appears in the same paragraph as information attributed to Chief Designer Yuri Kornilov and General Designer V. V. Pallo, both of the Salyut Design Bureau.

[†]Bobyrev's statement that the scale model laser would have "worked but not to total yield," because of power constraints comes from a Voice of Russia broadcast (www.vor.ru/Spanish/Cosmos/cosmos_sp_60.html). While there was some speculation that this was to be a free-electron laser, the large "terahertz" Soviet FEL was not built until about 2000, at the Budker Institute in Novosibirsk, and in any case would have been too large even for Polyus to accommodate.

"The launch, as I believe, was not so much a really technical undertaking as a political move in the big space 'game' between the USA and USSR," Peter Zarubin said. "The spacecraft was produced in great haste and it came to its logical end—malfunction. Since no real payload was available at the time of the launch, an imitation payload had to be quickly devised."[4] The dramatic speculations about Polyus's payload were little more than propaganda and outdated journalistic hype.

The crash must have been a bitter disappointment to Baklanov, who wanted to show off Soviet space capabilities not only to the world but to Gorbachev as well. But the general secretary had political (and doubtless economic) reasons for slowing down the militarized space race—Big Oleg just happened to lose ground in the process. Zarubin considers that neither man had a realistic knowledge of the status of space-based directed energy weapons (Baklanov built spacecraft, not lasers). "The space high-energy laser and other possible directed-energy weapons were at very early stages of development in several organizations, not only at Astrofizika," he insists, "and no real ground prototypes existed—only small-scale and poorly engineered laboratory test models."[5]

"If Polyus had gone into space, and even if it was really a bunch of junk," said Gerold Yonas, "they would have done the best psy-op of all, and we would have panicked."[6] Ever conscious of the dark side, he points out that even a laser-free Polyus *could* have contained small antisatellite mines and launched them into space before it ditched.

Polyus started out with a grand design—in fact several grand designs that had been developed over a twenty-year period—that remained a state secret until *Izvestia* disclosed its existence in 1991. While Polyus appears to have been little more than a Potemkin ruse, its abrupt demise may have prevented an entire set of Cold War escalations. What if the Soviets, regardless of whether it was a true statement, claimed it carried weapons? What if the Americans simply *believed* it carried weapons? Would Baklanov's folly have awakened a sleeping giant, or a faking giant, or would it have caused the United States to accelerate its offensive capability?

Having a laser-carrying "battle station" in orbit could have been promoted as a Soviet military-space spectacular—even if the laser was an underpowered dwarf—for its limited capabilities were hidden beneath a veil of secrecy. Then, if it had the capability and the will to shoot down Polyus, the United States could have found itself in a very difficult position. "The Soviets could have claimed," said Yonas, that "we would be starting a space war when all they were doing was some space science with lasers, for the good of mankind and in keeping with UN agreements between the peace-loving peoples of the world."[7]

Fortunately that possibility and a host of other problem scenarios were snuffed out with the failure of a piece of electronic gadgetry that had been hurriedly scavenged from a warehoused Cosmos spacecraft. The Polyus saga represented the final death throes of the Soviet "Star Wars" program.

Driven by Reagan's decision to beef up America's military capabilities early in his administration, U.S. nuclear might was building fast while research accelerated in the SDI laboratories. Minuteman III ICBMs were in full production and would reach their full complement of 528 by mid-year; the first developmental Trident II submarine-launched missile had been land-launched that January. Reagan had successfully proposed development of a rail-mobile Peacekeeper (MX) in December 1986, requiring the fifty missiles slated for duty in relatively vulnerable Minuteman silos to be placed instead in specially-designed railroad cars. The wagons could be secretly inserted in freight trains at times of impending conflict. Though derided by many, the idea would offer unprecedented flexibility and freedom from detection. In the Kremlin, Gorbachev and his reformist cohort realized reluctantly that they could not compete forever. Events started to happen that seemed strange and even disloyal.

REFORM AT THE KREMLIN

Without an inkling of the momentous changes he was unleashing, Gorbachev laid the groundwork for democratizing the Communist Party of the Soviet Union in January 1987. This early chink in the totalitarian armor of Soviet communism was destined to become a widening fracture. *Perestroika* (restructuring) and *glasnost* (openness) were seen optimistically in the West as bywords of a trend that could invest the Soviet Union with the hallmarks of Western-style democracy. But Gorbachev merely wanted to reform Soviet communism and bring it up to date with the rest of the world. He may have been more interested in using perestroika to promote propaganda and disinformation than in retooling his nation's creaky infrastructures.[8]

History was moving along its own path regardless. Thatcher had just returned from a spring visit to Moscow. She had accepted Gorbachev's invitation as the British prime minister and no more, yet she believed the Soviet leader would take her words as indicators of broader Western intent and opinion.

Thatcher did her homework. Russian rabbis, former *refuseniks* (individuals denied exit visas), and other intellectuals briefed her, as did Britain's leading Sovietologists. The dissident physicist Yuri Orlov, who had been deported to the United States in 1986, brought her up to date on Soviet human rights developments. General Abrahamson gave her the state of play on the Strategic Defense Initiative. Then she boarded her executive VC-10 airliner, the airborne annex to No. 10 Downing Street, determined, as she told the Conservative Central Council, to sue for "a peace based not on illusion or surrender, but on realism and strength."[9]

Despite the tough talk with her Conservative brethren—Gorbachev said the speech had been harsh enough to consider calling off her visit—she and other Western leaders suspected that the Soviet Union was now on the right track. Thatcher and West German Chancellor Helmut Kohl also shared a concern that Gorbachev might be deposed before he could bring about substantive reforms in the Soviet system.

Thatcher was continuing the role she had assumed as intermediary between Reagan and Gorbachev, though she made no secret of which side she favored. As usual, she and Gorbachev talked for protracted periods of time—unlike the general secretary's meetings with Reagan—and as usual they disagreed strongly on the issue of nuclear disarmament. Thatcher goaded Gorbachev along. She said that she "knew of no evidence that the Soviet Union had given up the Brezhnev doctrine or the goal of securing world domination for communism." The Soviets were supporting proxy wars in South Yemen, Ethiopia, Mozambique, Angola, and Nicaragua, and had occupied Afghanistan.[10] Gorbachev tried to deny that anything was amiss, but later conceded that she had been right.

On the second day of talks, Gorbachev claimed that Soviet computer technology was capable of competing with the American industry, and that the Soviets were ready to match U.S. advances in SDI weaponry. He gave no details, however, and the prime minister was not impressed.*

The Soviets could not lay claim to a single domestically-made supercomputer. Yet as the NSC's Gus Weiss commented, "The Soviets considered a supercomputer a 'strategic attribute,' the lack of which was inexcusable for a superpower."[11] So they pretended.

Between her official Moscow meetings, Thatcher stayed busy and

---

*In the spring of 1987, Gorbachev told a group of All-Union Congress Komsomol leaders that the first Soviet supercomputer had been successfully completed (the Chinese had already made such a claim). Apparently he had been misled by Academy President Guri Marchuk, who in turn may have been forced into the fabrication by Lev Zaikov, supervisor of the military-industrial complex.

visible. She appeared on television, met with dissidents, talked with ordinary citizens, and heard the sad tales of Jewish *refuseniks*. She commented that this had been "the most fascinating and important foreign visit I had made"; she sensed that "the ground was shifting under the communist system," that "something fundamental was happening under the surface."[12]

Thatcher was now in the peculiar position of having a "special relationship" with both heads of state, and though she liked Gorbachev as an individual, she was aware that continuing European street demonstrations in favor of nuclear disarmament could still help the Soviets to split the NATO alliance. As for Reagan, his leadership strength was ebbing. She was worried that he was losing some of his authority and felt she needed to step in, to curb Gorbachev's influence on public opinion.

Reagan was indeed losing his sparkle. "I believe Reagan began to fade bit by bit beginning in late 1985-early 1986," wrote the CIA's Robert Gates in his book *From the Shadows: The Ultimate Insider's Story of Five Presidents and How They Won the Cold War*. "I thought he was still on top of the issues, at least the major ones, but a quality I believed to be fairly magical was waning, day by day."[13]

GORBACHEV: A CHANGE IN STYLE

The CIA issued two reports in 1987 that, respectively, linked domestic Soviet change with external events and analyzed the Kremlin's problems with SDI. A July report observed that while internal problems were facing the Soviet Union, "external developments impinge on all of the decisions Gorbachev might make. . . . [E]ven progress on political and cultural reforms depends on the General Secretary's authority, which can be strengthened or eroded by what happens to his foreign policy initiatives."[14] In November, another report postulated that the Soviets feared SDI because it upset the correlation of forces in terms of both targeting and deterrence; it shifted military-technology capability from ICBMs to an area in which they would be hard pressed to compete, a response would likely be very costly; and SDI would spawn a variety of new technologies, including spin-offs into other areas.[15]

Dobrynin remarked that Gorbachev's style became "more authoritative and commanding" after Reykjavik, to the extent of making top-level decisions and putting them into effect without consulting the Politburo.[16] Some of his foreign policy dicta were considered by the Kremlin elite as unjustifiable concessions to American interests. Within weeks after Thatcher's visit, for example, Gorbachev agreed to include the new short-range SS-23 in the list of missiles to be destroyed under the INF treaty—though the Soviet military strongly wanted to retain them and Akhromeyev had counseled that their range was too short to qualify. When Shultz said the agreement had to include the SS-23, Gorbachev simply said yes, they could be scrapped along with the more powerful SS-20s. An acrimonious scene followed at the Kremlin, but Gorbachev held his ground.

"Without the military and economic pressure from the United States," commented Matlock, "it is most unlikely that Gorbachev could have persuaded his generals to acquiesce to the arms cuts the Soviet Union itself desperately needed, and without which internal re-form would have been unthinkable."[17]

The next month, speaking before the Politburo, Gorbachev re-flected, without naming names, on the relationship between himself, Reagan, and perhaps Thatcher:

> It is important that policymakers, including the leaders of states, of governments, if they really are responsible people, they also represent purely human qualities, the interests and the aspirations of common people, and that they can be guided by purely normal human feelings and aspirations. And in our day and age, this turns out to be of enormous importance. That is to say, literally, to incorporate the human factor in in-ternational politics.[18]

As the political scientist John Dumbrell put it, a "personal superpower diplomacy" was winding down the Cold War—a dynamic that in-cluded Gorbachev, Reagan, and, at the margin, Thatcher.[19]

It's true that Thatcher and Gorbachev were better at dealing with complex issues than Reagan, but the American leader held his own trump card. "The man was not only President, but in many ways the embodiment of his people's down-to-earth character, practicality, and optimism," wrote Colin Powell. "Wise fellow heads of state recog-nized this fact; more cynical leaders did not. And Mikhail Gorbachev was nobody's fool."[20]

Reagan's "easygoing manner masked one of the toughest and shrewdest political minds of our time," wrote Robert Gates.[21] Even Gorbachev was motivated to praise him in public. "You have to hand it to him," he said in a Discovery Channel program. "He believed in his country. He believed it was America's destiny to be victorious."[22]

Shultz commented that Reagan and Gorbachev "were both peo-ple who were self-confident enough to be very bold and not to be troubled if they broke away from the conventional wisdom."[23] One might speculate on whether, decades earlier, the summit talks between President Dwight Eisenhower and Premier Nikita Khrushchev could have evolved in a similar way. The two discussed Cold War problems in 1959 and were due to meet again in 1960. The human factor mentioned by Gorbachev conceivably could have ended the Cold War at that time, had it not been canceled following the interception over the Soviet Union of Gary Powers's U-2 spy plane.

Things didn't look nearly so rosy at the Soviet Ministry of Defense. "We became particularly worried by the end of 1987," Lt. Gen. Valentin Varennikov, chief of Soviet Ground Forces, told a CNN interviewer. "We saw that the country was not going in the direction it should. The situation of the people was getting worse and worse. The situation of the armed forces was no better."[24]

Despite Varennikov's gloomy viewpoint, the anti-Soviet strategies embodied in Casey's ruminations and the early decision directives had begun to wind down in early 1987. Part of this was due to collateral damage from Iran-Contra, but then the strategies, including the SDI campaign, had already done their jobs. Where the Cold War was concerned, the United States was definitely in the ascendancy—but at a price.

Two clouds fell over the U.S. domestic scene in the fourth quarter of 1987. On October 19—"Black Monday"—the stock market dropped five hundred points, a fall attributed partly to the nation's rising deficit. In November, Congress ruled that Reagan bore "ultimate responsibility" for the Iran-Contra affair, adding that his administration exhibited "secrecy, deception, and disdain for the law."

But on December 8 an international success was hailed when—to the disgust of the hawks—Reagan and Gorbachev signed the INF treaty in Washington. Hundreds of U.S. ground-launched cruise missiles and Pershing IIs now would be removed, as would be the Soviet intermediate-range nuclear weapons on the other side of the Iron Curtain. Gorbachev also agreed, unilaterally, to do away with SS-20s that were emplaced in Soviet Asia—yet another conciliatory step that enraged many in the Soviet leadership. In all, the new treaty called for the dismantling of 1,752 U.S. and 859 Soviet missiles.[25]

Standing at a White House podium, with Gorbachev at his side, Reagan recalled, "It was over six years ago, November 18, 1981, that I first proposed what I called a Zero Option. It was a simple proposal, one might say disarmingly simple. For the first time in history, the language of arms control was replaced by arms reduction, the complete elimination of an entire class of U.S. and Soviet nuclear missiles."

REAGAN, ABE, AND SDI

Abrahamson participated in presidential meetings three to four times yearly, at cabinet meetings or in special reviews held with selected members of the cabinet. But never in his career had the SDI chief had a chance for a one-on-one meeting with Reagan. Gorbachev's visit gave him that opportunity.

On this particular occasion, the White House needed a site for the president to make a strong speech before the general secretary arrived, to reinforce the point that SDI was not up for negotiation. Abrahamson suggested they travel to Colorado, where as a backdrop they could use an eighteen-foot wooden mockup of a space-based chemical laser, Zenith Star, at the Lockheed Martin (then Martin Marietta Astronautics) facility near Denver. "We would have an opportunity to tell Reagan that this was one of the things we are doing for his science program," Abrahamson explained. "We would try to make things real for him. I always thought I could make advanced technology understandable by explaining things carefully and hopefully in not too complex a way."

The president duly arrived for his November 24 visit, and Abrahamson supervised a "science fair," explaining various examples of SDI technology in what he considered to be layman's language. At the end of the day, the Lockheed chairman called him in. "I want to share a comment the president made," he said. "The president turned to me and said, 'Do you think General Abrahamson thinks I'm a rocket scientist?'"

Abrahamson was crestfallen. "I had failed dismally, and I didn't know it."[26]

That summer (1987), a Yonas article appeared in the *Los Angeles Times,* accompanied by a cartoon that depicted the SDI as a fake gun that frightened the Soviets. "Many of the necessary elements of a defense system have already been shown to be feasible," he wrote, "and I am convinced that we can resolve the outstanding issues one way or the other with a vigorous program."[27] But he was treading the edge as usual, for he also harbored a large measure of doubt. He was amazed by Abrahamson's steadfast belief in SDI's achievability. "We were able to convince the Soviets that we could beat the crap out of them, using viewgraphs that made no sense at all," Yonas said in 2002. "I remember Abe standing with Reagan in front of a silly cardboard mockup. That was many years ago, and it is still cardboard."[28]

"I don't know any technical person who believed all of the stuff we said," Yonas said. "We knew it was a game. But the Soviets believed it. They went around in public claiming it was nuts while privately worrying about the problem and trying to get us to give it up."[29]

"They tried the mind game, as well as the intimidation game, as well as the charm game, but none of it worked. If they had docked Polyus with Mir, they could have played the game, but we might have overplayed it as well. This enigmatic and ironic story is still untold. We had our Potemkin cardboard laser and they had their Potemkin Polyus."[30]

In 1987, Yonas was estimating the cost of a modest deployment of Smart Rocks—his own version of kinetic-kill interceptors launched from hundreds of orbiting "garages"—at $100 billion. This was cheap compared with a full-fledged DEW system that might cost $1 trillion.[31] The concept, which he proposed at Sandia in 1985 but did not publish, had a lineage that traced back to Project Defender and BAMBI, and to a similar program proposed by the Soviets in 1980. Lowell Wood briefed the similar Brilliant Pebbles concept to Abrahamson in November 1987, and to Reagan and his top aides in the summer of 1988. It was another Teller-inspired initiative. Brilliant Pebbles was designed to put his laboratory back into the defensive-weapon lead after the decline of the x-ray laser. Thousands of these very small, smart, cheap minisatellites would swarm around the earth, alert for the telltale signature of an unannounced rocket launch; if one were located, the satellite would become a kinetic energy weapon, locking onto the rocket and smashing the weapon to oblivion. Lowell Wood's proposed KEWs would each measure less than 40 inches and weigh about 120 pounds. The satellite carrying them would be orbiting at five miles a second, roughly ten times the velocity of a bullet, and would impart this energy to each of its missiles as they were released.

ANOTHER TIME AND ANOTHER ERA

The Kremlin's Hall of Facets is a sumptuous, chandeliered, tsarist relic covered from walls to ceilings with Byzantine paintings from Russian history and religion. The place was and is a monument to historic change. In 1988, one could have imagined that, even though the Soviet Union seemed firmly intact, a time of peace was emerging between the two superpowers. Change was again in the air.

It was here that Ronald Reagan returned Gorbachev's visit to Washington, six weeks after the official, UN.-mediated closure of the disastrous Soviet war in Afghanistan. The next day, June 1, 1988, the INF treaty would come into force. Gorbachev used the occasion to remark, "Realism is an important quality in President Reagan as a politician. . . . Who would have thought in the early eighties that it would be President Reagan who would sign with us the first nuclear-arms reduction agreement in history?"[32]

"I think the first great misconception of this period had to do with arms control measures," Abrahamson said. "The assumption was that arms control measures—such as the ABM treaty—are effective in reducing the nuclear threat. But there had never been a reduction in nuclear arsenals until SDI came along and was seriously advocated by Reagan.

"Another misconception was that the only logical course of action by someone faced by SDI is to build more missiles," he continued. "But we've seen that the Russians compromised when it came to this point."[33]

An American reporter approached as Reagan walked with the General Chairman in the bright sunshine of Red Square.

"You still think you're in an evil empire, Mr. President?" asked the reporter.

"No," said Reagan softly.

"Why not?"

"I was talking about another time and another era."[34]

He didn't know how right he was.

The atmosphere was almost surreal. "He began as number one enemy and he ended as—if I may put it this way—number one friend from capitalist world," commented Dobrynin. "They were shaking hands, strolling around Red Square."[35]

For all the apparent bonhomie of the "Moscow Spring," the final Reagan-Gorbachev summit achieved little of a substantive nature. Ironically, it ended somewhat uncomfortably, enough so to cause Paul Nitze to believe, as Strobe Talbott put it, "that the competition between the superpowers, in both its political and its military dimensions, would continue for a very long time to come."[36]

DRAMA AND GEOPOLITICS

Strangely, the leadership of neither the United States nor the Soviet Union seemed to have any idea that the Soviet Union was about to collapse. A CIA National Intelligence Estimate issued in December 1988 announced that, "to date . . . we have not detected changes under Gorbachev that clearly illustrate either new security concepts or new resource constraints are taking hold." The agency urged a wait-and-see attitude toward Moscow because "thus far, we see no convincing evidence that the Soviets under Gorbachev are making basic changes in their approach to actually fighting nuclear war."[37]

Apparently the report was written and printed before Gorbachev announced to the United Nations, on December 7, that the Soviet Union would reduce its armed forces by half a million men in the following two years—including six tank divisions based in East Germany, Czechoslovakia, and Hungary. This was a fairly dramatic statement, but other parts of the speech were remarkable in a truly historic sense. Gorbachev praised "pan-humanist values" and "global interdependence" Then, calling the 1917 Bolshevik revolution "a most precious spiritual heritage," he all but said it had outgrown its usefulness. "Today we face a different world, for which we must seek a different road to the future," he said. "We have entered an era when progress will be shaped by universal human interests. . . . World politics too should be guided by universal human values."[38]

"Reagan, always lucky," wrote Hendrik Hertzberg in the *New Yorker*, "was never luckier than to be on hand when a Soviet leader decided to lift the pall of fear and lies from his empire, thus permitting its accumulated absurdities and contradictions to come into plain view and shake it to pieces."[39]

In his UN speech, Gorbachev had redefined the status of the October Revolution and, indeed, the validity of Marxism-Leninism in the modern context. He believed that he could move the Soviet Union quickly into an era where communism could be modernized into some sort of socialist-capitalist blend. This dream would prove to be entirely unrealistic. "Gorbachev," said Anatoly Dobrynin, "showed himself increasingly helpless in the face of practical problems and tried to solve them by taking spontaneous, feverish, rash steps."[40]

"Gorbachev was an intelligent man, but he didn't think that he was taking a major risk by encouraging perestroika and glasnost because he thought everything was under such tight control," Dmitry Mikheyev explained.

"He was trying to get people to think, and find new resources to strengthen the USSR. But they didn't talk about solving problems: they began talking about politics. They didn't suggest ideas to strengthen the Party's control of the country, to make their rule more efficient—the things that Gorbachev was dreaming about.

"Once he encouraged the intelligentsia to speak out, scientists began informal debating societies by the thousand," he added. "In two years the whole Soviet ideology was finished, destroyed, not an element left untouched. They destroyed all the Soviet myth in two years. That's what Gorbachev could not possibly foresee. He didn't realize how deeply people resented the totalitarian system."[41]

Still, no one in the late 1980s could know how the Soviet solution would unfold, and SDI continued as if the Cold War were still in full spate. In February 1989, Abrahamson told Weinberger that research results had been "dramatic, and will soon yield major new cost reduction possibilities." He favored Brilliant Pebbles "because it will add defensive deterrence to our offensive capability at less cost than adding new survivability features to a part of our ICBM force." It would also provide "extended defensive deterrence" to the Allies, and "provide maximum leverage in arms control negotiation."[42]

"Some of our strongest Washington allies wanted to go quickly to a deployment program," Abrahamson recalled. "We had made enough progress that, shortly before we left—had there been political will and a majority of the Congress available to us—we could have started a real deployment effort."[43]

Lt. Gen. George L. Monahan Jr. succeeded Abrahamson as SDI director on February 1, 1989.

Gorbachev came face to face with reality that October, when he attended the observance of the fortieth anniversary of the creation of communist East Germany. A torchlight parade intended as a tribute to Marxism-Leninism turned the other way when people began to shout, "Gorby, help us!" After that, Gorbachev realized that the Soviet empire was finished. Two months later, at the Malta summit, he turned to the new president, George H. W. Bush, and said, "We don't consider you an enemy any more." Gorbachev's press spokesman then declared, "We buried the Cold War at the bottom of the Mediterranean."

Gorbachev still hoped to save the Soviet Union, even if it meant giving unprecedented freedoms to satellite states that, beginning with Poland, Czechoslovakia, Hungary, and the Baltic States, were turning against Moscow. The Berlin Wall, which went up in 1961, began to come down on the stroke of midnight on November 9, 1989. Steamrolled by history, Gorbachev ignored the Politburo when, in a July 1990 meeting with Chancellor Helmut Kohl at Arkhyz (Caucasus), he agreed to the unification of Germany. Amazingly, almost bizarrely, the East German states would henceforth owe their allegiance to NATO rather than the Warsaw Pact, though no NATO soldiers could be stationed there.

When asked why the general secretary surrendered East Germany so serenely, Valentin Falin of the Central Committee replied, "We are still waiting for the answer to that from Gorbachev. . . . He confided in no one."[44] Aleksandr Bessmertnykh said the decision was "one of the most hated developments in the history of Soviet foreign policy, and it will remain so for decades."[45]

Through the use of centralized state control, and by managing information given to outsiders, the Soviet system had for decades been able to garb itself with a thin veneer of success, artfully enough to fool more than one itinerant Western analyst. This could not last forever. The veneer was stripped away, slowly withdrawn—by necessity—as citizens tuned in to mass media, began to converse more freely, and awakened to the disparities between Soviet and Western lifestyles. Repeated Western calls for increased Soviet recognition of human rights, rooted in the all-but-ignored Helsinki Accords of 1975, were at last being answered. Glasnost and perestroika came along in the last moves of a transformative process that Mikhail Gorbachev, that would-be reformer of an unreformable system, began and then could not control. Laudably, Gorbachev felt he had to bring the Soviet Union into greater synchrony with the modern nation-states of Europe, North America, and Asia. But the ideologies of the Soviet Union were too unwieldy and too entrenched. The old system could not survive the change. Like a huge old cast-iron structure suddenly plunged into cold water, it split and broke.

Soviet diehards blamed the Soviet Union's fall from the superpower category on "blunders" and give-away foreign policy by Gorbachev and Shevardnadze. The *perestroishchiki* (Gorbachev's brain trust of pro-reform advisors) rebutted that the "universal crisis of socialism" had undermined the Soviet Union.

Sagdeev admits he feels "poignancy for the period of Mikhail Gorbachev, whom we thought to be the savior of the country, the reformer of the system." The great irony was that "It would be this savior who would inadvertently accelerate the collapse of the system."[46]

It was a bittersweet time, for in late 1989 "Gorbymania" was sweeping the world's media. He received the Nobel Peace Prize in 1990 for helping to end the Cold War, and *Time* chose him as Man of the Decade.

A reinvigorated Boris Yeltsin, elected to the new parliament in 1989, soon found himself in the all-powerful Supreme Soviet. Then, in 1990, he ascended to the presidency of the Russian Federation. He rode the great tsunami of change that accompanied an attempted coup in August 1991, increasing his popularity while asking the world not to support the rebellion. He was very visibly present, confident and smiling, when the parliament disbanded the Communist Party of the Soviet Union that month.

Gorbachev returned from a brief house arrest, but his time in the sun was over. In December, he and Yeltsin consummated another unthinkable act: they dissolved the Soviet Union and transferred power to a Commonwealth of Independent States. The so-called Velvet Revolution was over. Gorbachev resigned in a television address on December 25, and Yeltsin began his troubled and contentious nine-year reign as head of a struggling state.

BLUFF, FEAR, CONFUSION, AND HOPE

The terror created by weapons has never stopped man from employing them. For each new weapon a defense has been produced, in time.
—Bernard Baruch, 1946

The U.S.–Soviet Union arms race ended at Reykjavik in 1987, after the two sides agreed to scrap their intermediate-range nuclear missiles in Europe.

It may be said that the Cold War ended at the same time—or when, at the 1989 Malta summit, Gorbachev told President George H. W. Bush, "We don't consider you an enemy." That spring, the *New York Times* ran a series of op-ed columns centered on the question, "Is the Cold War Over?" The *Times* answered its own question in the affirmative. In his 1990 New Year's address, Gorbachev himself pronounced 1989 the "year of ending the Cold War."

But the Soviet Union staggered on until, shortly after an attempted August 1991 coup, Soviet diehards finally conceded that they could not bring Bolshevism back to life. The Soviet Union officially ceased to exist on December 31, 1991.

It had not been a "war" by previous definitions, for it had been waged with arms races, proxy wars, and simulations, with rhetoric and summitry. But then what was it? Evgeny Velikhov, who, despite his sometimes-irreverent attitude to politicians, was science advisor to Mikhail Gorbachev at all of his summits, called it a "virtual war."[1] Then who won it? The knee-jerk Western answer is that the United States (or maybe NATO) emerged victorious. But this is going a mite too far. The Soviets were doing a pretty good job of ruining their own system long before the Great Communicator vowed to bring an end

217

to it. There is merit in the view that Reagan, though extraordinary in so many ways, had "victory" handed to him on a silver platter. However, a different leader might not have recognized the opportunity or been able to summon the political will and determination to take it on.

That said, the last act of the Cold War featured an amazing cast of players. Gorbachev was a history-making phenomenon in spite of himself; other Western players were remarkable, too. Herb Meyer comments on the pivotal political roles played by a most unlikely trio—a Polish Pope, a woman prime minister, and an ex-actor. "Thatcher was important because she was smart, she wanted to win, she was not American, and she was the president's strong right arm," he says. "She and Reagan and the Pope were utterly determined to end this thing."[2]

Gerold Yonas agreed: "All had very significant ideas but little understanding of complex technology, which is not nearly as important as a great idea. Ironically, the Pope knew as much about SDI as he needed to know, which was nothing, and yet he posed a threat to the Soviet Union."[3]

"Strangely," wrote John Lewis Gaddis, professor of history at Yale University, "of all the external efforts to promote internal reform in the Soviet Union through external pressure, SDI—which was never even intended for that purpose—may have been the most effective." The multifaceted U.S. offensive further weakened Moscow's faltering ability to function; then, Gaddis wrote, "the prospect of SDI may well have pushed them over the edge."[4]

SDI was originally intended to support the first and third items in the three-part summary of U.S. policy that appeared in National Security Decision Directive 75: to bolster "external resistance to Soviet imperialism" and to reinforce U.S. interests during bilateral negotiations.[5] Using SDI for an economic or psychological assault on the Soviet system was never singled out as a mainstay of the official plan. When Shultz went to Moscow for talks in January 1985, he was reminded that the "overriding importance" of SDI centered on enhancing deterrence and the case for nuclear arms reductions.[6] But in the end analysis, SDI contributed most to NSDD 75's *second* imperative: to encourage internal pressure "to weaken the sources of Soviet imperialism."[7]

David Fishlock, former science editor of the *Financial Times*, encapsulated the SDI effect with a measured view that makes eminent good sense. "It's a well established principle that if you do a crash program on something that your rival is weakest at, you stand a chance of destabilizing them," he said. "The Russians were weakest on microelectronics and sophisticated electronic systems in general. And here was 'Star Wars,' which was effectively a crash program on electronics. It is true that popular interest focused on the ways of shooting down missiles with lasers, but the program was much broader than this."[8]

SDI somehow stood outside the definition of conspiracy. There is little or no evidence that any covert strategy lay behind the SDI scenario at its inception in 1983, though the announcement was kept secret until the last moment. What is known is that it exerted an internal pressure that the Soviet leadership was ill prepared to deal with, and could not shake from its collective psyche.

"The point of SDI," Thatcher wrote, "was to stop nuclear weapons from reaching their objective. The first nation that got it would have a tremendous advantage because the whole military balance would change."[9]

"It's clear that SDI accelerated our catastrophe by at least five years," Vladimir Lukhin, former chief of foreign relations for the Supreme Soviet and later ambassador to the United States, told Robert McFarlane.[10] But it was not clear to others. "I cannot agree that the SDI initiative had this much importance," snorted Gorbachev. "In the eyes of the people, especially the educated, the totalitarian system had run its course morally and politically. . . . This was the decisive factor, not SDI."[11]

"The idea that it accelerated the collapse of the Soviet Union is nonsense," agreed Evgeny Velikhov. "The reasons were completely internal."[12] Sagdeev told me he felt that "many in the West were persuaded that SDI intimidated the Soviets so much that that they decided to dismantle the communist system." He rightly called the notion ridiculous and "a kind of historic injustice."[13]

Edward Teller concurred with the Soviets—at least to the point of discounting SDI. "The obvious reasons for the failure of communism in Russia," he said in 1999, "were, first, misgovernment, and second, failure to acquire military superiority beyond Eastern Europe. Together, these two contributed to the downfall of the Soviet Union."[14]

When Teller was asked if he agreed with the opinion that SDI had hastened the dissolution of the Soviet empire by five years, he simply answered, "No." On the other hand, he said, "Star Wars" supported the cause of deterrence: "The SDI program tended to ensure the self-defense of the United States. One might make the statement that SDI was a good reason why Russia could not win the Cold War.

"The downfall of the Communist government was due partly to their failure of improving conditions in Russia which accelerated their failure to influence the rest of the world," he said.[15]

The role of MAD has a place here, too. It made invasion of one superpower by the other unthinkable, and it kept the Soviets from extending their European empire beyond the Iron Curtain. It contained the Soviet Union long enough that its internal bureaucracies rotted away. The Cold War had been de-fanged sometime in the 1970s, because no one in the leadership of either side truly believed that anyone on the other side would push the apocalypse button. The Strangelove syndrome was long gone.

The mass media also deserve a mention in the cauldron of ingredients that cooked up the end of the arms race, the Cold War, and the Soviet Union. While SDI did little to increase the appeal of Western culture to ordinary Soviet citizens, radio, print media, and television undoubtedly did. The Kremlin had worsened its own situation by subsidizing the purchase of television sets to watch the 1980 Moscow Olympics. Only the media, and the tough medicine of glasnost, could offer an opportunity to compare Soviet life with life elsewhere. When the Supreme Soviet banned censorship of the press on November 17, 1989, it was a nonevent. The people already knew, and it made them angry with their lot.

SDI was thus no more, and no less, than one of a number of substantive threats that Soviet hierarchs could not shake from their lives. As the Soviet Union weakened, SDI was another germ in the fever that already infected the great Soviet bear's ulcerated breast, eventually causing the beast to die from its many ailments. The infection remained until Soviet communism, old and irritable and sick, fell into the ravine of history.

Just what, and how much, the Strategic Defense Initiative contributed to the end of the Cold War is destined to remain an enigma. It seems that people all over the world, possibly all the way up to President Reagan himself, were captivated by a massive delusion—that an SDI system could *possibly* be in operation, protecting the United States from attack, before the end of the twentieth century. Partly orchestrated, partly improvised, the myth was not noticeably harmful to Western believers. And of course the West's ultimate desire was achieved—a Soviet Union imploded by an unbeatable amalgam of forces that included a profound uneasiness about SDI. It may be that, in the process, the American public also was deceived by the techno-political mirage. But with luck and a fair amount of agile thinking, it seemed their nation had won Velikhov's "virtual war." It hadn't been a war in the old-fashioned sense. It was the kind that now is of supreme interest to superpower planners and guerrilla generals alike. It was and is a war of fear, a high-stakes mind game.

Dissecting the SDI

Reagan's desire to protect the United States with radical new technologies fit well with the thinking of his spymaster, Director of Central Intelligence William J. Casey. Casey suspected that the president would have to come up with something completely new if he wanted to finish the Cold War. Reagan's plans to enlarge and modernize the armed forces would unsettle the Soviets, but the DCI reasoned that the USSR could only be brought to its knees "on the tangent"— that is, by means that were divergent or asymmetrical by comparison with conventional warfighting wisdom.*

The United States needed to come up with something that reached beyond the adjectives "new" or even "threatening." It needed something that was unexpected, unpredictable, unconventional, even off the wall. SDI fit that bill.

After the president's speech of March 23, 1983, Gerold Yonas said, "The Reagan initiative just sort of happened, with no real plan but with some fuzzy ideas that worked."[16] They worked partly because, in Moscow, certain powerful military industrialists hyped the SDI scheme for their own interests, generating and magnifying the impression that the Americans might prove successful. This was relatively easy because Soviet science had already spent huge amounts of money on SDI-like research and, while its efforts had been disappointing, it was suspected in some quarters that American expertise might be strong enough to pull the space-defense rabbit out of the hat.

In the mid-1980s, Soviets and Westerners alike were hypnotized by the rousing high-tech visions of SDI. But, like Yonas, Reagan-era National Security Council staffer Norman Bailey prefers to downplay the issue of SDI's technological feasibility, almost as though it were an incidental matter. The main thing was how the initiative was perceived. "As an element of military display," he wrote, "it was a brilliant success." It was, he added, "an act of leadership which revealed the president's solid grasp of Soviet vulnerabilities, reversed the 'preemptive cringe' approach to arms control which had become habitual to the U.S. in previous years, drew effectively on Western strengths and Soviet weaknesses, and elevated the national consciousness by rejecting the immorality inherent in traditional nuclear deterrence."[17]

At some point, very early in the game for some, much later for

---

*This wording comes from a paraphrase in Peter Schweizer's *Victory: The Reagan Administration's Secret Strategy that Hastened the Collapse of the Soviet Union* (The Atlantic Monthly Press, 1994), 7. In *Ethelberta* (1890), Thomas Hardy wrote of "those devious impulses or tangential flights that spoil the works of every would-be schemer who instead of being wholly machine is wholly half-heart."

others, it became evident that SDI was mostly a construct of possibilities. It held little chance of providing a comprehensive ballistic missile defense—let alone one that also would protect America's allies—within anyone's lifetime. Despite this, and for a variety of nontechnical reasons, the administration thought SDI was a great idea, and a fair proportion of the public favored it as well. The media, ever mindful of the public appeal of space wars and exotic weapons, gave SDI extensive coverage, so that the program assumed a greater aura of importance and promise even when journalists editorialized against it and, in their news columns, reported the criticisms of eminent U.S. scientists.

The blending of these varied perceptions gave rise to a special dynamic. It was this dynamic that began to manufacture the semblance of reality for something that (1) did not exist and (2) had no integrated game plan by which to bring it into existence. While a successful road map for a space-based SDI might be devised, sometime, it was well beyond the capability of twentieth-century science and technology.

While experts on the outside repeatedly condemned the expenditure of so much money on SDI projects, the insiders held their ground and kept on going. With lobbyist support, they steadily upped the ante even when they did not know how they would spend the money they were requesting. In this way they sent a subliminal message to the Kremlin—that these hand-picked SDI experts, supposedly the crème de la crème of American science, must know what they were doing. And they must be more successful, behind the scenes, than they cared to tell. Nothing could have rammed this message home more effectively than Reagan's summit performances. Reagan's aversion to nuclear weaponry was legendary. Thus, when he refused to hobble SDI in return for a Soviet agreement to do away with strategic nuclear missiles, he transmitted a powerful unspoken message. If he gave up this opportunity to do away with nukes, the American SDI program must be confidently tracking toward success.

Yet for Reagan SDI was something other than a mind game. "The president was very firm in his determination to pursue this research," Shultz reflected. "This was based on his own feelings, after having heard from people he considered qualified. As in other areas, it turns out he had thought it through beforehand. Also he had a pretty stiff backbone, and that helped him too."[18]

MORALITY, DECEPTION, AND STING THEORY

It is tempting to question the ethics of a government that knowingly allows its own people to believe that something will almost surely be achieved in the near future when in truth it is a long shot at best.

"Physics is based on integrity. Politics is based on perception," says Yonas. Yet science not infrequently crosses the line into the political sphere. When that happens, Yonas asks, "if a physicist messes with perception by setting the record straight and in doing this upsets the politics, can the physicist be said to be free of political accountability?"[19] It's a knotty question, in which "pure science" comes up against political reality and where one is reminded of Churchill's chastening remark that "scientists should be on tap but not on top." "We have used psy-ops in the past to trick our enemies, and sometimes we tricked ourselves in the process and have diminished the value of our principles," says Yonas, "but we achieved our goals in the end."[20]

The idea that the American public was being misled, or misleading itself, about SDI prompted no great outcry, though plenty of potshots were taken at individual parts of the program. Richard Garwin, no friend of SDI, repeatedly quoted the code of honor of the United States Military Academy, which, he said, "forbids not only lying but also . . . the use of words in such a way that they give a misleading impression of assurance, threat, etc.

"The myths of space technology," he said, "inhibit our putting an end to the extension of the arms race into space, and they deny modern societies the full productive civil and military [non-weapon] uses of space."[21]

"Human beings," Garwin warned on another occasion, "owe their society honesty and candor, and they should be very cautious before using their talents to deceive or mislead, especially in the service of a program of their government or society."[22]

The broad view is that, despite the honest dedication of exceptional people such as its first director, Gen. James A. Abrahamson, SDI was perpetuating a myth, with a few of its practitioners being more deceitful than others. Yonas, for one, worded his own public statements very carefully, and avoided outright lies. Other insiders either were not so subtle or talked themselves into believing certain untruths and managed to forget the frailty of their facts.

Yonas was charged several times with engaging in public deception, even to a degree that could undermine faith in American institutions and damage the country. "We were lying to the Russians," he explains. "They were lying to us. The Cold War was characterized by deception on all levels." The criticism was justifiable, however, and it was uncomfortable: "Our approach did require lying to a lot of people, so it was an ethical problem for them and us."[23]

The truth is that the promoters of SDI were playing with cards that were not so good as they were made out to be. In the process of misleading the Soviets with SDI, its supporters led some of the American public astray as well. Did these misconceptions extend to the presidency? It's a pretty safe bet that, if Reagan submitted to being misinformed, he did so selectively and willingly. The president, not a technical man, may have talked himself into believing in the future of SDI technology because it was simply a smart thing to do—which, indeed, it turned out to be. It is a hard and uncomfortable act to place blame when individuals become "true believers" in the things they say, because in their own minds they *are* true.

The scientific community had its own mix of attitudes toward SDI. Some scientists believed in it because, genuinely, there were important things to learn in their particular areas of expertise—basic information that could be proven to be more broadly applicable, as in the use of adaptive optics to improve images made by astronomers. Some were lured by prospects of money, fame, and glory. Others were simply drawn in by the system. "The politics of science is not laden with the dispassionate objectivity traditionally associated with the conduct of scientific research," wrote Daniel Greenberg. "Like generals pleading for new weapons, or highway contractors pining to pour concrete, many of the politicians of science employ the hard sell and a stretched tale or two to make their way in the competition for money, public and private."[24]

"The problem is how to make a convincing technical argument in a political environment," a former Sandia colleague, Charlie Winter, wrote in a letter to the *New York Times*. "This almost always requires taking some liberties with scientific truth because the audience will not take the time for a few semesters of science before hearing it."[25]

It was generally more difficult for engineers to become believers. The engineer, like the artist, is a translator of ideas into realities. He or she is a performer, entirely essential but mostly unseen, who communicates with the public in the noisy theaters of industry and public works, and his director may be an architect or an astrophysicist. Engineers would have to put together working systems for the ultrasophisticated, supercomplex devices that used SDI-specific science. SDI was a nightmare in the making for the systems integrators, who would have to orchestrate reconnaissance, target acquisition, tracking, beam control, and kill assessment—aided by yet-uninvented power supplies and hitherto undreamed-of computing capability.

Many scientists and engineers alike left the early SDI teams disillusioned, but most stayed on because for them this was the biggest game in town. And after all, they were following orders, doing a job that the president and commander in chief had given top priority, to end the arms race and obliterate the specter of nuclear Armageddon. They may not have had a clear vision of how this might come out, but then, that is what applied research is all about—looking for new ways of doing things better.

Early in the game, ABC's chief White House correspondent, Sam Donaldson, quoted Robert McFarlane—chief architect of Reagan's 1983 SDI announcement—to the effect that the program "would be the greatest sting operation in history." The remark was supposed to be off the record, or attributed to a "senior administration official." But McFarlane made similar comments to other journalist-authors of the time, including Lou Cannon and Strobe Talbott.

McFarlane defines a "sting" as "gaining an advantage by asserting, convincingly, that you can do something remarkable when you can't."[26] The definition is not unrelated to three given in *Webster's Third New International Dictionary:* "to get the better of in a financial dealing . . . to cause to suffer sharp mental pain; to stir or incite by a sharp often painful stimulus." It's a neat explanation. But it would be a mistake to suggest that everyone agrees with it.

"There was no sting since a sting is a conscious, well thought-out and carefully orchestrated game," rebuts Yonas. "We were all clueless but lucky, first with HOE-4 [the successful 1984 antimissile test] and the Russian overreaction, and then with the Congressional overreaction. This was followed by Reagan playing the game with Gorbachev and its perfect timing with the economic collapse of the Soviet Union."[27]

"There was no sting, there was no plan, but the story unfolded anyway. It happened because of people, not technology. It happened because the role of people—crazy, thoughtful, selfish, drunk, stupid, clever people—is to contribute unpredictability."[28]

"A sting?" asked Adm. James D. Watkins, who was chief of naval operations at the time he convinced the Joint Chiefs of Staff to champion strategic defense. "No, that was above my pay grade at the time. It didn't come up with me."[29]

SDI AND THE SOVIET CRASH

Arthur C. Clarke, who at times was an SDI critic, expressed admiration for the program in an essay he wrote for *Science* magazine. I suspect that President Reagan's 1983 'Star Wars' speech . . . will one day be regarded as an act of political genres," he wrote. "However shaky SDI's technological foundations, it may well have contributed to the end of the Cold War."[30] As SDI moved into gear, it helped inflate the fear factor that was necessary for the military-industrial, military, and intelligence chieftains of the Soviet Union to encourage internal misgivings and, incidentally, to line their own pockets. Thus the Soviets encouraged American SDI-backers mightily by reacting with unexpected, undisguised alarm, and the myth enlarged all by itself.

Evgeny Velikhov said that there was no time that the Soviet scientific intelligentsia thought of SDI as a hoax, or a trick, or a scam. "This never happened because we [Soviet scientist-academicians] had very close relations with our American friends, especially the Federation of American Scientists, and we could share their insights," he said. "So we took SDI more or less realistically. We could see the two camps— one camp was in favor, the other against. And we understood the philosophy of both of them."[31]

However, SDI was subject to continuous change. Yonas is fascinated by the huge potential for change that can be hidden in small events: "SDI could have come out differently if a few things had changed—if Harold Agnew really did not like my jokes when we had dinner together in 1982 and did not ask me to do the Fletcher study; if HOE-4 failed and the Russians did not overreact; if Cap got mad at the Army; if Abe quit because we couldn't get money. Things could have been different if the people acted differently. In the end, 'It's the people, stupid.' "[32]

Chaos was increasingly at work throughout the last years of the Cold War, as time-worn staples of superpower relationships—from warfighting methodology on one hand to trade relations and diplomacy on the other—were reshaped. Ronald Reagan was the chaosmonger, cheerfully accepting the caricatures of loose cannon and diplomatic dunce in the full knowledge that these distortions would increase the distress of a Soviet system that, to protect and extend its power, depended desperately on the ability to predict the behavior of its adversaries.

Sun Tzu advised, "In war, practice dissimulation and you will succeed."[33] Thus, at times attractive simulations of reality—modern-day Potemkin villages—will compete for acceptance against demonstrable fact and succeed. One wonders what would have happened if the Soviets' Polyus "orbital weapons platform" had been successfully launched in 1987. By all accounts it contained nothing of great consequence. But it was huge and it was dramatic, and no one outside a chosen few *knew* that it was only a Potemkin death star. Surely the INF treaty would have been at least temporarily abandoned. Would the United States, fearing the unknown, have shot Polyus down? Disaster could have come out of such a perception-versus-perception scenario, where reality was consigned to the back of the room.

Sun Tzu's philosophy won out in the end. As he wrote in *The Art of War*, "Supreme excellence consists in breaking the enemy's resistance without fighting." That is precisely what happened in the late 1980s. The United States exploited the Soviet Union's weaknesses across a broad front, persistently applying additional stress as its adversary's internal troubles expanded to the breaking point.

The success of Reagan's Cold War strategy centered on economics and *the practice* of technology—the Soviets' most vulnerable suits—and the use of information and disinformation that comes under the rubric of psychological warfare. It was the technical capability suggested by "Star Wars"—Arthur C. Clarke's "magic"—not SDI technology per se, that helped to unbalance the Soviet system. In other words, it wasn't the feasibility of SDI that did the trick—this was relegated to a side issue—it was the symbolism, the between-the-lines picture of untrammeled U.S. technical genius at work. The psychological success of SDI was truly remarkable, perhaps even a stroke of political genius. As Reagan said, "SDI wasn't conceived by scientists."[34]

There is no way of measuring how much SDI contributed to the Soviet Union's fall. But SDI *did* contribute, and the Cold War did end, peacefully, though, as Velikhov remarked, "at times we were getting very close to open conflict."

Following World War II, says SAIC's Michael Wheeler, "danger was not eliminated by any means, but the international community did not experience a third, civilization-threatening world war, nor did it stumble into nuclear Armageddon. The 'long peace,' to use John Lewis Gaddis's memorable phrase, was an extraordinary accomplishment."[35]

"The biggest success of our generation was that we avoided nuclear war," said Velikhov. "We avoided it, the catastrophe. What to do with this century is another question."[36]

BMD IN THE TWENTY-FIRST CENTURY

In May 1993, Defense Secretary Les Aspin declared "the end of the 'Star Wars' era." Then, with reference to the SCUD missile problem of the first Gulf War, he conceded that there was a continuing need for some kind of ABM defense, warning that "we may face hostile or irrational states that have both nuclear warheads and ballistic missile technology that could reach the United States."[37]

In Abrahamson's mind too, there is a continuing requirement for strategic defense, and a never-ending need for the technological creativity that will help ensure the continuation of a society based on democratic principles. Surely he is the most idealistic of cold warriors, picturing the nuclear weapon, the genie that cannot be stuffed back into its bottle, as the supreme horror that must be contained by people who know enough to visualize and believe in the ultimate desolation of nuclear warfare.

"Is SDI truly going to be the ultimate system, able to counter any kind of offensive action?" he asks. "No—but if your children are endangered by traffic as they go to school and you also have a swimming pool in the back yard, are you going to say you shouldn't build a fence around the swimming pool?"[38]

The U.S. ABM budget was held fairly constant immediately after the Cold War, with the Army soon was running the remnants of SDI through the Ballistic Missile Defense Organization (BMDO). Five years after Aspin's declaration, the Rumsfeld Commission reexamined the post–Cold War missile threat and in 1998 came up with a familiar conclusion: "Concerted efforts by a number of overtly or potentially hostile nations to acquire ballistic missiles with biological or nuclear payloads pose a growing threat to the United States, its deployed forces and its friends and allies. . . . They would be able to inflict major destruction on the U.S. within about five years of a decision to acquire such a capability."[39] This paved the way for the National Missile Defense Act of 1999, which stated U.S. intent "to deploy as soon as is technologically possible an effective National Missile Defense system capable of defending the territory of the United States against limited ballistic missile attack." The act also created the Missile Defense Agency (MDA), an entity reporting directly to the Department of Defense.

While many critics, at home and abroad, opposed the return of anything that looked remotely like SDI, a new president, George W. Bush, endorsed the optimistic new plan early in his administration, despite the fact that it was at odds with the ABM Treaty. The administration originally expressed interest in working with Moscow to amend the treaty, but soon decided to simply ignore it—a position also favored by the previous Clinton administration. Then Bush took the ultimate step. "We will withdraw from the ABM treaty on our timetable," he said in August 2001, "at a time convenient to America." He followed through on June 13, 2002.

The old arguments arose that missile defense could be foiled easily by countermeasures and would encourage potential adversaries to build more warheads and missiles as defenses against a putative U.S. first strike. Strategic Forecasting, Inc. (Stratfor), a respected organization that specializes in analysis of geopolitical, economic, and security affairs, argued that a new BMD thrust was unnecessary because threats from rogue states could be eliminated with existing technology. "If the United States genuinely believed that someone was planning to launch an ICBM at the United States," said an article in its Global Intelligence Update, "U.S. satellite intelligence would pick up the construction of the site months or even years before it was intact. The low-cost response would be to destroy the launch site, the missile factory and the nuclear facility with preemptive, preferably conventional, air strikes." Investment in space assets would be much more useful if applied to the protection of satellite systems. "Defending American cities against rogue states [with space assets] seems the wrong mission at the wrong time. Preemptive strikes and the promise of nuclear annihilation is a sufficient defense."[40]

But the new ballistic missile defense scenario was gradually unfolding, centered on use of kinetic-weapon devices which, through the use of miniaturized onboard computers, are designed to guide themselves to their targets and destroy them through the sheer force of impact. By 2005, the MDA had geared up a multi-faceted program for investigating a number of such systems, with initial emphasis on Ground-Based Midcourse Defense (GMD), Aegis Ballistic Missile Defense (Aegis BMD), and Patriot Advanced Capability (PAC-3).

The GMD, using silo-based interceptors now emplaced at Fort Greely in Alaska and Vandenberg Air Force Base in California, is designed for midcourse strategic missile interception. The Aegis BMD, deployed at sea on cruisers of that class, will intercept short- to intermediate-range missiles at mid-course. The U.S. Army's PAC-3, proven in battle and the most mature technology, will intercept relatively slow-moving missiles at relatively short range.

The most capable future system on the MDA's drawing boards is the extremely fast, high-acceleration Kinetic Energy Interceptor (KEI), which could conceivably come into service sometime in the 2010s. Deployable as a mobile land unit or at sea, it would be able to destroy missiles in the boost, ascent, and midcourse phases. Interest in the KEI was fueled at least partly because of increasing concern about the feasibility of fielding the Airborne Laser (ABL), a boost-phase defense that the Air Force designed for use in a modified Boeing 747-400 aircraft. The idea works—on the ground. But the full-scale system is dauntingly heavy, and the laser would need to be focused on its moving target for several seconds to destroy it. Still, in 2005, the MDA had the ABL on its books as "the primary boost-phase defense element."

The MDA "family of systems" is expected to expand to include at least two new concepts for defending troops and ground installations. One, the Theater High Altitude Area Defense (THAAD), is a mobile ground-based defense against short- and intermediate-range ballistic missile attack. The other, the Medium Extended Air Defense System (MEADS), under development by the United States, Germany, and Italy, will be a mobile system for air defense at lower altitudes.

Development of new launchers and warheads represents only the most visible part of the missile defense program. An effective system must also spot missile launches and follow their targets electronically until they are blasted out of the sky. To help address this immensely complicated challenge, two Space-Based InfraRed Satellite (SBIRS) constellations, able to discriminate between nuclear warheads and decoys as well as to find and follow the target missile, should be in place by 2012. They will be part of a "three-edged sword" that also takes advantage of information from advanced sea/land radars, some of which are already in place, and the sensor smarts of the kinetic energy warhead. In the comprehensive, integrated Ballistic Missile Defense Systems (BMDS) envisaged by the MDA, these would be interlinked with individual missile systems, providing a layered defense capable of countering threat missiles in all phases of flight.

Despite the generally poor performance typified by the GMD program's early years, midcourse interception is pictured as easier to accomplish than attacking an intercontinental missile during its boost phase. However, as in the SDI of the 1980s, boost-phase interception is favored because the rocket's plume of hot gases creates an easily identifiable infrared signal, indicating that a launch has occurred. Further, the target would be destroyed before it could release its confusing bundle of countermeasures, and debris from a destroyed missile might fall back on the country that launched it. But since the missile must be detected in the first few minutes of its flight, while its rockets are burning, this would require relatively close placement of a surface-based defensive system. To strike one possible target in North Korea, the ABM weapon would have to travel as much as 650 miles in the scant few minutes remaining after the offensive launch is detected and the defensive response authorized. Perhaps the KEI will be able to do this. On the other hand, it may be that only a space-based system, yet to be defined, would be able to destroy ICBMs rising from unexpected quarters or from the vastnesses of Asia.

"Some consider that boost-phase interception can only be achieved effectively for a global system with space-based interceptors," wrote Stanley Orman and Eugene Fox, two veterans of SDI-era missile defense, "if for no other reason than that surface-based interceptors, whether on land or at sea, cannot always be located close enough to launch sites to reach the attacking missiles in their boost phase."[41] (As commander of the Army Strategic Defense Command, Fox was responsible for the 1984 HOE-4 test.)

Earlier U.S. ballistic missile defense systems flourished for a while, only to die. The MDA program was roundly criticized in a January 2006 report by the Congressional Research Service. But the technologies of the twenty-first century are much improved and could permit eventual development of an acceptable, credible system. Provided it escapes the fate of its predecessors and its early technical problems are overcome, the new program will become one of many protective measures that the United States will deploy against potential aggressors. Even after it is improved and expanded, and even if someday it includes space defenses, it will fall far short of being 100 percent effective. But it still will enhance deterrence.

On Threats and the Will to Protect

All the SDI euphoria about lasers, neutral particle beams, and the rest of the directed-energy dream melted away long before the Rumsfeld Commission made its report. But it is worth noting that the innovations and systems know-how inherited from SDI, modernized and incorporated with technologies developed for MDA scenarios, miniaturized inertial guidance, propulsion, and controls incorporated in the MDA interceptor, integrated with heat-seekers and guidance computers, may make it possible to demonstrate an effective, deployable, *space-based* interceptor.[42] This idea has not been completely abandoned, though it has lost much of its luster, partly because of reminders by Garwin and others that space satellites are vulnerable to attack by antisatellite technology. "The very strong emotional objections to space-based interceptors seems to have influenced the MDA choice to opt instead for the surface based KEI (Kinetic Energy Interceptor) system," Fox and Orman wrote in *Defense News,* "although it is far from clear that this is the best solution from either a cost or an effectiveness standpoint."[43]

There is also absolutely no evidence that long- or medium-range missiles would be an attacker's weapons of choice. The current MDA system would not be able to protect against short-range missiles launched from freighter-style ships near the American coastline, or from the delivery of any weapon of mass destruction by such mundane means as a moving van. "It has always been very implausible to me that a rogue state would send one or two missiles over here," Kurt Gottfried, a Cornell University physicist and then-acting chair of the Union of Concerned Scientists, told reporter James Glanz. "It would be suicide."[44]

But the search for protection will continue, as it must. "There is ample evidence today of the centuries-old human spirit that manifests the incredible will, and the imagination, to protect and preserve," Abrahamson said. "The search for a workable missile defense system has brought us now through several presidencies, with a lot of people having passed the torch. These people believe that they are pursuing the best way to provide the greatest assurance that we will never again see a Hiroshima or a Nagasaki or, at worst, witness the beginning of the end of the world. You can see this spark of dedication in individuals at all levels—some ordinary people and some incredible people, probing, and probing, and probing to show that such a thing can be done."[45]

Lessons and Mysteries

The Star Wars enigma is tied up with the elusive but deceptively simple-sounding question of what it actually was. Jim Abrahamson and Gerold Yonas, two good friends and colleagues, disagree entirely on what SDI was from, say, 1985 onward. Abrahamson says it continued to be a technical program to defend the United States against missile attack, period; Yonas says it was a delusion that tricked the Soviet leadership into a weaker posture vis-à-vis the United States and struck fear into their midst. After all, what was Gorbachev's main agenda item at Geneva and Reykjavik, other than the drive to stall SDI in its tracks?

Why *did* Gorbachev rant on and on against SDI at those two summits? For a start, it would certainly upset the long-standing Soviet formula for maintaining its warfighting capability. This prospect was acute enough that the Soviet Union would at some time be likely to take some kind of action, even force, to prevent SDI's deployment, and Gorbachev wished to remove this potential ignition point in the East-West balance. Not only that, but the cost of responding to SDI, whether through developing countermeasures (relatively cheap), engaging in a military space race (impossibly expensive), or increasing the nuclear stockpile (more of the same) was simply too great, especially at a time when the Afghan war was taking an enormous toll on Soviet resources. The Kremlin's military space supporters were still lobbying for expensive new projects, and Gorbachev, in street vernacular, wanted to "get those guys off my back."

The enigma persists, and the sting theory still looks good. For Casey and others, it followed that the only sane way to end the Soviet state and protect the West was to hurry along the implosion that observers expected would eventually visit Russia's ragged socio-economic infrastructures. In the mind of George Shultz, an economist, "I think we won the Cold War because their system was essentially a bankrupt system."[46]

Eventually we come back to luck, and the wit to make the most of it. "The course of history," says Yonas in his laconic mood, "is determined by the evolution of circumstances that are controlled by nobody."[47]

Does the history of the Strategic Defense Initiative illustrate the victory of politics over science? Yonas persists that the real SDI story is really about human behavior, bluff, fear, confusion, and hope.[48] Science itself was all but relegated to a kind of stage-dressing. "All of our deterrence strategy is a psychological and strategic war to make war unlikely," he says. "Defense is part of a strategy. I believed that SDI was a grand strategy, but not a grand savior to protect us from nukes. Nothing can protect us from nukes. We are vulnerable and will always be vulnerable. The goal is to get the other guy to not even try."[49]

The details of just how the Soviet Union fell apart will likely be debated forever, though it is certain that domestic issues provided the lethal death blows—albeit with Western help. "All great powers from the Roman to the British Empire have disintegrated because of internal strife and not because of pressure from abroad," wrote Anatoly Dobrynin. "Nobody won the Cold War, and both sides paid a great price, but the end of the Cold War is our common victory."[50]

NOTES

CHAPTER 1

1. Evgeny Velikhov, interviews with the author, December 23 and 27, 2004; Roald Sagdeev, interview with the author, October 9, 2003.

2. Gerold Yonas, personal communication with the author, March 18, 2005.

3. James A. Abrahamson, interviews with the author, May 12 and May 23, 2001.

4. Stanley Orman, interview with the author, June 6, 2001.

5. See Atomic Archive site, www.atomicarchive.com (accessed February 24, 2006).

6. Thomas C. Reed, *At the Abyss: An Insider's History of the Cold War* (New York: Random House, 2004), 359.

7. David J. Hawkings, *Keeping the Peace: The Aldermaston Story* (Barnsley, England: Leo Cooper, 2000).

8. Quoted in notes for the PBS program "Citizen Kurchatov: Stalin's Bomb Maker." See www.pbs.org/opb/citizenk/siteindex.html (accessed February 24, 2006).

9. The full text of McNamara's speech is posted by the Atomic Archive, www .atomicarchive.com/Docs/Deterrence/Deterrence.shtml (accessed February 24, 2006).

10. Gerold Yonas, review of *The Shield of Faith: The Hidden Struggle for Strategic Defense*, by B. Bruce Briggs, *IEEE Spectrum*, November 1988.

11. Quoted by Henry Trofimenko in "The 'Theology' of Strategy." *Orbis* 21:3 (Fall 1977): 510.

12. Carl Sagan, *Pale Blue Dot* (New York: Random House, 1994), 213, 215.

CHAPTER 2

1. Robert McNamara, interview, December 13, 1998. Full text found at GWU National Security Archive, www2.gwu.edu/~nsarchiv/coldwar/interviews/ (accessed February 24, 2006).

2. Roald Z. Sagdeev, *The Making of a Soviet Scientist: My Adventures in Nuclear Fusion and Space From Stalin to Star Wars* (New York: John Wiley & Sons, 1995), 156.

3. P. V. Zarubin, "Academician Basov, High-Power Lasers, and the Antimissile Defence Problem," *Quantum Electronics* 32:12 (December 2002): 1053.

4. Quoted in Strobe Talbott, *The Master of the Game: Paul Nitze and the Nuclear Peace* (New York: Knopf/Borzoi Books, 1988), 97.

5. Gerold Yonas, personal communication with the author, October 29, 2004.

6. Thomas C. Reed, *At the Abyss: An Insider's History of the Cold War* (New York: Random House, 2004), 323.

7. See http://online04.lbl.gov/~telnov/htmls/akadem.html for notes on the history of Akademgorodok (accessed February 24, 2006).

8. Roald Sagdeev, interview with the author, October 9, 2003.

9. Sagdeev, interview with the author, October 9, 2003.

10. Evgeny P. Velikhov, interview with the author, March 6, 2003. See also Velikhov's "Science and Scientists for a Nuclear-Weapon-Free World." *Physics Today*, November 1969, 32–36

11. Peter Zarubin, personal communication with the author, November 3, 2004.

12. Zarubin, personal communication with the author, November 3, 2004.

13. B. Bruce Briggs, *The Shield of Faith: The Hidden Struggle for Strategic Defense* (New York: Simon & Schuster, 1988), 220.

14. Charles Herzfeld, personal communication with the author, February 16, 2005.

15. Information provided to the author by Donald Baucom, from Ballistic Missile Defense Program of the Advanced Research Projects Agency, *A Review of Project Defender for the Director of Defense Research and Engineering*, July 25–29, 1960, vol. I; and G. P. Sutton, "Summary of 1960 Defender Program Review," in *Project Defender*, 1960, Vol. II.

16. Herbert F. York, "Race to Oblivion: A Participant's View of the Arms Race." Available at www.learnworld.com/ZNW/LWText.York.Race.Ch07.html (accessed February 24, 2006).

17. Charles Herzfeld, personal communication with the author, February 28, 2005.

18. Herzfeld, personal communication with the author, February 16, 2005.

19. Herzfeld, personal communication with the author, February 16, 2005.

20. John Spratt, "Ballistic Missile Defense and National Security" (speech, American Institute of Aeronautics and Astronautics, January 20, 2000).

21. John Bosma, personal communication with the author, February 24, 2005.

22. Alton Frye, "Our Gamble in Space: The Military Danger." *The Atlantic* 212:2 (August 1963): 46–50.

23. Robert C. McFarlane and Zofia Smardz, *Special Trust* (New York: Cadell & Davies, 1994), 217.

24. Gould's long battle to win and retain his laser patents rights are documented in Nick Taylor's *Laser: The Inventor, the Nobel Laureate, and the Thirty-Year Patent War* (New York: Citadel Press, 2000).

25. Jeff Hecht, *Beam Weapons: The Next Arms Race* (New York: Plenum Press, 1984), 23.

26. Zarubin, "Academician Basov," *Quantum Electronics* 32:12 (December 2002): 1048–64.

27. Michael Ellman and Vladimir Kontorovich, eds., *The Destruction of the*

Soviet Economic System: An Insiders' History (Armonk, NY: M. E. Sharpe, 1998), 57–58.

28. National Intelligence Estimate, "The Soviet Space Program," Central Intelligence Agency, March 2, 1967. Posted at www.astronautix.com/articles/nie11167.htm (accessed February 24, 2006).

29. Ibid.

30. V. D. Sokolovsky, *Military Strategy* (Moscow, 1968), tr. by Harriet Fast Scott as *Soviet Military Strategy* (New York: Crane Russak & Co., 1975), 458.

31. C. K. N. Patel, "Continuous-Wave Laser Action on Vibrational-Rotational Transitions of CO_2," *Phys. Rev* 5A (1964): 1187–93.

32. Access George W. Sutton's "Early History of High Power Lasers" through www.sparta.com/sew/index.jsp?publications (accessed February 24, 2006).

33. Hans Mark, "The Airborne Laser from Theory to Reality," *Defense Horizons*, April 2002. Available at www.ndu.edu/inss/DefHor/DH12/DH12.htm (accessed February 24, 2006).

34. Ibid.

35. Department of Defense, "Fact Sheet: DoD High Energy Laser Program," February 1982, 2.

36. Bengt Anderberg and Myron L. Wolbarsht, *Laser Weapons: The Dawn of a New Military Age* (New York: Plenum Press, 1992).

37. Bruce Briggs, *Shield of Faith*, 141–42.

38. Stephen Weiner, "Systems and Technology," in Ashton B. Carter and David N. Schwartz, eds., *Ballistic Missile Defense* (Washington, DC: Brookings Institution, 1984), 51, 53.

39. Caspar Weinberger, *Fighting for Peace: Seven Critical Years in the Pentagon* (New York: Warner Books, 1990), 299.

40. Kenneth Alibek, statement before the Joint Economic Committee session on "Terrorist and Intelligence Operations: Potential Impact on the U.S. Economy," U.S. Congress, May 20, 1998. Posted at www.house.gov/jec/hearings/intell/alibek.htm (accessed February 24, 2006).

CHAPTER 3

1. See Inez Cope Jeffery, *Inside Russia: The Life and Times of Zoya Zarubina* (Austin, TX: Eakin Press, 1999).

2. National Intelligence Estimate, "The Soviet Space Program," Central Intelligence Agency, March 2, 1967. Posted at www.astronautix.com/articles/nie11167.htm (accessed February 24, 2006).

3. Quoted in Alton Frye, "Our Gamble in Space: The Military Danger." *The Atlantic* 212:2 (August 1963): 46–50.

4. See www.russianspaceweb.com/is.html (accessed February 24, 2006).

5. Wernher von Braun, Frederick I. Ordway III, and Harry H. K. Lange, *History of Rocketry & Space Travel (Revised Edition)* (New York: Crowell, 1969), 217.

6. Col. P. Sidirov, "The Leninist Methodology of Soviet Military Science,"

Voyennaya mysl' (June 1969): FPD 0008/70 trans. 1/30/70, p. 26 (Quoted in Joseph D. Douglass Jr. and Amoretta M. Hoeber, *Soviet Strategy for Nuclear War* (Stanford, CA: Hoover Institution Press, 1979).)

7. Peter Zarubin, interview with the author, November 24, 2003.

8. Roald Sagdeev, interview with the author, October 9, 2003.

9. Charles Townes, personal communication with the author, February 13, 2005.

10. Zarubin, interview with the author, November 24, 2003.

11. Evgeny Velikhov, interview with the author, November 27, 2003.

12. Zarubin, interview with the author, November 24, 2003.

13. Oleg Krokhin, interview with the author, November 25, 2003.

14. A. Karpenko, "ABM and Space Defense," *Nevsky Bastion* No. 4 (1999): 2–47. Posted at www.fas.org/spp/starwars/program/soviet/990600-bmd-rus .htm (accessed February 24, 2006).

15. Velikhov, interview with the author, March 6, 2003.

16. Zarubin, personal communication with the author, October 2, 2004.

17. J. V. V. Kasper and G. C. Pimentel, "Atomic Iodine Photodissociation Laser," *Applied Physics Letters* 5:11 (December 1994): 231.

18. Zarubin, personal communication with the author, February 9 and 10, 2005.

19. V. N. Mikhailov, *I Am a Hawk*, Chapter 1, "Arzamas-16—A Closed City." Posted at www.iss.niiit.ru/book/chap1.htm (accessed January 24, 2006).

20. Zarubin, interview with the author, November 24, 2003.

21. Evgeny P. Velikhov, "Science and Scientists in a Nuclear-Weapon-Free World." *Physics Today*, November 1989, 32–36. (Article adapted from the Soviet Foreign Ministry publication *International Affairs*.)

22. Krokhin, interview with the author, November 25, 2003.

23. Alexander Ignatyev, "Almaz Unveils Advanced Laser Technologies," *Military Parade*, November 2001. (Ignatyev was then Chief Designer and Head of the Special Design Bureau of Laser Technologies of the Almaz R&P Association, a descendant of the Soviet-era Almaz bureau.)

24. From "Strategic Defense Initiative—Space Race Between the Superpowers." NTV Russia television documentary, 2001.

25. George C. Wilson, "Soviets Reported Gaining in Space Weapons," *Boston Globe*, March 3, 1982, 9.

26. Department of Defense, *Soviet Military Power, 1983* (Washington, DC: Government Printing Office, March 1983), 68.

27. Herb Meyer, personal communication with the author, November 23, 2004.

28. Roald Sagdeev, interview with the author, October 9, 2003.

29. Gen. Maj. A. S. Milidov, ed., *The Philosohical Heritage of V. I. Lenin and Probems of Contemporary War (A Soviet View)*, tr. by U.S. Air Force, Soviet Military Thought Series No. 5. (Washington, DC: Government Printing Office, 1974), 235, 280. (Quoted in Douglass and Hoeber, 1979.)

30. Main nuclear correlation of forces equations were included in Major General I. Anurev in *Voyenna Mysl (Military Thought)* No. 6 (1967). See also Douglass and Hoeber, *Soviet Strategy for Nuclear War* ; and Simon P. Worden, *SDI and the Alternatives* (Washington, DC: National Defense University Press, 1991).

31. Edward Teller, personal communication with the author, June 7, 1999.

32. Jeff Hecht, *Beam Weapons: The Next Arms Race* (New York: Plenum Press, 1984), 301.

33. George J. Keegan Jr., "New Assessment Put on Soviet Threat," *Aviation Week & Space Technology*, March 28, 1977, 38–48.

34. John Pike, "The Death-Beam Gap: Putting Keegan's Follies in Perspective," *FAS*, October 1992. Posted at www.fas.org/spp/eprint/keegan.htm (accessed February 24, 2006).

35. Hecht, *Beam Weapons*, 33.

36. Simon P. (Pete) Worden, personal communication with the author, February 13, 2005.

37. Worden, personal communication with the author, February 1, 2005.

38. Robert Hotz, "Beam Weapon Threat," *Aviation Week & Space Technology*, May 2, 1977, 11.

39. Philip J. Klass, "Laser Destroys Missile in Test," *Aviation Week*, August 7, 1978, 16.

40. Edward Teller, "Where Are the Russians on SDI?" (speech, Commonwealth Club, November 24, 1986).

41. Fred I. Greenstein and William C. Wohlforth, eds., *Retrospective on the End of the Cold War* (Center of International Studies Monograph Series No. 6, Princeton University, 1996). (Report of a conference sponsored by the John Foster Dulles Program for the Study of Leadership in International Affairs.)

42. Robert C. McFarlane and Zofia Smardz, *Special Trust* (New York: Cadell & Davies, 1994), 218.

43. Ronald Reagan, *An American Life* (New York: Simon & Schuster, 1990), 547, 550.

CHAPTER 4

1. Jack F. Matlock Jr., *Reagan and Gorbachev: How the Cold War Ended* (New York: Random House, 2004), 114.

2. Ronald Reagan, *An American Life* (New York: Simon & Schuster, 1990), 605.

3. Matlock, *Reagan and Gorbachev*, 26.

4. Herb Meyer, personal communication with the author, November 24, 2004.

5. Matlock, *Reagan and Gorbachev*, 75–76.

6. Meyer, personal communication with the author, November 23, 2004.

7. Mark C. Cleary, *The Cape: Military Space Operations 1971–1992*, Chapter 1, Section 9, www.patrick.af.mil/heritage/Cape/Cape1/cape1-9.htm (accessed February 24, 2006).

8. See Adrian Blomfield, "Soviets 'Had Pope Shot for Backing Solidarity,'" *Daily Telegraph*, March 3, 2006, www.portal.telegraph.co.uk/news/main.jhtml?xml = /news/2006/0 3/03/wpope03.xml (accessed March 3, 2006).

9. Meyer, personal communication with the author, November 24, 2004.

10. Dennis Brown, "Notre Dame Commencement Speakers Past and Present" (news release, May 14, 2001, posted at www.nd.edu/cgi-bin/news.cgi?article = 200105141555 [accessed February 24, 2006]).

11. C. Paul Robinson, "Is There a Purpose for Deterrence After the Cold War?" (Speech, Project on Nuclear Issues, June 10, 2004).

12. Quoted in "The Reagan Legacy," produced by Derek Lapping Associates for the Discovery Channel, 1996.

13. Quoted in *The International Communist Movement*, a publication of the Communist Party of the Soviet Union, 1972.

14. Norman A. Bailey, *The Strategic Plan That Won the Cold War: National Security Decision Directive 75* (McLean, VA: Potomac Foundation, 1999), 18.

15. William J. Casey, *The Secret War Against Hitler* (Washington, DC: Regnery, 1988), xiv.

16. B. Byely et al., *Marxism-Leninism on War and Army (A Soviet View)*, tr. by U.S. Air Force, Soviet Military Thought Series No. 2. (Washington, DC: Government Printing Office, 1974), 12.

17. Gus W. Weiss, "The Farewell Dossier," www.odci.gov/csi/studies/96unclass/farewell.htm (accessed March 1, 2006); see also Nigel West's *Games of Intelligence* (New York: Crown, 1989).

18. Thomas C. Reed, *At the Abyss: An Insider's History of the Cold War* (New York: Random House, 2004), 269.

19. Jay Tuck, *High-Tech Espionage: How the KGB Smuggles NATO's Strategic Secrets to Moscow* (New York: St. Martin's Press, 1986), 109.

20. See Edmund Morris's remark in "The Unknowable," *New Yorker*, June 28, 2004, 51.

21. Peter Schweizer, *Victory: The Reagan Administration's Secret Strategy That Hastened the Collapse of the Soviet Union* (New York: Atlantic Monthly Press, 1994), 8.

22. C. Paul Robinson, "Is There a Purpose for Deterrence After the Cold War?" (speech, Project on Nuclear Issues, June 10, 2004).

23. National Security Directive 32, May 20, 1982, 3.

CHAPTER 5

1. For information on Operation Ryan, see Benjamin B. Fischer's "A Cold War Conundrum." (Center for the Study of Intelligence, Central Intelligence Agency, 1997, posted at www.cia.gov/csi/monograph/coldwar/source.htm (accessed March 1, 2006).)

2. Jeff Hecht, *Beam Weapons: The Next Arms Race* (New York: Plenum Press, 1984), 33.

3. Gerold Yonas, personal communication with the author, August 31, 2003.

4. Gerold Yonas, personal communication with the author, August 31, 2003.

5. Gerold Yonas, "One More Time From Russia." *Advanced Concepts Group News & Views*, September 2004, 1–3 (Sandia National Laboratories).

6. Yonas, personal communication with the author, August 31, 2003.

7. Jerry Pournelle, personal communication with the author, January 22, 2005.

8. See Jerry Pournelle, "Chaos Manor Debates," www.jerrypournelle.com/debates/nasa-sdi.html#space2 (accessed March 1, 2006).

9. John Bosma, personal communication with the author, February 24, 2005.

10. Edward Teller, personal meeting with author, May 2, 1999, Stanford, California.

11. William J. Broad, "Reagan's 'Star Wars' Bid: Many Ideas Converging," *New York Times*, March 4, 1985.

12. From Edward Teller, *Memoirs: A Twentieth Century Journey in Science and Politics* quoted in "The Ultimate Defense," *Hoover Digest*, no. 1, 2002. Available at www.hooverdigest.org/021/teller.html (accessed March 1, 2006).

13. For more information on this group's activities, see "Defense Dept. Experts Confirm Efficacy of Space-Based Laser," *Aviation Week*, July 28, 1980, 65–66.

14. Quoted by William Broad in *Teller's War* (New York: Simon & Schuster, 1992), 115.

15. "Strategic Defense, Strategic Choices: Staff Report of the Strategic Defense Initiative, Democratic Caucus of the U.S. House of Representatives." Report published by the Carnegie Nonproliferation Project, May 1988, www.ceip.org/files/projects/npp/resources/StrageticDefenseStrategicChoices.htm.

16. Richard Halloran, "Pentagon Draws Up First Strategy for Fighting a Long Nuclear War," *New York Times*, May 30, 1982.

17. William J. Broad, "Nuclear Power for the Militarization of Space." *Science* 218 (December 17, 1982):1199–1201.

18. "President Calls for Crusade," *Washington Post*, June 9, 1982.

19. Igor Tsarev, "A 'Diamond-Studded Sky.' Should the Military Who Maintains 'They Have Stopped Preparing for Star Wars' Be Trusted?" *JPRS Central Eurasia: CIS/Russian Military Issues* (October 20, 1993): JPRS-UMA-93-039.

20. A. Karpenko, "ABM and Space Defense," *Nevsky Bastion* No. 4 (1999): 2–47. Available at www.fas.org/spp/starwars/program/soviet/990600-bmd-rus.htm (accessed March 1, 2006).

21. Policy fact sheet available from the Reagan Library, at www.reagan.utexas.edu/ (accessed March 1, 2006).

22. The Erice Statement is posted at emcsc.ccsem.infn.it/ericestatement.html (accessed March 1, 2006).

23. Evgeny Velikhov, interview with the author, November 23, 2003.

24. Edward Teller, "Openness: A Contribution from Scientists." Paper delivered at International Nuclear War Seminar, August 19–24, 1982 in Erice, Italy.

25. Velikhov, interview with the author, November 27, 2003.

26. Edmund Morris, "The Unknowable," *The New Yorker*, June 28, 2004, 44.

27. Edward Teller, *Memoirs: A Twentieth-Century Journey in Science and Politics*, with Judith Shoolery (New York: Perseus, 2001), 531.

28. "Laser Talks," *Aviation Week & Space Technology*, September 20, 1982, 15.

29. Peter Schweizer, *Victory: The Reagan Administration's Secret Strategy That Hastened the Collapse of the Soviet Union* (New York: Atlantic Monthly Press, 1994), xvii.

30. Jack F. Matlock Jr., *Reagan and Gorbachev: How the Cold War Ended* (New York: Random House, 2004), 85.

31. William P. Clark, "NSDD-75: A New Approach to the Soviet Union," in *The Fall of the Berlin Wall: Reassessing the Causes and Consequences of the End of the Cold War*, ed. Peter Schweizer (Stanford: Hoover Institution Press, 2000), 69.

32. William P. Clark, "NSDD-75," 72.

33. Matlock, *Reagan and Gorbachev*, 5.

34. Norman Bailey, *The Strategic Plan That Won the Cold War* (McLean, VA: Potomac Foundation, 1999), 13.

35. James A. Abrahamson, interview with the author, May 16, 2001.

36. Quoted in "The Reagan Legacy," produced by Derek Lapping Associates for the Discovery Channel, 1996.

37. Ibid.

38. Adm. James Watkins, interview with the author, April 20, 1999.

39. Teller, *Memoirs*.

40. Watkins, interview with the author, April 20, 1999.

41. Ibid.

42. Robert C. McFarlane and Zofia Smardz, *Special Trust* (New York: Cadell & Davies, 1994), 228.

43. Caspar Weinberger, *Fighting for Peace: Seven Critical Years in the Pentagon* (New York: Warner Books, 1990), 304–5.

44. Quoted in "The Reagan Legacy."

45. Quoted in "The Reagan Legacy."

Chapter 6

1. Raymond Pollock, personal communication with the author, October 10, 2001.

2. Victor Reis, personal communication with the author, September 5, 2003.

3. Raymond Pollock, letter to Robert Helm, February 24, 1986.

4. Ibid.

5. Robert McFarlane, interview with the author, October 10, 2003.

6. Ibid.

7. Robert C. McFarlane and Zofia Smardz, *Special Trust* (New York: Cadell & Davies, 1994), 235.

8. Anatoly Dobrynin, *In Confidence: Moscow's Ambassador to America's Six Cold War Presidents (1962–86)* (New York: Times Books/Random House 1995), 528.

9. Raymond Pollock, personal communication with the author, November 9, 2003.

10. "Secretary of State Assails Scientists in Political Roles." *SGR (Science and Government Report)*, March 15, 1985.

11. Robert McFarlane, personal communication with the author, October 13, 2003.

12. McFarlane, interview with the author, October 10, 2003.

13. Reis, personal communication with the author, September 5, 2003.

14. Gerold Yonas, personal communication with the author, August 31, 2003.

15. Pollock, personal communication with the author, November 9, 2003.

16. Reis, personal communication with the author, September 5, 2003.

17. William J. Broad, *Teller's War* (New York: Simon & Schuster, 1992), 131.

18. George P. Shultz, *Turmoil and Triumph: My Years as Secretary of State* (New York: Macmillan, 1993), 246.

19. Shultz, "What Really Happened at Reykjavik," in Shultz, *Turmoil and Triumph*.

20. Caspar Weinberger, *Fighting for Peace: Seven Critical Years in the Pentagon* (New York: Warner Books, 1990).

21. Pollock, letter to Robert Helm.

22. Quoted in "The Reagan Legacy," produced by Derek Lapping Associates for the Discovery Channel, 1996.

23. Herbert Meyer, personal communication with the author, November 24, 2004.

24. Reis, personal communication with the author, September 5, 2003.

25. Raymond Pollock, personal communication with the author, August 4, 2005.

26. "Strategic Defense Strategic Choices: Staff Report of the Strategic Defense Initiative, Democratic Caucus of the U.S. House of Representatives." Report published by the Carnegie Nonproliferation Project, May 1988. Available at www.ceip .org/files/projects/npp/resources/StrageticDefenseStrategicChoices.htm (accessed March 1, 2006).

27. Robert Rankine, personal communication with the author, January 14, 2005.

28. Reis, personal communication with the author, September 5, 2003.

29. Peter Goodchild, *Edward Teller: The Real Dr. Strangelove* (London: Weidenfeld & Nicolson, 2004), 349.

30. McFarlane, interview with the author, October 10, 2003.

31. Charles H. Townes, *How the Laser Happened: Adventures of a Scientist* (New York: Oxford University Press, 1999), 165–67.

32. Charles Townes, personal communication with the author, February 13, 2005.

33. Edmund Morris, *Dutch: A Memoir of Ronald Reagan* (New York: Random House, 1999), 476.

34. See Stanley A. Blumberg and Louis G. Panos, *Edward Teller: Giant of the Golden Age of Physics* (New York: Charles Scribner's Sons, 1990), 10. Teller expanded on this theme in his article "SDI: The Last Hope," in the *Washington Post*'s *Insight* magazine, October 28, 1985.

35. Edward Teller, *Memoirs: A Twentieth-Century Journey in Science and Politics*, with Judith Shoolery (New York: Perseus, 2001), 532.

36. Hans Bethe, "No," in double feature titled "Can Star Wars Make Us Safe?" *Science Digest*, September 1985, 83.

37. Kenneth Gatland, *The Illustrated Encyclopedia of Space Technology* (New York: Harmony Books, 1981), 225. See also www.au.af.mil/au/awc/awcgate/au-18/au180040.htm#0040_0023 (accessed March 1, 2006).

38. B. Bruce Briggs, *The Shield of Faith: The Hidden Struggle for Strategic Defense* (New York: Simon & Schuster, 1988), 432.

39. Lou Cannon, "President Seeks Futuristic Defense Against Missiles," *Washington Post*, March 24, 1983.

40. Quoted in "The Reagan Legacy."

41. George Shultz, personal communication with the author, August 3, 2005.

42. Paul Lettow, *Ronald Reagan and His Quest to Abolish Nuclear Weapons* (New York: Random House, 2005), 83.

43. Ronald Reagan, press conference, March 25, 1983. *Public Papers of the Presidents: Ronald Reagan, 1983.* Book 1, 448–9.

44. Ronald Reagan, press conference, March 29, 1983. *Public Papers of the Presidents: Ronald Reagan, 1983.* Book 1, 465.

45. "Poll finds 7 out of 10 Imagine Outbreak of Soviet Nuclear War," *Washington Post,* September 7, 1981, 17

46. George Gallup, *The Gallup Poll: Public Opinion 1981* (Wilmington: Scholarly Resources, 1982), 163; *The Gallup Poll: Public Opinion 1983* (Wilmington: Scholarly Resources, 1983), 266.

47. Meyer, personal communication with the author, November 24, 2004.

48. Yonas, personal communication with the author, November 28, 2004.

49. Simon P. (Pete) Worden, personal communication with the author, February 13, 2005.

50. John Bosma, personal communication with the author, February 10, 2005.

51. Herbert Meyer, personal communication with the author, November 23, 2004.

52. Dmitry Mikheyev, interview with the author, November 26, 2003.

53. From "Messengers from Moscow," a Barraclough Casey production for BBC/PBS.

54. *Cold War,* Episode 22: "Star Wars." CNN Perspective series. Posted at www.cnn.com/SPECIALS/cold.war/episodes/22/script.html (accessed March 1, 2006).

55. E. P. Velikhov and A. A. Kokoshin, "A New Cycle of the Arms Race?" *New Perspectives Quarterly,* Fall–Winter 1985. Available at http://www.digital npq.org/archive/1984_85_fall_winter/new_cycle.html (accessed March 1, 2006).

56. Quoted in "The Reagan Legacy."

57. "Possible Soviet Responses to the US Strategic Defense Initiative." Interagency Intelligence Assessment NIC M 83-10017, September 12, 1983. Posted by Federation of American Scientists at fas.org/spp/starwars/offdocs/m8310017 .htm (accessed March 1, 2006).

58. Edward Teller, testimony before House Armed Services Committee, April 28, 1983.

59. Department of Defense, *Soviet Military Power 1983* (Washington, DC: Government Printing Office, March 1983), 75.

60. Meyer, personal communication with author, November 23, 2004.

61. Carl Sagan, *Pale Blue Dot* (New York: Random House, 1994), 208.

62. Press release, "JFK Library Releases White House Tape on Space Race." Posted at www.jfklibrary.org/pr_jfk_tapes_tape63.html (accessed March 1, 2006).

63. See study guide for *Messengers From Moscow* Program Four, issued by the National Bureau of Asian Research, 4518 University Way NE, Suite 300, Seattle, WA 98105.

64. Bruce Briggs, *Shield of Faith,* 437.

65. Yonas, personal communication with the author, July 19, 2001.

66. Robert Scheer, *With Enough Shovels* (New York: Random House, 1983), quoted in Peter Schweizer, *Reagan's War* (New York: Doubleday, 2002).

67. Anatoly Chernyaev, *Moya zhizn' I moyo vrema* (Moscow: Mezhdunarodnye otnosheniya, 1995), discussed in Jack F. Matlock Jr., *Reagan and Gorbachev: How the Cold War Ended* (New York: Random House, 2004), 180–1.

68. Quoted by Dobrynin in *In Confidence*, 517–18.

69. Roald Sagdeev, interview with the author, October 9, 2003.

70. Quoted in Schweizer, *Reagan's War*, 212. From a speech given by Andropov in Prague, VA-01/40473, Budesarchiv-Militararchiv, Freiburg.

71. Steven J. Zaloga, "Red Star Wars," *Jane's Intelligence Review*, May 1, 1997.

72. Broad, *Teller's War*, 21.

73. Raymond Pollock, letter to Robert Helm, February 24, 1986.

74. Pollock, personal communication with the author, November 9, 2003.

75. Townes, *How the Laser Happened*, 167.

76. McFarlane, interview with the author, October 10, 2003.

77. Blumberg and Panos, *Edward Teller*.

78. Edward Teller, interview with the author, May 2, 1999.

79. Hedrick Smith, *The Power Game: How Washington Works* (New York: Harper & Row, 1988), 604.

80. Strobe Talbott, *The Master of the Game: Paul Nitze and the Nuclear Peace* (New York: Knopf/Borzoi Books, 1988), 201.

81. John Lewis Gaddis, *The United States and the End of the Cold War* (New York: Oxford University Press, 1992), 62.

82. Herb Meyer, personal communication with the author, November 24, 2004.

83. Yonas, personal communication with the author, November 28, 2004.

84. Stanley Orman, interview with the author, June 6, 2001.

CHAPTER 7

1. Robert Rankine, personal communication with the author, January 14, 2005.

2. Simon P. (Pete) Worden, personal communication with the author, February 1, 2005.

3. Rankine, personal communication with the author, January 14, 2005.

4. Gerold Yonas, personal communication with the author, February 19, 2000.

5. Caspar Weinberger, remarks to Paul Lettow on August 1, 2001, quoted in Lettow, *Ronald Reagan and His Quest to Abolish Nuclear Weapons* (New York: Random House, 2005), 103.

6. Hedrick Smith, *The Power Game: How Washington Works* (New York: Harper & Row, 1988), 612.

7. Victor Reis, personal communication with the author, September 5, 2003.

8. Edward Teller, letter to President Ronald Reagan, July 23, 1983.

9. Gerold Yonas, personal communication with the author, August 31, 2003.

10. Harold Agnew, personal communication with the author, February 14, 2004.

11. Ibid.

12. Yonas, personal communication to N. Hey and N. Singer, January 3, 2003.

13. Yonas, personal communication with the author, January 14, 2004.

14. Ibid.

15. Gerold Yonas, interview with the author, March 3, 2000.

16. Yonas, personal communication with the author, August 31, 2003.

17. Yonas, interview with the author, March 3, 2000.

18. Gerold Yonas, personal communication with the author, February 19, 2000.

19. Yonas, personal communication with the author, August 31, 2003.

20. Gerold Yonas, "Strategic Defense Initiative: The Politics and Science of Weapons in Space." *Physics Today*, June 1985, 24.

21. Ibid.

22. Yonas, interview with the author, March 3, 2000.

23. Rankine, personal communication with the author, January 14, 2005.

24. Central Intelligence Agency, "DCI Report: Possible Soviet Responses to the U.S. Strategic Defense Initiative," September 12, 1983. Declassified document NIC M 83-10017, posted at www.fas.org/spp/starwars/offdocs/m8310017.htm (accessed March 1, 2006).

25. Rankine, personal communication with the author, January 14, 2005.

26. Caspar Weinberger, *Fighting for Peace: Seven Critical Years in the Pentagon* (New York: Warner Books, 1990), 311.

27. Rankine, personal communication with the author, January 14, 2005.

28. James A. Abrahamson, interview with the author, May 16, 2001.

29. James A. Abrahamson, personal communication with the author, September 2, 2003.

30. James A. Abrahamson, personal communication with the author, July 19, 2001.

31. Abrahamson, personal communication with the author, September 2, 2003.

32. Abrahamson, interview with the author, May 16, 2001.

33. Abrahamson, personal communication with the author, September 2, 2003.

34. Fred Hiatt, "Defense Secretary Restates Support for ABM System," *Washington Post*, March 28, 1984.

35. Edward Teller, testimony, House Armed Services Committee, April 28, 1983.

36. Abrahamson, interview with the author, May 16, 2001.

37. Rankine, personal communication with the author, January 14, 2005.

38. James C. Fletcher, "The Strategic Defense Initiative," testimony before the Subcommittee on Research and Development of the Committee on Armed Services, U.S. House of Representatives, March 1, 1984.

39. Gerold Yonas, letter to Edward A. Torrero, technical editor, *IEEE Spectrum*, August 2, 1985.

40. Gerold Yonas, "Yes," in double feature titled "Can Star Wars Make Us Safe?" *Science Digest*, September 1985, 34.

41. Edward Teller, interview with the author, May 2, 1999.

42. Dmitry Mikheyev, *The Soviet Perspective on the Strategic Defense Initiative* (McLean, VA: Pergamon-Brassey's International Defense Publishers, 1987), 2–3.

43. Ibid., 50.

44. Dmitry Mikheyev, interview with the author, November 26, 2003.

45. Michael Ellman and Vladimir Kontorovich, eds., *The Destruction of the Soviet Economic System: An Insider's History* (Armonk, NY: M. E. Sharpe, 1998), 50.

46. Jacob W. Kipp, "Forecasting Future War: Andrei Kokoshin and the Military-Political Debate in Contemporary Russia," Foreign Military Studies Office, Fort Leavenworth, Kansas, January 1999. Available through the FMSO website, fmso.leavenworth.army.mil/ (accessed March 1, 2006).

47. See Sasha Telnov, "History of Akademgorok," at http://costard.lbl.gov/~telnov/htmls/history.html (accessed March 1, 2006).

CHAPTER 8

1. Allen Bloom, *The Closing of the American Mind* (New York: Simon & Schuster, 1987).

2. Dennis Healey, *The Time of My Life* (New York: W. W. Norton, 1989), 517.

3. Office of Technology Assessment, "Ballistic Missile Defense Technologies," 052-003-001008-9 (Washington, DC: Government Printing Office, September 1985).

4. See "Parallel History Project on NATO and the Warsaw Pact," compiled by the Center for Security Studies at ETH Zurich and the National Security Archive at George Washington University on behalf of the PHP network. Posted at www.isn.ethz.ch/php (accessed March 1, 2006).

5. See William Burr, ed., "U.S. Planning for War in Europe, 1963–64" (National Security Archive Electronic Briefing Book No. 31), posted at www2.gwu.edu/~nsarchiv/NSAEBB/NSAEBB31/#_edn1 (accessed March 1, 2006).

6. "Secrets and Humor: Keeping Things in Perspective," *Advanced Concepts Group Newsletter*, Sandia National Laboratories, August 1999.

7. Fred I. Greenstein and William C. Wohlforth, eds., *Retrospective on the End of the Cold War*, Center of International Studies Monograph Series No. 6, Princeton University, 1996. (Report of a conference sponsored by the John Foster Dulles Program for the Study of Leadership in International Affairs).

8. Stanislav Menshikov, "Missile Defense: A Russian Perspective," ECAAR-Russia Paper, July 21, 2002.

9. Hans Bethe, "No," in double feature titled "Can Star Wars Make Us Safe?" *Science Digest*, September 1985, 83.

10. Guyla Horn, quoted in "Frühe Zweifel," *Der Spiegel*, September 2, 1991, 110–11.

11. Section titled "Star Wars/SDI," from the TV series *Messengers From Moscow*.

12. Gerold Yonas, personal communication with the author, February 14, 2000.

13. Robert M. Gates, *From the Shadows: The Ultimate Insider's Story of Five Presidents and How They Won the Cold War* (New York: Simon & Schuster, 1996), 266.

14. Ibid., 539.

15. George Shultz, personal communication with the author, August 3, 2005.

16. Charles H. Townes, *How the Laser Happened: Adventures of a Scientist* (New York: Oxford University Press, 1999), 167–68.

17. Richard Pipes, "Can the Soviet Union Reform?" *Foreign Affairs,* Fall 1984, 47–61.

18. *Izvestia,* September 24, 1999, quoted in Christopher Andrew and Vasili Mitrokhin's *The Sword and the Shield* (New York: Basic Books, 1999), 214.

19. Yuri B. Shvets, *Washington Station: My Life as a KGB Spy in America* (New York: Simon & Schuster, 1994), 75.

20. Ibid., 74.

21. Reported in *Pravda* (October 28, 1985) and *Literaturaya Gazeta* (June 20, 1986), in Peter Schweizer, *Victory: The Reagan Administration's Secret Strategy That Hastened the Collapse of the Soviet Union* (New York: Atlantic Monthly Press, 1994), 197.

22. Herbert E. Meyer, "Why Is the World So Dangerous?" Memo to William Casey, Director of Central Intelligence, November 30, 1983.

23. Healey, *Time of My Life,* 517.

24. Evgeny Velikhov, interview with the author, November 27, 2003.

25. Jack F. Matlock, Jr., *Reagan and Gorbachev: How the Cold War Ended* (New York: Random House, 2004).

26. Mikhail Gorbachev, *Memoirs* (New York: Doubleday, 1995).

27. William M. Arkin and Richard W. Fieldhouse, *Nuclear Battlefields: Global Links in the Arms Race* (Cambridge, MA: Ballinger Publishing Co., 1985).

28. Quoted from "The Reagan Legacy," produced by Derek Lapping Associates for the Discovery Channel, 1996.

29. Col. Gen. (Ret.) Yu. V. Votintsev, "Unknown Troops of the Vanished Superpower," *Voyenno-Istoricheskiy Zhurnal* No. 9 (1993): 26–38.

30. Matlock, *Reagan and Gorbachev,* 172.

31. See Thomas Powers, "Who Won the Cold War?" Review of *From the Shadows* by Gates, *New York Review of Books,* June 20, 1996.

32. Anatoly Dobrynin, *In Confidence: Moscow's Ambassador to America's Six Cold War Presidents (1962–86)* (New York: Times Books/Random House, 1995), 548–49.

33. Ibid., 550.

34. James A. Abrahamson, interview with the author, May 16, 2001.

35. James A. Abrahamson, personal communication with the author, July 19, 2001.

36. Gerold Yonas, personal communication with the author, July 20, 2001.

37. Gerold Yonas, personal communication with the author, July 18, 2001.

38. Daniel S. Greenberg, *Science, Money, and Politics* (Chicago: University of Chicago, 2001), 282.

39. Evgeny Velikhov, interview with the author, November 27, 2003.

40. Ibid.

41. Evgeny Velikhov, Roald Sageev, and Andrei Kokoshin, eds., *Weaponry in Space: The Dilemma of Security* (Moscow: Mir Publishers, 1986). (Report of the Soviet Scientists' Committee for the Defense of Peace Against Nuclear Threat.)

42. Evgeny Velikhov, interview with the author, November 23, 2003.

43. Velikhov, interview with the author, November 27, 2003.

44. Roald Sagdeev, interview with the author, October 9, 2003.

45. Quoted from Velikhov's London press conference on the book *Weaponry in Space* (date unknown).

46. Stanislav Menshikov, "Missile Defense: A Russian Perspective," ECAAR-Russia Paper, July 21, 2002.

47. Peter Zarubin, personal communication with the author, September 2, 2003.

48. P. V. Zarubin, "Academician Basov, High-Power Lasers and the Antimissile Defence Problem," *Quantum Electronics* 32:12 (December 2002): 1050.

49. Sagdeev, interview with the author, October 9, 2003.

50. Ibid.

51. Gerold Yonas, personal communication with the author, August 31, 2003.

52. Velikhov, interview with the author, November 27, 2003.

53. Ibid.

CHAPTER 9

1. Daniel Graham, Commonwealth Club speech, July 6, 1984.

2. James A. Abrahamson, interview with the author, May 23, 2001.

3. Gerold Yonas, interview with the author, March 3, 2000.

4. Simon P. (Pete) Worden, personal communication with the author, February 1, 2005.

5. James A. Abrahamson, interview with the author, May 16, 2001.

6. James A. Abrahamson, personal communication with the author, July 19, 2001.

7. Gerold Yonas, personal communication with the author, August 31, 2003.

8. Yonas, interview with the author, March 3 2000.

9. Gerold Yonas, interview with the author, February 19, 2000.

10. Gerold and Jane Yonas, private discussion with the author, January 12, 2003.

11. Jane Yonas, private discussion with the author, January 12, 2003.

12. Gerold Yonas, "What I Learned From Star Wars," unpublished paper, May 21, 1996, and personal correspondence of February 19, 2000.

13. Yonas, private correspondence with the author, April 7, 2002.

14. Yonas, interview with the author, March 3, 2000.

15. Ibid.

16. Ibid.

17. Fred Hoffman, James A. Abrahamson, and Simon P. Worden, "Technologies for Effective Multilayer Defenses," in Hoffman, Albert Wohlstetter, and David S. Yost, eds., *Swords and Shields: NATO, the USSR, and New Choices for Long-Range Offense and Defense* (Washington, DC: Lexington Books, 1987), 184.

18. Yonas, private correspondence with the author, April 7, 2002.

19. Yonas, private correspondence with the author, December 14, 1999.

20. Eugene Fox, "Homing Overlay Experiment: Setting the Record Straight," *Army*, November 1994, 12–13.

21. Col. Gen. Yu. V. Votintsev, "Unknown Troops of the Vanished Superpower," *Voyenno-Istoricheskiy Zhurnal* No. 9 (1993): 26–38.

22. Caspar Weinberger, *Fighting for Peace: Seven Critical Years in the Pentagon* (New York: Warner Books, 1990), 312.

23. Ibid., 313.

24. James C. Fletcher, "The Technologies for Ballistic Missile Defense," *Issues in Science and Technology* 1 (Fall 1984): 15–29.

25. G. J. Nunz, "Beam Experiments Aboard a Rocket (BEAR) Project," final report, volume 1, project summary, Los Alamos National Laboratory, January 1990.

26. Quoted by Strobe Talbott, *The Master of the Game: Paul Nitze and the Nuclear Peace* (New York: Knopf/Borzoi Books, 1988), 217.

27. Richard L. Garwin, "Space Technology: Myth and Promise" in *Ways Out of the Arms Race*, edited by J. Hassard, T. Kibble, and P. Lewis, Proceedings of the Second International Scientists' Congress held at Imperial College of Science, Technology & Medicine, University of London, December 2–4, 1988.

28. Fletcher, "Technologies for Ballistic Missile Defense," 15–29.

29. James D. Watkins, interview with the author, April 20, 1999.

30. Christopher Andrew and Vasili Mitrokhin, *The Sword and the Shield* (New York: Basic Books, 1999), 229.

31. Herbert E. Meyer, "What Should We Do About the Russians?" Memo to William Casey, Director of Central Intelligence, June 28, 1984.

32. George A. Keyworth II, "The Case of Strategic Defense: An Option for a World Disarmed," *Issues in Science and Technology* 1 (Fall 1984): 30.

33. Yonas, private communication to N. Hey and N. Singer, January 3, 2003.

34. "The History of the Creation of 'Polyus.'" Posted at Molniya website, http://www.buran.ru/htm/molniya.htm (accessed March 1, 2006).

35. Gerhard Kowalski, "Kosmoplan, Killer Satellites and a Battle Station," *Flug Revue*, December 2000: 56. Also see A. Karpenko, "ABM and Space Defense," *Nevsky Bastion* No. 4 (1999): 2–47; translation posted by the Federation of American Scientists at www.fas.org/spp/starwars/program/soviet/990600-bmd-rus.htm (accessed March 1, 2006).

36. Quoted from "Strategic Defense Initiative—Space Race Between the Superpowers," NTV Russia television documentary, 2001.

37. William J. Broad, *Teller's War: The Top-Secret Story Behind the Star Wars Deception* (New York: Simon & Schuster, 1992), 199.

38. See DIA report, *Soviet Military Power, 1983*, Chapter 4 "Soviet Space Systems," posted at FAS website, www.fas.org/irp/dia/product/smp_83_ch4.htm (accessed March 1, 2006).

39. Soviet technology lag is documented in Roald Z. Sagdeev, *The Making of a Soviet Scientist* (New York: John Wiley & Sons, 1994), 298–301.

40. Matt Fellowes, "Public Opinion and American Foreign Policy: 1980–1990," Washington, DC: Winston Foundation, 1999.

41. Quoted in Leslie H. Gelb, "Vision of Space Defense Posing New Challenges," *New York Times*, March 3, 1985.

42. Philip M. Boffey, "Dark Side of 'Star Wars': System Could Also Attack," *New York Times*, March 7, 1985.

43. Gerold Yonas, "The Strategic Defense Initiative: The Politics and Science of Weapons in Space," *Physics Today*, June 1985, 25.

44. Ibid., 27.

45. Roald Sagdeev, interview with the author, April 15, 2004.

46. Evgeny Velikhov, interview with the author, November 27, 2003.

47. See DIA report, *Soviet Military Power, 1985*, Chapter 3 "Strategic Defense and Space Programs," posted at www.fas.org/irp/dia/product/smp_85_ch3.htm (accessed March 1, 2005).

48. Worden, personal communication with the author, February 13, 2005.

49. Yonas, private discussion with the author, August 24, 2002.

50. James A. Abrahamson, interview with the author, May 23, 2001.

51. Yonas, interview with the author, March 3, 2000.

CHAPTER 10

1. Margaret Thatcher, *The Downing Street Years* (New York: HarperCollins, 1993), 466.

2. Ibid., 382.

3. "1984: Tory Cabinet in Bright Bomb Blast," BBC dispatch, posted at news.bbc.co.uk/onthisday/hi/dates/stories/october/12/newsid_2531000/25 31583.stm (accessed March 1, 2006).

4. James A. Abrahamson, interview with the author, May 12, 2001.

5. Abrahamson, interview with the author, May 23, 2001.

6. Sir Charles Powell, interview with the author, June 8, 1999.

7. Thatcher, *Downing Street Years*, 463.

8. "Defrosting the Old Order," *New Perspectives Quarterly*, Winter 1996. See also comments from Mikhail Gorbachev, Margaret Thatcher, George Bush, François Mitterrand, Brian Mulroney, Fidel Castro.

9. Powell, interview with the author, June 8, 1999.

10. Thatcher, *Downing Street Years*, 467.

11. Ibid.

12. Ibid., 468.

13. George Shultz, personal communication with the author, August 3, 2005.

14. Robert C. McFarlane, interview with the author, October 10, 2003.

15. Ibid.

16. Powell, interview with the author, June 8, 1999.

17. Thatcher, *Downing Street Years*, 466.

18. Roald Sagdeev, interview with the author, October 9, 2003.

19. See DIA report, *Soviet Military Power, 1985*, Chapter 3 "Strategic Defense and Space Programs," posted at www.fas.org/irp/dia/product/smp_85 _ch3.htm (accessed March 1, 1996).

20. Robert M. Gates, *From the Shadows: The Ultimate Insider's Story of Five Presidents and How They Won the Cold War* (New York: Simon & Schuster, 1996), 329–30.

21. Powell, interview with the author, June 8, 1999.

22. James A. Abrahamson, personal communication with the author, July 19, 2001.

23. Abrahamson, interview with the author, May 12, 2001.

24. Thatcher, *Downing Street Years*, photo on 435.

25. William F. Broad, *Teller's War: The Top-Secret Story Behind the Star Wars Deception* (New York: Simon & Schuster, 1992), 144.

26. George E. Brown Jr., "Questions of Integrity at Livermore Laboratory," *Congressional Record*, December 10, 1987, E4745.

27. "The President's Strategic Defense Initiative," *Department of State Bulletin* 85: 65–72, March 1985

28. William J. Broad, "Science Showmanship: A Deep 'Star Wars' Rift," *New York Times*, December 16, 1985.

29. Gerold Yonas, interview with the author, October 24, 2003.

30. See Gerold Yonas, "The Strategic Defense Initiative," in *Recollections for Tomorrow* (Albuquerque, NM: Sandia National Laboratories, 1989), 40.

31. Jay Winik, *On the Brink: The Dramatic, Behind-the-Scenes Saga of the Reagan Era and the Men and Women Who Won the Cold War* (New York: Simon & Schuster, 1996), 362.

32. Thatcher, *Downing Street Years*, 466.

33. Quoted by Strobe Talbott, *The Master of the Game: Paul Nitze and the Nuclear Peace* (New York: Knopf/Borzoi Books, 1988), 208.

34. Winik, *On the Brink*, 366.

35. Abrahamson, interview with the author, May 12, 2001.

36. Abrahamson, personal communication with the author, July 19, 2001.

37. Herbert E. Meyer, "Can Gorbachev Pull It Off?" Memo to William Casey, Director of Central Intelligence, April 1985.

38. Charles Mohr, "What Moscow Might Do in Replying to 'Star Wars,'" *New York Times*, March 6, 1985.

39. Gerold Yonas, letter to Edward A. Torrero, technical editor, *IEEE Spectrum*, August 2, 1985.

40. Gerold Yonas, "Yes," in double feature titled "Can Star Wars Make Us Safe?" *Science Digest*, September 1985, 30.

41. Ibid., 74.

42. Gerold Yonas, interview with the author, March 3, 2000.

43. Abrahamson, personal communication with the author, July 19, 2001.

44. Stanley Orman, interview with the author, June 6, 2001.

45. Gerold Yonas, personal communication with the author, May 18, 2001.

46. Gerold Yonas, personal communication with the author, October 31, 2004.

47. Gerold Yonas, personal communication with the author, January 20, 2005.

48. Michael Ellman and Vladimir Kontorovich, eds., *The Destruction of the Soviet Economic System: An Insider's History* (Armonk, NY: M. E. Sharpe, 1998), 59.

49. Vladimir Shlapentokh, "How Colossus Fell: The Collapse of the Soviet Empire," www.msu.edu/~shlapent/sovhistory.htm (accessed March 1, 2006).

50. Gerold Yonas, personal communication with the author, February 1, 1999.

51. Yonas, interview with the author, March 3, 2000.

52. Roald Sagdeev, interview with the author, October 9, 2003.

53. John Newhouse, "Test," *The New Yorker*, July 1985.

54. Stanley Orman, interview with the author, July 24, 2001.

55. Orman, interviews with the author, June 6 and July 24, 2001.

56. Peter Schweizer, *Victory: The Reagan Administration's Secret Strategy That Hastened the Collapse of the Soviet Union* (New York: Atlantic Monthly Press, 1994), 16.

57. Gerold Yonas, interview with the author, February 13, 1999.

58. Edward Teller, "Where Are the Russians on SDI?" (speech, Commonwealth Club, November 24, 1986).

59. Orman, interview with the author, June 6, 2001.

60. Ibid.

61. Ibid.

62. Ibid.

63. Orman, interview with the author, July 24, 2001.

64. Orman, interview with the author, June 6, 2001.

65. Gerold Yonas, "What I Learned from Star Wars," unpublished paper, May 21, 1996.

66. Abrahamson, interview with the author, May 16, 2001.

67. Orman, interview with the author, June 6, 2001.

68. Gerold Yonas, review of *The Shield of Faith: The Hidden Struggle for Strategic Defense*, by B. Bruce Briggs, *IEEE Spectrum*, November 1988.

69. Yonas, "What I Learned from Star Wars."

70. Daniel S. Greenberg, *Science, Money, and Politics* (Chicago: University of Chicago, 2001), 289.

71. Meyer, "Can Gorbachev Pull It Off?"

72. Ibid.

CHAPTER 11

1. Samuel Florman, "Technology and the Tragic View," *Alternative Futures* 2 (Spring 1980): 3.

2. Both quoted in "The Reagan Legacy," produced by Derek Lapping Associates for the Discovery Channel, 1996.

3. Mikhail Gorbachev, *On My Country and the World* (New York: Columbia University Press, 2000), 177–79.

4. Robert M. Gates, *From the Shadows: The Ultimate Insider's Story of Five Presidents and How They Won the Cold War* (New York: Simon & Schuster, 1996), 378.

5. Robert McFarlane, interview with the author, October 10, 2003.

6. George P. Shultz, *Turmoil and Triumph: My Years as Secretary of State* (New York: Macmillan, 1993), 702.

7. Anatoly Dobrynin, *In Confidence: Moscow's Ambassador to America's Six Cold War Presidents (1962–86)* (New York: Times Books/Random House, 1995), 583.

8. Strobe Talbott, *The Master of the Game: Paul Nitze and the Nuclear Peace* (New York: Knopf, 1988), 284–85.

9. Michael Duffy and Nancy Gibbs, "The Real Reagan," *Time*, September 29, 2003, 62. Book excerpt from Kiron K. Skinner, Annelise Anderson, and Martin Anderson, *Reagan: A Life in Letters* (New York: Free Press, 2003).

10. McFarlane, personal communication with the author, November 10, 2003.

11. Duffy and Gibbs, "The Real Reagan," 62.

12. Robert C. McFarlane and Zofia Smardz, *Special Trust* (New York: Cadell & Davies, 1994), 317.

13. Dobrynin, *In Confidence*, 588.

14. Quoted from "The Reagan Legacy."

15. Dmitry Mikheyev, interview with the author, November 26, 2003.

16. Ronald Reagan, *An American Life* (New York: Simon & Schuster, 1990), 650.

17. Quoted from "The Reagan Legacy."

18. Ibid.

19. Herb Meyer, personal communication with the author, November 24, 2004.

20. Mikhail Gorbachev, *Memoirs* (New York: Doubleday, 1995).

21. Dobrynin, *In Confidence*, 589–90.

22. Ibid., 591.

23. McFarlane, personal communication with the author, October 21, 2003.

24. Quoted in Fred I. Greenstein and William C. Wohlforth, eds., *Retrospective on the End of the Cold War*, Center of International Studies Monograph Series no. 6, Princeton University, 1996. (Report of a conference sponsored by the John Foster Dulles Program for the Study of Leadership in International Affairs).

25. Gerold Yonas, personal communication with the author, December 13, 1999.

26. Gerold Yonas, interview with the author, February 13, 1999.

27. Dobrynin, *In Confidence*, 479.

28. Ibid., 592.

29. Edmund Morris, "The Unknowable," *The New Yorker*, June 28, 2004, 44.

30. Meyer, personal communication with the author, November 24, 2004.

31. Max Kampelman, "The Ronald Reagan I Knew" *Weekly Standard*, November 24, 2003.

32. Stanley Orman, interview with the author, July 24, 2001.

33. McFarlane and Smardz, *Special Trust*, 331.

34. Jack F. Matlock Jr., *Reagan and Gorbachev: How the Cold War Ended* (New York: Random House, 2004), 188.

35. Reagan, *An American Life*, 650.

36. Dobrynin, *In Confidence*, 620.

37. Notes from the CPSU Central Committee session of March 24, 1986, in Peter Schweizer, *Reagan's War* (New York: Doubleday, 2002). Anatoly Chernayev diary, courtesy of the Gorbachev Foundation.

38. See Peter Schweizer, *Victory: The Reagan Administration's Secret Strategy That Hastened the Collapse of the Soviet Union* (New York: Atlantic Monthly Press, 1994), 240.

39. James D. Denton and Peter Schweizer, "Murdering SDI," *National Review*, July 31, 1987, 37–39.

40. Herbert E. Meyer, "Why is the World So Dangerous?" Memo to William Casey, Director of Central Intelligence, November 30, 1983.

41. Denton and Schweizer, "Murdering SDI," 37–39.

42. From "Oma im Altkauter," *Der Spiegel* 24 (1990), in Schweizer, *Reagan's War*.

43. Meyer, personal communication with the author, November 24, 2004.

44. Matlock, *Reagan and Gorbachev*, 243.

45. Herb Meyer, "What's Wrong with the CIA?" lecture at seminar titled *The History, Purpose and Propriety of U.S. Intelligence Activities*, Hillsdale College, September 14–18, 2003. Available at www.siegeofwesternciv.com/hillsdale.htm (accessed March 1, 2006).

46. From *Simpson's Contemporary Quotations* (New York: Houghton Mifflin, 1988), quoted in *Washington Post*, May 13, 1986. See www.bartleby.com/63/68/468.html (accessed March 1, 2006).

47. Roald Sagdeev, interview with the author, October 9, 2003.

48. Ibid.

49. Quoted in Mona Charnel, *Useful Idiots* (Washington, DC: Regnery, 2003).

50. Evgeny Velikhov, interview with the author, November 23, 2003.

51. Sagdeev, interview with the author, October 9, 2003.

52. Michael Ellman and Vladimir Kontorovich, eds., *The Destruction of the Soviet Economic System: An Insider's History* (Armonk, NY: M. E. Sharpe, 1998), 56.

53. Ibid.

54. Velikhov, interview with the author, November 23, 2003.

55. Sagdeev, interview with the author, October 9, 2003.

56. Roald Sagdeev, remarks following Truman Lecture, Sandia National Laboratories, October 24, 2003.

57. Yonas, personal communication with the author, February 26, 2005.

58. "Ministry," chapter 5 of V. N. Mikhailov, *I Am a Hawk*. Posted at www.iss.niiit.ru/book/chap5.htm (accessed March 1, 2006).

59. Yonas, personal communication with the author, January 12, 2005; and Yonas, "The Strategic Defense Initiative," *Daedalus* 114:2 (Spring 1985): 89.

60. Gerold Yonas, interview with the author, March 3, 2000.

Chapter 12

1. Ronald Reagan, remarks at the high school commencement exercises in Glassboro, New Jersey, June 19, 1986. Available at www.reagan.utexas.edu/archives/speeches/1986/61986e.htm (accessed March 1, 2006).

2. Gerold Yonas, "SDI: Prospects and Challenges," speech delivered at the Commonwealth Club, March 7, 1986, www.commonwealthclub.org/missile defense/yonassp.html (accessed March 1, 2006).

3. Reagan, Remarks at the High School Commencement Exercises in Glassboro.

4. Michael Duffy and Nancy Gibbs, "The Real Reagan," *Time*, September 29, 2003, 62. Book excerpt from Kiron K. Skinner, Annelise Anderson, and Martin Anderson, *Reagan: A Life in Letters* (New York: Free Press, 2003).

5. Roald Sagdeev, "Science and Revolutions," one of the Tanner Lectures on Human Values, delivered at Brasenose College, Oxford University, March 9–16, 1992.

6. James A. Abrahamson and Simon P. Worden, "Technologies for Effective Multilayer Defenses," in Fred Hoffman, Albert Wohlstetter, and David S. Yost, eds., *Swords and Shields: NATO, the USSR, and New Choices for Long-Range Offense and Defense* (Washington, DC: Lexington Books, 1987), 193.

7. Fred I. Greenstein and William C. Wohlforth, eds., *Retrospective on the End of the Cold War*, Center of International Studies Monograph Series no. 6, Princeton University, 1996. (Report of a conference sponsored by the John Foster Dulles Program for the Study of Leadership in International Affairs.)

8. Quoted in "The Reagan Legacy," produced by Derek Lapping Associates for the Discovery Channel, 1996.

9. Simon P. (Pete) Worden, personal communication with the author, February 1, 2005.

10. Jack F. Matlock Jr., *Reagan and Gorbachev: How the Cold War Ended* (New York: Random House, 2004), 237–38.

11. Simon P. Worden, "What Can We Do? When Can We Do It?" *National Review*, December 31, 1986, 40. Preprints of this article were distributed before the Reykjavik Summit.

12. Worden, personal communication with the author, February 1, 2005.

13. Yuri B. Shvets, *Washington Station: My Life as a KGB Spy in America* (New York: Simon & Schuster, 1994), 158–60.

14. Simon P. Worden, *SDI and the Alternatives* (Washington, DC: National Defense University Press, 1991), 175.

15. Mark C. Cleary, *The Cape: Military Space Operations 1971–1992*, chapter 3, section 5, at www.patrick.af.mil/heritage/Cape/Cape3/cape3-5.htm.

16. James A. Abrahamson, personal communication with the author, May 23, 2001.

17. See Stanley A. Blumberg and Louis G. Panos, *Edward Teller: Giant of the Golden Age of Physics* (New York: Charles Scribner's Sons, 1990), 255.

18. Robert M. Gates, *From the Shadows: The Ultimate Insider's Story of Five Presidents and How They Won the Cold War* (New York: Simon & Schuster, 1996), 409.

19. Shvets, *Washington Station*, 161.

20. Peter Schweizer, *Victory: The Reagan Administration's Secret Strategy That Hastened the Collapse of the Soviet Union* (New York: Atlantic Monthly Press, 1994), 279.

21. Strobe Talbott, *The Master of the Game: Paul Nitze and the Nuclear Peace* (New York: Knopf, 1988), 324.

22. Worden, personal communication with the author, January 17, 2006.

23. George P. Shultz, "What Really Happened at Reykjavik," in *Turmoil and Triumph: My Years as Secretary of State* (New York: Macmillan, 1993), 751.

24. George Shultz, personal communication with the author, August 3, 2005.

25. Mikhail Gorbachev, *Memoirs* (New York: Doubleday, 1995).

26. Nancy Reagan, *My Turn: The Memoirs of Nancy Reagan*, with William Novak (New York: Random House, 1989).

27. Paul Lettow, *Ronald Reagan and His Quest to Abolish Nuclear Weapons* (New York: Random House, 2005), 245–46.

28. Robert McFarlane, personal communication with the author, April 29, 2005.

29. Gorbachev, *Memoirs*.

30. Margaret Thatcher, *The Downing Street Years* (New York: HarperCollins, 1993), 470–71.

31. Ronald Reagan, *An American Life* (New York: Simon and Schuster, 1990), 651, 683–84.

32. Anatoly Chernyaev, *My Six Years With Gorbachev* (University Park: Pennsylvania State University Press, 2000), 51, as translated from the Russian in Matlock, *Reagan and Gorbachev*, 180.

33. Anatoly Dobrynin, *In Confidence: Moscow's Ambassador to America's Six Cold War Presidents (1962–86)* (New York: Times Books/Random House, 1995), 610.

34. William E. Odom, *The Collapse of the Soviet Military* (New Haven, CT: Yale University Press, 1998), 132.

35. Herb Meyer, personal communication with the author, November 24, 2004.

36. Thatcher, *Downing Street Years*, 471.

37. Christopher Ogden, *Maggie: An Intimate Portrait of a Woman in Power* (New York: Simon & Schuster, 1990), 241.

38. Sir Charles Powell, interview with the author, June 8, 1999.

39. Margaret Thatcher, "Courage," speech delivered at the Heritage Foundation's "Leadership for America" Gala, December 10, 1997.

40. Thatcher, *Downing Street Years*, 473.

41. Ibid., 474.

CHAPTER 13

1. Simon P. (Pete) Worden, personal communication with the author, February 13, 2005.

2. B. I. Gubanov, *The Triumph and Tragedy of "Energia": Reflections of the Chief Engineer*, Vol. 3, *Energia-Buran* (Nizhnij Novgorod: NIER publishers, 1998).

3. From "Strategic Defense Initiative—Space Race Between the Superpowers," NTV Russia television documentary, 2001.

4. Peter Zarubin, personal communication with the author, March 1, 2005.

5. Ibid.

6. Gerold Yonas, personal communication with the author, February 5, 2004.

7. Gerold Yonas, personal communication with the author, March 16, 2005.

8. See Brian Crozier, *The Rise and Fall of the Soviet Empire* (Rocklin, CA: Forum, 1999), 404.

9. Margaret Thatcher, *The Downing Street Years* (New York: HarperCollins, 1993), 477.

10. Ibid., 481.

11. Gus W. Weiss, "The Farewell Dossier," www.odci.gov/csi/studies/96unclass/farewell.htm (accessed March 1, 2006).

12. Thatcher, *Downing Street Years*, 485.

13. Robert M. Gates, *From the Shadows: The Ultimate Insider's Story of Five Presidents and How They Won the Cold War* (New York: Simon & Schuster, 1996), 573.

14. Central Intelligence Agency, "Gorbachev: Steering the USSR into the 1990s," Intelligence Assessment, CIA Directorate of Intelligence, July 1987, 1–2, included in CIA, *Analysis of the Soviet Union, 1947–1991*, vol. 2.

15. Central Intelligence Agency, "Soviet SDI Response Options: The Resource Dilemma," research paper, CIA Directorate of Intelligence, November 1987, 1–2, included in CIA's *Analysis of the Soviet Union, 1947–1991*, vol. 2.

16. Anatoly Dobrynin, *In Confidence: Moscow's Ambassador to America's Six Cold War Presidents (1962–86)* (New York: Times Books/Random House, 1995), 622.

17. Jack F. Matlock Jr., *Reagan and Gorbachev: How the Cold War Ended* (New York: Random House, 2004), xiii.

18. Quoted by Anatoly Chernayev in *Retrospective on the End of the Cold War*, Fred I. Greenstein and William C. Wohlforth, eds., Center of International Studies Monograph Series no. 6, Princeton University, 1996. (Report of a conference sponsored by the John Foster Dulles Program for the Study of Leadership in International Affairs.)

19. John Dumbrell, *A Special Relationship* (New York: St. Martin's Press, 2001), 93–94.

20. Colin Powell, *My American Journey*, with Joseph E. Persico (New York: Random House, 1995), 366.

21. Gates, *From the Shadows*, 573.

22. Quoted in "The Reagan Legacy," produced by Derek Lapping Associates for the Discovery Channel, 1996.

23. Greenstein and Wohlforth, eds., *Retrospective on the End of the Cold War*.

24. See www.cnn.com/SPECIALS/cold.war/episodes/22/script.html (accessed March 1, 2006).

25. The INF treaty is posted at www.state.gov/t/np/trty/18432.htm.

26. James A. Abrahamson, interview with the author, May 23, 2001.

27. Gerold Yonas, "Despite the Battering, SDI Deserves a Determined Effort," *Los Angeles Times*, June 26, 1987.

28. Gerold Yonas, personal correspondence with the author, August 4, 2002.

29. Gerold Yonas, personal correspondence with the author, August 3, 2002.

30. Gerold Yonas, personal communication with the author, March 16, 2005.

31. Bruce van Voorst, "From Star Wars to Smart Rocks," *Time*, February 23, 1987.

32. Dusko Doder and Louise Branson, *Gorbachev: Heretic in the Kremlin* (New York: Viking Penguin, 1990), 319.

33. James A. Abrahamson, interview with the author, May 16, 2001.

34. Quoted in "The Reagan Legacy."

35. Ibid.

36. Strobe Talbott, *The Master of the Game: Paul Nitze and the Nuclear Peace* (New York: Knopf/Borzoi Books, 1988), 391.

37. NIE 11-3/8-88, *Soviet Forces and Capabilities for Strategic Nuclear Conflict Through the Late 1990s* (1 December 1988), 6, 3, 7, 8.

38. Quoted in Dennis Healey, *The Time of My Life* (New York: W. W. Norton, 1989), 531.

39. Hendrik Hertzberg, "Winner," *The New Yorker*, June 28, 2004, 34.

40. Dobrynin, *In Confidence*, 627.

41. Dmitry Mikheyev, interview with the author, November 26, 2003.

42. Caspar Weinberger, *Fighting for Peace: Seven Critical Years in the Pentagon* (New York: Warner Books, 1990), 317–18.

43. Abrahamson, interview with the author, May 12, 2001.

44. David Pryce-Jones, *The Strange Death of the Soviet Empire* (New York: Metropolitan Books/Henry Holt and Company, 1995), 292.

45. Quoted in Michael R. Beschloss and Strobe Talbott, *At the Highest Levels: The Inside Story of the End of the Cold War* (Boston: Little, Brown, and Company, 1993), 240.

46. Roald Z. Sagdeev, *The Making of a Soviet Scientist: My Adventures in Nuclear Fusion and Space from Stalin to Star Wars* (New York: John Wiley & Sons, 1995), 273.

CHAPTER 14

1. Evgeny Velikhov, interview with the author, March 6, 2003.

2. Herb Meyer, personal communication with the author, November 24, 2004.

3. Gerold Yonas, personal communication with the author, November 28, 2004.

4. John Lewis Gaddis, *The United States and the End of the Cold War* (New York: Oxford University Press, 1992), 43–44.

5. See NSDD-75, "U.S. Relations with the USSR," Office of the President, January 17, 1983.

6. NSDD-153, "Instructions for the Shultz-Gromyko Meeting in Geneva," Office of the President, January 1, 1985.

7. NSDD-75, "U.S. Relations with the USSR," Office of the President, January 17, 1983.

8. David Fishlock, personal communication with the author, February 28, 1999.

9. "Defrosting the Old Order," *New Perspectives Quarterly*, Winter 1996. See also comments from Mikhail Gorbachev, Margaret Thatcher, George Bush, François Mitterrand, Brian Mulroney, Fidel Castro.

10. Robert C. McFarlane and Zofia Smardz, *Special Trust* (New York: Cadell & Davies, 1994), 235.

11. "Defrosting the Old Order."

12. Velikhov, interview with the author, November 27, 2003.

13. Roald Sagdeev, interview with the author, October 9, 2003.

14. Edward Teller, interview with the author, May 2, 1999.

15. Edward Teller, personal correspondence with the author, June 7, 1999.

16. Gerold Yonas, personal communication with the author, January 8, 2005.

17. Norman Bailey, *The Strategic Plan that Won the Cold War* (McLean, VA: The Potomac Foundation, 1999), 20–21.

18. George Shultz, personal communication with the author, August 3, 2005.

19. Gerold Yonas, personal communication with the author, November 9, 2002.

20. Gerold Yonas, personal communication with the author, October 3, 2002.

21. Richard L. Garwin, "Scientist, Citizen, and Government—Ethics in Action (or Ethics Inaction)," Richard L. Horwitz Lecture, Illinois Mathematics and Science Academy, May 4, 1993.

22. Richard L. Garwin, "Space Technology: Myth and Promise," in *Ways Out of the Arms Race*, edited by J. Hassard, T. Kibble, and P. Lewis, Proceedings of the Second International Scientists' Congress held at Imperial College of Science, Technology & Medicine, University of London, December 2–4, 1988.

23. Yonas, private communication with the author, August 20, 2001.

24. Daniel S. Greenberg, *Science, Money, and Politics* (Chicago: University of Chicago, 2001), 6.

25. Charlie Winter, letter in response to a *New York Times* article, November 7, 1988.

26. Robert McFarlane, interview with the author, October 10, 2003.

27. Gerold Yonas, personal communication with the author, January 8, 2005.

28. Gerold Yonas, personal communication with the author, January 14, 2004.

29. James D. Watkins, interview with the author, April 20, 1999.

30. Arthur C. Clarke, "Presidents, Experts, and Asteroids," Essays on Science and Public Policy, *Science*, www.sciencemag.org/cg/content/fall/280/5369/1532.

31. Evgeny Velikhov, interview with the author, November 27, 2003.

32. Yonas, personal communication with the author, January 14, 2004.

33. Sun Tzu, *The Art of War,* edited by James Clavell (New York: Delacorte Press, 1983), 32.

34. Ronald Reagan, *An American Life* (New York: Simon & Schuster, 1990), 547.

35. Michael Wheeler, comments in "Nuclear Weapons: Keeping the Peace—Past and Future" (50th Anniversary International Colloquium, Sandia National Laboratories, November 2, 1999).

36. Velikhov, interview with the author, November 27, 2003.

37. Quoted in Richard Butler, *Fatal Choice: Nuclear Weapons and the Illusion of Missile Defense* (Boulder, CO: Westview Press, 2001).

38. Abrahamson, interview with the author, May 16, 2001.

39. D. Rumsfeld et al., "Report of the Commission to Address the Ballistic Missile Threat to the United States (1998)." Available at www.fas.org/irp/threat/missile/rumsfeld/toc.htm (accessed March 1, 2006).

40. "National Missile Defenses: Fighting the Last War," SRATFOR Global Intelligence Update, January 24, 2000, www.stratfor.com (accessed March 1, 2006).

41. Eugene Fox and Stanley Orman, "Where is BMD headed?" *Defense News,* August 9, 2004, 29.

42. This claim was made by Gerold Yonas in his paper "SDI: Past, Present, and Future," presented at the WDRG Conference, Washington, DC, February 18, 1989.

43. Eugene Fox and Stanley Orman, "Globalizing BMD," *Defense News,* November 8, 2004, 36.

44. James Glanz, "Military Research: Missile Defense Rides Again," *Science* 284:5413 (April 16, 1999): 416–20.

45. Abrahamson, interview with the author, May 16, 2001.

46. Shultz, personal communication with the author, August 3, 2005.

47. Gerold Yonas, personal communication with the author, December 13, 1999; Gerold Yonas, "One More Time From Russia," Advanced Concepts Group *News & Views,* September 2004 (Sandia National Laboratories).

48. Gerold Yonas, personal communication with the author, July 22, 2000.

49. Gerold Yonas, personal communication with the author, May 30, 2001.

50. Anatoly Dobrynin, *In Confidence: Moscow's Ambassador to America's Six Cold War Presidents (1962–86)* (New York: Times Books/Random House, 1995), 612.

GLOSSARY

ABM	anti-ballistic missile
ASAT	anti-satellite
AWE	Atomic Weapons Establishment (UK)
BAMBI	Ballistic Missile Boost Intercept
BMD	Ballistic Missile Defense
CISAC	Committee on International Security and Arms Control
COF	correlation of forces
COIL	chemical oxygen iodine laser
CPD	Committee on the Present Danger
CPSU	Communist Party of the Soviet Union
DARPA	Defense Advanced Research Projects Agency
DCI	director of central intelligence
DEW	directed energy weapon
DOE	Department of Energy
EMP	electromagnetic pulse
FALCON	Fission-Assisted Laser Concept
FIAN	Lebedev Institute of the Russian Academy of Sciences
FOBS	fractional orbital bombardment system
GAO	General Accounting Office
GLCM	ground-launched cruise missiles
GOI	Vavilov State Optical Institute
GRU	Main Intelligence Administration of the Soviet military General Staff
HOE	Homing Overlay Experiment
ICBM	inter-continental ballistic missile
IKI	Soviet Space Institute
IRBM	intermediate-range ballistic missile
JCS	Joint Chiefs of Staff
KEW	kinetic energy weapon
KGB	Committee for State Security (USSR)
LANL	Los Alamos National Laboratory
LLNL	Lawrence Livermore National Laboratory
MAD	mutual assured destruction

MEG	magnetic explosion generator
MFTI	Moscow Physical-Technical Institute
MHD	magnetohydrodynamics
MIC	Military Industrial Commission
MICOM	U.S. Army Missile Command
MINATOM	Department of Energy (Soviet/Russian)
MIRV	multiple independently targetable re-entry vehicle
MKBS	multimodule orbital base (USSR)
MOD	Ministry of Defense (UK)
MOP	Soviet Ministry of Defense Industry
NIF	National Ignition Facility
NKVD	People's Commissariat of Internal Affairs (Soviet predecessor of KGB)
NORAD	North American Air Defense
NPB	neutral particle beam
NSC	National Security Council
NSDD	National Security Decision Directive
NSPG	National Security Planning Group
OMB	Office of Management and Budget
OSS	Office of Strategic Services
OSTP	Office of Science and Technology Policy
PDL	photodissociation laser
RADLAC	radial-pulse-line accelerator
RV	re-entry vehicle
SALT	Strategic Arms Limitations Treaty
SCADA	supervisory control and data acquisition
SDI	Strategic Defense Initiative
SDIO	Strategic Defense Initiative Office
SLBM	submarine-launched ballistic missile
SPAD	Space Patrol Active Defense
SRBM	short-range ballistic missile
TEL	transporter erector launcher
THEL	tactical high-energy laser
TKS	manned transport spacecraft (USSR)
TRG	Technical Research Group
TRW	Thompson Ramo Wooldridge
VNIIEF	All-Union Research Institute of Experimental Physics (USSR)
WFS	World Federation of Scientists
WHSC	White House Science Council

SELECTED BIBLIOGRAPHY

This selected list of books, reports, and articles consulted in the preparation of *The Star Wars Enigma* offers readers opportunities for further study. World Wide Web URLs are given in some cases, with the caveat that these addresses may be changed or cancelled at any time and that therefore a more exhaustive computer search may be required.

Anderberg, Bengt, and Myron L. Wolbarsht. *Laser Weapons: The Dawn of a New Military Age.* New York: Plenum Press, 1992.

Andrew, Christopher, and Vasili Mitrokhin. *The Sword and the Shield.* New York: Basic Books, 1999.

Arkin, William M., and Richard W. Fieldhouse. *Nuclear Battlefields: Global Links in the Arms Race.* Cambridge, MA: Ballinger Publishing Co., 1985.

Bailey, Norman A. *The Strategic Plan That Won the Cold War.* McLean, VA: Potomac Foundation, 1999.

Baucom, Donald. *Ballistic Missile Defense Program of the Advanced Research Projects Agency: A Review of Project Defender for the Director of Defense Research and Engineering,* 25–29 July 1960, vol. I. Washington, DC: Government Printing Office, 1960.

———. *The Origins of SDI, 1944–1983* (Modern War Studies). Lawrence: University Press of Kansas, 1992.

Beschloss, Michael R., and Strobe Talbott. *At the Highest Levels: The Inside Story of the End of the Cold War.* Boston: Little, Brown, and Company, 1993.

Bethe, Hans. "No," in "Can Star Wars Make Us Safe?" *Science Digest,* September 1985.

Blumberg, Stanley A., and Louis G. Panos. *Edward Teller: Giant of the Golden Age of Physics.* New York: Charles Scribner's Sons, 1990.

Broad, William J. *Star Warriors.* New York: Touchstone, 1986.

———. *Teller's War: The Top-Secret Story Behind the Star Wars Deception.* New York: Simon & Schuster, 1992.

Brown, George E. Jr. "Questions of Integrity at Livermore Laboratory," *Congressional Record,* December 10, 1987.

Bruce Briggs, B. *The Shield of Faith: The Hidden Struggle for Strategic Defense.* New York: Simon & Schuster, 1988.

Butler, Richard. *Fatal Choice: Nuclear Weapons and the Illusion of Missile Defense.* Boulder, CO: Westview Press, 2001.

Byely, B., et al. *Marxism-Leninism on War and Army (A Soviet View).* Translation. U.S. Air Force for Soviet Military Thought Series no. 2. Washington, DC: Government Printing Office, 1974.

Canavan, Gregory H. *Missile Defense for the 21st Century.* Washington, DC: Heritage Foundation, 2003.

Cannon, Lou. *President Reagan: Role of a Lifetime.* New York: Simon & Schuster, 1991.

Cleary, Mark C. *The Cape: Military Space Operations 1971–1992,* chapter I, section 9. www.patrick.af.mil/heritage/Cape/Cape1/cape1-9 .htm.

Crozier, Brian. *The Rise and Fall of the Soviet Empire.* Rocklin, CA: Forum, an imprint of Prima Publishing, 1999.

"Defrosting the Old Order." *New Perspectives Quarterly,* Winter 1996. Comments from Mikhail Gorbachev, Margaret Thatcher, George Bush, François Mitterrand, Brian Mulroney, Fidel Castro.

Denton, James D., and Peter Schweizer. "Murdering SDI." *National Review,* July 31, 1987.

Dobrynin, Anatoly. *In Confidence: Moscow's Ambassador to America's Six Cold War Presidents (1962–86).* New York: Times Books/Random House, 1995.

Doder, Dusko, and Louise Branson. *Gorbachev: Heretic in the Kremlin.* New York: Viking Penguin, 1990.

Douglass, Joseph D., Jr., and Amoretta M. Hoeber. *Soviet Strategy for Nuclear War* (Stanford, CA: Hoover Institution Press, 1979).

Dumbrell, John. *A Special Relationship.* St. Martin's Press, 2001.

Dyson, Freeman J. *Weapons and Hope.* New York: Harper & Row, 1984.

Dyson, George. *Project Orion: The True Story of the Atomic Spaceship.* New York: Henry Holt, 2002.

Ellman, Michael, and Vladimir Kontorovich, eds. *The Destruction of the Soviet Economic System: An Insider's History.* Armonk, NY: M. E. Sharpe, 1998.

"Fact Sheet: High Energy Laser Program." Department of Defense, February 1982.

FitzGerald, Frances. *Way Out There in the Blue.* New York: Simon & Schuster, 2000.

Fletcher. James C. "The Strategic Defense Initiative." Testimony before the Subcommittee on Research and Development of the Committee on Armed Services, U.S. House of Representatives, March 1, 1984.
———. "The Technologies for Ballistic Missile Defense." *Issues in Science and Technology,* Fall 1984.

Fox, Eugene, and Stanley Orman. "Globalizing BMD." *Defense News,* November 8, 2004.

———. "Where Is BMD headed?" *Defense News*, August 9, 2004.

Frye, Alton. "Our Gamble in Space: The Military Danger." *The Atlantic* 212: 2 (August 1963).

Gaddis, John Lewis. *The Cold War: A New History*. New York: Penguin Press, 2005.

———. *The United States and the End of the Cold War*. New York: Oxford University Press, 1992.

Garwin, Richard L. "Holes in the Missile Shield." *Scientific American*, October 25, 2004.

———. "Scientist, Citizen, and Government—Ethics in Action (or Ethics Inaction)." A Richard L. Horwitz Lecture, Illinois Mathematics and Science Academy, May 4, 1993.

Gates, Robert M. *From the Shadows: The Ultimate Insider's Story of Five Presidents and How They Won the Cold War*. New York: Simon & Schuster, 1996.

Glanz, James. "Military Research: Missile Defense Rides Again." *Science* 284:5413 (April 16, 1999).

Goodchild, Peter. *Edward Teller: The Real Dr. Strangelove*. London: Weidenfeld & Nicolson, 2004.

Gorbachev, Mikhail. *Memoirs*. New York: Doubleday, 1995.

Greenberg, Daniel S. *Science, Money, and Politics*. Chicago: University of Chicago, 2001.

Greenstein, Fred I., and William C. Wohlforth, eds. *Retrospective on the End of the Cold War*. Center of International Studies Monograph Series no. 6, Princeton University, 1964.

Gubanov, B. I. *The Triumph and Tragedy of "Energia": Reflections of the Chief Engineer*. Vol. 3, *Energia-Buran*. Nizhnij Novgorod: NIER Publishers, 1998.

Hassard, J., T. Kibble, and P. Lewis, eds. "Ways Out of the Arms Race." *Proceedings of the Second International Scientists' Congress*. Imperial College of Science, Technology & Medicine, University of London, December 2–4, 1988.

Hecht, Jeff. *Beam Weapons: The Next Arms Race*. New York: Plenum Press, 1984.

Hoffman, Fred, Albert Wohlstetter, and David S. Yost, eds. *Swords and Shields: NATO, the USSR, and New Choices for Long-Range Offense and Defense*. Washington, DC: Lexington Books, 1987.

Karpenko, A. "ABM and Space Defense." *Nevsky Bastion*, no. 4, 1999. www.fas.org/spp/starwars/program/soviet/990600-bmd-rus.htm.

Keegan, George J. Jr. "New Assessment Put on Soviet Threat." *Aviation Week & Space Technology*, March 28, 1977.

Keyworth, George A. "The Case of Strategic Defense: An Option for a World Disarmed," *Issues in Science and Technology*, Fall 1984.

Kipp, Jacob W. "Forecasting Future War: Andrei Kokoshin and the Military-Political Debate in Contemporary Russia." Foreign Military Studies Office, Fort Leavenworth, KS, January 1999. http://fmso .leavenworth.army.mil/.

Kowalski, Gerhard. "Kosmoplan, Killer Satellites and a Battle Station." *Flug Revue*, December 2000.

Lettow, Paul. *Ronald Reagan and His Quest to Abolish Nuclear Weapons.* New York: Random House, 2005.

Mark, Hans. "The Airborne Laser from Theory to Reality." *Defense Horizons*, April 2002. http://www.ndu.edu/inss/DefHor/DH12/ DH12.htm.

Matlock, Jack F. Jr. *Reagan and Gorbachev: How the Cold War Ended* New York: Random House, 2004.

McFarlane, Robert C., and Zofia Smardz. *Special Trust.* New York: Cadell & Davies, 1994

Menshikov, Stanislav. "Missile Defense: A Russian Perspective." ECAAR-Russia Paper, July 21, 2002. www.ecaar-russia.org/UNdraft.PDF.

Meyer, Herb. "What's Wrong With the CIA?" Lecture at seminar titled *The History, Purpose and Propriety of U.S. Intelligence Activities*, Hillsdale College, Hillsdale, MI, September 14–18, 2003. www .siegeofwesternciv.com/hillsdale.htm.

Milidov, A. S., ed. *The Philosohical Heritage of V. I. Lenin and Problems of Contemporary War (A Soviet View).* Translation U.S. Air Force for Soviet Military Thought Series no. 5. Washington, DC: Government Printing Office, 1974.

Mikheyev, Dmitry. *The Soviet Perspective on the Strategic Defense Initiative.* McLean, VA: Pergamon-Brassey's International Defense Publishers, 1987.

Morris, Edmund. *Dutch: A Memoir of Ronald Reagan.* New York: Random House, 1999.

"National Missile Defenses: Fighting the Last War." SRATFOR Global Intelligence Update, January 24, 2000. www.stratfor.com.

Odom, William E. *The Collapse of the Soviet Military.* New Haven, CT: Yale University Press, 1998.

Ogden, Christopher. *Maggie: An Intimate Portrait of a Woman in Power.* New York: Simon & Schuster, 1990.

Pike, John. "The Death-Beam Gap: Putting Keegan's Follies in Perspective." Federation of American Scientists, October 1992. www.fas .org/spp/eprint/keegan.htm.

Pipes, Richard. "Can the Soviet Union Reform?" *Foreign Affairs*, Fall 1984.

"Possible Soviet Responses to the US Strategic Defense Initiative." Interagency Intelligence Assessment NIC M 83-10017, 12. www.fas .org/spp/starwars/offdocs/m8310017.htm.

Powell, Colin, with Joseph E. Persico. *My American Journey*. New York: Random House, 1995.

"The President's Strategic Defense Initiative," *Department of State Bulletin* 85: 65-72, March 1985.

Pryce-Jones, David. *The Strange Death of the Soviet Empire*. New York: Metropolitan Books/Henry Holt and Company, 1995.

Reagan, Ronald. *An American Life*. New York: Simon & Schuster, 1990.

Reed, Thomas C. *At the Abyss: An Insider's History of the Cold War*. New York: Random House, 2004.

Rumsfeld, Donald, et al. "Report of the Commission to Address the Ballistic Missile Threat to the United States (1998)." www.fas.org/irp/threat/missile/rumsfeld/toc.htm.

Sagdeev, Roald. *The Making of a Soviet Scientist: My Adventures in Nuclear Fusion and Space From Stalin to Star Wars*. New York: John Wiley & Sons, 1995.

———. "Science and Revolutions." The Tanner Lectures on Human Values, delivered at Brasenose College, Oxford University, Oxford, UK, March 9–16, 1992.

Schweizer, Peter, ed. *The Fall of the Berlin Wall: Reassessing the Causes and Consequences of the End of the Cold War*. Stanford: Hoover Institution Press, 2000.

———. *Reagan's War*. New York: Doubleday, 2002.

———. *Victory: The Reagan Administration's Secret Strategy That Hastened the Collapse of the Soviet Union*. New York: Atlantic Monthly Press, 1994.

Shlapentokh, Vladimir. "How Colossus Fell: The Collapse of the Soviet Empire." www.msu.edu/~shlapent/sovhistory.htm.

Shultz, George P. *Turmoil and Triumph: My Years as Secretary of State*. New York: Macmillan, 1993

Shvets, Yuri B. *Washington Station: My Life as a KGB Spy in America*. New York: Simon & Schuster, 1994.

Sokolovsky, V. D. *Soviet Military Strategy*. Translated by Harriet Fast Scott. New York: Crane Russak & Co., 1975.

Soviet Military Power, 1983. U.S. Department of Defense publication. Washington, DC: Government Printing Office, March 1983.

"The Soviet Space Program." National Intelligence Estimate, Central Intelligence Agency, March 2, 1967. www.astronautix.com/articles/nie11167.htm.

Spratt, John. "Ballistic Missile Defense and National Security." Speech, American Institute of Aeronautics and Astronautics, Monterey, CA, January 20, 2000. www.house.gov/spratt/newsroom/99_00/s10624.htm.

"Strategic Defense, Strategic Choices: Staff Report of the Strategic Defense Initiative, Democratic Caucus of the U.S. House of Represen-

tatives." Carnegie Nonproliferation Project, May 1988. www
.ceip.org/files/projects/npp/resources/StrategicDefenseStrategic
Choices.htm.

Talbott, Strobe. *The Master of the Game: Paul Nitze and the Nuclear Peace*. New York: Knopf/Borzoi Books, 1988.

Taylor, Nick. *Laser: The Inventor, the Nobel Laureate, and the Thirty-Year Patent War*. New York: Citadel Press, 2000.

Teller, Edward. *Memoirs: A Twentieth-Century Journey in Science and Politics*. With Judith Shoolery. New York: Perseus Books, 2001.

Thatcher, Margaret. *The Downing Street Years*. New York: HarperCollins, 1993.

Townes, Charles H. *How the Laser Happened: Adventures of a Scientist*. New York: Oxford University Press, 1999.

Trofimenko, Henry. "The 'Theology' of Strategy." *Orbis* 21:3 (Fall 1977).

Tsarev, Igor. "A 'Diamond-Studded Sky': Should the Military Who Maintains 'They Have Stopped Preparing for Star Wars' Be Trusted?" *JPRS Central Eurasia: CIS/Russian Military Issues*, October 20, 1993. JPRS-UMA-93-039.

Tuck, Jay. *High-Tech Espionage: How the KGB Smuggles NATO's Strategic Secrets to Moscow*. New York: St. Martin's Press, 1986

Velikhov, E. P., and A. A. Kokoshin. "A New Cycle of the Arms Race?" *New Perspectives Quarterly*, Fall-Winter 1985. www.digitalnpq .org/archive/1984_85_fall_winter/new_cycle.html.

Velikhov, Evgeny P. "Science and Scientists in a Nuclear-Weapon-Free World." *Physics Today*, November 1989, 32–36.

Velikhov, Evgeny, Roald Sageev, and Andrei Kokoshin, eds. *Weaponry in Space: The Dilemma of Security*. Moscow: Mir Publishers, 1986.

Weinberger, Caspar. *Fighting for Peace: Seven Critical Years in the Pentagon*. New York: Warner Books, 1990

Weiss, Gus W. "The Farewell Dossier." www.cia.gov/csi/studies/96un clas/farewell.htm.

Winik, Jay. *On the Brink: The Dramatic, Behind-the-Scenes Saga of the Reagan Era and the Men and Women Who Won the Cold War*. New York: Simon & Schuster, 1996.

Worden, Simon P. *SDI and the Alternatives*. Washington, DC: National Defense University Press, 1991.

———. "What Can We Do? When Can We Do it?" *National Review*, December 31, 1986, 40.

Yonas, Gerold. "The Strategic Defense Initiative," *Daedalus* 114:2 (Spring 1985).

———. "The Strategic Defense Initiative: The Politics and Science of Weapons in Space." *Physics Today*, June 1985.

———. "Yes," in "Can Star Wars Make Us Safe?" *Science Digest*, September 1985.

Zarubin, P. V. "Academician Basov, High-Power Lasers and the Antimissile Defence Problem," *Quantum Electronics* 32:12 (December 2002).

INDEX

About the Author

Nigel Hey is a writer of nonfiction books about science and technology. After an early journalistic career in Britain, the United States, and Bermuda, he joined Sandia National Laboratories, one of America's three large nuclear weapon laboratories. He was a Sandia senior administrator (internal consultant) at the time of his retirement in October 2001. His writings include four published books, several reference works, and hundreds of articles in magazines ranging from *Smithsonian* to *New Scientist* and the *Sunday Times* (London).

His other books include *The Mysterious Sun* (Putnam); *How We Will Explore the Outer Planets* (Putnam); *How Will We Feed the Hungry Billions?* (Messner); and *Solar System* (Weidenfeld & Nicolson). He has founded and edited a number of periodical publications and was a contributing author for *The Science Book* (Weidenfeld & Nicolson) and *The McGraw-Hill Security Handbook*. A native of England, he now resides in New Mexico.